A Cultural Psychology of Music Education

A Cultural Psychology of Music Education

Edited by

Margaret S. Barrett

School of Music
The University of Queensland
Queensland, Australia

OXFORD
UNIVERSITY PRESS

OXFORD
UNIVERSITY PRESS

Great Clarendon Street, Oxford OX2 6DP

Oxford University Press is a department of the University of Oxford.
It furthers the University's objective of excellence in research, scholarship,
and education by publishing worldwide in

Oxford New York

Auckland Cape Town Dar es Salaam Hong Kong Karachi
Kuala Lumpur Madrid Melbourne Mexico City Nairobi
New Delhi Shanghai Taipei Toronto

With offices in

Argentina Austria Brazil Chile Czech Republic France Greece
Guatemala Hungary Italy Japan Poland Portugal Singapore
South Korea Switzerland Thailand Turkey Ukraine Vietnam

Oxford is a registered trade mark of Oxford University Press
in the UK and in certain other countries

Published in the United States
by Oxford University Press Inc., New York

© Oxford University Press, 2011

The moral rights of the authors have been asserted

Database right Oxford University Press (maker)

First published 2011

British Library Cataloging in Publication Data
Data available

Library of Congress Cataloging in Publication Data
Data available

Typeset in Minion by Glyph International, Bangalore, India
Printed in Great Britain
on acid-free paper by
the MPG Books Group, Bodmin and King's Lynn

ISBN 978–0–19–921438–9

10 9 8 7 6 5 4 3 2 1

Whilst every effort has been made to ensure that the contents of this book are as complete,
accurate and up-to-date as possible at the date of writing, Oxford University Press is not able
to give any guarantee or assurance that such is the case. Readers are urged to take appropriately
qualified medical advice in all cases. The information in this book is intended to be useful to
the general reader, but should not be used as a means of self-diagnosis or for the prescription of
medication.

Foreword

The contributions that comprise this volume are from internationally leading authors, each of whom has spent his or her professional life thinking about and researching aspects of musical development that might shape a much more complete understanding of the nature and purpose of music education. Collectively, this new conception of a cultural psychology of music education provides a rigorous yet accessible means for explaining how the self and the cultural and social worlds of musicians and of those learning music are inseparable, and how explanations of these various interdisciplinary insights allow us to rethink common assumptions in a way that will lead to much deeper understandings of the diversity that characterizes music education around the world, the influences which shape current thinking, and of what all of this might mean for improving music education theory and practice.

Included within the eleven chapters is a wealth of information across a range of dimensions. From various contexts and intersecting perspectives, our understandings are broadened by insights about how children learn traditional music and dance, how they make meaning through their various forms of play, how they become attuned to the musical culture that surrounds them, how teachers' actions enhance or impede students' learning, why it is important for learners to attend to the cultural tools (such as symbols and cultural artefacts) that can be used to enhance their learning, how we might challenge longstanding conceptions of music listening, how greater understandings of the self in and through culture can further understandings of culture and self (as well as self as other), and how cross-cultural research of music learning and development can be used to frame more complete understandings of musical development from novice to expert levels.

Transformative changes occur infrequently in any discipline. But when they do occur, they reshape thinking in ways that move a discipline forward and enliven research. *A cultural psychology of music education* is one of those publications that will transform how we think about and practice our craft. With the focus very much on understanding the impact of culture, tradition and social practices, the ten contributions which encompass this volume provide a much-needed new pathway for understanding how various cultural and social practices across divergent forms of music education shape the development of children's cognitive processes and musical activity in various ways. As such, the volume is a timely contribution that freshens and transforms thinking in ways that make a profound impact on music education practice and scholarly debate.

Gary E. McPherson
Ormond Professor,
University of Melbourne

Acknowledgements

Each chapter was independently reviewed by the editor and three expert reviewers, including other authors from this book and anonymous external reviewers. Beyond those contributing to the book, I acknowledge the work of Göran Folkestad, Lucy Green, Joyce Gromko, David Hargreaves, Raymond MacDonald, Gary McPherson, Janet Mills, Adam Ockelford, Bennett Reimer, R. Keith Sawyer, Rosalynd Smith, Sandra Stauffer, Robert Walker, and Susan Young. To all, I convey my sincere appreciation of your efforts and expert advice and commentary.

In preparing this book, I was fortunate to have the assistance of the editorial team at Oxford University Press. I am grateful to OUP commissioning editor Martin Baum and his assistants, initially Carol Maxwell, and, following her retirement, Charlotte Green, for their interest in and support of this project, and their assistance in addressing all those queries that arose in the preparation of the final manuscript. Their work is much appreciated.

I take this opportunity to single out the efforts of Dr Tammy Jones, the editorial assistant on this project. Tammy's insight, organization, and attention to detail have been invaluable, and her good humour much appreciated throughout this project.

To each author I extend my heartfelt thanks for your interest in and enthusiasm for the topic, and your commitment to the fulfilment of this project.

It is my hope that this book contributes to the larger conversations of music, cultural psychology, and music education, and generates further interest and work in this area.

Margaret S. Barrett
April 2010

Contents

Contributors

Margaret S. Barrett is Professor and Head of the School of Music at The University of Queensland. Her research interests include the investigation of the role of music and the arts in human thought and activity, creativity and the pedagogy of creative thought and activity, aesthetic decision-making, young children's musical thinking and identity work in and through music, and the meaning and value of the arts for young people. This research has been funded through grants from the Australian Research Council, the Australia Council for the Arts, and the British Academy, and has been published in the key journals and monographs of the discipline. Recent and forthcoming publications include *Narrative inquiry in music education: troubling certainty* (Springer, 2009, with Sandra Stauffer), Section Editor of the Appreciation Section in the *International handbook on research in arts education* (Springer, 2007), and the Early Childhood Section of the *Oxford handbook of music education* (2011 forthcoming). She is President-elect of the International Society for Music Education (becoming President in 2012) and has held positions as National President of the Australian Society for Music Education, a commissioner for the Research Commission of the ISME, and an elected Board member of the ISME. Margaret is Editor of *Research Studies in Music Education*, Associate Editor for *Psychology of Music*, and a member of the editorial boards of key journals in the discipline.

Patricia Shehan Campbell is Donald E. Peterson Professor of Music at the University of Washington, where she teaches courses at the interface of education and ethnomusicology. Her scholarly interests include the musical cultures of children, world music pedagogy, and ethnomusicological method in the study of music education practices. She is author of *Songs in their heads: music and its meanings in children's lives* (1998, 2nd edition 2010), *Musician and teacher* (2008), *Tunes and grooves in music education* (2008), *Teaching music globally* (2004) (and co-editor with Bonnie Wade of the Oxford Global Music Series), *Lessons from the world* (1991/2001), *Music in cultural context* (1996), and co-author of *Music in childhood* (3rd edition, 2006). She is a board member of Smithsonian Institution's Folkways, a member of the editorial boards of *Psychology of Music*, *Research Studies in Music Education*, and the *Journal of Research in Music Education*, and is Vice-President of the Society for Ethnomusicology.

Peter Dunbar-Hall is an Associate Professor in the Music Education Unit of Sydney Conservatorium of Music, University of Sydney. His research interests include Australian Aboriginal music, the history and philosophy of music education, Australian cultural history, and Balinese music and dance. His research has been funded through the Arts Council of Australia, and the Australian Research Council. Publications by Peter include the biography of Australian soprano, Strella Wilson, and *Deadly sounds, deadly places: contemporary Aboriginal music in Australia*. Peter is a member of the editorial panels of various journals, including *Research Studies in Music Education* and the *Journal of Historical Research in Music Education*. He is a performing member of the Sydney-based Balinese gamelan group, Sekaa Gong Tirta Sinar.

Magne Espeland is Professor in Music and Education at Stord/Haugesund University College (HSH) in Western Norway. His specialities are curriculum studies, music methodology for the general classroom and research methodology for arts education. His research interests have been, and are, the role, characteristics, and secrets of music listening, music composition, and the use of technology in music classrooms. He was the Chair for ISME Bergen 2002, the 25th World Conference in Music Education and is an immediate past board member of this organization. He is a member of the international advisory group for the *British Journal of Music Education*, has been an editorial board member on the *International Journal of Education & the Arts* from its start, and he was Section Editor of the Assessment and Evaluation Section in the *International handbook on research in arts education* (2007). Currently he is Project Chair of the research programme 'Culture, Arts and Creativity in Education' at HSH and leader of MusicNet West, a network for higher education staff involved in music studies and research in Western Norway.

Susan Hallam is Professor of Education at the Institute of Education, University of London, and currently Dean of the Faculty of Policy and Society. She pursued careers as both a professional musician and a music educator before completing her psychology studies and becoming an academic in 1991 in the Department of Educational Psychology at the Institute. Her research interests include disaffection from school, ability grouping and homework, and issues relating to learning in music, practising, performing, musical ability, musical understanding, and the effects of music on behaviour and studying. She is the author of several books including *Instrumental teaching: a practical guide to better teaching and learning* (1998), *The power of music* (2001), *Music psychology in education* (2005), editor of the *Oxford handbook of psychology of music* (2009), and the forthcoming *Music education in the 21st century in the United Kingdom: achievements, analysis and aspirations* and has written more than one hundred other scholarly contributions. She is past editor of *Psychology* *of Music*, *Psychology of Education Review* and *Learning Matters*. She has twice been Chair of the Education Section of the British Psychological Society, and is past treasurer of the British Educational Research Association, an auditor for the Quality Assurance Agency and an Academician of the Learned Societies for the Social Sciences.

Cecilia Hultberg is Professor in Music Education and Chair of Research and Research Studies in Music Education at The Royal College of Music in Stockholm. She has a background as a performing chamber musician, and teacher, educated at Hochschule der Künste, West Berlin (music performance, flute), and Malmö Academy of Music, Lund University (music education), Sweden. In her doctoral thesis (2000) she explored pianists' approaches to music notation. Further studies concern learning conditions and individual approaches to learning and teaching on different levels. Specifically, she explores learning and competence development in learning by playing instruments. She is leading comprehensive collaborative research projects, such as 'Instrumentalists' musical competence development' (Swedish Research Council) and 'Students' ownership of learning' (Authority for Networks and Cooperation in Higher Education).

Kathryn Marsh is Associate Professor of Music Education at the Sydney Conservatorium of Music, University of Sydney, where she teaches subjects relating to primary music education, cultural diversity in music education, and music education research methods. With a PhD in ethnomusicology and a professional background in music education, her research interests include children's musical play, children's creativity, music in the lives of refugee children and multicultural music education. She has written numerous scholarly publications, including her book, *The musical playground: global tradition and change in children's songs and games* (2008), published by Oxford University Press and winner of the Folklore Society's Katherine Briggs Award. She has been actively involved in curriculum development and teacher training for many years and has presented internationally on a regular basis. She has been the recipient of major national research grants which have involved international cross-cultural collaborative research into children's musical play in Australia, Europe, the UK, USA, and Korea, and was a member of an interdisciplinary research team that conducted the National Review of School Music Education in Australia. She is a member of the editorial boards of key international journals in the discipline.

Susan O'Neill is Associate Professor at Simon Fraser University's Faculty of Education. She is Director of Research for Youth, Music & Education, which is currently funded by the Social Sciences and Humanities Research Council of Canada. She is Senior Editor of the Canadian Music Educator's Book Series,

Research to practice. She has published widely in the fields of music psychology and music education, including chapter contributions to eleven edited books by Oxford University Press. Her research interests focus on the way young people value music-making and the impact of youth music engagement on motivation, identity, well-being, and cultural understanding.

Graham F. Welch holds the Institute of Education, University of London Established Chair of Music Education and is Professor and Head of the Institute's Department of Early Childhood and Primary Education. He is elected Chair of the internationally based Society for Education, Music and Psychology Research (SEMPRE), President of the International Society for Music Education (ISME) (2010–2012), and past Co-Chair of the Research Commission of ISME. Current Visiting Professorships include the Universities of Queensland (Australia), Limerick (Eire), as well as Canterbury Christ Church, Coventry, Roehampton, UEL and the Royal College of Music in the UK. He is also a member of the UK Arts and Humanities Research Council's (AHRC) Review College for music. He has acted as a specialist consultant on: (i) aspects of children's singing and vocal development for the USA National Center for Voice and Speech (NCVS) in Denver, the Swedish Voice Research Centre in Stockholm, as well as UK and Italian government agencies; (ii) the British Council in the Ukraine and Ministry for Education and Youth in the United Arab Emirates on education and teacher development; and (iii) the National Research Foundation of South Africa and British Council in Argentina on the development of these national research cultures in music. Publications number more than 260 and embrace musical development and music education, teacher education, the psychology of music, singing and voice science, and music in special education and disability. He is on the editorial boards of the world's leading journals in music education, including *International Journal of Music Education, Journal of Research in Music Education, Research Studies in Music Education, British Journal of Music Education,* and *Music Education Research.*

Jackie Wiggins is Professor of Music Education and Chair of the Department of Music, Theatre and Dance at Oakland University. Known for her work in constructivist music education theory and practice, children's musical creativity, and technology in the music classroom, Wiggins has been an active clinician, presenter, and author in local, state, national, and international settings. As a researcher, she studies the nature of students' experiences composing and improvising in music learning settings and the role of the teacher in these settings. Among her publications are: *Teaching for musical understanding* (McGraw-Hill, 2001; CARMU, Oakland University, 2009), *Composition in the classroom* (MENC, 1990), *Synthesizers in the elementary music classroom*

(MENC, 1991), and numerous journal articles and book chapters. Wiggins is a contributor to the *Handbook of research in arts education*, edited by Liora Bresler (Springer, 2007) and the forthcoming *Oxford handbook for music education*. An active reviewer, she serves on the editorial boards the *Bulletin of the Center for Research in Music Education*, the *International Journal of Education and the Arts*, and the *Asia–Pacific Journal for Arts Education*.

Chapter 1

Towards a cultural psychology of music education

Margaret S. Barrett

Introduction

Cultural psychology is an idea that is at once both old and new; a tension and ambiguity that is captured powerfully in the subtitle of Michael Cole's seminal book *Cultural psychology: the once and future discipline* (1996). Cole's reference to a 'once and future' discipline acknowledges that the origins of the contemporary field of cultural psychology lie in the work of earlier scholars such as the eighteenth century Neapolitan philosopher Giambattisto Vico (1725/1948). Vico sought to develop a science of human nature that was distinct from a science of the natural world and suggested that the investigation of social and cultural phenomena, our lived worlds, required a different approach to that employed in the study of the physical world. Cole summarizes this approach as one in which 'human nature must necessarily be understood through an historical analysis of language, myth, and ritual' (1996, p. 23). This notion has been influential in the study of human endeavour in many domains, for example, those of anthropology and ethnography; domains that seek to understand the individual human in and through the social and cultural settings in which s/he lives and works. Cole traces the development of historical, locally contingent theories of mind, and the cultural–historical sciences, and contrasts these with ahistorical, universal theories of mind in his outlining of a possible cultural psychology. His text may be viewed as one of a number of significant markers in a (re)turn to cultural psychology in the late twentieth and early twenty-first centuries.

The (re)turn to cultural psychology may be attributed in part to the 're-discovery' in the early 1960s, and onwards, of the work of Soviet psychologists Vygotsky, Leontiev, Luria and their colleagues. The translation and publication of these researchers' theoretical and empirical works into a range of languages, including English and German, precipitated a growing interest in a cultural perspective on the theory and practice of psychology. The impact of this event is evident in domains such as educational psychology (Bruner, 1990, 1996), developmental psychology (Rogoff, 2003; Schweder, 1991; Schweder et al., 1998), and social psychology (Fiske, Kitayama, Markus, & Nisbett, 1998), in which the principles of a cultural psychology underpin the work of a number of scholars. Despite growing interest in the tenets and practices of a cultural psychology approach, that cultural psychology is still viewed as an emerging domain is evidenced in the range of interrelated terms that are applied to the field, including sociocultural psychology, cultural–historical psychology, and cultural–historical activity theory (CHAT). Chaiklin (2001), who uses the term cultural–historical psychology, suggests that the field has yet to be 'institutionalized'. He comments: 'Cultural–historical psychology is young as an institutionalized practice, even if it is old as an intellectual practice' (2001, p. 16), and suggests that the lack of an institutionalized structure for cultural–historical psychology rests in the 'suppression of the Vygotskian tradition in the Soviet Union starting officially from 1936 with the Pedagogical Decree and continuing until the mid-1950s' (2001, p. 18). Regardless of which term or label researchers employ to identify their work, an alignment with the Vygotskian tradition, and contemporary developments from that tradition, tends to be a common and integral component of their work.

A field might be viewed to be coming of age when a Handbook is published. Such an event tends to mark out the territory, identify what is thought and known at a particular point in time, and indicate those areas that are ripe for further exploration. The field of cultural psychology has been marked by two such Handbook publications (Kitayama & Cohen, 2007; Valsiner & Rosa, 2007). It is not my intention here to provide a comparative analysis of the approaches taken in these publications; rather, my purpose is to identify some markers of the field's current growth, and to acknowledge the wide-ranging views and positions that attend to contemporary studies in and of cultural psychology. This overview provides a context for considering potential and actual applications of a cultural psychology of music education.

Accounts of cultural psychology

Cultural psychology has been described and defined in diverse ways. Chaiklin suggests that cultural psychology is 'the study of the development of psychological functions through social participation in societally-organized practices' (Chaiklin, 2001, p. 21). This definition proceeds from the study of the individual, to the sociocultural context, and might be viewed as a form of methodological individualism. Cultural psychology might also be viewed as the study of social and cultural practices, and the relationships that hold between social and cultural practices and the development of individual and collective psychological processes. Cultural psychology approaches acknowledge the role of material culture (including objects, artefacts, and the structures and rules by which these might be used), social culture (the social institutions of a culture, and the rules of behaviour that regulate these), and subjective culture (the shared ideas and knowledge of particular social groups) in shaping individual and collective thought and action (Chiu & Hong, 2006).

A central concern of psychology is the search to explain the nature and development of human thought and activity. Historically, social scientists engaged in this search have focused on the individual, often in isolation from others and/or the cultural/historical settings in which they live and work. To address each of these issues in turn, individuals rarely live and work in isolation; we are enmeshed in social networks both physically proximate and virtual, from the beginning of our existence. These social networks range from the formally constituted, as experienced in institutions (including schools and workplaces) and organizations (such as political parties and special interest groups), through to those more informal networks that emerge through family, friendship, and affinity groupings. There has been increasing recognition that an individual's thoughts and behaviours vary considerably when participating across the range of these groupings, reflecting the shaping force that engagement in such groups has on thought and behaviour. Embedded in social networks are sets of cultural practices that are embodied in ways of thinking and acting, and those tools and artefacts that support and extend culturally specific thought and action.

At the core of a cultural psychology is the recognition that the self and the social worlds are inseparable; that the psychological and the sociocultural are 'mutually constituting' (Schweder, 1990; see also Markus & Hamedani, 2007), in an ongoing process of interaction between individuals, and their social and cultural worlds. Through the processes of mutual constitution, individuals and groups not only shape the contexts and settings in which they live and work, they are in turn shaped by them. In such a view, context and setting are integral to the constitution of human thought and activity, rather than variables to be taken into account when investigating a phenomenon. In short, we cannot separate mind and cognition from culture and context, values and beliefs, and a culturally mediated identity.

Cultural psychology and education

In the preface to *The culture of education*, Jerome Bruner states his 'central thesis is that culture shapes mind, that it provides us with the toolkit by which we construct not only our worlds but our very conceptions of our selves and our powers' (1996, p. X). For Bruner, a cultural psychology view of education is not one that requires constant cultural comparisons between diverse educational settings and practices; rather 'it requires that one consider education and school learning in their situated, cultural context' (p. X). In outlining the features of a cultural psychology, Bruner reasserts the inherently social nature of mental activity, commenting that 'Mental life is lived with others, is shaped to be communicated, and unfolds with the aid of cultural codes, traditions, and the like' (p. XI). Bruner raises a number of questions that are asked of and through a 'culturalist' approach to education suggesting that such an approach:

> asks first what function 'education' serves in the culture and what role it plays in the lives of those who operate within it. Its next question might be why education is situated in the culture as it is, and how this placement reflects the distribution of power, status, and other benefits . . . culturalism also asks about the enabling resources made available to people to cope, and what portion of these resources is made available through 'education,' institutionally conceived. And it will constantly be concerned with constraints imposed on the process of education—external ones like the organization of schools and classrooms or the recruitment of teachers, and internal ones like the natural or imposed distribution of native endowment, for native endowment may be as much affected by accessibility of symbolic systems as by the distribution of genes. (Bruner, 1996, p. 11)

Culturalist views of learning and development recognize that development is not 'eternal', defined and determined by biology and chronology alone; rather, that it is 'historical', and is determined and defined by participation in sociocultural practices and the use of 'tools and signs' (Vygotsky, 1978). As Rogoff reminds us, 'people develop as participants in cultural communities. Their development can be understood only in light of the cultural practices and circumstances of their communities—which also change' (Rogoff, 2003, pp. 2–3).

The premise that informs the discipline of cultural psychology asserts that human experience is social and situated, both formative of and formed by culture. Rather than viewing the person strictly in terms of evolutionary and biological explanations of behaviour, a cultural psychology recognizes the social and, specifically, cultural aspects of human behaviour, and the ways by which we are engaged in culturally specific systems of meanings and practices. In early writings on this topic, Bruner described cultural psychology as 'an interpretive psychology [that] seeks out the rules that human beings bring to bear in creating meanings in cultural contexts' (1990, p. 12).

In this reading of human experience and meaning-making, psychological processes and the products, artefacts, and events that are fashioned through such processes are interdependent with the cultural practices and shared meanings (both public and private) in which these processes are embedded. A cultural psychology view of learning recognizes the diversity of human action and meaning-making and the ways in which cultural contexts influence the meaning-making processes we employ (the tools by which we think and act) and the resultant products of such processes. The objects, images, ideas, and rituals of our milieu constitute the materials that shape our thinking in the very process of using these to shape our cultural interaction.

Through a cultural psychology lens, we are able to admit that an event may be interpreted in a range of ways, dependent upon the different cultural contexts in which the event is situated. The cultural psychology agenda may be described as one that seeks to illuminate the ways in which cultural practices and meanings, and human agency—made up of psychological processes and structures—are interrelated, and reinforce and sustain each other.

A cultural psychology of music education

What can we learn when we bring the principles of cultural psychology to bear on music education? At one level, the investigation of diverse music education settings and practices provides opportunities for music educators to question some of the taken-for-granted assumptions that have shaped music education, and to reconsider the aims, theories, and practices of music education. At a more complex level, a cultural psychology approach to music education provides opportunities to look more deeply into the practices of music education in order to understand the role that culture plays in shaping: children's musical learning and thinking; teachers' music teaching and learning; the formal and informal institutions and structures within and through which learning and teaching occur; and the intersection of these processes in the development of musical thought and practice. A cultural psychology of music education might assist us in identifying the characteristic features of an 'enabling culture' (Bruner, 1996, p. XV) of music learning.

Recent studies in music education have sought to investigate the ways in which different constituencies construe music, music-making, and music education, and the ways in which these constructions are culturally bound (see for example Green, 2001, 2008; Marsh, 2008). These studies have revealed a number of anomalies between the ways in which, for example, children engage in music-making when working in children's communities of cultural practice, as opposed to those communities that are part of the institutionalization of formal education, or the experimental laboratory.

In recognizing that development is an interactive process between the child and surrounding environment—defined socially and culturally—the ways in which music education is construed, the institutions through which it is effected, and the musical values such education purports to promote warrant a culturalist scrutiny.

This volume seeks to explore the ways in which the 'once and future discipline' of cultural psychology may contribute to our understandings of the ways in which music education and engagement occur in a range of cultural settings, the shaping influences and forces of these cultural settings, and the subsequent implications of such understanding for the theory and practice of music education. The volume draws together the work of a number of music education researchers whose work references a cultural psychology framework; it does not purport to be a handbook of cultural psychology in music education; rather it seeks to provide an introductory perspective in this developing field, and to indicate some future investigative pathways for a cultural psychology of music education.

Plan of the book

Music education is interdisciplinary by nature. Increasingly, music education scholars and researchers have turned to disciplines beyond music and education, including psychology, sociology, and, more recently, anthropology in order to develop further investigative tools and theoretical frames through which the fundamental questions of music education might be addressed. Questions concerning the nature of musical development, music learning and teaching, the culture(s) of music and music education, the relationships that exist between identity and music learning, and musical childhoods have been re-examined from varying disciplinary perspectives, providing increased insight into the complexities of these issues.

In this volume, music education scholars and researchers have addressed the notion of a cultural psychology of music education through the intensive investigation of the interaction of culture, context, and setting on music learning. Peter Dunbar-Hall and Kathryn Marsh examine two distinctive musical cultures in which children participate, those of the Balinese music tradition, and the children's playground, in order to identify the ways in which music learning practices are shaped by the values, identities, and cultural practices of these settings. In a similar vein, Patricia Shehan Campbell provides an overview of the ways in which differing cultural groups in the USA value and practice forms of music-making and music education. These three researchers all bring an ethnomusicological lens to the cultural psychology of music, reflecting the complementary nature of some ethnographic and cultural psychology approaches (Cole, 1996).

Peter Dunbar-Hall employs a cultural psychology lens to explore the ways in which Balinese children's learning of traditional music and dance is shaped by their culture's uses and valuing of music, and beliefs and practices concerning teaching and learning. Drawing on more than a decade of fieldwork in Bali,

Dunbar-Hall demonstrates that the purposes, methods, and outcomes of music education in this setting position children's music-making as central to the cultural practices of Balinese society. The point of music education is 'to be able to recreate examples of repertoire, and to recreate them within strictly held guidelines of style and aesthetics' (Dunbar-Hall, this volume, p. 23) in order to perform this repertoire as a valued participant in ritual and cultural practices. Dunbar-Hall's careful description and analysis of the 'culturally or socially embedded expectations of learners' (this volume, p. 19) and their communities, illustrates the mutually reinforcing nature of these expectations and the practices that arise from them. He demonstrates the ways in which children's participation in learning traditional Balinese music and dance not only provides them with a means to participate in music activity in ritual and ceremony, but also of learning the codes and conventions of Balinese society, and of being and becoming Balinese.

Kathryn Marsh's chapter examines the ways in which children make meaning through musical play. In locating play as a cultural construct, Marsh focuses on three key issues, those of appropriation, transculturation, and identity, in order to highlight the nature and extent of children's agency in the interactive pedagogy of the playground. The role of play as a shaping force in the development of children's thought and action has been recognized for some time: what is less well understood are the musical dimensions of such play, and the ways in which children exercise cultural agency through the self-initiated musical play that occurs in the informal spaces and places of schools and communities. Marsh argues that playgrounds not only draw on the surrounding musical cultures created by adults, but also generate their own unique musical culture, within which particular formulae of musical generation and performance are created and enacted. Such a process, she argues, constitutes the generation of a 'cultural toolkit' on which children draw progressively in their ongoing musical development and maturation. Marsh emphasizes the range and diversity of influences that young children encounter through their increasing access to and interaction with various forms of media, and the increasingly global nature of the populations of many schools and communities. These influences include:

> parents, siblings, and other relatives; mediated sources found on television, CDs, cassettes, films, DVDs, videos, the radio, and Internet; peers in the playground and classroom; teachers, and the materials which form part of school curricula; and experiences which may be gained in countries of birth, on visits to countries of cultural origin, or on holidays in other localities (Marsh, this volume, p. 43).

Marsh suggests that all of these influences feed back into the culture of the playground, where children exercise autonomy beyond that experienced in the adult-mediated world. She provides numerous illustrations of the ways in which children are active agents in meaning-making in and through their musical play. She suggests that such play experiences generate a child-directed pedagogy that might inform those learning and teaching practices enacted in the classroom.

In her chapter, **Patricia Shehan Campbell** investigates the ways in which children become attuned to a collective musical culture. Using the concept of 'musical enculturation' (Herskovits, 1949), Campbell traces the musical pathways traversed by children from a range of cultural traditions: from the beginnings of musical speech in infancy and early childhood, through their encounters with media and technology, to their engagement with and in American 'ethnic' cultures. Writing in the context of growing multiculturalism in the USA, Campbell focuses the inquiry lens on immigrant children and their families, groups who are 'still close to an identifiable and distinctive culture that is based upon the *mores* and values of a particular ethnicity' (this volume, pp. 66). For the purposes of Campbell's chapter, five 'ethnic' traditions are examined; those of Irish-Americans, Mexican-Americans, Vietnamese-Americans, African-Americans, and Native Americans. Through this exploration, Campbell provides examples of the diverse nature and practices of musical parenting, enculturation, and socialization, and the ways in which children make musical meaning from these experiences. Campbell, along with a growing body of scholars (Barrett, 2003, 2006, 2009; Marsh, 2008; Young, 2008), acknowledges the diverse and rich musical skills, knowledge, and resources that children bring to their formal music learning in school settings, and seeks to provide some insights into the nature and extent of these skills, knowledge and resources, and the environments and sociocultural practices that foster these. Campbell draws on two key theories that have sought to incorporate sociocultural elements and influences into the investigation of learning and development: Urie Bronfenbrenner's (1979; Bronfenbrenner & Morris, 1998) ecological systems theory and Arjun Appadurai's (1996) theory of '-scapes'. While acknowledging the broad dimensions of each of these theories, Campbell's interest lies in those that children encounter most readily, the micro- and meso-systems of the home, family, school, and neighbourhood (Bronfenbrenner & Morris, 1998), and the ethno-, techno-, and media 'scapes' (Appadurai, 1996) that shape children's interactions in these systems of home, school, family, and neighbourhood. Campbell suggests that children's musical worlds comprise a 'complex auditory ecosystem' (this volume, p. 77) that warrants further investigation in our endeavours to understand children's musical learning.

Jackie Wiggins, Cecelia Hultberg, Magne Espeland, and Susan O'Neill draw on the Vygotskian tradition of cultural psychology—specifically, the ways in which this has been taken up in educational theory and practice through the work of scholars such as Jerome Bruner. Their work reflects a concern with the concepts of scaffolding (Wiggins), cultural tools as embedded in technological advances (Espeland) and pedagogical traditions and techniques (Hultberg), and the mediation of identity through place and shared space (O'Neill).

Jackie Wiggins' study of teacher-supported collaborative songwriting events provides a context for the investigation of learner agency and teacher scaffolding in children's musical learning. Wiggins works from the premise that learning is an interactive social process that is characterized by negotiation and mutuality (Bruner, 1996; Wenger, 1998), undertaken in a community of practice (Lave & Wenger, 1991), and located in physical settings (often classrooms) that in turn shape the nature, intent, and purposes of interaction. Through a careful analysis of her own and others' actions as teachers scaffolding children's musical learning, Wiggins explores the ways in which teacher actions may enable and/or constrain student learning and sense of agency in the music-making process, and the ways in which learners draw on the cultural signs and tools at their disposal to make meaning from these experiences. Wiggins' presentation of scaffolding as a teaching strategy acknowledges contrasting views of the pedagogical intentions and learning outcomes of scaffolding. These include a view of scaffolding as an enabling learning strategy that supports and empowers learners (Woods, Bruner, & Ross, 1976), and one that presents scaffolding as an intrusion on learners' thought and activity (Allsup, 2002), a form of control and constraint. Wiggins points to the need to be cognizant of the potentiality of both these perspectives, citing Bruner's view that 'pedagogy is never innocent' (1996, p. 63). Wiggins also considers the different dimensions of scaffolding—musical and social—and points to the ways in which these forms of scaffolding can work in tandem to support and extend student interaction and learning. She suggests that careful attention to these two views of scaffolding is needed in order to balance the potential tensions that may exist between strategies that aim to promote learner agency and those that reflect the structuring and directive processes of teacher scaffolding.

Cultural psychology approaches recognize the role that 'cultural tools' such as signs, symbols, and artefacts play in shaping thought and action. Drawing on Vygotsky's cultural historical theory (Vygotsky, 1978, 1986), **Cecilia Hultberg** reminds us of the complex relationships that exist between sign, symbol, artefact, and the need to consider these in interaction rather than isolation. The central thesis of the Russian cultural–historical school rests in the view that 'the structure and development of human psychological processes emerge through culturally mediated, historically developing, practical activity' (Cole, 1996, p. 108). Attention to the interactive relationships between the concepts of (a) mediation through artefacts, (b) historical development (as evidenced in enculturation and the transmission of cultural knowledge and ways of being through successive generations), and (c) practical activity, emphasizes the social origins of learning and development (Cole, 1996, p. 111). Hultberg examines two teachers' ways of working—one in a notation-based music environment, the other in an aural-based music environment—in order to illustrate the complex interplay between, and varying functions of, tools and artefacts such as notated (printed scores) and aural (performances) presentations of musical works. She interrogates the ways in which these teachers draw on their knowledge as culture bearers of the musical (Western classical music and Zimbabwean marimba ensemble respectively) and pedagogical (Suzuki piano instruction and aural-based group teaching) traditions within which they work, in order to use notated, aural, and embodied presentations of the music to prompt student thought and practical activity. In these environments, the teachers use student performances as cultural tools for reflection and understanding in their own learning as teachers, as well as that of their students. Hultberg also illustrates the varying functions a musical instrument might play in students' learning, as, for example, a mechanical tool for practising or experiencing specific aspects of technique, or as a cultural tool for the expression of musical meaning. Importantly, she emphasizes the need to draw students' attention to the interplay of cultural tools in music learning, as, for example, in the interplay between cultural tools, such as conventions of structuring musical ideas, conventions of expressing musical ideas, notations of musical ideas, and the sound-making possibilities of musical instruments.

Magne Espeland draws on Bruner's (1996) nine tenets of a cultural psychology in order to frame the history of music listening practices in music education and outline a potential application of the tenets to future music education work. Espeland affirms that listening is fundamental to music experience, but makes some distinction between (a) listening in and through performance and composition, (b) what he terms 'other "listening" disciplines' (this volume, p. 146), such as music history, music analysis, and music theory, and (c) 'educational music listening' (this volume, p. 146). This latter is defined by Espeland as 'different ways of educating young people into recognizing, understanding, and appreciating central aspects of the sounding essences of particular pieces of music and their respective contexts' (Espeland, this volume, p. 146), and is the focus of the chapter.

Espeland's historical account of 'educational music listening' illustrates the ways in which cultural tools embedded in technological advances, for example the gramophone, shape the ways in which we engage with music and music learning. He identifies three major issues that have emerged in approaches to educational music listening: (a) the parenthetical position in music listening, (b) absolute, or referential meaning-making, and (c) the role of masterpieces of music. Drawing on the early work of English academic Stewart MacPherson (1910), Espeland describes the early 'parenthetical position' as one that combines aural skill development (ear training and music theory) with music appreciation, and contrasts this with those approaches that emphasize the child's personal emotional response to the exclusion of other considerations. This distinction between emotional/referential response to music listening, and more formal or 'absolute' approaches is also evident in the second issue identified by Espeland, that of the relative roles of absolute or referential meaning-making, and teachers' use of these in pedagogy. The advent of the gramophone and the radio democatized music, allowing anyone with the financial resources to access the 'masterpieces' of Western music. Espeland provides an overview of the debates that ranged over when and how the masterpieces of music should be introduced, and, in this process, demonstrates the complex and nuanced views of educational music listening that were in place from the early part of the twentieth century.

'What music to listen to? And how?' are fundamentally cultural questions, indeed, psychocultural questions, as well as educational questions. In pointing to possible worlds of educational music listening, Espeland draws on Dissanayake's notion of 'artification' (Dissanayake, 2007), described as 'making use of and responding to aesthetic operations' (2007, p. 793). For Espeland, artification, evidenced in practices that are student-centred, eliciting student responses, involving artistic expression, interpretive reasoning, discovery, and problem-solving, provides a means to revitalising and making relevant music listening practices in contemporary music education. Such practices draw on many of Bruner's tenets of a cultural psychology, and, Espeland foreshadows, challenge the music education community to rethink current music listening theory and practice.

Susan O'Neill commences her discussion of culture and learning in and through music performance by highlighting the potentially conflicting social agendas with which educators are asked to work: those of 'acknowledging and mediating the unique identity of individuals or groups while at the same time occupying a shared space where all people, regardless of their cultural background, feel a sense of value and belonging' (this volume, p. 179). O'Neill asks us to consider the practical challenges of recognizing and working with cultural difference, and the ways in which we might address these in learning and teaching contexts. In a multidisciplinary approach, O'Neill draws together ideas from multicultural educational theory and practice, social psychology, and cultural psychology to interrogate what is understood and intended by multicultural music education. She argues that dialogic approaches to music performance learning provide opportunity for the engagement of the self in and through culture, which in turn may prompt greater understanding of culture, self, and other, including self as other (the dialogic self).

The final three chapters in this volume draw on variants of cultural psychology to investigate musical learning and development, and the acquisition of musical expertise. Susan Hallam considers research in cross-cultural studies of music learning and development in order to consider the potential interplay between 'universal' aspects of human learning, the role of culture, and genetic inheritance. Both Graham Welch and Margaret Barrett investigate the cultural settings and practices of the English cathedral choir in order to identify the characteristic features of learning in these settings, and the sociocultural structures that support and shape these.

Susan Hallam interrogates notions of musicality and musical expertise through the lenses of neurological and psychological research, in order to consider the role and function of culture in musical learning and development. Approaches to the study of culture and behaviour have ranged from relativist views that suggest that human behaviour is defined by cultural settings, to absolutist views that culture plays little part in shaping human behaviour. Hallam points to middle-ground views between these two extremes, specifically universalist and ecoculturalist views, that suggest that whereas there are aspects of psychological thought and activity common to all humans, these are shaped differently by the cultural contexts into which we are born and live. Hallam provides an overview of research investigating both commonalities and differences in musical thought and behaviour across and within cultures in order to interrogate different cultural perceptions of 'musicality' and the ways in which these might change in time and place. Commencing from the viewpoint that 'the propensity for musical development and . . . musicality is as universal as linguistic ability' (this volume, p. 203), Hallam illustrates the interaction between culture, development, and the acquisition of musical expertise through the analysis of a broad range of research. She presents a number of points, including the view that prolonged music engagement, particularly as performers, shapes neurological structures and processes in ways that reflect our 'learning biographies' in and through culture. Hallam outlines the ways in which musical expertise is acquired in communities of practice in which particular forms and processes of musical participation are culturally valued. She suggests that musical expertise might be explained, in part, by the amount of time spent in deliberate practice, and consideration of the complex interactions between individual knowledge, experience, and motivation, and culturally specific beliefs concerning the nature of musical ability and musicality.

Cultural–historical activity theory (CHAT) provides the lens through which **Graham Welch** examines a significant cultural change in the centuries-old tradition of the English cathedral choir; the introduction of female choristers. CHAT also provides a means to interrogate the ways in which this change has been enacted and understood in contemporary life, and to consider the affordances and constraints of the cathedral in shaping the musical life and learning of female choristers. Welch traces the considerable history of the all-male choral tradition and provides a careful analysis of the social, cultural, educational, and musical factors that gave impetus to the introduction of female choristers to English cathedral choirs in the late twentieth century. This 'cultural shift' has not been without controversy. Welch draws on the Scandanavian approach to CHAT (Engeström, 2001) to analyse the 'activity system' of the English cathedral choir (including cultural artefacts, member-ship of groups within the cathedral community, established traditions and rules—including the ways in which the 'labour' of the choir is divided between members—and the goals and outcomes of the activity), to explain how the cultural change has been effected, and to illustrate the effect of this change on both the tradition of the English cathedral choir, and those who participate in that tradition. Welch's longitudinal case study of Wells Cathedral provides the data to focus on the latter point, specifically, chorister development for female choristers. Welch suggests that chorister development in this setting is 'nur-tured, shaped, and constrained by systemized cultural practices' (this volume, p. 244) which operate reflexively to perpetuate a system while accommodating change.

The English cathedral choir also provides the context and setting for **Margaret Barrett's** investigation of the acquisition of early expertise. She con-siders the ways in which cultural systems shape human engagement and inter-action, in order to illustrate the ways in which the cultural system of an English cathedral choir shapes the boy choristers' musical learning, identity, and devel-opment. Research suggests that the key to the development of expertise rests in two factors; (a) environmental conditions, including positive and supportive family values and structures, and early and continuous access to resources and education; and (b) appropriate education, including deliberate practice that is goal-focused, and critiqued and monitored by an expert other. Barrett's nar-rative analysis of a longitudinal case study of one English cathedral choir illustrates the ways in which these components are established in that setting. She also provides some insights into the personal costs of participating in this community of practice, and the affordances and constraints encountered through participation.

In this opening chapter, I have endeavoured to provide a brief overview of the ways in which cultural psychology has re-emerged, and been taken up in the study of human thought and activity. This brief overview has surveyed the application of the theory and practice of cultural psychology to music education. The ensuing chapters provide a rich preliminary account of work in the field and shall, I hope, encourage further engagement and debate.

References

Allsup, R. E. (2002). *Crossing over: mutual learning and democratic action in instrumental music education.* Unpublished doctoral dissertation, Teachers College, Columbia University, New York.

Appadurai, A. (1996). *Modernity at large: cultural dimensions of globalization.* Minneapolis, MN: University of Minnesota Press.

Barrett, M. S. (2003). Meme engineers: children as producers of musical culture. *International Journal of Early Years Education, 11*(3), 195–212.

Barrett, M. S. (2006). Inventing songs, inventing worlds: the 'genesis' of creative thought and activity in young children's lives. *International Journal of Early Years Education, 14*(3), 201–20.

Barrett, M. S. (2009). Sounding lives in and through music: a narrative inquiry of the 'everyday' musical engagement of a young child. *Journal of Early Childhood Research, 7*(2), 115–34.

Bronfenbrenner, U. (1979). *The ecology of human development: experiments by nature and design.* Cambridge, MA: Harvard University Press.

Bronfenbrenner, U., & Morris, P. A. (1998). The ecology of developmental processes. In W. Damon & R. M. Lerner (Eds.), *Handbook of child psychology* (Vol. 1, pp. 993–1028). New York: Wiley.

Bruner, J. (1990). *Acts of meaning.* Cambridge, MA: Harvard University Press.

Bruner, J. (1996). *The culture of education.* Cambridge, MA: Harvard University Press.

Chaiklin, S. (2001). Cultural–historical psychology as a multinational practice. In S. Chaiklin (Ed.), *The theory and practice of cultural–historical psychology* (pp. 15–34). Aarhus, Denmark: Aarhus University Press.

Chiu, C.-Y., & Hong, Y.-Y. (2006). *Social psychology of culture.* New York: Psychology Press.

Cole, M. (1996). *Cultural psychology: the once and future discipline.* Cambridge, MA: The Bellknapp Press of Harvard University Press.

Dissanayake, E. (2007). In the beginning: pleistocene and infant aesthetics and 21st century education in the arts. In L. Bresler (Ed.), *International handbook of research in arts education* (pp. 783–95). Dordrecht: Springer.

Engeström, Y. (2001). Expansive learning at work: toward an activity theoretical reconceptualisation. *Journal of Education and Work, 14*(1), 133–56.

Fiske, A. P., Kitayama, S., Markus, H. R., & Nisbett, R. E. (1998). The cultural matrix of social psychology. In D. T. Gilbert, S. T. Fiske & G. Lindzey (Eds.), *Handbook of social psychology* (4th edn, pp. 915–81). New York: McGraw-Hill.

Green, L. (2001). *How popular musicians learn: a way ahead for music education*. Aldershot, UK: Ashgate.

Green, L. (2008). *Music, informal learning and the school: a new classroom pedagogy*. Aldershot, UK: Ashgate.

Herskovits, M. (1949). *Man and his works*. Evanston, IL: Northwestern University Press.

Kitayama, S., & Cohen, D. (Eds.). (2007). *Handbook of cultural psychology*. New York: Guilford Press.

Lave, J., & Wenger, E. (1991). *Situated learning: legitimate peripheral participation*. Cambridge: Cambridge University Press.

MacPherson, S. (1910). *Music and its appreciation, or the foundations of true listening*. London: Joseph Williams.

Markus, H. R., & Hamedani, M. G. (2007). Sociocultural psychology: the dynamic interdependence among self systems and social systems. In S. Kitayama & D. Cohen (Eds.), *Handbook of cultural psychology* (pp. 3–39). New York: Guilford Press.

Marsh, K. (2008). *The musical playground: global tradition and change in children's songs and games*. Oxford: Oxford University Press.

Rogoff, B. (2003). *The cultural nature of human development*. New York: Oxford University Press.

Schweder, R. A. (1990). Cultural psychology—what is it? In J. W. Stigler, R. A. Shweder & G. Herdt (Eds.), *Cultural psychology. Essays on comparative human development* (pp. 1–42). Cambridge: Cambridge University Press.

Schweder, R. A. (1991). *Cultural psychology: thinking through cultures*. Cambridge, MA: Harvard University Press.

Schweder, R. A., Goodnow, J., Hatano, G., LeVine, R., Markus, H., & Miller, P. J. (1998). The cultural psychology of development: one mind, many mentalities. In W. Damon (Ed.), *Handbook of child psychology*, Vol. 1, *Theoretical models of human development* (5th edn, pp. 865–937). New York: Wiley.

Valsiner, J., & Rosa, A. (Eds.) (2007). *The Cambridge handbook of sociocultural psychology*. New York: Cambridge University Press.

Vico, G. (1725/1948). *The new science* (T. G. Bergin & M. H. Fish, Trans.). Ithaca, NY: Cornell University Press.

Vygotsky, L. S. (1978). *Mind in society: the development of higher psychological processes* (Eds. M. Cole, V. John-Steiner, S. Scribner & E. Souberman). Cambridge, MA: Harvard University Press.

Vygotsky, L. S. (1986). *Thought and language* (new rev. trans. by A. Kozulin). Cambridge, MA: MIT Press.

Wenger, E. (1998). *Communities of practice: learning, meaning and identity*. New York: Cambridge University Press.

Woods, P., Bruner, J., & Ross, G. (1976). The role of tutoring in problem-solving. *Journal of Child Psychology and Psychiatry, 17*, 89–100.

Young, S. (2008). Lullaby light shows: everyday musical experience among under-two-year-olds. *International Journal of Music Education, 26*(1), 33–46.

Chapter 2

Children's learning of music and dance in Bali: an ethnomusicological view of the cultural psychology of music education

Peter Dunbar-Hall

Introduction

It is midday in Ubud, a southern Balinese village known for its arts activity, and with a handful of other tourists I am watching a group of girls rehearse a dance. Close by, a *gamelan*, played by boys, is running through the music for the girls' dance. The two activities, although simultaneous, are not coordinated. The dance teachers move among the girls, correcting their posture and steps. Similarly, *gamelan* teachers move among the boy instrumentalists checking their parts and fixing mistakes. There are many repetitions of the music and the dance. If mistakes are identified, they are corrected during the next repetition of the music; at no time is the music or dance slowed down as a pedagogic strategy. Tourist cameras are working overtime, a usual occurrence when Balinese children are learning, rehearsing or performing music and dance. Eventually everything stops and a complete performance of *Tari Kijang Kencana* (Shining Deer Dance) is given—although it is without costumes for either the dancers or the *gamelan* players. Within a few days these children will perform this dance in the children's section of the Annual Bali Arts Festival. Everyone is intent on winning.

This vignette, typical of children's interactions with the learning and teaching of music and dance in Bali, encapsulates aspects that seem the same as those observable wherever children are learning music; intense practise, concentration, mistake correction, teacher direction, group effort. However, the purposes, methods, and outcomes of learning and teaching in this case are strongly influenced and acquire meanings from socially and culturally influenced understandings of the roles and values of music, of teaching strategies, and of learning styles. To understand how this reading of the rehearsal I observed can be obtained, it is necessary to interpret the teaching and learning of music and dance to children in Bali through a cultural psychology lens that is ethnomusicological in nature.

While the cultural psychology of music education can appear as a recent offshoot of the psychology of music, it has a history in the work and findings of ethnomusicologists who have investigated music learning and teaching in a range of culturally specific settings, and through this have provided understanding of how culture affects the content and structure of music experience that is pedagogic in either intent or outcome. The idea that cultural context is a factor in the ways people approach music, aestheticize music, learn and teach music, think about music and its effects on their lives, and think about how they learn music is not unusual to ethnomusicologists, especially those who include study of music transmission in their research. In this way, a wide literature on the cultural psychology of music education and models for analysing it exists, even if this area of music study is only implicitly referenced, is referred to under other headings, or is embedded in texts that focus on other aspects of music. For example, Ellis discusses cultural aspects of the psychology of music education when she explains the learning of music among Australian Pitjantjatjara Aborigines (Ellis, 1985). Rice (1994) discusses aspects of music cognition among Bulgarian musicians, while the ways that Javanese musicians theorise the deepest levels of Javanese gamelan music, and their own learning and teaching processes, are a focus of Perlman's (2004) work. In his investigation of jazz improvisation as a music culture, Berliner (1994) includes a chapter on jazz musicians' learning experiences and how these reflect the musical ethos of the jazz community. Earlier, Berliner (1981) had analysed cultural perspectives of the ways in which Shona people learn and teach the *mbira* in Zimbabwe, devoting a complete chapter to this as integral to the complementary nature of the relationship between a player and his *mbira*. In a more holistic manner, Brand (2006) summarizes a range of ways that music is taught in Asian contexts, Szego (2002) discusses music transmission, and North, Hargreaves and Tarrant (2002) provide an overview of music education through a social psychology lens that references Western and other contexts, drawing specific attention to the work of ethnomusicologists. Among others, Folkestad (2002) writes about how individual people perceive learning music as a factor of national identity construction. Addressing this area from a psychology of pedagogy perspective, writers who bridge the space between ethnomusicology and music education provide examples of how, and perhaps why, children learn music in 'communities of musical practice' (Barrett, 2005, p. 261; see for example Campbell, 1998; Marsh, 1995). Writing through the lens of the psychology of music, Hargreaves, MacDonald and Miell (2005) indicate that what they call 'situations and contexts' (p. 8), including 'social and cultural contexts' (p. 15), are at the primary level of factors influencing response to music and the meanings of music performance.

The influences of social and cultural contexts form the basis of this discussion, which investigates the learning and teaching of music and dance among children in Bali. In many ways this reinforces the view of researchers, such as Vygotsky, whose belief is that childhood is best understood through examination of children's place and participation in the sociocultural contexts that surround them. Barrett sums this up in the statement:

> in a socio-cultural view, culture is no mere 'add-on,' or casual factor; rather, it is formed by and formative of human thought and action, and inseparable from human development.
>
> (Barrett, 2005, p. 263)

In line with this, what follows is an explanation of how the learning of music and dance by children in Bali adheres to and exemplifies expectations placed on Balinese people as members of a religiously influenced cultural context. Rather than propose that the example of Balinese music learning and teaching can be generalized and therefore become the basis of broad theorizations about how culture affects musical experience, this example is of the type that Dowling and Harwood (1986, p. 225) define as 'description of real-life behaviour of people in rich and complex social contexts'. It is representative of what van Manen (2003) calls 'researching lived experience', and is a case study of music learning and teaching in one setting, but one which raises questions applicable to all music pedagogy. Especially, it raises concerns about analyses of music pedagogy that focus on the learning of music without reference to culturally or socially embedded expectations of learners. For example, expectations that performers will gain skills through which they can participate in performances requisite for religious observances that underpin daily life. It demonstrates alternate, subversive ways of theorizing the purposes, methods and outcomes of the learning and teaching of music. The discussion begins by emphasizing reasons for children's learning of music and the methods through which children acquire music with reference to literature on Bali that since the 1930s has tangentially alluded to children as learners and performers. It then interprets aspects of Balinese culture and society as sites of music learning and teaching that are culturally specific. This demonstrates how children's music activities are important contributions to the life of Balinese communities and how community expectations mandate teaching strategies and learning styles. Much of the discussion is based on my fieldwork in Bali between 1999 and 2007.

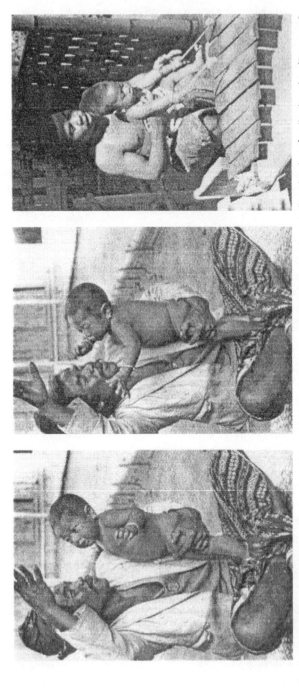

Fig. 2.1 Three photos by Gregory Bateson and Margaret Mead showing a child's dance and music learning in a family situation (Bateson & Mead, 1942, p. 85).

Balinese children as musicians—historical perspectives

In 1942, Gregory Bateson and Margaret Mead published their *Balinese character: a photographic analysis*, which consists of several hundred photographs of Balinese village activity as Bateson and Mead recorded it in the late 1930s. Throughout these photographs, musical activity is a regular occurrence and children's involvement in musical activity can readily be seen. In their written notes for the photographs, these researchers draw attention to the learning of music and dance by children. For example, to explain a set of three photographs of a father teaching his child dance movements and a musical instrument (Fig. 2.1), they write:

> A father teaches his son to dance, humming a tune and posturing with his hand. In the first picture, the father shapes his face to a typical dance smile and the son looks at the raised hand. In the second picture, the son tries to grasp the arm … the same father teaches his son to play the xylophone.
>
> (Bateson & Mead, 1942, p. 84)

Elsewhere, Mead wrote about the involvement of Balinese children in religious ritual, noting that:

> The Balinese may comment with amusement but without surprise if the leading metallophone player in a noted orchestra is so small that he has to have a stool in order to reach the keys: the same mild amusement may be expressed if someone takes up a different art after his hands have a tremor of age to confuse their precision. But in a continuum within which the distinction between the most gifted and the least gifted is muted by the fact that everyone participates, the distinction between child and adult—as performer, as actor, as musician—is lost, except in those cases where the distinction is ritual, as where a special dance form requires a little girl who has not reached puberty.
>
> (Mead, 1970a, p. 199; see also Sullivan, 1999)

This noticing of children's musical activity, and its similarities and interconnections to that of adults, also underpins writings by Bateson and Mead's contemporaries in Bali. Beryl de Zoete and Walter Spies (1938, p. 6) noted the participation of children in music activities, and that this was a primary means of learning:

> Children sit between their father's knees in the gamelan before they can walk, and their tiny hands strike the cymbals or metal keys or hold the drum-sticks, enclosed in their father's. It almost seems that they absorb directly into their bodies the melody and the complicated rhythms, just as they absorb the rhythms and postures of the dance.

Describing his time in Bali in the same decade, Canadian composer Colin McPhee wrote analytically about children's interactions with music, calling his description 'Children and music in Bali' (McPhee, 1970, pp. 212–239).

He included descriptions of Balinese children's music activities in his autobiographical *A house in Bali* (McPhee, 1947) and turned these descriptions into a children's novella, *A club of small men* (McPhee, 1948 [2002]), in which a group of boys acquires the instruments of a gamelan and, after various adventures, performs on them for the local raja. Jane Belo, McPhee's wife, uses photographs of child musicians and dancers in her anthropological study of the significance of *Rangda* and *Barong* (Balinese theatrical representations of evil and good respectively) (Belo, 1949), and includes photographs of child performers alongside detailed analysis of children's participation in specific dance rituals in her *Trance in Bali* (Belo, 1960). Similarly, American writer on dance Katherine Mershon provides photographs of child performers and discussion of their parts in religious rituals and age-related rites of passage in southern Bali in the 1930s (Mershon, 1971).

More recently, other writers have included reference to the music activities of children as parts of their texts on Balinese music. Tenzer (1998, pp. 107–108) explains aspects of children's engagement with the learning of Balinese music. He describes the imitation of adults that often underlies the first attempts to play, the role of enculturation and exposure to music that assist in acquiring repertoire, the social benefits of music activity, and the importance of family-based learning. Dibia and Ballinger (2004, pp. 38–39), in a chapter titled 'Children's gamelan and dance groups', describe the performing arts activities of Balinese children, noting McPhee's involvement in the late 1930s in the establishment of the first children's gamelan and subsequent growth of children's learning and performance so that today it is not unusual to see public performances and participation in arts festivals and contests by children's groups. My analysis of the meanings ascribed to children's performances of gamelan music and dance furthers this line of research (Dunbar-Hall, 2006). McIntosh (2006a, 2006b) analyses a range of Balinese children's music activities and uses his research into children's dance, music and song in south-central Bali to debate issues of ethnomusicological research method.

The picture that emerges from the literature as far back as the 1930s is that children's participation in music activities and their learning of music have been and continue to be standard components of daily life in Bali. They are considered so normal as to be unremarked on by Balinese. Yet the purposes and cultural outcomes of learning, apart from acquisition of physical skills and repertoire, remain less discussed. In Bali, these are often based on clear agendas of religious belief and cultural maintenance; they also contribute to socially accepted modes of behaviour and relate to expectations of the roles of families as the source of music learning. It is these purposes and cultural outcomes that form the focus of this discussion.

Learning and teaching music in Bali

In Bali, the learning and teaching of music and dance are significant aspects of people's lives and the teaching of these activities to children is entrenched. While, as Bateson and Mead (1942) and de Zoete and Spies (1938) noticed, this occurs in family settings where music and/or dance pass from parent to child, there are also structured programmes for instructing children. These programmes are run by museums and art galleries, by private studios set up by a musician and/or dance teacher, and by village-based community organizations. Observation of teaching and learning in these programmes could give the impression that they are similar to the ways music is learnt and taught in other locations (for example, the presence of teachers, regular lessons, rehearsals leading to performances, cohort-based teaching situations, repertoires graded by difficulty, performances used as assessments of levels of ability); however, they are culturally differentiated and reflect elements of Balinese social structures. They also demarcate children's learning of music in Bali from that in many other contexts, especially that of the Western world which dominates the literature of music teaching and learning and the psychology of music.

Literature on the psychology of music learning concentrates on a set of issues that become, by implication, definitional of this field of study. These include: how learners deal with notation (Mills & McPherson, 2006; Sloboda, 2005), beginners' choices of instrument (McPherson & Davidson, 2006), the desire to learn and to continue to learn music (Austin, Renwick & McPherson, 2006; Davidson, 1999), the role of and methods for practising (Barry & Hallam, 2002; Gruson, 1988), personal identity theory relating to concepts of being a musician (MacDonald, Hargreaves & Miell, 2002), music cognition (Davidson & Scripp, 1988; Sloboda, 2005), and learners' uses of and engagements with creativity (often in the form of improvisation) (Pressing, 1988; Sternberg, 1999). These issues rarely apply in the learning of Balinese music by Balinese children or adults. Notation is not used in teaching and learning situations or for performance—instead, music is memorized by teachers and transmitted to learners who also memorize it. Embodiment, rather than cognitive processing of how to perform, is the basis of learning. This situation refutes one of the mainstays of the psychology of music, that 'the ability to read music is, if not essential, an irreplaceable asset to anyone who indulges in musical activity' (Sloboda, 2005, p. 3). The point of learning to play in a gamelan or to dance is to be able to recreate examples of repertoire, and to recreate them within strictly held guidelines of style and aesthetics; concepts of individualism inherent in the use of creativity and the development of one's personal performance style (as is prominent in much Western music education) do not adhere. The concept of individual practice is almost unknown for a number of reasons. It is highly unlikely that individuals or families own instruments (even Balinese musicians from whom I learnt did not own instruments); generally, sets of instruments are communally owned and are kept in public spaces such as temples and *balai* (Balinese: village meeting pavilions). Practising is rarely done without a leader/teacher present, so in effect, a practice session is a learning session or a rehearsal for a performance. Even if the members of a small group of musicians practise their parts from a piece of music apart from a *gamelan*, this automatically requires the presence of other players and tends to focus on running through a piece a number of times, not breaking down a piece into short segments for intensive clinical work. The necessity of practising with other players is also related to the tunings of instruments in pairs with a slight pitch discrepancy—to play one instrument by itself does not make acoustic sense as it is needs its partner instrument to produce the correct sound of Balinese music. The approach to preparation for performance by repetition may reflect the underlying nature of the music, which is cyclical—once a mistake is identified it can be corrected (microcosmically) on subsequent repetitions of a cycle within a piece of music, or it can be remedied (macrocosmically) the next time the piece is played through. This gives a particular contextual style to mistake identification and correction, removing focus from the immediate to the eventual. In my experience as a learner in Bali, this ethos drives teaching, giving it its own sense of time and direction.

Music acquisition

Ways of learning music and of functioning as a musician reinforce socially exemplified relationships of mutual dependence and holistic effort. A number of music learning and teaching issues can be used to demonstrate this. The purposes of music acquisition are perhaps chief among these. As learning and/or teaching music imply choices of intent, the purposes of music acquisition can be read as indicators of culturally influenced motivational factors. By learning to perform as an instrumentalist or dancer, Balinese people gain access to participation in activities through which spiritual, communal and personal needs can be achieved—generally this commences in childhood, so there is a continual expectation that children are involved in music activity. That some dances for performance in temple rites must be performed by prepubescent girls reinforces the need to instruct children from an early age and helps to emphasize general expectations that children will be involved in learning music and dance. A flourishing 'industry' for teaching music and dance to children exists, including specialist teachers, *sanggar* (Balinese: arts organizations) that include training of instrumentalists and dancers among their activities, and commercial production of recordings of dance repertoire especially for the teaching of dance.

Balinese Hinduism demonstrates a strong reliance on the regular and correct observance of religious events through which world balance is maintained. Geertz notes that:

> Balinese life is . . . irregularly punctuated by frequent holidays, which everyone celebrates, but by even more frequent temple celebrations . . . this makes for a fairly busy, not to say frenetic, ritual life.
>
> (Geertz, 1973, p. 395)

Performance as a *gamelan* player or dancer provides a means through which a person, or performing group, can contribute to the fulfilment of these religious expectations, among them, temple festivals, funeral rites, life cycle rites of passage, and village calendric activities, which all rely on the provision of music and dance if these events are to be effective. Children are regular performers in these events. This not only adds to local village-based requirements, but assists in achievement of a bustling communal ethos called *ramai* (Indonesian: celebratory liveliness) which is considered a sign of performative success, and aids an individual in the acquisition of *sakti* (Indonesian: spiritual grace, supernatural power). It must be remembered that performance of Balinese music and dance is not principally addressed to those visibly present in the seen world (what Balinese refer to as *sekala*) but more importantly is an offering, a welcoming gesture and sign of respect, to visiting deities and spirit beings of the unseen world (*niskala*). Researchers into Balinese music and dance regularly discuss them as links between *sekala* and *niskala*, and as essential components of religious observance (Bandem & de Boer, 1995; Becker, 2004; Eiseman, 1990; Harnish, 1991; Hobart, 2003; Ramstedt, 1993). For example, Harnish (1991, pp. 9–10) writes:

> Nearly all traditional Balinese performing arts are ultimately rooted in religion and are ascribed functions relating to religious practices. The major theatre, dance and musical performances . . . are frequently presented at festivals to enhance the event's ritual power . . . The performing arts also constitute refined and actualised offerings of cosmological configurations to the deities. They act to entice the deities to remain in the temple throughout the festival, engaging their ears and eyes just as fruit and food offerings engage their palate. The arts offer the rich and complex imagery that encompasses the cosmos and address the various aspects of the divine in fulfilment of the festival experience.

Outcomes of music learning: contests, tourist performances, politics and group collaboration

Adding to the religious and communal complexities of the meanings of music and dance are four other outcomes of learning to perform. The first of these is participation in *lomba* (Indonesian: contests) in performing arts; the second is performance for tourists; third are agendas of political statement; and fourth is fulfilment of social expectations known as *gotong royong* (Indonesian: collaborative contribution).

Highly contested music and dance *lomba* are regular occurrences in Bali, and children's groups are trained intensively to take part in them (and win!). Success at a *lomba* has both intrinsic and extrinsic benefits. For a village to be able to say that their children's *gamelan* or dancers are the winners of a *lomba* is a thing of immense local pride; such success can also be used to advertise performances and commercial recordings (CDs, VCDs and DVDs), linking *lomba* to the second outcome of children's learning of music and dance: performance for tourists.

The coincidental ability to perform for tourists in exhibitions of supposed authentic culture brings a certain level of economic benefit to a community. As was noted above, even rehearsals are positioned as opportunities for tourists to watch Balinese music and dance. That tourists are encouraged to attend these is reinforced by notices in the programme leaflets of tourist performances, for example:

> The performance is taking place in the Ancak Saji Palace South Yard which was built in the 16th century, where also every Sunday and Tuesday the Ubud children have performance and art lessons ... organized by Tedung Agung Performance Institution.
>
> (Sekaa Gong Jaya Swara Ubud, undated, p. 2)

Monies earned by a group are rarely devolved to individuals—rather they are used to pay expenses (the costs of teaching; hire of a truck to transport instruments and performers; repairs to or purchase of instruments and dance costumes, which are communally owned)—providing another avenue through which individuals can make a contribution to those around them. It should be noted that even in the context of tourist performances, levels of the religious importance of music and dance are acknowledged—as can be witnessed by the blessing of performance spaces by *pemangku* (Balinese: village priest) before any performance for tourists commences.

On a political level, performance of music and dance provides Balinese people with a means of asserting Balinese identity as distinct from centrally set cultural policies of federal Indonesianism, seen by Balinese as emanating from Jakarta and therefore less than desirable. Teaching music and dance to children ensures that Balinese (as opposed to generic Indonesian) culture is strongly maintained. This political agenda has other levels that require acknowledgement. It will be noticed that the repertoire I refer to in this discussion is what is loosely defined as 'traditional'—that is, even if it is recently created it uses the historical styles of Balinese performing arts. That children are inculcated into the sounds, dances and costumes typical of Balinese tradition is reification of policies through which views of Bali as a culturally authentic remnant of some former 'golden age' are maintained. Children, in this reading, are used in the furthering of agendas set well above them.

Another aspect of learning and teaching music is reification of social ideologies and practices known as *gotong royong*—expectations through which Balinese people participate in activities as groups of equally responsible people. Performance in a *gamelan* is an example of this in musical terms (for example, in the ways that the individual instrumental parts integrate rhythmically and melodically with the rest of an ensemble); the accompaniment of dancers by a *gamelan* is also an example of *gotong royong*; learning and teaching methods, which occur in group settings and rarely individually, are other examples of *gotong royong* in practice. In their learning of gamelan and dance, children enter this world of cultural politics and reification of Balinese social mores such as that of *gotong royong*. Thus, learning music and dance become ways of learning how Balinese society works, how an individual functions as a member of a collective identity, and what the unspoken 'rules' of being Balinese are.

One final aspect of learning to become a performer requires explanation— the concept of *taksu* (Balinese: inspiration resulting from divine assistance). For a performance to be successful, it requires that its performer(s) have experienced and exhibited *taksu*. The term 'inspiration' robs *taksu* of its spiritual implications: it is the essence of a performance that is recognizable as a quality of having achieved desired levels of religious offering. In a context where performance of music and dance is therapeutic, both in the everyday physical sense and in the sense of psychic wellbeing, *taksu* is the essential power of a performance to acquire efficacy (see Hobart 2003; Sugriwa, 2000). *Taksu*, like so much in Balinese religious thinking, derives from belief in the power of one's deified ancestors to contribute to everyday existence and give it meaning and purpose. Balinese house compounds include a shrine to a family's ancestors, called a *kemulan taksu* (Balinese: ancestor shrine)—this references the continuing belief in the power of one's ancestors and the need to recognize them through perceiving actions as offerings to them. *Taksu* results from this position and remains the ultimate intention of any performance (see Eiseman, 1990; Herbst, 1997; Racki, 1998). Again, through participation in learning to play a *gamelan* instrument or to dance, Balinese children not only gain access to a pathway to *taksu*, they experience the cultural system which relies on belief in *taksu* as one of its core elements.

My vignette of a *gamelan* and dance rehearsal in Ubud exhibits many of these factors of learning and teaching music in Bali. The simultaneous, but uncoordinated, practising of the music and dance of *Tari Kijang Kencana* is an example of the socially desirable feeling of *ramai*; the activity was aimed at participation in a Bali-wide *lomba*; the presence of tourists was welcomed (but largely ignored); groups of teachers were working with the children; clear gender lines could be observed; there were numerous repetitions of the music and dance before a final 'performance' was given; the music and dance were never practised at a slower speed than would be expected in performance; whereas the dance is suitable for girls, it presages choreographies required in an adult dance role; the music is a typical *gamelan* piece, not in any way simplified or simple.

In these ways it is possible to interpret the learning and teaching of music in Bali as human experiences that demonstrate aspects of Balinese social norms and which are strongly related to culturally accepted ways of living and growing as a Balinese person. This provides the means for understanding Balinese music pedagogy as a culturally specific meaning system. Children learn music—at the same time they learn by experience the reinforcements of social and cultural frameworks that underpin Balinese life.

Learning and teaching in practice

Three examples of the purposes of children's learning of music and dance can be used to demonstrate how these theoretical explanations take effect in real-life situations. The first of these relates to Balinese reactions to the first Bali bombing of 12 October 2002. This example helps explain ways in which beliefs, especially those relating to the *sekala-niskala* dualism of the world, are borne out in and influence approaches to cultural expression.

I returned to Bali only months after this bombing. Immediately I could see increased cultural activity in the village of Ubud, where my fieldwork is centred, in comparison to my previous research trips. More dance and gamelan classes for children were occurring; more performances of Balinese music and dance staged for tourists were being scheduled; more children's groups were performing for tourists; new gamelan instruments had been commissioned; new pieces were being added to performing groups' repertoires; new performance venues were being built and brought into use; children's performances of dance were being integrated into those presented by adults. When asked about this visible increase in arts activity, especially increased involvement of children in lessons and performances, local Balinese confirmed that this would indicate to the Balinese deities, who live in the *niskala* realm, that recent neglect of traditional culture, perceived as a reason for the bombings, was being redressed by Balinese people. The teaching of music and dance to children was particularly singled out as important here—not only would this indicate attention to performance for deities, it would ensure continued ability to fulfil religious requirements of music and dance into the future. It confirms for those from non-spiritualist backgrounds that belief in the power of performance is the basis of Balinese aesthetics of music and dance, the significance of being a musician, and the importance of transmission of music and dance to children.

The second example is of children's participation in the religious festival of *Galungan*, the most important religious event in the Balinese *Pawukon* 210 day calendar, one of numerous simultaneous calendars by which Balinese life runs. *Galungan* occurs on the Wednesday of the eleventh week of this calendar, but involves festivities over a 10-day period. It celebrates the supremacy of *dharma* (Balinese: the power of righteousness and correct religious duty) over *adharma* (Balinese: godless existence and neglect of religion); it welcomes and honours visiting ancestral deities and invigorates spiritual energy. As music and dance are offerings with religious significance, the ten-day *Galungan* period includes many music and dance events (Bandem & de Boer, 1995; Becker, 2004; Covarrubias, 1973; de Zoete & Spies, 1938; Eiseman, 1990; Hobart, 2003; Mabbett, 2001). During this time, *barong* roam village streets with their own groups of accompanying instrumentalists. A *barong* is a mythical creature with an animal face danced by two men inside a large costume. While the face can be of an animal such as a dog or a pig, the most usual representation is lion-like; this form of *barong* is known as *Barong Ket* (or *Keket*). *Barong Ket* is symbolic of the powers of good. He is often a figure in danced theatre in which he is opposed to the powers of evil, usually represented by a witch-like figure, *Rangda*. During their wanderings, *barong* engage in *ngelawang* (Balinese: go from gate to gate), by stopping outside homes and businesses to dance or enact a short dramatic scene. For these scenes a *barong* will be joined by performers dressed as monkeys (in danced performances a *barong* is often joined by a group of such dancers with whom he engages in pantomimic behaviour—in adult performances these 'monkeys' are danced by child performers). *Barong* wandering village streets expel evil powers and reassure villagers that the powers of good are supreme, reinforcing the beneficial effects of *Galungan*.

While a village *sekaa taruna* (Balinese: young men's club) will be responsible for *ngelawang* with a communally owned *barong* and instruments of a *gamelan* (gongs, drums and *ceng-ceng* (small mounted cymbals)), it is common for groups of boys to make their own *barong*, to scrounge whatever musical instruments they can to accompany it, and set off on *ngelawang*. McPhee (1947), Mead (1970b) and McIntosh (2006b) all describe children's *sekaa barong*

(Balinese: *barong* clubs) during *Galungan*. Observing children's *sekaa barong*, I do not see these as imitative of adult musical behaviour, rather, as children performing something that they see as a natural part of *Galungan* festivities and expectations. That is, through preparation of and performance by a *barong*, children demonstrate the religious implications of contributing to a community's wellbeing at a time of heightened religious awareness at the same time that they fulfil a means to a level of personal *sakti*. That the members of a children's *sekaa barong* might receive payment as they *ngelawang* adds another dimension to Balinese cultural and religious activity.

The third example of the teaching of music and dance to Balinese children is the work of an arts organization. Many arts organizations run programmes for the teaching of *gamelan* and dance. This example refers to such a programme at the Agung Rai Museum of Art (ARMA) in Pengosekan, a village adjacent to Ubud. One of the aims of ARMA is Balinese cultural maintenance, and classes for children are couched by ARMA as a means to fulfilling this aim. Teachers in ARMA's children's *gamelan* and dance classes include *seniman tua* (Indonesian: senior artists), and through this inclusion, traditions of the past are channelled into the present and the future. The aim of these classes is defined by ARMA as to provide 'opportunities, free of charge, for Balinese children to become actively involved in cultural programs of classical dance, *gamelan* and drawing' (ARMA, undated, p. 1). To achieve this:

> ARMA has developed links with local schools to encourage extra-curricular programs. It provides space and the teachers who train the children in classical forms of dance which might otherwise disappear. Peliatan has been famous for Balinese dance for decades, and the classes at ARMA are provided to sustain that internationally recognised excellence. Older dancers are frequently brought in to teach the teachers who then pass the skills on to the young children ... though tourism continues to increase, the arts of Bali will also continue thriving into the next century. (ARMA, undated, p. 2)

Demonstration of the learning outcomes of this programme occurs in public performances (often aimed directly at tourist audiences, who have money to pay to attend concerts and thus can become an unwitting source of funding for the support of cultural preservation).

Pedagogic processes and strategies

Having unpacked some of the motivational forces which guide children's involvement as learners of music and dance, the present section describes processes and strategies employed by teachers in Bali. In many cases, these also rely on societal paradigms and expectations.

The imitation by children of adult music and dance activities remains a regular aspect of children's musical learning in Bali, so that in many cases a child learns elements of an instrument or a dance by witnessing rehearsals or performances over a period of time. Often, such observation is followed by attempts to play an instrument or mimic a dance as it is performed. It is converted into the ability to perform through formalized means at a later time. There is a strong tradition of music and dance teaching within families, and numerous musicians with whom I have worked attest to the capacity of their parents and/or grandparents as musicians who were able to teach them music. These types of learning are supplemented by structured teaching programmes in schools and arts organizations. For example, in the southern Balinese village of Ubud, recognized as a centre of arts activity, numerous community-based programmes for teaching music and dance to children exist. In these, it is usual for boys to learn *gamelan* and both boys and girls to learn dance. Usually fewer boys than girls learn to dance in these programmes (but see below for discussion of gender politics in Balinese music and dance). Teaching of both boys and girls exhibits the following:

- Learning is by imitation of models presented by teachers.
- Copying older students is an accepted way to learn.
- Rote learning is the major means of acquiring information.
- Teachers talk of developing automatic performance, saying that the music must '*masuk*' (Indonesian: enter) the body, highlighting the physicality of learning.
- Learning is always a group activity—it would be almost unthinkable for a learner to have an individual lesson.
- There is conscious emphasizing of group identity among learners, including the use of a group uniform consisting of a T-shirt.
- There is an explicit reliance on repertoire that can be defined as traditional.
- Teaching is often delivered by more than one teacher at the same time (this means that in a group situation, individual teachers work with small groups of children within the overall group).
- Learners are divided into 'cohorts' by age and/or ability; younger children learn by observing and copying their older peers (in this way children have 'learnt' *gamelan* pieces and/or dances before they receive the attention of an adult teacher).
- Regular public performance by children's groups, either for village events in family or temple settings, is integral to and an expected outcome of the learning process.
- In many cases, tourists attend and photograph or film rehearsals, which are easily accessible. Balinese do not deter tourists from this and see it as a sign

of the acceptability of what is happening. Children, therefore, become used to dancing/playing in front of audiences from very early ages.

- There are no technical exercises, and learning is through performance of complete pieces.

- There is little or no 'teacher talk'—children learn by repetition and by having music and/or movement demonstrated to them—it is their job to imitate and memorize.

- There is a hierarchy of pieces of music and dances used to teach basic movements and playing methods, but only a few of these are considered children's pieces; the majority of repertoire can also be seen performed by adult performers.

- Teachers have strong control of learning situations, in content and in pedagogic style.

- Issues of gender mirror those in wider Balinese society, so that while stereotyping exists, it is challenged.

Many of these strategies mark the learning and teaching of music and dance to Balinese children as different from that in Western contexts. Learning and teaching are very public activities; audiences are welcomed. A group ethos governs the enterprise and is reinforced through *sanggar* 'uniforms'. Memory and physical automaticity are guiding principles of learning. In contrast to pedagogic practice in many other parts of the world, there is a practice of teaching whole pieces: technical exercises divorced from the reality of repertoire are not used and performance technique is acquired as necessary to perform a piece at the same time that a piece is learned. While there are dances that are performed by children (e.g. *Tari Kelinci* (Rabbit Dance), *Tari Kijang Kencana* (Shining Deer Dance), *Tari Kupu-Kupu* (Butterfly Dance)), these introduce young female dancers to choreographies and characterizations necessary for dances performed by adults. For example, in *Tari Kupu-Kupu*, girl dancers are required to perform wearing gauze 'butterfly wings' on their arms. The wing movements they learn in this dance are the same as those required to dance the part of the bird of ill omen in *Legong Kraton (Lasem)*—one of the demanding roles required of young female adult performers. Similarly, the movements required to simulate a deer 'dancing' in *Tari Kijang Kencana* are the same as those needed by a young adult performer for the part of the deer in *Kecak* performances that include acting out of the Rama-Sita story from the *Ramayana*. What appear as children's dances are in effect preparation for adult repertoire.

As was noted previously, teaching does not usually allow the speed of music or dance to be slowed down while they are learnt. At the same time, it can be observed that expressive strategies in music and dance (dynamics, accentuation, etc.) are taught as the music/dance is learnt—they are not added after the piece has been learnt purely as notes or movement. Holism of music is the aim of teaching/learning situations.

Performance practices for Balinese *gamelans* and dancers are an element of group dynamic, both for the performers and for their audiences. *Gamelans* are usually set up around a performance space of three to four metres square. Instruments are usually organized along two or three sides of this square; dancers perform in the space between the instruments. Audience members sit/stand around the performance space usually in close proximity to the *gamelan* musicians. That *gamelan* players face each other and can see each other and the dancers during performances is crucial, as in some dances links between choreography and music rely on cues exchanged between dancers and drummers (who indicate structural characteristics of the music to the other players in a group). In some dances, for example, *Tari Baris Tunggal* (a male warrior dance), the dancer establishes his *agem* (Balinese: dance style and character) in an open-ended musical section of the dance before entering the dance space proper. This requires the two drummers of a gamelan to watch the dancer until he makes a physical sign that he is prepared to move into the performance space proper and start the substantive sections of the dance. These links between movement and music are best heard and seen in *angsel* (Balinese: rhythmic gestures) as coincidental dance movement and musical cue. In some dances, the dancer indicates that (s)he wants an *angsel* through formulaic movements; at other times, the drummers indicate that an *angsel* is about to happen. As children's groups learn to perform in this physical arrangement, children learn through responding to visual and aural cues that indicate the structure of the music being performed. Learning to perform is thus dependent on what North, Hargreaves and Tarrant (2002) refer to as the interindividual/situational level of performance.

Challenges to the status quo through children's music activities in Bali

As has been noted numerous times in this discussion, there are strong gender implications of what is learnt by whom in Balinese music and dance; whereas both boys and girls might learn to dance, it is rare for girls to be taught as *gamelan* instrumentalists. This situation echoes gender-based music roles in wider Balinese society. However, as these gender roles are challenged among adult Balinese, so, too, children's learning questions gender stereotyping in Balinese performing arts.

Bali is a society in which traditionally shaped gender roles are strongly delineated and reinforced. For example, the making of *banten* and *canang sari* (Balinese: forms of offerings to deities) is the domain of women; the preparation of food for *ngaben* (Balinese: cremations and funerary rites) remains the responsibility of men. In music, predominantly, males perform on instruments in *gamelans* and women are dancers. There are also male dancers, although even male dance exhibits negotiations of gender with *Tari Baris Tunggal*, the quintessential male dance, now regularly learnt and performed by girls. In my experience, children mostly divide by gender into musical roles of boys as *gamelan* members (and some dancers) and girls as dancers. In learning situations for dance, there are usually fewer boys than girls involved. McIntosh's (2006b) fieldwork experience confirms this. Over the past decades, however, these gender roles in performing arts have been challenged, particularly in development of *gamelan wanita* (Indonesian: women's *gamelan* groups), that position women publicly in activity once the domain of men. However, players in women's *gamelans* have begun learning and performing as adults, whereas male *gamelan* performers have usually learnt since childhood. This provides some explanation of the less than favourable comments of some Balinese about women's *gamelans*; that they do not play 'like men'.

Challenges to boys as the sole learners of *gamelan* exist, as can be seen by the teaching programme of *sanggar* Çudamani, in Pengosekan. Like ARMA, Çudamani espouses an agenda of cultural maintenance through teaching and performing:

> members (of Çudamani) see themselves as a community of leaders who, through their music and dance, positively contribute to the artistic, cultural and political life of their village . . . the group traces its roots from the 70s when the children of Pengosekan . . . gathered after school to play music in the village *balai* (pavilion). Over the years these independent-minded children formed a new kind of organization that has become a pride of the village . . . Çudamani maintains that the vitality of Balinese arts relies on the connection of performance to the religious and social life of the village.
>
> (Çudamani, 2006)

Also implicit in their work is a contemporary ethos of encouraging girls to learn *gamelan*. This was described by Emiko Susilo, from Çudamani, in the following way:

> It is still very unusual for girls to learn *gamelan* from a young age . . . We have a great response from the girls and the teachers . . . about six years ago we started with this group . . . it was obvious to us that training is a big factor. I was raised in the USA, so I was always frustrated by the assumption that women will always play badly simply because they are incapable.
>
> I suppose one of the most important things with us with the girls' gamelan is giving the girls the opportunity to really learn to love and understand the richness and depth

of Balinese gamelan, and the huge benefit of playing Balinese gamelan well is you learn to cooperate with others, listen carefully, value your fellow musicians . . . the interdependency nurtures a mutual respect and a sense of shared accomplishment.
(Personal communication, 17 December 2006)

She also commented on other benefits of girls' participation in a *gamelan*:

Çudamani is a community, a family, and it is important for us to have that sense of shared commitment and shared pride . . . we have found that our girls who have studied gamelan have a strong sense of that. And I cannot emphasise enough the importance of the commitment of a team of teachers, because unlike teaching boys *gamelan*, which is a normal thing to do as everyone thinks 'they may become great musicians one day,' teaching girls *gamelan* did not have that as a draw. Our teachers worked for years and years to teach the girls basic techniques, and developed a way to teach them that fits the girls' personalities like a glove. The warmth of their relationship is beautiful as I think the girls are starting to realise what it meant for these musicians to spend so many hours, months, years teaching them . . . the training of this girls' *gamelan* is one of Çudamani's greatest accomplishments. Who knows whether they will become 'professional' musicians? But they love *gamelan*, they perform with great joy, equally important they respect and admire their teachers, and they have learned how much they need one another . . . it allows the girls to play with other young women of different age groups and also allows students of different abilities to play together, with the shy, newer ones on simpler instruments, and the ones with stronger talent experience and love of the 'front row' in prominent positions. (Emiko Susilo, personal communication, 17 December 2006)

As this discussion demonstrates, music activity by Balinese children is not without agendas of cultural politics and challenges to the status quo. Teaching and learning, which are highly controlled in many cases, are propelled by local and island-wide objectives and expectations. Rivalry between villages and between the *banjar* (Balinese: village wards) within villages often drives the agendas behind teaching activity. Behind the façade of public performance, valued by both Balinese and by tourists, lie problematic situations. For example, a children's gamelan and dance troupe from Gianyar rehearsing to represent their *kebupaten* (Balinese: region) in the 2006 Festival Gong Kebyar exhibited 'enthusiasm . . . fabulous *gaya* (Indonesian: spirit) . . . and an electric energy and confidence that riveted the audience' (Worthy, 2006). The children's performance was beneficial to the festival (as children's groups tend to be at these events) and provided the children with a significant opportunity to perform in public. However, as Worthy points out, such groups often do not continue to practise and perform after public appearances such as this; he notes that the objectives of such festivals are suspect, and perhaps are addressed only to 'a small arts elite that is mostly associated with the governmental arts institutions' (Worthy, 2006). He points out that boys played instruments and girls danced in the example he describes, and this only served to reinforce gender-based music roles in Bali which are continually challenged by the existence of women's gamelan groups (see Bakan, 1997/1998; Dibia & Ballinger, 2004; McGraw, 2004) and by teaching of *sanggar* such as Çudamani (above). Such women's groups, while acceptable to tourists who may be more attuned to issues of gender equity, are not always strongly supported in Bali. In this way, children's *gamelans* (which favour boys as players) may act as a means of engendering and continuing the strong gender bases of Balinese society whereas a girls' *gamelan* may be seen as a challenge and a way through which the learning and teaching of music reflects Bali as a changing society.

Conclusion

In much of the literature of the psychology of music, attention is paid to the processes through which children learn and to the products of learning (especially when this involves individual musical creativity). Discussion often focuses on the learning and teaching of music as a pedagogic activity seemingly for its own ends; what those ends are often remains ambiguous. In the cultural psychology of music education, recognition is made that the purposes, methods and outcomes of music teaching and learning reflect sociocultural contexts. Thus, an ethnomusicological approach provides insights into children's acquisition of skills and repertoires in specific settings, demonstrating the need to read music teaching and learning through the lens of localized music aesthetics. This requires alternative paradigms for considering why music is taught and learnt and how the product of teaching and learning is used by a community's members. To consider children and music in Bali demonstrates how such a paradigm functions. It acknowledges the deep relationship between Balinese culture and Balinese performing arts. This relationship can be used to explain issues that regularly occur as topics of the psychology of music, but elucidates them as culturally influenced: the scope of children's learning of music and dance in Bali, ways that teachers work with learners, the existence of organizations for the teaching of music and dance, children's learning styles, socially driven agendas of the involvement of children in the learning of music and dance, and outcomes of the enterprise.

Through understanding of the social and cultural contexts in which music exists and is taught, it is possible to read the opening vignette of this chapter through Balinese eyes as something more than instruction in instrumental repertoire and dance movement: the purposes behind the event and the levels of meaning Balinese people could ascribe to it qualify its intentionality on many levels—personal, familial, for the performing groups involved, for the teachers, for the community and for the wider maintenance of Balinese culture and religion. To comprehend this reading, it is necessary to investigate the religious, social and political implications of music and dance and to interpret these links as influential in Balinese people's desires to learn music and dance, and for their children to learn them as well. That arts organizations, from privately run studios to *sanggar* and large museums and art galleries, concentrate so much energy on the teaching of music and dance demonstrates their belief in its importance and necessity for the continuation of Balinese wellbeing. A better motivation for music education would be difficult to find.

Acknowledgements

My understandings of Balinese music and dance rely on the advice and assistance of Anak Agung Anom Putra, Cokorda Raka Swastika, Cokorda Sri Agung, Emiko Saraswati Susilo, I Ketut Cater and I Wayan Tusti Adnyana.

References

Agung Rai Museum of Art (ARMA) (undated). Museum prospectus.

Austin, J., Renwick, J., & McPherson, G. (2006). Developing motivation. In G. McPherson (Ed.), *The child as musician: a handbook of musical development* (pp. 211–38). Oxford: Oxford University Press.

Bakan, M. (1997/1998). From oxymoron to reality: agendas of gender and the rise of Balinese women's *gamelan beleganjur* in Bali, Indonesia. *Asian Music, XXIX*(1), 37–85.

Bandem, M., & de Boer, F. (1995). *Balinese dance in transition: kaja and kelod*. Singapore: Oxford University Press.

Barrett, M. (2005). Musical communities and children's communities of musical practice. In D. Miell, R. Macdonald & D. J. Hargreaves (Eds.), *Musical communication* (pp. 281–99). Oxford: Oxford University Press.

Barry, N., & Hallam, S. (2002). Practice. In R. Parncutt & G. E. McPherson (Eds.), *The science and psychology of music performance* (pp. 151–65). New York: Oxford University Press.

Bateson, G., & Mead, M. (1942). *Balinese character: a photographic analysis*. New York: New York Academy of Sciences.

Becker, J. (2004). *Deep listeners: music, emotion, trancing*. Bloomington: Indiana University Press.

Belo, J. (1949). *Bali: rangda and barong*. New York: J. J. Augustin.

Belo, J. (1960). *Trance in Bali*. New York: Columbia University Press.

Berliner, P. (1981). *The soul of mbira: music and traditions of the Shona people of Zimbabwe*. Berkeley: University of California Press.

Berliner, P. (1994). *Thinking in jazz: the infinite art of improvisation*. Chicago: University of Chicago Press.

Brand, M. (2006). *The teaching of music in nine Asian nations*. Lewiston: Edwin Mellen Press.

Campbell, P. (1998). *Songs in their heads*. Oxford: Oxford University Press.

Covarrubias, M. (1973). *Island of Bali*. Singapore: Periplus Editions.

Çudamani. (2006). *Gamelan music and dance of Bali*. Retrieved 12 December 2006 from www.cudamani.org

Davidson, J. (1999). Self and desire: a preliminary exploration of why students start and continue with music learning. *Research Studies in Music Education, 12*, 30–37.

Davidson, L., & Scripp, L. (1988). Young children's musical representations: windows on music cognition. In J. Sloboda (Ed.), *Generative processes in music: the psychology of performance, improvisation and composition* (pp. 195–230). Oxford: Clarendon Press.

de Zoete, B., & Spies, W. (1938). *Dance and drama in Bali*. London: Faber & Faber.

Dibia, W., & Ballinger, R. (2004). *Balinese dance, drama and music: a guide to the performing arts of Bali*. Singapore: Periplus.

Dowling, J., & Harwood, D. (1986). *Music cognition*. San Diego: Academic Press.

Dunbar-Hall, P. (2006). Reading performance: the case of Balinese baris. *Context: Journal of Music Research, 31*, 81–94.

Eiseman, F. (1990). *Bali—sekala and niskala: essays on religion, ritual and art* (Vol. 1). Singapore: Periplus Editions.

Ellis, C. (1985). *Aboriginal music—education for living: cross-cultural experiences from South Australia*. St Lucia, Australia: University of Queensland Press.

Folkestad, G. (2002). National identity and music. In R. MacDonald, D. Hargreaves & D. Miell (Eds.), *Musical identities* (pp. 151–62). Oxford: Oxford University Press.

Geertz, C. (1973). *The interpretation of cultures*. New York: Basic Books.

Gruson, M. (1988). Rehearsal skill and musical competence: does practice make perfect? In J. Sloboda (Ed.), *Generative processes in music: the psychology of performance, improvisation and composition* (pp. 91–112). New York: Oxford University Press.

Hargreaves, D., MacDonald, R., & Miell, D. (Eds.) (2005). *Musical communication*. Oxford: Oxford University Press.

Harnish, D. (1991). Balinese performance as festival offering. *Asian Art, 4*(2), 9–27.

Herbst, E. (1997). *Voices in Bali: energies and perceptions in vocal music and dance theatre*. Hanover, CT: Wesleyan University Press.

Hobart, A. (2003). *Healing performances of Bali: between darkness and light*. New York: Berghahn Books.

Mabbett, H. (2001). *People in paradise: the Balinese*. Singapore: Pepper Publications.

MacDonald, R., Hargreaves, D., & Miell, D. (Eds.) (2002). *Musical identities*. Oxford: Oxford University Press.

Marsh, K. (1995). Children's singing games: composition in the playground? *Research Studies in Music Education, 4*, 2–11.

McGraw, A. (2004). Playing like men: the cultural politics of women's gamelan. *Latitudes, 47*, 12–17.

McIntosh, J. (2006a). How dancing, singing and playing shape the ethnographer: research with children in a Balinese dance studio. *Anthropology Matters, 8*(2). Retrieved 24 October 2006 from www.anthropolgymatters.com/journal/2006-2mcintosh_2006_how.htm

McIntosh, J. (2006b). *Moving through tradition: children's practice and performance of dance, music and song in south-central Bali*. Unpublished PhD thesis, School of History and Anthropology, Queen's University, Belfast.

McPhee, C. (1947). *A house in Bali*. Oxford: Oxford University Press.

McPhee, C. (1948/2002). *A club of small men: a children's tale from Bali*. Singapore: Periplus.

McPhee, C. (1970). Children and music in Bali. In J. Belo (Ed.), *Traditional Balinese culture* (pp. 212–39). New York: Columbia University Press.

McPherson, G., & Davidson, J. (2006). Playing an instrument. In G. McPherson (Ed.), *The child as musician: a handbook of musical development* (pp. 331–51). Oxford: Oxford University Press.

Mead, M. (1970a). Children and ritual in Bali. In J. Belo (Ed.), *Traditional Balinese culture* (pp. 198–211). New York: Columbia University Press.

Mead, M. (1970b). The strolling players in the mountains of Bali. In Jane Belo (Ed.), *Traditional Balinese culture* (pp. 137–45). New York: Columbia University Press.

Mershon, K. (1971). *Seven plus seven: mysterious life-rituals in Bali*. New York: Vantage Press.

Mills, J., & McPherson, G. (2006). Musical literacy. In G. McPherson (Ed.), *The child as musician: a handbook of musical development* (pp. 155–71). Oxford: Oxford University Press.

North, A., Hargreaves, D., & Tarrant, M. (2002). Social psychology and music education. In R. Colwell & C. Richardson (Eds.), *The new handbook of research on music teaching and learning* (pp. 604–25). Oxford: Oxford University Press.

Perlman, M. (2004). *Unplayed melodies: Javanese gamelan and the genesis of music theory*. Berkeley, CA: UCLA Press.

Pressing, J. (1988). Improvisation: methods and models. In J. Sloboda (Ed.), *Generative processes in music: the psychology of performance, improvisation and composition* (pp. 129–78). Oxford: Clarendon Press.

Racki, C. (1998). *The sacred dances of Bali*. Denpasar, Indonesia: Buratwangi.

Ramstedt, M. (1993). Traditional performing arts as *yajnya*. In B. Apps (Ed.), *Performance in Java and Bali: studies of narrative, theatre, music and dance* (pp. 77–87). London: School of Oriental and African Studies, University of London.

Rice, T. (1994). *May it fill your soul: experiencing Bulgarian music*. Chicago: University of Chicago Press.

Sekaa Gong Jaya Swara Ubud (undated). *The soul of Bali* (tourist performance program leaflet). Ubud, Indonesia: Ubud Tourist Information/Bina Wisata Foundation.

Sloboda, J. (2005). *Exploring the musical mind: cognition, emotion, ability, function*. Oxford: Oxford University Press.

Sternberg, R. (Ed.) (1999). *Handbook of creativity*. Cambridge: Cambridge University Press.

Sugriwa, S. (Ed.) (2000). *Nadi: trance in the Balinese art*. Denpasar, Indonesia: Taksu Foundation.

Sullivan, G. (1999). Margaret Mead, Gregory Bateson and highland Bali: fieldwork photographs of Bayung Gede, 1936–1939. Chicago: University of Chicago Press.

Szego, K. (2002). Music transmission and learning: a conspectus of ethnographic research in ethnomusicology and music education. In R. Colwell & C. Richardson (Eds.), *The new handbook of research on music teaching and learning* (pp. 707–29). Oxford: Oxford University Press.

Tenzer, M. (1998). *Balinese music*. Singapore: Periplus.

Van Manen, M. (2003). *Researching lived experience: human science for an action sensitive pedagogy*. London: Althouse Press.

Worthy, K. (2006, April 24). Gamelan anak-anak. Message posted to GamelanListserv electronic mailing list, archived at http://listserv.dartmouth.edu/scripts/wa.exe?A0=GAMELAN (login required).

Chapter 3

Meaning-making through musical play: cultural psychology of the playground

Kathryn Marsh

Introduction: play and learning

For many children, play of varying kinds provides a means for engaging with the world around them. Children can observe and play out patterns of behaviour and other social and cultural phenomena, sometimes as a solitary pursuit, but frequently in the company of others. In the very early years, their 'playmates' may be adults, but, as children's social sphere grows, increasingly their play is conducted in conjunction with other children. In play between peers, children interact both with each other and with their environment, gradually acquiring competence to deal with their physical and social world and constructing knowledge related to this. 'They develop increasingly sophisticated and meaningful understandings and skills as they solve problems and meet new challenges . . . Play provides a mechanism allowing them to move from what they already know and can master to more advanced knowledge' (Glover, 1999, pp. 6–7). Thus play is not only an enjoyable and intrinsically motivated activity, but also a way of incorporating the 'new with the known' (Rogers & Sawyers, 1988, p. 2) to create novel understandings. Children's play has been seen as a 'vehicle for cultural learning', both indicating and reflecting children's development within a culture (Lew & Campbell, 2005, p. 58).

In articulating his view of cultural psychology, Bruner states that 'learning and thinking are always situated in a cultural setting and always dependent upon the utilization of cultural resources' (1996, p. 4). It should be noted that, in this context, constructs of culture are multifaceted and can be deemed to be processual rather than static. They are part of 'an adaptive process that accumulates the partial solutions to frequently encountered problems' (Cole, 1996, p. 129). Culture is seen by Bruner to 'shape the minds of individuals' in order to enable them to assign individual and collective meanings to artifacts or occurrences (1996, p. 3). In this chapter, I examine the ways in which school-aged children construct meaning through the generation and performance of musical play forms, both drawing on and transforming cultural influences. Issues of appropriation, transculturation and identity as manifested in musical play are addressed. The interactive pedagogy of the playground, through which children's agency is fully realized in processes of mutual learning and teaching, is also demonstrated.

Musical play and culture in the playground

Musical play as a form of expressive practice has been the focus of increasing attention by interdisciplinary researchers in many different contexts, particularly over the last two decades (Addo, 1995; Bishop & Curtis, 2001, 2006; Campbell, 1991, 1998; Gaunt, 2006; Harwood, 1998a, 1998b; Kim, 1998; Lew & Campbell, 2005; McIntosh, 2006; Minks, 2006a, 2006b; Prim, 1989; Riddell, 1990). While some researchers (such as Campbell, McIntosh, Minks, and Lum, 2007) have investigated multiple forms of children's musical engagement in varied settings, my research has focused on forms of children's self-initiated musical play that occur primarily in the context of the school playground or in the informal times and spaces between school lessons. Forms of musical play for children of primary school age range from dance and songs derived from adult influences in the classroom, audiovisual media and the sports field through to the more structured sung and chanted games that are part of an oral tradition, such as clapping and jump-rope games, ring and line games.

I have endeavoured to develop an understanding of the characteristics of contemporary playground games, their modes of transmission, children's ways of generating them, and aspects of the children's environments that influence current forms of musical play (Marsh, 1995, 1999, 2001, 2002, 2005, 2006, 2008; Marsh & Young, 2006). I have explored these issues through cross-cultural study of children's musical play in urban Australia, the UK, Norway, USA and South Korea, and in remote schools with predominantly Aboriginal populations in central Australia. In each location I have observed and video-recorded children at play in school playgrounds and adjacent indoor sites, interspersing these observations with discussions with the children regarding their observed play practices. More than 2000 game performances, in addition to other forms of musical play, have been recorded and discussed with children in this manner.

The playground may be seen not only to draw on a surrounding culture created by adults but to have its own culture, evidenced by 'shared values, assumptions, rules, and social practices that make up and contribute to personal and collective identity and security' (Lull, 2000, p. 284). Perhaps the most prominent forms of musical play that are associated with the culture of the playground itself are the playground singing games and chants that are owned, performed and orally transmitted by children. These games share a number of characteristics with other orally transmitted forms, in particular the maintenance of a tradition within which there is constant change.

In oral-formulaic theory, change is effected by means of 'composition in performance' (Lord, 1995, p. 11). In this process, performers recreate a performance artefact, such as a singing game, by drawing on a 'generative matrix' (Treitler, 1986, p. 46) created using 'traditional tools' (Edwards & Sienkowicz, 1990, p. 13), which include particular expectations regarding the overall pattern of the performance, the use of formulae and certain types of language, music and metre. Formulae are the building blocks of oral performances, segments of text, music or movement that are combined in a variety of ways in performance. Whether they are linguistic, rhythmic, melodic or metrical, formulae are imbued with a particular meaning for both performers and listeners who belong to that culture. Within the culture of the playground, formulae could therefore be seen to be a manifestation of a 'cultural toolkit' (Bruner, 1996) through which children not only construct new performative artefacts (varied and novel game forms) but also create new meanings for themselves in the process.

Bruner indicates that 'culture shapes mind, that it provides us with the toolkit by which we construct not only our worlds but our very conceptions of our selves and our powers' (1996, p. X). In the case of children's games in the playground, children draw on cultural influences from the multiple sources that inform their world for the musical, textual and kinesthetic tools through which they can manipulate and construct their own meanings. Such meaning-making, and, indeed, identity formation, results from a fluid process that reflects the rapidly changing nature of the world in which it takes place (J. Marsh, 2005). Increasingly, new technologies create access to a continually expanding range of cultural artefacts and practices, which influence and interact with localized versions to produce 'new cultural hybrids' in a process termed 'transculturation' (Lull, 2000). Similarly, processes of cultural borrowing and hybridity are enhanced by the migration that is characteristic of global populations in the twentieth and twenty-first centuries.

Cultural influences on children's musical play and meaning-making therefore include parents, siblings, and other relatives; mediated sources found on television, CDs, cassettes, films, DVDs, videos, the radio, and Internet; peers in the playground and classroom; teachers, and the materials which form part of school curricula; and experiences which may be gained in countries of birth, on visits to countries of cultural origin, or on holidays in other localities. Through the processes of transformation of material derived from these cultural influences, children use them both to express their own meanings and to attain a form of mastery over the original artefacts, achieving a level of power that is often denied them in the larger world controlled by adults. These processes have been observed in children's play in many localities, including the UK (Bishop & Curtis, 2006); the USA (Gaunt, 2006); Singapore (Lum, 2007); Bali (McIntosh, 2006); and Nicaragua (Minks, 2006a, 2006b).

Co-construction and musical play

In musical play, empowerment is partly achieved through collaboration between children in order to co-construct new games and game variants over which they can exert complete ownership. As Harwood (1998a) and Barrett (2005) have indicated, children engaging in musical play in the school playground form a 'community of practice' (Wenger, 1998, as cited in Barrett, 2005, p. 268) in which members of the group operate within a 'domain of knowledge' (p. 268), mediating that knowledge through shared practice and using it to develop greater levels of expertise. This is most explicitly evident when children are working together to invent or vary their games, as outlined by two girls (aged 8 and 9 years) in West Yorkshire, UK in 2002:

> *Janice*:[1] You don't usually make it up on your own. You usually make it up with a group so they know it.
> *Hayley*: 'Cause then all of the people can have, like, ideas to put in it and then you get more things to use in it . . . you can't really think for yourself as much as in a group.

An example of collaborative practice and the manipulation of different elements drawn from varied societal sources can be seen in the composition of a new clapping game by a group of 10-year-old girls in a school in Stavanger, Norway, in 2002. Although the provenance and novelty of games has sometimes been disputed (for example, by Opie & Opie, 1985), that this game was entirely new to the playground was clearly apparent, because the subject of the game was my recent appearance as a researcher in the school. The, song, entitled *To Kathryn from Charlotte* was performed in both Norwegian and English as follows:

Performance in Norwegian	Performance in English
Katrine, Katrine, Katrine, Katrine	Kathryn Kathryn Kathryn Kathryn
Vi liker deg her på skolen vårv	We love you here in the school
Og vi håper du blir her lenger	And we hope you will be there longer
Tra la la la la la	Tra la la la la la
Og vi håper du blir her lenger	And we hope you will be there longer
Tra la la la la la	Tra la la la la la la[2]
(B KK 02 2 AV, recorded 2002)	

[1] Schools and children's names are referred to by pseudonyms.
[2] This was the girls' performative translation, their own version as they performed the clapping game in English. It differs slightly from a direct translation from the Norwegian.

The girls' vocal performance was accompanied throughout by a variety of clapping patterns. Charlotte, its instigator, described her process of singing the game into being, then with the help of other friends, adding formulae and refining the material:

> *Charlotte*: I think I will have a song with you. And so I just begin and sing. And so I sing and sing and sing. And I made it. I find up a song for you.
> *Ine*: With clapping . . .
> *K* (researcher): OK. So you just sang it until it all came together, did you?
> *Charlotte*: Yes . . . and so I came to the song's melody. And so I found up a melody from another song and so I sing it.
> *K*: OK. So that melody comes from another song?
> *Charlotte*: Yes, from an English CD . . . And so I think I can take that melody. And so I found up 'Kathryn Kathryn Kathryn Kathryn' and 'we love you here in the school' but . . . today I found up the whole song with another. She's name Hege but I found it up and she help me . . .
> *K*: And how did you work out the clapping?
> *Charlotte*: I think of some other clapping game. And so I take some from that and some from that.

Charlotte's use of terms is influenced by the fact that English is a less familiar language for her. And yet her expression for the generative process, 'found up', is illustrative of the processes at work, combining as it does the idea of 'thought up' with finding and selecting materials from the generative matrix provided by existing game formulae (clapping patterns) and the media-influenced sonic environment (song melody). The process of refinement is enacted through trialling by performance with friends and the progressive implementation of their suggested additions and amendments until a satisfactory performative product is reached. Such an approach exemplifies the 'interactive, intersubjective pedagogy' advocated by Bruner (1996, p. 22), in which, he suggests, 'works-in-progress create shared and negotiable ways of thinking in a group' (p. 23).

Although this community of practice focuses on children, there are circumstances in which it is expanded to include adults in the mutual construction of song material. One example of this was observed in 2002 at a tiny school serving an indigenous community of Jingili and Mudburra people in the remote Barkly Tablelands of the Northern Territory, Australia.[3] The strong kinship bonds of Aboriginal peoples in this area mean that games are frequently transmitted by siblings, 'cousins', and 'aunties' within an intricate network of kinship affiliations. Thus games are more readily learnt from or played with

---

[3] Aboriginal people in this area, as in other areas of central Australia, are referred to by their language groups. In the particular part of the Barkly Tablelands under discussion, the predominant language groups are Jingili and Mudburra.

adults or older children at home or on visits elsewhere and the divide between child and adult in co-construction is less widely marked. One 8-year-old Aboriginal girl in another small school in the area told me that she had not only learnt *Chocolate cake* (a clapping game in local circulation) from her mother, but that she and her mother made up clapping games to 'them Bible songs', exemplified by a song entitled *Here's Lord*.

The example of co-construction that I witnessed on this occasion was not actually a game but the conversion of a story from the Dreaming (the beginning of time in Aboriginal belief systems) into a song (translated as *Long ago*) to be taught to the other children in the school, as part of a programme of indigenous language maintenance in the local Mudburra language. What prompts my discussion of this song here is the similarity of its generative process to that described by Charlotte in the previous example. The song was once again sung into being, by repeated testing out of melodic phrases, with both the 11-year-old girl, Erin, and two adults (Erin's aunt and uncle) trying out and modelling phrases, making occasional suggestions about text setting, word underlay, melody and rhythm over repeated renditions. The two adults had both been members of an Aboriginal country band, so drew strongly on the musical conventions of this genre for the melody and chordal accompaniment on the guitar. Yet, Erin's contributions were equally important, and the song gradually evolved into a coherent and elaborated form through collaborative composition in performance over a period of more than 30 minutes in a quiet space at the edge of the playground.

Boundary crossing: play and identity

The contributions of adults to playground games are more usually at a remove from the playground itself, though once again, in instances where there is intergenerational play in the home, this may be immediately adopted or adapted for use among peers at school. Thus the Punjabi clapping game *Zig zag zoo* is learnt by many children from mothers, aunts or grandmothers in the home environment in Anglo-Punjabi enclaves in a West Yorkshire town in the UK, but its acceptance in the playground is influenced by the prevailing conditions in the school. Ellington Primary School, which I visited in 2002, had a population made up largely of Anglo-Punjabi and Anglo-Bengali children. In this school *Zig zag zoo* and a number of other Punjabi and Bengali games flourished in the playground, with multiple variants resulting from its popularity. However, in St Stephen's, a nearby ethnically mixed primary school with dominant Anglo population, the Punjabi games were played in a much more covert manner, without the variety found at Ellington.

At Ellington school, games such as *Zig zag zoo* were used by children almost as markers of identity, a manifestation of children's comfort with their bilingual, bicultural world. This might be partly attributed to their majority ethnic status and the strong maintenance of language and ethnic heritage by adults within the school. Children of both sexes demonstrated considerable flexibility in their play, with performance of some games vacillating between two languages. For example, a counting out game in which children's fingers, spread on the floor, were gradually eliminated through successive pointing by the game leader, was performed with both Punjabi and English texts, often recited cyclically in close succession:

Game text	Translation
Akkar bakkar pahmba poh	Akkar bakkar pahmba poh (vocables)
Chori mari poorey sow.	Done some stealing makes a full hundred
Akkar bakkar pahmba poh	Akkar bakkar pahmba poh
Assee navay poorey sow . . .	Eighty, ninety, full hundred.
(Punjabi)	
Eeny meeny miny more	
Put the baby on the floor	
If it cries slap it twice	
Eeny meeny miny more . . .	
(English)	
(EA AK 02 4 AV, EA EM 02 2 AV, recorded 2002)	

Other renditions of this game were bilingual, incorporating both English and Punjabi text with equal insouciance, for example:

Scooby dooby doo went to the loo	Bacha = child
Out came a bacha with a kala tuhu.	Kala = black
Scooby dooby doo went to the loo	Tuhu = bum
Out came a bacha that was you . . .	
(English and Punjabi)	
(EA SDD 02 2 AV, recorded 2002)	

In discussing similar examples of linguistic code-switching within the play of Miskitu children on the coast of Nicaragua,[4] Minks (2006b) notes that 'borrowed words enable children and other speakers to integrate knowledge from different spheres of social interaction, and they are never simply borrowed but always "re-accentuated" in the emerging discourse . . . borrowed words encode histories of intercultural social relations and inflect speech with other contexts of use' (p. 125).

---

[4] Code switching may be defined as the alternation between two languages within a conversation (or language exchange) between bilingual people (Milroy & Muysken, 1995).

By contrast, in the St Stephen's playground, the Anglo-Punjabi children's bicultural identity was subsumed into the dominant Anglo mainstream, to some extent because of their demographic minority but also because biculturalism was not endorsed with the same enthusiasm by school policies and practices. Musical play at this school appeared to be a manifestation of an assimilated identity whereas at home the resumption of dual identities was enabled through musical play, among other forms of activity.

Although most of the Anglo-Punjabi children in both schools had been born in England, many of them made regular trips with their families to Pakistan where their repository of games was replenished. There was thus an ever-expanding generative matrix of musical games and game formulae (textual, kinesthetic and musical) to add to that already maintained through intergenerational play in the home.

Bicultural children may use musical play as a way of reinforcing identity and cultural practices from their birth countries but may also use it as a mechanism for adopting new cultural practices and for working through the transitions between the two. In children's playful interactions, 'complex, multi-layered, and continually emergent subjectivities are forged in the intercultural practices of border-making and border-crossing' (Minks, 2006a, abstract). At a multi-ethnic school in Seattle, where there was an English Language Learners (ELL) class, comprising Spanish-speaking children aged from 5 to 9 years, I encountered an example of this process of both figurative and literal 'border-crossing'. These Latino children, newly arrived from Mexico and South America, formed a tightly knit group within the playground. Clapping games, ring games and line games, originally learnt in their countries of origin, were all played in their first language of Spanish. Many of these games, such as the clapping game *Me caí de un balcón* (I fell from the balcony) maintained certain verbal formulae that linked to previously known cultural practices.

Spanish	English translation
Me caí de un balcón, con, con	I fell from the balcony, -cony, -cony
Me hice un chichón, chon, chon	It gave me a bump, bump, bump
Vino mi mama me quiso pegar	My mother came and wanted to hit me
Vino mi papa me quiso horcar	My father came and wanted to choke me
Vino mi abuelita la pobre viejita	My grandma came, the poor old thing
Me dio un centavito y me hizo callar	She gave me a cent and made me be quiet
Calla, calla, calla	Quiet, quiet, quiet
Cabeza de papaya	Head of a papaya
(HV MCB 04 1 AV, recorded 2004)	

The final formula in this game 'Calla, calla, calla, Cabeza de papaya' (Quiet, quiet, quiet, head of a papaya) invoked the chant often sung by central American parents while they rock and sooth a child who has hurt his or her head. In this instance, it is possible that the comfort derived from the reference to this familiar practice in the game extended beyond the performance of the game to the reinforcement of a sense of belonging to this microcommunity, within the larger community operating in the playground.

In contrast to the clapping games, all jump-rope games played by the members of this class were performed in English, because they had been newly acquired in the Seattle playground from English-speaking peers. It seemed that the Latino children were enacting a transition into a new form of cultural and linguistic practice by the adoption of this new genre of musical play in all its linguistic integrity.

The transitional act of migration itself was encoded in several of the Latino girls' clapping games. One example of this was *Frankenstein*, the text of which juxtaposed the frightening figures of Frankenstein and vampires with the fear and uncertainty of border-crossing to the promised land of California:

Spanish	English translation
Frankenstein	Frankenstein
Fue a ver	Went to see
Al Castillo	To the castle
Del vampiro	Of the vampire
Se asusto	He was frightened
Y grito:	And he shouted:
A la ver, a ver, a ver	To see, to see, to see
De la mar, de la mar	To the sea, to the sea
Por la culpa de pasar	For the fault of passing here
Lo' de delante corre mucho	Those at the front run fast
Lo' de atrás se quedaran, tras, tras, tras	Those behind, will stay behind, behind, behind
California, California	California, California
Estados Unidos	USA
Viajes presumidos	Trips cancelled
California, California	California, California
Blanco chúpate un mango	White (man) suck a mango
Se callo de la silla (OW!)	He fell from the seat (OW!)
(HV FR 04 1 AV, recorded 2004)	

At the culmination of the game, the 'white man', with his apparently boundless authority to determine the outcome of the journey to the USA, is disempowered in one single textual swoop, the ridicule reversing this power relationship between the immigration authorities and the children who have successfully negotiated this literal rite of passage.

From classroom to playground

The only clapping game that I observed being sung in English by the Latino children in the Seattle school had been devised to accompany the song *There was an old lady who swallowed a fly*, learnt in school music classes. Although teachers might be seen to operate as outsiders to the playground, they can sometimes join the community of practice for a short time, contributing games that have longevity in the playground beyond their initial performance. Once in the playground such games take on a life of their own, with new meanings ascribed by the ever-increasing circle of performers as the games are transmitted from child to child. For example, the game *Da da dexi*, recorded in performance by groups of children of different ages at a Sydney school in 1990 had been taught by a classroom teacher:

> *Tara:* We learnt it from our . . . We had a teacher, Miss Stillianos. She was Greek.
> *K:* Uh huh.
> *Clara:* And she taught us that.
> *Matu:* Yeah, she taught us.
> *K:* Oh. She taught you that one, did she? Did she teach you the game, or just the words, or what?
> *Tara:* The actions.
> *Matu:* The actions.
> *K:* Oh right. Is it a Greek game?
> *Tara:* Yeah.
> *Clara:* No, it's more . . . it's more Italian.
> *Tara:* It's more Italian.
> *Clara:* Yeah. 'Si signorina' . . .
> *K:* So, when did you have her?
> *Several:* Year 2
> *Clara:* I didn't have her.
> *Tara:* I didn't have her either.
> *Matu:* I did.
> *K:* So you think that's how that one came to the school, then?
> *Clara:* Yes, definitely,'cause I've never ever heard it . . .
> *Tara:* Yeah. I've never heard it before–just from her.
>
> (Interview, Year 6 girls, 1994)

It can be seen from this example that children create and attribute their own meaning at will to adult-derived material. The brief game text, with the exception of 'Si signorina', was almost certainly composed completely of vocables, or syllables with negligible semantic content:

Da da dexi
Dexi dexi da
Si signorina
Upona dexi da hey!

(SH DX 90 1 AV, recorded 1990)

Despite this, children imbued the text with meaning by attributing it to a language. The most popular language for such attributions in this playground was Italian, as an Italian LOTE[5] programme had been operating in school classrooms for several years. It should be noted that many languages were spoken by children in this multi-ethnic school, but the language sanctioned by classroom teaching was seen by the children to be almost all-purpose in its use. In other schools, vocables were deemed to belong to another 'official' language. Interestingly, despite their bilingualism, the Punjabi speaking children at Ellington school in West Yorkshire designated all vocables in their Punjabi games as English. English, in this sense, meant 'other', a language to some extent removed from the children's sense of self by being equated with its omnipresence in the classroom.

This is not to say that songs learnt in the classroom were exempt from use in the playground. As can be seen from the instances above, songs taught in the classroom were appropriated as playground games with some frequency. Indeed, they seemed to attain greater currency if they were then subverted, or had a nonsensical or subversive element in their initial form. One example of this was the game *Waddly archer*, which contained a large proportion of vocables and tricky hand movements. This game, originally learnt from the music teacher, was popularly performed in the playground of one West Yorkshire school. In a school in Bedford, in south-east England, a cycle of appropriation was exemplified by the adaptation of an action song learnt in the classroom.

Twinkle twinkle chocolate bar
My Dad drives a rusty car
Press the button. Pull the choke
Off we drive in a cloud of smoke
Twinkle twinkle chocolate bar
My Dad drives a rusty car

(SP TTC 02 1 AV, recorded 2002)

The song was a textual parody, probably originating in a playground, though not necessarily in this school.[6] Its performance in the classroom had been

---

[5] Languages other than English.

[6] A number of parodies of the nursery rhyme *Twinkle twinkle little star* appear in collections of children's playlore (see, for example, Turner, Factor & Lowenstein, 1978).

suggested by a male member of the class on the day that I had later seen it played. It had been briefly adopted for classroom teaching purposes, then reverted to the playground, where it was immediately converted into a clapping game, performed with the ubiquitous three-beat clap[7] by a group of 8-year-old girls.

The real and the imagined: appropriation and the media

Similar cycles of appropriation operate in relation to children's use of media sources. Barrett (2005) states that 'we participate in a number of intersecting communities of musical practice. These include localized communities that feature direct human interaction, and "globalized" virtual communities where interaction is mediated through electronic media such as MTV and sound recordings' (p. 269). In children's musical play these 'localized' and 'globalized' communities intersect, as children listen to music on CDs; watch televised popular music programmes, often aimed specifically at the 'tweenage' market; absorb background songs and music from other television programmes and movies; and download sound files and song lyrics from the Internet (Carrington, 2006; Mitchell & Reid-Walsh, 2002).

In Seattle, a 10-year-old girl told me how she downloaded songs from the Internet to share with her friends. These songs constituted source material for the wide range of song and dance routines generated by this very prolific group of girls, who were often to be found in the playground devising and performing clapping games, cheers and movement routines to songs. Their sources included movies and sports chants, but one source seemed to be a favourite. This was the website associated with KZOK, a local radio station specializing in classic rock. A programme that held a particular fascination for these girls was one that featured 'Twisted Tunes', parodies of well-known popular songs in which, according to the girls 'they, like, make up words to different songs but they put funny words in' (Interview, 2004). The song parodies could be downloaded as audio files or as song lyrics. They were then subjected to further creative manipulation by the girls, who varied the texts and invented

---

[7] This pattern was the most frequently used clapping pattern observed in all field schools except those in Korea. It consists of three successive clapping movements performed on the beat:

1. right hand claps down while left hand claps up (hands horizontal);
2. clap partner's hands (hands vertical);
3. clap own hands together.

This pattern has been noted by many other researchers into children's musical play, especially in the UK and USA (Bishop & Curtis, 2006; Campbell, 1991, 1998; Gaunt, 2006; Merrill-Mirsky, 1988).

movement routines to accompany them (see Marsh, 2006, for a further discussion of this phenomenon).

While some of the parodic texts were adopted almost in entirety, others were garnered for their textual and melodic formulae in order to form very different entities. The result of one such creative endeavour was a song *Scooby dooby do*, accompanied by a choreographed dance sequence:

> Scooby dooby do did a poo
> Shaggy thought it was candy
> Shaggy took a bite and turned all white
> And that's the end of the story.
> [Faster tempo]
> And from the start they go YMCA
> From the start they go YMCA
> You can eat Siamese, you can eat a poo
> But that doesn't matter when you're all together.
>
> (HV SD 04 1V, recorded 2004)

The song was an eclectic mix, having been drawn from a range of sources, as explained by the girls:

> *K*:   OK, so where did that one come from?
> *Alicia*:   We made it up.
> *K*:   You made it up did you?
> *Chrissie*:   Well, I kind of taught them that.
> *K*:   How did you make it up, Chrissie?
> *Chrissie*:   I didn't make it up. My sister told me . . .'cause her friend told her.
> *K*:   OK, so did she tell you the whole thing or did you add some bits to it?
> *Chrissie*:   Oh, we added the last part, the [sings] 'YMCA'.
> *K*:   The 'YMCA'. OK. How did you decide to add that bit?
> *Chrissie*:   Just, me and Rania were at my house and we were thinking of dances to do for the talent show. Then we thought of that.
> *Alicia*:   Then at school we made up [demonstrates song and movements] 'You can eat Siamese'.

The song incorporated a parody of the theme music of a television cartoon series, *Scooby doo*,[8] text and the iconic movements (letter shapes) from the 1978 disco hit, *YMCA*, by the Village People, and a text line developed from another parody song appropriated from KZOK, *Cats in the kettle*, which mentioned a 'fat Siamese' cat as food served up in a Chinese restaurant. The girls went on to perform their version of *Cats in the kettle* immediately after *Scooby dooby do*. Both performances emphasized the parodic nature of the songs with

---

[8]   Other similarly scatological parodies of this same theme song by children in a Yorkshire (UK) school are discussed by Bishop and Curtis (2006).

lavish mimetic movements interspersed between more standard dance moves, to increase the level of subversion of adult norms and musical forms. The solidarity achieved by enactment of this 'miniature rite of rebellion' (McDowell, 1999, p. 55) was reinforced by the final line, 'But that doesn't matter when you're all together' at which point the girls moved together and embraced.

The power generated by collaboration could be further enhanced by the association with a media-endorsed image, a form of extended 'mimesis', characterized as 'part reproduction and part re-creation, part fidelity and part fantasy' (Goldman, 1998, as cited in Bishop & Curtis, 2006, p. 4). The girls who had created the *Scooby doo* parody described how a game show format incorporating chants had developed as they were rehearsing in the playground.

> *Chrissie:* We used to have this little thing called GT . . .
> *K:* Yeah? What was that?
> *Alicia:* Girl Talk.
> *Rania:* We used to have this little thing called GT. But then people started calling it something else. It was supposed to be Girl Talk.
> *Chrissie:* They started calling it something bad.
> *K:* Did they? So what was GT? Tell me about it.
> *Alicia:* It's like a game show thing and we just perform chants and stuff.
> *K:* So was this something that you just made up, like in your group?
> *Alicia:* Yeah.
> *K:* Yeah. And where do you do this? …
> *Chrissie:* Recess.
> *K:* At recess?
> *Alicia:* Yeah.
> *Chrissie:* We didn't never even want to have this show but . . .
> *Rania:* People started saying 'GT, GT'.

The game show format gave the girls' play an extra cachet. However, even such illustrious constructions as television game shows could be subject to ridicule, with boys in the playground changing the title to 'something bad', so that eventually this game was abandoned. Children are quite capable of subverting each other's play, as well as collaborating. I observed a pair of girls excluded from a group devising dance routines to popular hits in a Bedford (UK) school playground. The two girls performed on the periphery of the group using highly exaggerated movements to parody the others, achieving their own form of personal vengeance for the exclusion. In a West Yorkshire school, a less malicious parody was provided by a member of a group of girls singing the Madonna song, *Like a prayer*, who effortlessly interpolated the phrase 'Mamma mia' (from the eponymous ABBA song) at various points of (otherwise) textual rest.

As demonstrated by the examples above, material appropriated from the media is rarely retained in its initial form, but is used for the children's own purposes. During my 2001 visit to a school in a small desert town in central Australia, children were preparing for the annual school sports carnival. Preparations included the creation of sports chants and accompanying dances with which to rally participants from different sports 'houses' or teams as they participated in athletics races. I observed a small group of older girls devising an appropriate dance routine to the song *I'm a believer*, from the soundtrack recording of the movie *Shrek*. It is notable that, although this town was 500 kilometers away from the nearest cinema, the movie and soundtrack were already well-known to the children through a video outlet in the town. Another group explained to me that they were changing the lyrics to a cheer from the movie, *Bring it on*, to include the name of their sports house, again to use during the sports carnival. The cycle of appropriation was further demonstrated on the day of the sports carnival when two 6-year-old girls were seen in the playground at recess performing a clapping game that incorporated one of the sports chants they had just observed on the sports field, which ended emphatically with the anthemic line 'We will, we will rock you' from the song by the 1970s rock group Queen.

A similar transition from screen song and dance to playground dance routine, followed by transmutation to clapping game, was found in the play of a number of groups of Anglo-Punjabi and Anglo-Bengali girls in the Ellington school playground in West Yorkshire. The girls, along with other members of their families, were avid consumers of Bollywood[9] movies, notable for their colourful and highly choreographed song and dance sequences. These sequences were re-enacted in the playground by girls of different ages, sometimes with remarkable accuracy. However, they were also used as the basis for clapping games that immediately enabled the girls to attain ownership of these mediated musical materials. Frequently the kinesthetic characteristics of the original sequence (such as full body twirls) were interpolated between clapping movements to retain traces of the game's progenitor, while creating something that was idiomatically the girls' own.

Ownership of mediated material was most obviously demonstrated by the appropriation of another popular song, *That's the way I like it* by girls in

---

[9] Bollywood is the name given to the Indian film industry that generates a large number of movies, predominantly in Hindi but also in Urdu and other languages. The movies are popular not only within India and Pakistan but also with the diaspora from the Indian subcontinent.

Bedford and West Yorkshire, UK and Stavanger, Norway. *That's the way I like it* was a disco hit released in 1975 by the American group KC and the Sunshine Band, but made familiar to children of this generation by constant reappearance in the soundtracks of advertisements and movies. The song is identifiable by the iconic text of its chorus:

That's the way (uh huh uh huh) I like it (uh huh uh huh).

In children's use of this text to create a clapping game (of which there were many examples), the appropriated text line is used to endorse markers of the individual player's identity, typically indicated in the Bedford school by sporting preferences, as performed by two 8-year-old girls:

> [*Both*]
> A B C hit it
> That's the way (uh huh uh huh) I like it (uh huh uh huh)
> That's the way (uh huh uh huh) I like it (uh huh uh huh)
>
> [*Chloe*]
> My name is Chloe and … my game is football
> Boys are never on my mind so
>
> [*Both*]
> That's the way (uh huh uh huh) I like it (uh huh uh huh)
> That's the way (uh huh uh huh) I like it (uh huh uh huh)
>
> [*Danielle*]
> My name is Danielle and my game is netball
> Boys are never on my mind so
>
> [*Both*]
> So that's the way (uh huh uh huh) I like it (uh huh uh huh)
>
> (SP TTW 02 7 AV, recorded 2002)

The appropriated text line both endorses these identity markers and emphasizes the accomplishment of the players, borne out by their management of an intricate interweaving hand pattern involving alternate clapping and gripping. It is as if their mastery of this difficult pattern is also a manifestation of their individual and collective power, which they chorus together in triumph. In this version, 'girl power' is also demonstrated by their dismissal of boys as a complete irrelevance.

Another version of this game by 9-year-old girls in a West Yorkshire school was more subversive, with 'That's the way I like it' endorsing transgressive behaviour:

> [*Both throughout*]
> One two three hit it
> That's the way (uh huh uh huh) I like it (uh huh uh huh)
> That's the way (uh huh uh huh) I like it (uh huh uh huh)

My name's Saiqa, I'm really really cool
When I'm out shoppin' my friends are still at school, so
That's the way (uh huh uh huh) I like it (uh huh uh huh)
That's the way (uh huh uh huh) I like it (uh huh uh huh)

(ST TTW 02 7, recorded 2002)

By outwitting both adults and other children the girls exemplified in their verbal play the epitome of 'coolness' reaching a pinnacle of social standing, which was just 'the way [they] like it'.

Conclusion: from playground to classroom

Through musical play, children process and synthesize many different aspects of their worlds. Play enables them to mediate knowledge obtained through exposure to parents and other adults and relatives, child peers, the classroom, and audiovisual media, and to generate their own understandings. It provides a mechanism through which they can exercise control over their knowledge, accommodating differences through collaboration within various communities of practice. Learning within these interrelated communities is achieved by the interdependent contributions of its members, with interpretation leading to transformation, and the creation of new social meanings, in addition to musical forms and styles.

Bruner has noted that, too often, schools fail to take account of 'the enabling nature of human culture as a toolkit for active, questing children seeking mastery over their worlds' (1996, p. 81). The playground can provide a model of ways in which a 'community of learners' can develop agency, identity and self-esteem (pp. 38–39) within its participant members, which schools may do well to emulate. In the subcommunity of the playground there are multiple teacher/learners who engage in a mutual, two-way process of teaching, learning and meaning-making through symbolic use of language, music and gesture. The playground is a place where 'learners help each other, each according to her abilities', and where 'the teacher does not play that role as a monopoly' but 'learners "scaffold" for each other as well' (p. 21). Although the content of learning may be vastly different, the processes of interactivity and agency found in the playground can only be of benefit when applied to the classroom.

Teachers need to recognize that children are not only learners but also expert teachers within their own milieu, and to accept that children bring these skills into the classroom, where they may be put to use. The adoption of a more flexible approach to teaching, where there is accommodation of differing practices and solutions to problems that are posed, is also an important catalyst to learning. Such flexibility uses the potential developed within children's communities of practice, engendering success and a feeling of achievement in learners.

Teachers can adopt a scaffolding rather than directive role, providing new materials for performance, listening, and composition, which acknowledges children's observed current musical skills and knowledge, and takes them further. Equally important is the acknowledgement that children's understandings are sophisticated, reflecting a diversity of cultural influences derived from global and local sources. Just as playground culture is permeable, so the culture of the classroom can draw on divergent sources for musical and pedagogical enrichment.

References

Addo, A. O. (1995). Ghanaian children's music cultures: a video ethnography of selected singing games (Doctoral dissertation, University of British Columbia, Canada, 1995). *Dissertation Abstracts International*, 57/03, AAC NN05909.

Barrett, M. S. (2005). Musical communities and children's communities of musical practice. In D. Miell, R. MacDonald & D. J. Hargreaves (Eds.), Musical Communication (pp. 260–80). Oxford: Oxford University Press.

Bishop, J. C., & Curtis, M. (2001). *Play today in the primary school playground*. Buckingham: Open University Press.

Bishop, J. C., & Curtis, M. (2006, July). Participation, popular culture and playgrounds: children's uses of media elements in peer play at school. Paper presented at 'Childhood and Youth: Participation and Choice' conference, University of Sheffield.

Bruner, J. (1996). *The culture of education*. Cambridge, MA: Harvard University Press.

Campbell, P. S. (1991). The child-song genre: a comparison of songs by and for children. *International Journal of Music Education*, 17, 14–23.

Campbell, P. S. (1998). *Songs in their heads: music and its meaning in children's lives*. New York: Oxford University Press.

Carrington, V. (2006). *Rethinking middle years: early adolescents, schooling and digital culture*. Crows Nest, Sydney: Allen & Unwin.

Cole, M. (1996). *Cultural psychology: a once and future discipline*. Cambridge, MA: Harvard University Press.

Edwards, V., & Sienkowicz, T. J. (1990). *Oral cultures past and present: rappin' and Homer*. Oxford: Blackwell.

Gaunt, K. D. (2006). *The games black girls play: learning the ropes from double-Dutch to hip-hop*. New York: New York University Press.

Glover, A. (1999). The role of play in development and learning. In E. Dau (Ed.), Child's play: revisiting play in early childhood settings (pp. 5–15). Sydney: MacLennan & Petty.

Harwood, E. (1998a). Music learning in context: a playground tale. *Research Studies in Music Education*, 11, pp. 52–60.

Harwood, E. (1998b). Go on girl! Improvisation in African-American girls' singing games. In B. Nettl & M. Russell (Eds.), In the course of performance: studies in the world of musical improvisation (pp. 113–25). Chicago: University of Chicago Press.

Kim, Y.-Y. (1998). Traditional Korean children's songs: collection, analysis and application. Unpublished doctoral dissertation, University of Washington, Seattle.

Lew, J. C.-T., & Campbell, P.S. (2005). Children's natural and necessary musical play: global contexts, local applications. *Music Educators Journal*, 91(5), 57–62.

Lord, A. B. (1995). The singer resumes the tale. Ithaca, NY: Cornell University Press.

Lull, J. (2000). *Media, communication, culture: a global approach*. Cambridge: Polity Press.

Lum, C.-H. (2007). Musical networks of children: an ethnography of elementary school children in Singapore. Unpublished doctoral dissertation, University of Washington, Seattle.

Marsh, J. (2005). Ritual, performance and identity construction: young children's engagement with popular cultural and media texts. In J. Marsh (Ed.), Popular culture, new media and digital literacy in early childhood (pp. 28–50). London: Routledge.

Marsh, K. (1995). Children's singing games: composition in the playground? *Research Studies in Music Education*, 4, 2–11.

Marsh, K. (1999). Mediated orality: the role of popular music in the changing tradition of children's musical play. *Research Studies in Music Education*, 13, 2–12.

Marsh, K. (2001). It's not all black or white: the influence of the media, the classroom and immigrant groups on contemporary children's playground singing games. In J. C. Bishop & M. Curtis (Eds.), Play today in the primary school playground (pp. 80–97). Buckingham: Open University Press.

Marsh, K. (2002). Observations on a case study of song transmission and preservation in two Aboriginal communities: dilemmas of a 'neo-colonialist' in the field. *Research Studies in Music Education*, 19, 1–10.

Marsh, K. (2005). Worlds of play: the effects of context and culture on the musical play of young children. *Early Childhood Connections*, 11(1), 32–36.

Marsh, K. (2006). Cycles of appropriation in children's musical play: orality in the age of reproduction. *The World of Music*, 48(1), 8–23.

Marsh, K., & Young, S. (2006). Musical play. In G. McPherson (Ed.), The child as musician: a handbook of musical development (pp. 289–310). Oxford: Oxford University Press.

Marsh, K. (2008). *The musical playground: global tradition and change in children's songs and games*. New York: Oxford University Press.

McDowell, J. H. (1999). The transmission of children's folklore. In B. Sutton-Smith, J. Mechling, T. W. Johnson & F. McMahon (Eds.), Children's folklore: a source book (pp. 49–62). Logan: Utah State University Press.

McIntosh, J. A. (2006). Moving through tradition: children's practice and performance of dance, music and song in South-Central Bali. Unpublished doctoral dissertation, Queen's University, Belfast.

Merrill-Mirsky, C. (1988). Eeny meeny pepsadeeny: ethnicity and gender in children's musical play. Unpublished doctoral dissertation, University of California, Los Angeles.

Milroy, L., & Muysken, P. (1995). *One speaker two languages: cross-disciplinary perspectives on code-switching*. New York: Cambridge University Press.

Minks, A. (2006a). Interculturality in play and performance: Miskitu children's expressive practices on the Caribbean coast of Nicaragua. Unpublished doctoral dissertation, Columbia University, New York.

Minks, A. (2006b). Mediated intertextuality in pretend play among Nicaraguan Miskitu children. *Texas Linguistic Forum*, 49, 117–27.

Mitchell, C., & Reid-Walsh, J. (2002). *Researching children's popular culture: the cultural spaces of childhood*. London: Routledge.

Opie, I., & Opie, P. (1985). *The singing game*. Oxford: Oxford University Press.

Prim, F. M. (1989). The importance of girl's singing games in music and motor education. *Canadian Journal of Research in Music Education, 32*, 115–23.

Riddell, C. (1990). Traditional singing games of elementary school children in Los Angeles. Unpublished doctoral dissertation, University of California, Los Angeles.

Rogers, C. S., & Sawyers, J. K. (1988). *Play in the lives of children*. Washington, DC: National Association for the Education of Young children.

Treitler, L. (1986). Orality and literacy in the music of the European Middle Ages. In Y. Tokumaru & O. Yamaguta (Eds.), The oral and literate in music (pp. 38–56). Tokyo: Academia Music.

Turner, I., Factor, J., & Lowenstein, W. (1978). *Cinderella dressed in yella* (Rev. ed.). Melbourne, Australia: Heinemann.

Chapter 4

Musical enculturation: sociocultural influences and meanings of children's experiences in and through music

Patricia Shehan Campbell

Children are born into the musical worlds of their home, family, and neighbourhood environments, and their immersion within their sonic surrounds shapes their musical expressions (Campbell & Lum, 2007). They begin the formation of their musical identities within the nuclear culture of their families, and their network of musical influences grows to encompass extended family, family friends, neighbours, and most certainly the media. They sing the songs to which they have been exposed, and they vocalize in personally creative ways in accordance with the musical speech and songful melodies that they have heard (Barrett, 2003, 2006; Welch, 2000, 2006). The rhythms children manifest are likewise a part of the sonic weave of their homes and neighborhoods, which are notable both audibly and visibly in the ways they bounce and sway, step and skip (Campbell, 2007; Marsh & Young, 2006). The musical instruments that they may later learn to play, and with which they have greatest familiarity, are often those that they recall from their earliest years of music listening (MacKenzie, 1991). Children are quite naturally drawn to music, and it is the nature and extent of their musical experience within the family, among friends, and from the media that shapes their musical selves. Even as they adjust the music they know to their playful situations, stretching and bending the musical components to make them fit their expressive needs, children are also anchored to the values and practices of the adults who raise them. Adults and adolescents, alike, often take comfort in the music they were weaned on, and base their musical identities at least partly in the music that surrounded them as young children. This chapter probes scholarship relevant to children's musical enculturation and socialization in families, and pays tribute to theories that suggest pathways to understanding children's musical worlds.

Children, family, social networks and cultural contexts

In a consideration of children's musical worlds, the full extent of their social networks is worthy of examination. All children live in multiple contexts, and an understanding of children in all of their dimensions necessitates an examination of these varied contexts. Cultural pedagogy recognizes that children learn in school but also in other social and cultural contexts (Katsuri, 2002), and thus educators are increasingly challenged to understand the knowledge children bring to school. They seek to integrate children's in-school and out-of-school experiences, to validate the various learning settings, and to transfer and convert knowledge from one context to another.

Urie Bronfenbrenner theorized that children's development, including their musical thought, occurs within an ecological environment which he describes as a 'set of nested structures, each inside the other like a set of Russian dolls' (1979, p. 3). Proximal environments nestle within systems that are increasingly distant to the child, including the school system (beyond the individual neighborhood school), the local economy, and the national policies and infrastructures in place for children's health, education, and welfare (Bronfenbrenner & Morris, 1998). The most immediate environment of the child—the microsystem—encompasses the home and family, and also the culture of the neighbourhood and school. It is in the interactions with parents, siblings, neighbours, teachers, and friends within this microsystem that a child develops his or her social and cultural reality. Time spent in school (and preschool), on the playground, at the mall, in religious institutions, help to shape identity. Bronfenbrenner refers to the relationships between the child's contexts of home, school, and neighborhood as the mesosystem, and considers the influences of government policy and media (exosystem) and the dominant beliefs of a culture (macrosystem) on the child's development. His model of the environmental influences on a child offers an ecological perspective, such that forces near and seemingly far (such as the larger sociocultural milieu) are all to be accommodated by the developing child in understanding self and others.

Another theory that addresses the social and cultural processes of people's everyday lives, and which is relevant to an understanding of the environmental influences in children's development, is the notion of '-scapes', or 'landscapes', as proposed by anthropologist Arjun Appadurai (1996). Appadurai recognized the impact of globalization on societal changes, particularly those due to developments in transportation and communications, and saw that the world was developing into a web of interconnections that made changing conceptions of self and other, and reshaping local identities, possible. It was Appadurai's contention that the world is no longer a collection of autonomous and monadic spaces, that thinking of people and cultures is now a more complex task; one that requires consideration of nuances, hybrids, and resultant products of many mixed influences.

In formulating a framework of five '-scapes' that influence the folkways of adults and children alike, Appadurai suggested facets that surround and influence individuals everywhere: (a) ethnoscapes, the people of our world, including immigrants, refugees, and tourists; (b) technoscapes, the technological developments that deliver worldwide information; (c) finanscapes, the movement of money, goods, and trade across cultures; (d) mediascapes, the electronic distribution of cultural information, images and attitudes; and (e) ideoscapes, the floating images of political positions on constructs of freedom, welfare, citizens' rights, and democracy. These strands of influence encircle children, adding colourful pieces to the complex mosaic-like identities of the adults they will become.

Two significant projects, Lew (2006) and Lum (2007), have sought to examine the music-educational applications of both Appadurai's and Bronfenbrenner's theories of social and cultural networks within the contexts of young children's musical lives.

Lew (2006) conducted an ethnography of Malay, Chinese, and Indian children in a Malaysian preschool, and in the homes of four preschool-enrolled children. She found that Bronfenbrenner's set of nested structures, or systems, operated within the realm of children's musical utterances, rhythmic play, and repertoire of 'heritage songs'. All utterances were traceable to musical sources in the home or at school. These sources included parental music choices, entertainment by mediated sources such as TV and videos, teachers and their decisions of what constituted child-appropriate music, as well as the influences exerted by peers, who introduced new musical material for imitation and adaptation. Young children's mediascapes, as per Appadurai's description, were particularly influential in the music they spontaneously made at play.

Lum (2007) applied Bronfenbrenner's micro–macro model in tandem with the techno-, media-, and ethnoscapes proposed by Appadurai in his study of a class of 7-year-old first-grade children enrolled in an elementary school in Singapore. He noted that not only did home and school figure prominently in children's musical arenas of activity, but that the larger social systems of school, driven as they are by politics and cultural identity (Bronfenbrenner's exosystem and macrosystem), also played a role in the music that figured both officially in the curriculum and within teachers' personal choices to share with children. Appadurai's dimensions were evident within the families of three Singaporean children selected by Lum as subjects for case studies. In their free-play, these children were engaged in the use of various electronics and media sources, including portable karaoke machines, DVDs, CDs, and TV.

That these research studies (Lew, 2006; Lum, 2007) should independently underscore facets of children's networks of influence is validation of the relevance of these social theories to children's musical development.

Children are born within the intimacy of families, and it is there in this closest and most constant of social units that children first learn the cultural patterns that define them. The structure of the family involves the distribution of status, authority, and responsibility within the nucleus of father, mother, and child(ren) and encompasses also the network of kin relationships that link members of the extended family (McAdoo, 1993). Children learn their current and eventual roles, rights, and responsibilities within the family, and they are recipients of family values and preferences that shape their decisions (Freeman, 2000). Issues that concern individual achievement, lifestyle, and educational or occupational aspirations spring from the family, and the family's ethnicity, race, and religious beliefs are usually central in the mediation of values to children.[1] As a result of family upbringing, children possess a cultural reservoir of motivations, skills, attitudes and behaviours that follow them through their childhood and youth, out of their family of origin into the adult world they will come to know (Lareau, 2003).

The music of the family that envelops children from before birth, through infancy, and onward, is linked to the larger cultural community that generates the 'sonic surrounds' of children's musical sensibilities. A variety of the family's demographic characteristics may be pertinent to children's exposure to and experience in culture and the arts, including music. Fundamental traits, including patterns of marriage, family size and fertility, and roles assumed by members of the nuclear family, are influences on the musical behaviours, inclinations, and tastes of children. Even more relevant to children's musical development may be the socio-economic and employment factors of parents (Can they afford private lessons? Or the cost of a concert ticket?), the influence of religious beliefs and practices (What are the musical dimensions of the prayers, praise-songs, rites-of-passage, and other rituals upheld by the family?), and the presence and care of the elders within the family circle—especially grandparents (What is the song repertoire that they pass on to their grandchildren?). Of further consideration are the traditional and changing behaviours of families that adhere to heritage, assimilate, or even rediscover (and sometimes remake) their cultural identities. Finally, the child-rearing practices of families quite naturally affect children's family experiences in music (Are there lullabies at bedtime?

---

[1] This stance on family influences has been questioned by Harris (1995), who has suggested that children are strongly influenced by their peers rather than by their parents.

Is music-making part of the family's recreational activities? Do children learn to value music as rewards for their socially appropriate behavior?).

From the birth of the child forward, a family's influence embeds the subconscious foundation of reality within the scope of acceptable and valued behaviours. A web of attitudes, created through attunement over time within a family and a community, and the larger culture and community, are called into play as children and youth make their decisions. Children receive massive amounts of information both circumstantially and as actively sought by them, and they turn the data into a series of generalizations, stereotypes and theories that they use to navigate their way through life. A young girl, for example, whose family has naturally resorted to singing and dancing at parties and family reunions may be prone to such musical merry-making while at play at home or on the schoolyard, as amusement, a diversion. This joyous impulse may be so 'in the blood' as to be unable to be repressed. A boy who grows up in a home where he is emotionally secure may be more likely to pursue his musical interests in the face of teasing by his friends than one who suffered emotional rejection. This might particularly be the case in relation to a more gender-specific instrument such as flute or piano; he may feel free to choose his own course regardless of peer preferences. Children of families who value music are often taught by example that musical choices concern not *whether* one will make music but on which instrument(s) music will be learned and performed (Davidson, Howe, & Sloboda, 1995). As Edward T. Hall postulated, 'the acquisition of culture begins with birth', and is a 'process [that] is automatic', learned but not taught (1992, p. 225). He argued that 'acquired information is so basic and so fundamental' as to be a part of the self, with behaviour patterns that are automatic and unable to be dissected (p. 225). Linked as they are to subconscious and communal values, behaviours are not always conscious and individual (Hall, 1992). Indeed, the behaviours and attitudes of a family are continuously projecting themselves to children, whose individual perceptions, attitudes, and choices are thus deeply affected by the behaviours they internalize from their home surroundings (Eshleman, 1988; Lareau, 2003).

Children's musical development is enhanced through formal music-educational activity at school. Yet whereas teachers are charged with the delivery of thoughtfully planned lessons, the musical enculturation and socialization of children occurs prior to and in lieu of schooling in informal and unplanned ways. Of these processes, enculturation is the more informal; individuals achieve cultural competence by way of osmosis, absorbing the many facets of their home environment, learning by virtue of living within a family, community, or culture (Campbell, 1998, 2006, 2007; R. Gibson & P. S. Campbell, unpublished study). They absorb language and dialect, food preferences, ways of dress, and moral behaviours within the orbit of their family through an enculturation process that is, typically, natural and nearly effortless. Anthropologist Melville Herskovits described musical enculturation (1949) as so informal a circumstance as to appear as ambient sounds such as singing and pitch-inflected speech. A second and related phenomenon, socialization, was defined by Alan P. Merriam (1964) as 'the process of social learning as it is carried on in the early years of life' (p. 162). Children are musically socialized in ways that overlap enculturative processes; this occurs through the presence of music that is intended by parents to entertain children, to generate social inter-activity and language development, and to teach them concepts such as numbers, body parts, friends and neighbours (Minks, 2006). Enculturation has been a less commonly used concept than socialization in recent years, as the latter suggests children's direct engagement as learners rather than a more passive role as mere accumulators of cultural knowledge. Socialization requires members of a social group (parents and grandparents, for example) to interact with children in order to inculcate the beliefs and values of that social group, whereas enculturation 'happens' as part of a lifelong process by which a personal and cultural identity is shaped (Jorgensen, 1997). In either case, however, the role of the family as principle agent (among other influential '-scapes', ecological environments, and agents within a social network) is certain and strong in the formation of children's musical behaviours and identities.

Children and American 'ethnic' families: social–historical matters

Because the family is the primary locus of children's musical meaning-making, a closer examination of the phenomenon of family is warranted. In the USA, as in the UK, Australia, Canada, and much of the contemporary world, the importance of ethnic group identification in the family has become increasingly clear. Since the composition of many young American families today is multicultural, especially in the 30 years following the rise of multiculturalism in the USA, a study of children in American 'ethnic' families is useful in understanding something of the enculturative and socializing processes these children experience. The descriptor, 'ethnic', refers to those families who continue, by habit or by choice, the cultural behaviours that distinguish them by their ethnicity or race. Rather than study families who are the mainstream 'all-American' average, an examination of families still close to an identifiable and distinctive culture that is based upon the *mores* and values of a particular ethnicity allows for a deeper understanding of the social networks of children's enculturation and socialization.

Beyond the tables and bar graphs of demographic statistics that depict ethnicity and race by region, religious, or socio-economic status, certain social and cultural patterns are evident and relevant to our knowledge of diverse American families, including their children. The continuous stream of immigration to America, and the processes that families undergo as they are transplanted from 'the old country' to their new homeland, have made for adaptations and transformations to the family, as the principal social unit to which adults and children belong. Whether people trace their roots to Africa, Asia, Europe, or Latin America, children are at the core of the family unit, and are most fully affected by the economic and demographic developments of the family. Those families in the midst of their migration and resettlement, and sometimes even several generations removed from this process, may adhere to traditional child-rearing practices linked to ethnicity as well as to a retention of language and cultural traditions, including music, stories, and dance.

Beginning in the 19th century and continuing into the 21st century, the USA has exerted a magnetic force on immigrants and refugees alike. Add to the émigrés from Europe, Asia, and Latin America the forced migration of millions of Africans and the evolution of a distinctive African-American culture, as well as the transformation of Native American society by government regulations, and the population of 'the new world' can be seen as having been drastically and rapidly altered. Throughout most of the 20th century, young immigrants arrived, married, and set about bringing children into the world. Their families grew large (six to eight children were not too many), as did families seeking political asylum. Children were potentially economic assets, or, their creation was seen as a religious duty by some (Mindel, Habenstein, & Wright, 1988). Then, as now, mothers took on primary responsibilities for childcare, especially if not working outside the home, while grandmothers and mothers' sisters (their children's aunts) were also important to the extended kinship systems within which the nuclear family was embedded (Gordon, 1978). The traditional socialization process of child-rearing continues for families newly arriving today in the USA from Mexico, Central America, East Africa, and elsewhere. Embedded within the realm of the family and the kinship systems have been the songs, stories, poetry, dance, and folk arts, along with traditional foodways and apparel—all expressions of the heritage carried onward, preserved, and evolved in a new world (Lareau, 2003).

Young children of immigrant families in the USA are less likely than non-immigrant families to attend formal education and recreation programmes prior to school age. Non-immigrant children may catch up on formal learning, however, after their entrance to kindergarten, especially if they are encouraged by their parents to give their attention to performing well in academic courses. Almost immediately, immigrant children experience the Americanization process at school: they learn American-style English, American history, and American approaches to the study of mathematics, science, the social studies, the humanities, and the arts. They may observe Ramadan or celebrate Cinco de Mayo or Chinese New Year, but they also celebrate American national holidays such as Thanksgiving, Martin Luther King Day, President's Day, and Memorial Day. By middle childhood, they may be performing in American-style school music ensembles, too: choirs, orchestras, and marching and concert bands. For some immigrant children, a violin, snare drum, trumpet, or saxophone are emblematic of an American way of 'musical' life, and so they join school ensembles at least partially for the purpose of demonstrating their yearning to 'belong' to the citizenry of their new nation (Campbell, 1994).

Many children of immigrant families begin their shifting to work experience in their middle childhood, while still in elementary school, often in the family business or in low-skilled part-time restaurant jobs. By the time they are 14 years old, and have graduated from grammar or grade school, in most American states they are eligible for a work permit (Feldstein & Costello, 1974). Following the needs of the family, defined largely by their father who interprets the family's economic status and needs, young Mexicans, Khmers, Nicaraguans, and Somalis may go on to work at a remarkably young age compared with their US-descended peers. Their after-school and weekend work activities often prevent their involvement in extracurricular activities that include sports, clubs, and performances (and sometimes rehearsals) of various ensembles. Thus, while they seek Americanization, some may be unable to fully participate in the very experiences of their school years that are deemed so 'All-American' (Campbell, 1993). While these young working people continue their formal schooling, their allegiances may remain with their families until they leave high school for college, jobs, and life (Campbell, 1993).

For many children, the family home is the safe haven from the anxieties of life in school, on playgrounds and sports fields, and in various other extracurricular events (Scott-Jones, 1986).

For immigrant children in 'ethnic' families whose languages and cultures do not conform to the American mainstream, even while they acquire the characteristics that constitute their 'American-ness', their refuge is the home and family where they can relax into their mother tongue and all of the familiar cultural trappings with which they have grown up. As they grow, children dance between cultures of home and school, and some may be embarrassed by their family's first language and cultural customs as they themselves strive for the mainstream popular culture that is reinforced in school. Children code-switch in and out of the realm of family, and return each day to parents, grandparents, siblings, and others who have made even subsidized housing, tight and temporary spaces, and overcrowded apartments the comfortable home in which they learned their primary cultural view of the world. The codes of their culture are burned into the essence of their being, and a deep level of cultural learning transpires over the years of their childhood within their 'ethnic' families.

Music in American 'ethnic' families: particularities

Five American ethnic communities are briefly noted here for their perspectives on child-raising, the musical genres with which they widely identify, and ways in which children are musically nurtured to know the expressions of their heritage. Of course, the spectrum of American ethnic communities, let alone individual 'ethnic' families, is vast and varied, and any attempt to describe facets of their functions and interests may be blamed for teetering on the edge of generalizations. The descriptions that follow are verifiable, however, and are based in multiple cases emerging from fundamental research for this chapter or as reported in the literature, all of which cluster according to the culture-specific patterns that emerge from them.

Irish-Americans

From their surge as part of a widely documented flight from famine beginning in the mid-nineteenth century, to the comparative trickling of new arrivals, the Irish have become a significant demographic population in America, making up one of the largest of all European-American groups. About two-fifths of Americans trace at least one strand of their ancestry to Ireland, and thus are eligible to claim rights to an Irish-American identity. They define this identity variously, by their 'wearing of the green' on St Patrick's Day, their listening preferences for Irish traditional music, and their genealogical trips back to Ireland in search of family roots. Children in Catholic Irish-American homes, especially among those recent émigrés, tend to know firm and moralistic mothers who are kind and consistent in their care (Clark, 1991). These mothers, still tied to 'the emerald isle', and to moral behaviours steeped in conservative Catholicism, stress obedience and have an expectation of respect in their approach to child-rearing. First-generation Irish-American parents, regardless of the time of their arrival, have tended to emphasize physical activity for their children, with suggestions to play outdoors as they themselves did in the Irish towns and rural outposts they remember; places where families knew one another and 'stranger-danger' was not the concern it is among more settled Americans (Alba, 1990). Through until at least the mid-twentieth century, young Irish-American boys were encouraged to look ahead to both college opportunities and their future work, while young girls were encouraged to learn how to run a household and raise a family (Clark, 1991). Today's Irish-American families have modernized, even as they also have become egalitarian in their views of education and work for their young. Keeping a stable and harmonious household is important to young Irish-American families, so that children will grow up feeling loved and responsive to the needs of others (McMahon, 1995).

One of Ireland's chief exports is its traditional music, much of which is received into the American recording market and performed on concert stages, in community centres, and in clubs and bars. The musical identity of Irish-Americans, for those who seek it out, is associated with learning traditional Irish dance, including both hard and soft shoe styles. Young girls (more than boys), typically between the ages of 5 and 15 years, are transported to weekly lessons, and learn the steps and geometric pathways of an ensemble of dancers to the recordings of standard jigs, hornpipes, and reels. Less so, some families arrange for their children to pursue musical training in *sean-nos* singing, on fiddle, flute, and concertina, and more rarely the uillean pipes and Celtic harp. The organization called Comhaltas Ceotoiri Eireann (or just Comhaltas), established in Ireland in 1951 to promote the transmission of Irish heritage music, dance, and language to children and youth, has gone international, to the extent that branches of the organization have sprung up in American cities including Baltimore, Boston, Chicago, Denver, New York, Philadelphia, and San Francisco (Hast & Scott, 2004). At week-long festivities celebrating St Patrick's Day, performances of traditional music and dance feature children on indoor and outdoor platforms and in parades through the city streets. Also, competitions on all major traditional instruments, 'lilting' (single vocables to dance tunes), *sean-nos* singing, and dance are sponsored throughout the year by the Comhaltas branches for children and youth of all ages (Campbell, 2006). Children too young for training participate on the sidelines; they watch and listen, and try out the jig steps or the fiddler's arm movement. Some integrate the 'diddle-dee-dum-dee-diddle-dee-dum' vocables in sing-song ways as they play on swings, in sandboxes, with dolls, and while constructing their Lego-worlds. For Irish-American families who hope to maintain or build back the links to their old-world culture, participation by their children in Ireland's traditional dance and its music is a valued means of attaining this goal (Shannon, 1963; Scott and Hast, 2004).

Mexican-Americans

More than sixty per cent of all Hispanics living in the USA are of Mexican origin, and a significant influx of Mexicans has arrived within a single generation (since the late 1980s). Mexican-Americans learn their gender roles as children, with the male as protector and breadwinner and the female as a supportive wife and mother (Williams, 1990). Mexican-American children attend school, and yet there is an elevated dropout rate among high school students (Garcia, 2004). The importance of familial solidarity is characteristic of Mexican Americans, such that families often live near to relatives and have frequent interactions with them. Basic religious beliefs and values of Mexican-American culture are preserved through traditional ceremonies and celebrations, including *Cinco de Mayo, Dia de los Muertos, Navidad* (Christmas), *Quinceaneara* (the coming-of-age festivity of 15-year-old girls), and even church holidays and selected feast days of the saints. Even for those families who appear to have quietly erased their associations with Mexico, holidays are meaningful times for instilling in children the meaning of Mexican-American identity (McWilliams, 1990).

The music of special events and holidays varies, and is dependent upon family preferences, the extent of the family's removal from (or connection to) Mexico, and the community in which they live. Children grow up surrounded by standard holiday songs and family favourites, their homes veritable walls of Mexican-flavoured music surrounding them from various media including radio, CDs, and TV. Families of Mexican-American Texans, or Tejanos, may select *conjunto* music over genres such as *mariachi, cancion ranchera, banda,* and *son jarocho* music as background or for dance entertainment.

West coast Mexican-Americans who are drawn to pop-rock genres may prefer the sounds of Otzamotli or Los Lobos over the music of Mariachi Cobre (or conjunto artist Eva Ybarra). The rhythms, textures, and instrumentation of Mexican-American music are differentiated by the genres and artists, but connecting them all is a penchant for diatonic major and minor-keyed melodies, tonic and dominant chordal harmonies, and strophic Spanish language poems (Sheehy, 1998). Children may learn to play some of the instruments of the various ensembles, including *mariachi*-style trumpet or violin; *bajo sexto, vilhuela,* or accordion of *conjunto* music; and the omnipresent guitar. They learn the techniques and repertoire by osmosis, 'by ear', in the informal ways of oral transmission by family members who play for the enjoyment of it (Sheehy, 2006). Moreover, because singing and dancing is so common a part of these repertoires, children grow up with a rich selection of Spanish-language songs and rythms to perform for affirming their identities as Mexican-Americans (Campbell, 1996; Gonzalez, 2009).

Vietnamese-Americans

After Vietnamese families fled their homeland in the 1960s and 1970s, many learned about America and Americans through a daily diet of television that beamed into the cramped spaces of their tiny US apartments (P. T. Nguyen, 1995). Some Vietnamese were still arriving in American port cities by boat through the 1980s, and thus resettlement efforts by government agencies and church groups continued in an effort to Americanize these new arrivals to the extent necessary to secure them employment (Strand & Jones, 1985). As these immigrants/refugees sought economic stability through their jobs within the communities in the country of their adoption, Vietnamese parents were often too busy working to have the time to teach their children all the subtleties of traditional Vietnamese culture (Reyes-Schramm, 1986). What came naturally from parents (and stay-at-home grandparents) to children was what they acquired— food and language, and selected folktales, songs, and traditional values, such as a strong work ethic and respect for one's elders (P. T. Nguyen & Campbell, 1991). Vietnamese-American children, with childhoods spent somewhere within the three-decade period of resettlement (1960–1990), stood teetering at the edge of two cultures, with the traditions of their elders balanced by the images and experiences they were acquiring through the media and their American schooling. With two types of traditional Vietnamese families evident—the scholar family and the peasant family, which coexisted in their adopted American setting just as in their homeland—there was the tendency to expect children to excel at school (the scholar family) or to learn farming, fishing, household maintenance, and the work associated with such American economic enterprises as restaurants, dry cleaning, and housekeeping (the peasant family) (T. D. Nguyen, 1991). It was also not unusual for Vietnamese-American children to live out both the expectations of study and work in the transitional time of their families (Reyes, 1999).

More than instrumental music, it is the Vietnamese songs—traditional and popular—that have had staying power with children and youth, even as they have grown into adulthood. A generation further on, the children of the resettlement period are now raising their own children, who know Vietnam only through the memories shared with them by their parents and grandparents— elders who experienced the movement of their families from a war-torn homeland to a new American way of life. Today's Vietnamese-American children revisit the traditions of their elders on special occasions such as *Tet* (Vietnamese New Year) rather than as daily routine (P. T. Nguyen & Campbell, 1991). At Tet, extended family meals are accented by recordings of Vietnamese music, and meal-time conversations may eventually break into songfests and karaoke contests of music-minus-one renditions to newly arranged folk songs (P. T. Nguyen, 1995). Families of moderate income may afford lessons in *dan tranh* zither or traditional dance (for daughters more often than sons), which result in performances in church and community venues, and at local festivals that feature traditional and folk arts. Today's Vietnamese-American children, most of them two generations removed from Vietnam, have largely assimilated into the mainstream of American culture. They may recognize a few folk melodies due to their prominence in community performances, and on recordings, such as *Co La* ('The egret is flying'), *Ly Ngua O* ('Song of the black horse'), and an instrumental piece, *Vong Co* ('Longing for the past') (P. T. Nguyen & Campbell, 1991).

African-Americans

Because a larger proportion of African-Americans do not marry (this likely due to a sex-ratio imbalance that is created by teen deaths, male incarceration, and poor health), African-American children have a one-in-five chance of growing up with two parents (Bumpass, as cited in Ingrassi, 1993). Many African-American families have traditionally formed families that include a single parent (usually a mother), grandparents, aunts and uncles, and it is frequently grandparents who become the primary caregivers for young children. Middle-class families more than those of lower socio-economic levels tend toward intact two-parent families (Kitwana, 2002; McAdoo, 1997). While there may be no one value system for African-American families, parents of young children often value self-sufficiency, a strong work orientation, positive African-American racial attitude, perseverance, and respect for the mother's role in the family (Hill, 1971).

The church, whether Baptist, Methodist, or another denomination, has been one of the special strengths of African-American families, where not only reinforcement of positive social values but also solace, relief, and support can be found (Hill, 1971). It is in church that children are most likely to encounter the live music of gospel, as well as elements of the genres that have influenced this music—blues, rhythm-and-blues, and jazz (Boyer, 2000). From infancy onward, children from church-going families are exposed on a weekly basis to the toe-tapping, hand-clapping, head-nodding grooves of powerhouse choirs and the instrumental combos that accompany them. African-American church-going children are immersed in the blues-coloured melodies and syncopated rhythms of this music, and are embraced by congregations that take seriously the participatory and improvisatory nature of African-American music. Because they are surrounded by pews of church-goers who sing and respond through movement to gospel song, they learn that music is something one does as a component of their African-American identity.

The popular styles of mass-mediated music in the USA have long been associated with, or are derived from, African-American musical sensibilities.[2]

---

[2] While there is considerable research surrounding issues of the media and technology, it is beyond the scope of this chapter to address this subject in detail. In order to further explore the presence of media and technology in children's lives, see works by Holloway & Valentine (2003), and Cannella & Kincheloe (2002).

From nineteenth century spirituals and the blues and ragtime music of the early twentieth century, to gospel, to a wide assortment of jazz styles, rhythm-and-blues, early rock-and-roll, soul, and hip hop, these styles are rooted in the sliding tones of blues scales, syncopations and multitextured cross-rhythms, with vocal inflections situated between speech and song. The texts of African-American songs in any of these styles often tell the stories of hard times, oppression, and the challenges of life on the streets and in societies where the vision of equality is yet more rhetoric than real. All children, including African-American children, are likely repositories for the sounds of Tupac and Beyonce, and it is common for the family radio and iPods of African-American children to be tuned to the sounds of other reigning dynamos of hip hop (Kitwana, 2002). These sounds evidence themselves in the creative expressions of young African-American children, whose playground songs and singing games are typically more numerous, more syncopated, and more likely to make use of formulaic introductions than those of Euro-American, Asian, or Latino children (Corso, 2003; Gaunt, 2006). While most American schoolchildren—especially girls—enjoy a repertoire of singing games in their musical play, much of it can be traced to the styles and characteristics of African-American music.

Native Americans

With the Native American family, there is a six-category continuum of family types based on preferred language (native or colonial, typically English but occasionally Spanish in the American Southwest), religious beliefs (native, pan-Indian, and Christian), attitudes about land (sacred or utilitarian), family structure (extended, fictive, and nuclear), and health beliefs and behaviours (native health practices versus Anglo-European medical care) (Nagel, 1997). There is the Traditional Indian family, the Neotraditional family, the Transitional family, the Bicultural family, the Acculturated family, and the Panrenaissance family—six family types spanning a spectrum from continuing a lifestyle and heritage that is anchored in the past, to a loss of that heritage, a blend of older and contemporary Indian and non-Indian values, or even a renewal of heritage in a pan-Indian way (Nagel, 1997). Detailed descriptions of these family types are offered by Red Horse (1988), but it is sufficient here to note that the spectrum makes for varied pathways and 'projectories' for children and youth of Native American heritage, so much so that misinterpretations by outsiders of Native American identity are common (Red Horse, 1988). Thus, educational programmes are sometimes confused in their delivery by even the best-intentioned teachers. Still, it may be said that children are socialized into Native American culture as it is defined by the family and tribe or local community, and that this socialization generally operates on the principle of 'the inviolability of the individual' (Downs, 1964), in which light discipline by persuasion, ridicule, or shaming is utilized instead of corporal punishment. Socialization of Native American children occurs largely through non-verbal means, and learning by example is the expected norm by which children learn to share, to respect their elders, and to contribute to the group (Nagel, 1997).

Even in less traditional Native American families, lullabies featuring the indigenous language have been continued by mothers and grandmothers who more usually care for their infants and young children. Transmission of musical culture in this way allows for fundamental linguistic and musical phrases (commonly of just three or four pitches falling over a small range) to form children's early sonic environment (Campbell, 1989). Localized forms of 'traditional indigenous knowledge' are typically embedded in songs for children and adults alike, and these typically embody fundamental beliefs about cosmology, social life, values, and relationships (Diamond, 2008). Music is a communal event, so that when tribal families gather for worship, the honouring of elders, and social occasions such as pow-wows, group-owned songs are sung and drummed as a means of passing on local wisdom, religious beliefs, matters of lineage, and significant events in the history of the tribe (Sijohn, 1999). Stories are valued for their metaphorical meaning, and while important cultural knowledge about ancestors, family, animals, waterways, and plants are transmitted through the narrations, the morals and lessons are underscored by singing them. Because music is also part of one's personal identity, children may be raised to understand that they will one day give birth to their own song; one that expresses their unique role in the world and their communion with the world beyond this life (Diamond, 2008; Miller, 1999).

Children and youth living on Native American reservations are more likely to participate in singing, dancing, and drumming than their urban kin (Nagel, 1997). In tribal schools, there are heritage classes that feature the making of hand drums, beaded belts, brooches, earrings, and the jingle-dresses of sewn metal cones that create tinkling sounds as the girls dance (Campbell, 2001). Public schools on or near reservations may have a 'culture room', but unless the population is highly indigenous, the transmission of traditional Native American culture is usually sporadic and superficial. Because popular forms of music are very much integrated within these communities, much of the music children are weaned on may resemble country or rock music, with vocables as well as Native flutes and drums interwoven (Campbell, 2001). Young Native Americans are often in between cultures, trying to make sense of older layers of music and culture, once or even still evident within their families, in a changing world (Campbell, 1991).

Their musical worlds

If the pervasive theory is that culture, including musical culture, is acquired by children at home, it then follows that there is ample evidence that children evince facets of their culture in their play, social interactions, and spontaneous expressions. Indeed, the research is rich on music that children make, as members of various cultures, and that they do so naturally. Without the immediate stimulation or direction by adults to do so, the culture of children's ecological environment—their social networks—comes forward. Children sing, chant, and musically babble some of the linguistic, melodic, and rhythmic phonemes and phrases to which they have grown accustomed. As they bounce across the kitchen floor, 'animate' their toys, and even play with their food, their music resembles the music of their surroundings. While it may be that children find unique and individual meanings in their very own personal music, which is evident in portrayals by Crafts, Cavicchi and Keil (1993), and Campbell (1998), the sonic features of a Vietnamese-American children's singing game is easily distinguished from those of Mexican-American children. Likewise, when first-generation Irish-American toddlers engage in expressions that hover between speech and song, theirs is distinctive from the sounds of Native American toddlers by virtue of the separate musical environments in which they live. Children, in particular very young children on the brink of learning their spoken and musical languages, quite naturally express the nuances of the motherese (or parentese), that infant-directed musical speech of their caretakers, which they have known as a constant stream of sound projected to them since birth (Fernald, 1991) Their expressive music, then, is related to the music they have received.

It has been persuasively argued, however, that families are not in complete control of their children's cultural experiences, and that home-culture (and the musical culture within the family) is no longer exclusively the up-front and personal encounter of child-and-parent that it once was (Cannella & Kincheloe, 2002; Kincheloe, 2002; Lury, 2002). Bronfenbrenner's theory is testimony to this in his conceptualization of an exosystem in which the media as well as governmental policy is a potentially powerful orbit of influence on children's interests and values. In fact, governmental policy dictates the nature of programming on public-funded TV and also, to an extent, on commercial stations. The barrage of visual and sonic information, components of Appadurai's mediascape, conveys information and attitudes to children, and its influence emerges in their speech, movement, and song style. Their musical play, in particular some of their collectively composed songs, singing games, and parodies of familiar songs, are laden with the music they have come to know on TV shows, movies, the Internet, and video games (Lum, 2007). Mediated music encompasses the songs of *Barney and friends* and music by pop stars Shakira, Kanye West, and Chris Brown, for singing with, and moving and grooving to. By the time children reach school age, as 5-year-olds, their child-produced activities fall within the realm of the media's influence. While the media radiate their messages to children in the home and within the family, it is generated from outside the home, and is thus fairly separate from the traditional sense of home influence as live music-making from parent to child. Traditional conceptions of childhood as a time of adult dependency are thus altered by children's access to mediated pop culture (Campbell, 2010).

Children will continue to be musically enculturated, and to be active participants in the music socialization process that surrounds them every day, even as the 'scapes' of their environment are impacted—even transformed—by technology, the media, and the circumstances of their families. The characteristics of their ethnicities, the economic status of their families, the child-rearing practices that are passed down generation by generation are all influences on the songs they will know, the dancing they will do, the music they will make. Their musical education, the directed learning of music that happens in schools, will transpire even as the unplanned and informal music streams into their lives at home. In fact, it may be said that alongside the sequential instruction in music that happens as early as kindergarten and which runs through the elementary grades of school, there are also occasions for children's socialization through music as classroom teachers feature music as social signalling, rewards for good behaviour, and tools for teaching non-music concepts such as maths and language arts (Lum & Campbell, 2007). The world of children at home, in their local communities, and even as it is constructed at school, is a complex auditory ecosystem that deserves attention and continued study by those who concern themselves with children's learning and development in music. This ecosystem includes the web of social processes that are rich with musical content that help to shape children's expressive selves.

Acknowledgements

I am grateful to the scholarship of Dr Chee-Hoo Lum, Dr Jackie Chooi-Theng Lew, and Dr. Rachel Gibson, and to the conversations we have had on the subject of music in children's in-school and out-of-school lives.

References

Alba, R. (1990). *Ethnic identity: the transformation of White America*. New Haven, CT: Yale University Press.

Appadurai, A. (1996). *Modernity at large: cultural dimensions of globalization*. Minneapolis, MN: University of Minnesota Press.

Barrett, M. S. (2003). Meme engineers: children as producers of musical culture. *International Journal of Early Years Education, 11*(3), 195–212.

Barrett, M. S. (2006). Inventing songs, inventing worlds: the 'genesis' of creative thought and activity in young children's lives. *International Journal of Early Years Education, 14*(3), 201–20.

Boyer, H. C. (2000). *The golden age of gospel.* Urbana, IL: University of Illinois Press.

Bronfenbrenner, U. (1979). *The ecology of human development: experiments by nature and design.* Cambridge, MA: Harvard University Press.

Bronfenbrenner, U., & Morris, P. A. (1998). The ecology of developmental processes. In W. Damon & R. M. Lerner (Eds.), *Handbook of child psychology* (Vol. 1, pp. 993–1028). New York: John Wiley & Sons.

Campbell, P. S. (1989). Music learning and song acquisition among Native Americans. *International Journal of Music Education, 14,* 24–31.

Campbell, P. S. (1991). *Lessons from the world: a cross-cultural guide to music teaching and learning.* New York: Schirmer Books.

Campbell, P. S. (1993). Cultural issues and school music participation: the new Asians in American Schools. *Quarterly Journal of Music Teaching and Learning, 4*(2), 45–56.

Campbell, P. S. (1994). Musica exotica, multiculturalism, and school music. *Quarterly Journal of Music Teaching and Learning, 4*(2), 65–75.

Campbell, P. S. (1996). Steve Loza on Latino music. In P. S. Campbell (Ed.), *Music in cultural context: eight views on world music education* (pp. 58–65). Reston, VA: Music Educators National Conference.

Campbell, P. S. (1998). *Songs in their heads.* New York: Oxford University Press.

Campbell, P. S. (2001). Lessons from the Yakama. *Mountain Lake Reader,* 46–51.

Campbell, P. S. (2006). Global practices. In G. E. McPherson (Ed.), *The child as musician* (pp. 415–37). New York: Oxford University Press.

Campbell, P. S. (2007). Musical meaning in children's cultures. In L. Bresler (Ed.), *International handbook of research in arts education* (pp. 881–94). New York: Springer.

Campbell, P. S., & Lum, C. H. (2007). Live and mediated music meant just for children. In K. Smithran & R. Upitis (Eds.), *Listen to their voices: research and practice in early childhood music* (pp. 319–29). Waterloo, Ontario: Canadian Music Educators Association.

Campbell, P. S. (2010). *Songs in Their Heads, second edition.* New York: Oxford University Press.

Cannella, G., & Kincheloe, J. (Eds.) (2002). *Kidworld: Childhood studies, global perspectives, and education.* New York: Peter Lang.

Clark, D. (1991). *Erin's heirs: Irish bonds of community.* Lexington, KY: University Press of Kentucky.

Corso, D. T. (2003). 'Smooth as butter': practices of music learning amongst African-American children. Unpublished doctoral dissertation, University of Illinois at Urbana-Champaign.

Crafts, S., Cavicchi, D., & Keil, C. (1993). *My music: explorations of music in daily life.* Middletown, CT: Wesleyan University Press.

Davidson, J., Howe, M., & Sloboda, J. (1995). The role of parents and teachers in the success and failure of instrumental learners. *Bulletin of the Council for Research in Music Education, 127,* 40–44.

Diamond, B. (2008). *Native American music in eastern North America*. New York: Oxford University Press.

Downs, J. F. (1964). *Animal husbandry in Navajo society and culture*. Berkeley, CA: University of California Press.

Eshleman, J. R. (1988). *The family: an introduction* (5th edn). Boston: Allyn & Bacon.

Feldstein, S., & Costello, L. (Eds.) (1974). *The ordeal of assimilation: a documentary history of the White working class*. Garden City, NJ: Doubleday, Anchor Books.

Fernald, A. (1991). Prosody in speech to children: prelinguistic and linguistic functions. *Annals of Child Development, 8*, 43–80.

Freeman, J. (2000). Families: the essential content for gifts and talents. In K. A. Heller, F. J. Monks, R. J. Sternberg, & R. F. Subotnik (Eds.), *International handbook of giftedness and talent* (pp. 573–85). New York: Elsevier.

Garcia, E. E. (2004). Educating Mexican American students; past treatment and recent developments in theory, research, policy, and practice. In J. A. Banks (Ed.), *Handbook of research on multicultural education* (2nd edn, pp. 372–87). San Francisco: Jossey-Bass.

Gaunt, K. (2006). *The games black girls play: learning the ropes from double-Dutch to hip-hop*. New York: New York University Press.

Gonzalez, M. (2009). *Zapateado* Afro-Chicana *Fandango* Style: Self- Reflective Moments in *Zapateado*. In: O. Najera-Ramirez, N.E. Cantu, & B.M. Romero (Eds.), *Dancing Across Borders: danzas y bailes Mexicanos* (pp. 359-378). Urbana-Champaign: University of Illinois.

Gordon, M. (Ed.) (1978). *The American family in social–historical perspective*. New York: St Martin's Press.

Hall, E. T. (1992). Improvisation as an acquired, multilevel process. *Ethnomusicology, 36*, 151–69.

Harris, J. R. (1995). Where is the child's environment? A group socialization theory of development. *Psychological Review, 102*(3), 458–89.

Hast, D. E., & Scott, S. (2004). *Music in Ireland*. New York: Oxford University Press.

Herskovits, M. (1949). *Man and his works*. Evanston, IL: Northwestern University Press.

Hill, R. (1971). *The strengths of Black families*. New York: Emerson Hall.

Holloway, S. L., & Valentine, G. (2003). *Cyberkids: children in the information age*. London: Routledge.

Ingrassi, M. (1993). A world without fathers: the struggle to save the Black family [Special report]. *Newsweek*, 30 August, pp. 16–29.

Jorgensen, E. R. (1997). *In search of music education*. Urban: University of Illinois Press.

Katsuri, S. (2002). Constructing childhood in a corporate world: cultural studies, childhood, and Disney. In G. S. Cannella & J. L. Kincheloe (Eds.), *Kidworld: Childhood studies, global perspectives, and education* (pp. 39–58). New York: Peter Lang.

Kincheloe, J. L. (2002). The complex politics of McDonald's and the new childhood: colonizing kidworld. In G. S. Cannella & J. L. Kincheloe (Eds.), *Kidworld: Childhood studies, global perspectives, and education* (pp. 75–121). New York: Peter Lang.

Kitwana, B. (2002). *The hip hop generation: young Blacks and the crisis in African American culture*. New York: Civitas.

Laureau, A. (2003). *Unequal Childhoods: Class, Race, and Family Life*. Berkeley: University of California Press.

Lew, J. C. T. (2006). The musical lives of young Malaysian children: in school and at home. Unpublished doctoral dissertation, University of Washington, Seattle.

Lum, C.-H. (2007). Musical networks of children: an ethnography of elementary school children in Singapore. Unpublished doctoral dissertation, University of Washington, Seattle.

Lum, C.-H., & Campbell, P. S. (2007). The sonic surrounds of an elementary school. *Journal of Research in Music Education, 55*(1), 31–47.

Lury, K. (2002). Chewing gum for the ears: children's television and popular music. *Popular Music, 21*, 292–311.

MacKenzie, C. G. (1991). Starting to learn to play a musical instrument: a study of boys' and girls' motivational criteria. *British Journal of Music Education, 8*(1), 15–20.

Marsh, K., & Young, S. (2006). Musical play. In G. E. McPherson (Ed.), *The child as musician* (pp. 289–310). New York: Oxford University Press.

McAdoo, H. (Ed.) (1993). *Family ethnicity: strength in diversity*. Newbury Park, CA: Sage.

McAdoo, H. (1997). *Black families* (3rd edn). Newbury Park, CA: Sage.

McMahon, E. M. (1995). *What parish are you from? A Chicago Irish community and race relations*. Lexington, KY: University of Kentucky Press.

McWilliams, C. (1990). *North from Mexico* (revised edn). Westport, CT: Greenwood Press.

Merriam, A. P. (1964). *The anthropology of music*. Evanston, IL: Northwestern University Press.

Miller, B. S. (1999). Seeds of our ancestors. In W. Smyth & E. Ryan (Eds.), *Spirit of the first people* (pp. 25–43). Seattle, WA: University of Washington Press.

Mindel, C., Habenstein, R., & Wright, R. (Eds.) (1988). *Ethnic families in America: patterns and variations* (2nd edn). New York: Elsevier.

Minks, A. (2006). Afterword. In S. Boynton & R.-H. Min (Eds.), *Musical childhoods and the cultures of youth* (pp. 209–218). Middletown, CT: Wesleyan University Press.

Nagel, J. (1997). *American Indian ethnic renewal: Red power and the resurgence of identity and culture*. New York: Oxford University Press.

Nguyen, P. T. (1995). *Searching for a niche: Vietnamese music at home in America*. Kent, OH: Viet Music.

Nguyen, P. T., & Campbell, P. S. (1991). *From rice paddies and temple yards: traditional music of Vietnam*. Danbury, CT: World Music Press.

Nguyen, T. D. (1991). *A Vietnamese family chronicle: twelve generations on the banks of the Hat River*. Jefferson, NC: McFarland.

Red Horse, J. G. (1988). Cultural evolution of American Indian families. In C. Jacobs & D. D. Bowles (Eds.), *Ethnicity and race: critical concepts in social work* (pp. 86–110). Silver Spring, MD: National Association of Social Workers.

Reyes-Schramm, A. (1986). Tradition in the guise of innovation: music among a refugee population. In D. Christensen (Ed.), *Yearbook for Traditional Music, 18*, 91–101.

Reyes, A. (1999). *Songs of the Caged, Songs of the Free*. Austin, TX: University of Texas Press.

Scott-Jones, D. (1986). The family. In J. Hanaway & M. E. Lockheed (Eds.), *The contributions of the social sciences to educational policy and to practice, 1965–1985* (pp. 11–31). Berkeley, CA: McCutchan.

Shannon, W. (1963). The American Irish: a political and social portrait. Amherst, MA: University of Massachusetts Press.

Sheehy, D. (1998). Mexico. In A. Arnold (Ed.), *The Garland encyclopedia of world music*, Vol. 2: *South America, Mexico, Central American, and the Caribbean*, (pp. 600–25). New York: Garland.

Sheehy, D. (2006). *Mariachi music in Mexico*. New York: Oxford University Press.

Sijohn, C. (1999). The circle of song. In W. Smyth & E. Ryan (Eds.), *Spirit of the first people* (pp. 45–49). Seattle, WA: University of Washington Press.

Strand, P. J., & Jones, W., Jr (1985). *Indochinese refugees in America: problems of adaptation and assimilation*. Durham, NC: Duke University Press.

Welch, G. (2000). Singing development in early childhood: the effects of culture and education on the realization of potential. In P. J. White (Ed.), *Child voice* (pp. 27–44). Stockholm: Royal Institute of Technology.

Welch, G. (2006). Singing and vocal development. In G. E. McPherson (Ed.), *The child as musician* (pp. 311–29). New York: Oxford University Press.

Williams, N. (1990). *The Mexican American family: tradition and change*. New York: General Hall.

Chapter 5

When the music is theirs: scaffolding young songwriters

Jackie Wiggins

Introduction

Twenty-two first-grade students sat bunched around my feet, as close to the piano and to me as they could get without sitting on one another. We had met for the first time when they entered the room a few minutes before. We were to write a song together—the first song they had ever written in a music class setting. I asked them what our song would be about. Children know that songs are *about* something, which usually makes this a comfortable place to begin with first-time songwriters, and they volunteered their ideas with ease.

One child suggested that we write about a dog, which precipitated (as it often does) suggestions that produced a rather lengthy list of different animals. After listing eight or ten on the board, I tried to abbreviate the process by saying, 'People seem to be naming lots of different kinds of animals. Perhaps we could just make the song about animals so we can use all the ideas?' There were many cries of 'Yes! Yeah!' that were quickly silenced by one rather piercing announcement: 'But *I* wanted to make a song about a *princess*!' A 6-year-old diplomat from the midst proposed, 'An *animal* can be a princess.' Once again the room erupted with simultaneously proposed ideas. 'The king could be a lion!', 'The queen could be . . .', 'The monkeys could be the guards.' (And then that same piercing voice) '*No. I* want the guards to be *cheetahs*!' Within moments, we decided to call the song, 'The Animal Palace'. The idea could have been a child's or mine (I don't recall) but it was avidly embraced and I wrote it on the board, careful to speak each word aloud as I wrote, for those who needed that support.

To scaffold a transition to the construction of song lyrics, I suggested, 'When people hear this song, they need to know what it is about, so maybe we should start with something like, "Once there was a palace . . ."' Within the cries of agreement, a small voice spoke up to finish my sentence: '. . . with animals in it!' With these two phrases written on the board, the rest of the lyrics flowed—each suggested by one child, sometimes modified by a peer, but more often than not, written on the board the way it was articulated by the contributor:

The Animal Palace

Once there was a palace
With animals in it.
The palace was guarded by cheetahs and pigs.
The king was a crocodile.
The queen was a duck.
The prince was a moose.
The princess was a unicorn.
The jester was a monkey.

I ventured that we probably had enough words to make a song and the response was a chorus of suggestions about how we should perform it. Many wanted to 'make up the movements', assuming that the song would have motions or be acted out in some way. I was trying to say that we had not yet written the music part of the song, that we had finished only the words—but they were so busy making suggestions to one another (some had already begun moving around on the floor like cheetahs and monkeys and crocodiles) that for the moment, they did not realize I was trying to speak.

Amidst this excited commotion, a voice tried to get my attention. '*Wait!* This isn't a song it's a *poem*! We need to *sing* it to make a song!' I was amazed. This is the way I usually choose to describe this situation to young children. In the thirty-plus years during which I had written songs with young children, I could not remember ever hearing a child this young articulate the problem in quite this way. This child had succeeded in getting the attention of his peers, when my own attempts had failed. In the quiet that ensued, I said I thought that Scott was right: that so far we had only made a poem and that we needed to make our voices go up and down in order to make the poem into a song. We needed to decide how we would sing it.

I walked to the piano and played a G major chord with the D above middle C as the highest pitch. As I played the chord, I asked, 'How shall we sing it? How should it go?' One voice responded loud and clear (Fig. 5.1):

Fig. 5.1

I immediately played what the child had sung, playing and singing the melody while sustaining the same G major chord. Just as I stopped, a second child from the other side of the group finished the line (Fig. 5.2):

with an - i - mals in it.

Fig. 5.2

'Yeah!' Everyone approved. This child had sung her suggestion complete with arm gestures out to the side in a way that resembled a pop singer. There was also a definite sense of an underlying pulse evident in her singing and in her body.

I then played the two phrases consecutively, accompanying the second phrase with an Em chord. This time, instead of sustaining block chords, I took my lead from the body motion of the girl who had created the second phrase and accompanied the melody with an oom-pah bass to provide forward motion. I had intentionally let the students establish the meter and tempo, but once they had done that with their opening suggestions, I decided to provide a bit more momentum in the accompaniment to keep the ideas and the communal sense of the song flowing. On each repetition, I sang and played the melody from the beginning to help the children understand where we were within the whole, melodically and harmonically.

The third and fourth lines were written in this same manner. I sang and played what had already been suggested and, each time, one child finished the line with a new melodic suggestion. First (Fig. 5.3):

The pal - ace was guard-ed by cheet-ahs and pigs,

Fig. 5.3

and then the fourth line, sung with a definite sense of closure and resolution (with arm gestures that one might do when exclaiming 'ta-DAH!') (Fig. 5.4):

The king was a croc - o - dile.

Fig. 5.4

Then, as I played the newly created melody with an oom-pah chordal accompaniment, the whole class sang through the first part of the song in its entirety. Their singing was extremely accurate and clearly enthusiastic. Because of the nature of the cadence of the fourth line, several students seemed to assume we were finished. I thought the children might be about to lose the level of concentration they had been sustaining, so I decided to ask them whether they would prefer to just repeat the music we had already written for the last four lines of lyrics. They immediately protested. Among the 'no's' was one voice that said, 'No, it doesn't *go* that way.'[1]

So once again I played and we sang the original four lines. As soon as we had sung the fourth line, a child went on with the fifth, making a choice that eventually led to a shift in tonal centre (Fig. 5.5):

Fig. 5.5

Right on her heels, someone fleshed out the idea by adding animal sounds accompanied by a gesture of two hands held up on either side of her head, opening and closing like the beak of a duck, once for each quack (Fig. 5.6).

Fig. 5.6

Because we seemed to be pursuing a new line of (musical) thinking, I played the duck line only (instead of returning to the beginning of the song) and paused for a second. Someone filled the space with a perfect sequence (Fig. 5.7):

Fig. 5.7

---

[1] This is a comment that one frequently hears when children are composing in classrooms—suggesting that they do seem to have a preconceived notion of what the work will sound like and can tell immediately when a suggested idea contradicts their vision of the work in progress. I know this from over 30 years of my own teaching and composing with children, from my research (e.g. Wiggins, 1992, 1994, 1995, 1999a, 2001, 2002, 2003, 2009), and from the practice and research of other teachers who have composed with their students.

Not wanting to destroy the momentum of the moment with a big discussion about the sound a moose makes that could finish the sequence in a way that would parallel the 'quack, quack', I contributed 'whsht, whsht!' while wiggling my fingers, my hands on either side of my head, like antlers (the only thing I could think of that quickly). They accepted my suggestion with giggles.

We once again returned to the beginning of the song, pausing just before 'The princess was . . .' They really seemed to understand the routine into which we had fallen—that I would play what we had created so far, pause, take my hands off the piano, and someone would contribute a line. In my experience of writing songs with children, although this is often the way more sophisticated composers work collaboratively, it was unusual that I did not have to intervene or make many suggestions, especially with such young and inexperienced composers. This group of youngsters just flowed with the process and seemed to be able to take full responsibility. My only role seemed to be reminding them of what they had already created.

As I paused this time, a little girl sang out loud and clear (and very much in tune, sustaining the high E in a lovely clear voice) (Fig. 5.8):

The   prin - cess was   a   u - ni - corn.

Fig. 5.8

I was amazed, but also a bit dismayed, wondering whether anyone would be able to resolve that line in a manner that would bring the song to a reasonable close. I returned to my role at the piano, leading the singing of the parts we had already written (from the beginning of the song). As we paused before the last line of lyrics, a boy on the far side of the room sang out triumphantly (Fig. 5.9):

The   jest - er   was   a   mon - key.

Fig. 5.9

The melodic range of this suggestion was impressive and his intonation flawless. Most of all, his idea finished the melody in a way that succeeded in resolving all the tension generated by its shape and progression throughout its course. It was the definitive ending—even though the song had started out implying G as tonic but finished clearly in D major. That he understood how to do this based on his understanding of the music of his experience at such a young age was surprising, but also exciting to see.

Now we were really finished. We all sang the song with energy. When we stopped, the children once again announced that we needed to make up motions for the song. Some were thinking we would act out the whole scene as we sang. They were busy volunteering for who would play the part of each animal, with conflicts beginning to arise. The classroom teacher was due momentarily, so I suggested that they each make up motions for all the animal characters as we sang (which, of course, they did with glee and enthusiasm) (Fig. 5.10).

The Animal Palace

Meadow Brook 1st Graders

Fig. 5.10

When the classroom teacher returned to the music room, they sang the song in its entirety along with their invented motions, which changed continually with each repetition of the song. I am not sure their teacher believed they had actually composed the song—or could compose such a song. Yet the children, while quite proud of their product, seemed to take the process completely in stride. It seemed to be as natural to them as breathing. They did not seem to think they had done anything out of the ordinary.

The 'Animal Palace' composers were engaged in a holistic, authentic musical experience that was personally meaningful to them. Bruner (1990) might characterize the experience as an opportunity for these learners to make their own meaning in a musical context—to create their own musical narrative—to construct their own understanding through a 'pedagogy of mutuality' (p. 56) as a 'community of mutual learners' (1996, p. 24). The song was produced through a process of 'interpersonal negotiation' (Bruner, 1986, p. 122) shaped by various layers of culture: the culture of the school and classroom, the culture of the children's local shared experience, the culture of their experience with the media, and their cultural experience with music in general. The musical product and the children's suggestions for its performance—the pop-style gestures that accompanied some of their ideas and their desire to set the song into a larger 'acted-out' context—reflect their shared understanding of the nature of songs in their experience, both in school and out.

This song composition process was also influenced by my decisions and actions as teacher because the process of creation occurred in the context of a classroom in which I, as teacher and also as member of the learning community, significantly influenced the environment, both musically and socially. Under any circumstances, collaborative composing is a social and musical process in which ideas are initiated and shared through musical, verbal, and sometimes gestural interaction (Wiggins, 2006). However, when collaborative composing (or any other experience, for that matter) takes place in the context of a classroom or other formal learning situation, it is additionally influenced by the nature of the environment established by the teacher. While a learning environment includes physical qualities (e.g. in the 'Animal Palace' vignette, where the proximity of students to teacher and to one another was intentional, designed to enable ideas of more reticent students to be noticed and heard), the more critical qualities are social, since learning is primarily a social process—a central premise of cultural psychology, articulated by many, including Bruner (1990, 1996), Cole (1996), Lave & Wenger (1991), Rogoff (1990, 2003), Rogoff and Lave (1984), and Vygotsky (1978). As such, the social, pedagogical, and, in this case, musical decisions and actions of the teacher play a significant role in establishing the context in which the students' processes occur. Even in the healthiest of learning situations, students and teachers find themselves in a constant state of negotiation, seeking a productive mutuality that will enable all parties to move forward toward their goals.[2] Wenger (1998) describes this kind of negotiation as 'an accomplishment that requires sustained attention and readjustment' (p. 53).

---

[2] The 'Animal Palace' songwriting experience seemed to require less negotiation than many similar processes in which I have engaged with young composers in school settings. (I have composed songs with elementary general music students since I first entered the classroom in 1972. Over the years, I have participated with students in some capacity in the composition of over 900 songs, plus more than 1000 instrumental pieces.) In the 'Animal Palace' story, more negotiation seemed to take place during the creation of the lyrics than during that of the melody. From my experience composing songs with children, I know that this is not always the case, but it is often true of upper-elementary-aged students for whom the choice of topic or theme is often heavily burdened with their concerns about creating a song that will be perceived by their peers as 'real', 'cool', and properly representative of who they perceive themselves to be socially and culturally.

Envisioning learning, teaching, and composing as culturally and socially embedded processes reflects a cultural psychology perspective. As Barrett so aptly describes in her introductory chapter, this perspective 'may be described as one that seeks to illuminate the ways in which cultural practices and meanings and human agency made up of psychological processes and structures are interrelated and reinforce and sustain each other' (p. 5). In the analysis that comprises this chapter, the cultural practice under consideration is teacher-supported, collaborative songwriting in the context of classroom learning. The analysis seeks to illuminate the intrinsic meaning-making processes of the participants and, in particular, to consider learner agency in the context of teacher scaffolding. The central issue here is the negotiation of the delicate balance between, on the one hand, establishing an environment that *engenders and honours the personal agency* that learners require to be able to invent meaningful musical ideas and, on the other, designing instruction that *provides the appropriate scaffolding* that learners may need, and have a right to receive in the formal learning setting that is school. Tensions that live at the intersection of teacher scaffolding and learner agency have many faces, even within the relatively narrow focus that is the scope of this chapter. Decisions about how these critical tensions are to be negotiated most often reside with the teacher—who is primarily responsible for establishing and sustaining a classroom environment that engenders learning.

Writing this chapter gave me an opportunity to reconsider some specific collaborative songwriting instances from over 30 years of composing with students through a cultural psychology lens. Data were drawn from a variety of settings collected across a number of years, in the form of audio-recordings, notated artefacts of student-composed songs, video-recordings, and field notes that captured real-life classroom learning experiences in which teachers were engaged in scaffolding collaborative songwriting efforts. All data were collected in American elementary general music classrooms during classes taught by music specialists. Many were instances of my own teaching in a variety of settings (e.g. Wiggins 1992, 1994, 1995). Some were collected in classrooms of other music teachers who were engaged in similar kinds of activity with their students (e.g. Wiggins, 1999a, 2001, 2002, 2003, 2009). Some were recordings made incidentally as part of the process of 'saving' ideas during collaborative composing sessions. Others (e.g. the 'Animal Palace' story) were recordings made while I was a guest teacher in another teacher's classroom, modelling this process for purposes of pre-service or in-service teacher education. In all, there were about 400 recordings and/or notated versions of songs composed by elementary children as part of their regular general music experiences.

From the collection of recordings, I selected the most salient instances of student/teacher interaction during compositional process, and transcribed both the musical and verbal interactions. I then analysed all transcripts and field notes for emergent themes reflective of the central learning and teaching issues evident in the data. The analysis that follows was born of reflection on the data in the context of my long-term experience with the process and therefore is representative of my own perspective as both teacher and researcher. My interpretation is deeply embedded in my beliefs about the nature of learning and teaching and reflects my thinking both 'on my feet' as a teacher and as a researcher reflecting on what it is to be teaching in these situations and settings.

Learner agency

If learning is an act of the individual, then in order to act on one's own volition an individual needs to feel sufficiently empowered. To be able to engage in a meaning-making process, 'we need to conceive of ourselves as 'agents' impelled by self-generated intentions' (Bruner, 1996, p. 16). Agency, a central issue in cultural psychology, can be described as the intentionality and control an individual feels she has over her own circumstances in a particular situation or at a given time in that situation. Freire (1970/2002) describes intentionality as the essence of consciousness and proposes a 'problem-posing' education because it allows for and fosters intentionality (p. 79). For Bruner (1996), agency is one universal aspect of selfhood in that selfhood 'derives from the sense that one can initiate and carry out activities on one's own' (p. 35).

> People experience themselves as agents . . . It is a 'possible self' that regulates aspiration, confidence, optimism, and their opposites . . . Since agency implies not only the capacity for initiating, but also for completing our acts, it also implies skill or know-how. Success and failure are principal nutrients in the development of selfhood (Bruner, 1996, p. 36).

Agency is at the core of capacity for learning, as has been demonstrated poignantly in critical works such as *Women's ways of knowing* (Belenky, Clinchy, Goldberger, & Tarule 1997), a collaborative study of learning processes of women, and *The dreamkeepers* (Ladson-Billings, 1994), a study of successful teaching and learning of African-American students.

If learning process requires learner agency, teaching process must be designed to foster and enable learner agency, thereby empowering learners (e.g. Freire, 1970/2002; 2003). Nealon and Giroux (2003) remind us that sociocultural contexts do not always empower agency and that, depending on the intent of social forces involved, our agency may be 'both *constrained* and *enabled* by the contexts in which we find ourselves' (p. 195). In my own work (e.g. Wiggins, 2006) and in the work of others who have studied students' compositional process (e.g. Allsup, 2002; Barrett, 2003; Burnard, 1999; Davis, 2005; Espeland, 2006; Faulkner, 2001, 2003; Ruthmann, 2006; Savage, 2004), it has become clear that a sense of agency and opportunity for intentionality are critical to students' ability to compose original music. Consequently, music teachers who are engaged in scaffolding students' compositional processes must remain cognizant of their own actions and decisions to be sure that they are enabling learner agency and not inadvertently constraining it.

Personal agency is socioculturally embedded, as is evident in the ways scholars envision its qualities. Bruner (1996) discusses personal agency in the context of a discussion of collaboration, because he sees these concepts as intertwined and interdependent. Wertsch, Tulviste and Hagstrom (1993) suggest a vision of agency that 'extends beyond the skin' in that it is 'often socially distributed or shared' and always culturally embedded (p. 352). Bakhtin (1981) went so far as to suggest that the mind itself is not bounded by skin and skull, but rather that what we know and understand is intrinsically linked to what others know and understand. For Bakhtin, our ideas are 'half someone else's' and do not become our own until we populate them with our own intent (p. 293). Rogoff (1990) identifies shared understanding or intersubjectivity as essential to teaching/learning process. In my own work (Wiggins, 1999a), I have demonstrated what musical intersubjectivity can look like in collaborative creation in music. Espeland (2006) describes children's compositional process as grounded in creative agency embedded within sociocultural process.

Wertsch et al. (1993), after Vygotsky (1978), propose a vision of agency as mediated by the signs and tools of the culture suggesting that there is often no boundary between individuals and the mediational means they employ (e.g. between a blind man and his stick, an example generated by Bateson, 1972, cited by Wertsch et al.). For Wertsch et al., mediated agency in a sociocultural context is an individual's ability to operate with mediational means (signs and tools) in an interactional social context—building on the ideas and understanding of others and, through the process, extending his or her own ideas and understanding (p. 346). More simply, 'mediation is the mechanism through which external, sociocultural activities are transformed into internal, mental functioning,' the source of mediation being a material tool, a symbol system, or an action of another human being in social interaction (Huong, 2003, p. 33).

Vygotsky (1978) suggests that as children begin to internalize and own verbal language, speech mediates thought. As their ability to use language as a means of organizing thought increases, children also increase their ability to function at higher levels of psychological process. For Vygosky, the processes of speech and thought are interactive in that speech organizes thought while, at the same time, thought underlies speech. The same is true of musical thinking.

Engaging in the musical processes of performing, creating, and listening mediate musical thought, enabling individuals to organize musical thought, but at the same time, musical thought underlies engaging in musical process. Vygotsky (1978) describes verbal thinking as 'inner speech' and identifies egocentric speech (talking aloud to oneself while trying to figure something out) as transitional between external speech (dialogue) and internal speech (verbal thinking) (p. 27). In my initial research (Wiggins, 1992), I found more than 100 instances of students' singing aloud to themselves while engaged in solving musical problems, which I identified as transitional between external collaborative musical experience and inner hearing of music (musical thinking).

If speech mediates thought, engaging in musical process mediates musical thought. We learn both speech and ways of interacting with music from others in our culture. Part of what enables individuals to develop the ability to internalize ideas (understand concepts) is interaction with others utilizing the particular signs and tools of a particular way of thinking (verbal, musical, etc.). Bruner (1996) suggests that the 'agentive mind is not only active in nature, but it seeks out other active minds' (p. 93). Further, he sees skill as 'the instrument of agency acquired through collaboration,' noting that 'without skill we are powerless' (p. 94). Freire (1970/2002) suggests that teachers and students 'become jointly responsible for a process in which all grow'; that 'people teach each other, mediated by the world' (p. 80). One of the primary means of mediation is scaffolding.

Teacher scaffolding

Bruner (1966; Wood, Bruner, & Ross, 1976) first used the term *scaffolding* to describe the support that mentors provide for learners. A cultural psychology perspective defines learning and teaching as sociocultural processes. Within this frame, scaffolding represents one of the primary roles of an individual who is teaching or supporting the learning of another. Bruner (1986) describes scaffolding as 'a negotiable transaction' (p. 76) in which the teacher 'remains forever on the growing edge of the child's competence' (p. 77), pushing her to higher and higher levels of competence each time mastery of some small part is achieved. Scaffolding enables a learner to participate in the actual practice of an expert while assuming responsibility for only those aspects of the practice that are within reach for the learner, with support (Lave & Wenger, 1991). Greenfield (1984) describes the teacher's role of support as 'selective intervention' that extends the learner's skills, allowing him to accomplish successfully a task not otherwise possible (p. 118). For the process to be the most productive, the teacher needs to provide 'the minimum necessary scaffolding for the learner to produce new skill components that are understood but not yet performed' (pp. 118–119). Then, 'ultimately, the scaffold becomes internalized, enabling independent accomplishment of the skill of the learner' (p. 135).

Rogoff and Gardner (1984) describe the process as teacher structuring of instruction to provide a framework for student (or collaborative) solution of a problem (p. 98). Cole (1996) describes the synergistic relationship between mediated and unmediated action where mediated action does not replace students' natural ideas, but rather students incorporate mediation into their own efforts (p. 119). Stone (1993) suggests that scaffolding is a 'subtle phenomenon . . . that involves a complex set of social and semiotic dynamics' (p. 180). He describes 'a fluid interpersonal process in which the participants' communicative exchanges serve to build a continually evolving mutual perspective on how to conceive the situation at hand' (p. 180).

Rogoff (1990) used *guided participation* instead of scaffolding to describe both formal and informal learning, because her understanding of Bruner's use of scaffolding was that it usually occurred when teaching was intentional. In her more recent explanations of guided participation (Rogoff, 2003), however, she sees the process as being more mutual than was previously thought, with the learner taking more initiative and responsibility, which makes an even stronger case for the need for a learning environment that supports learner agency (p. 285). I use the metaphor of scaffolding to describe the nature of the teacher's work in these data because the process was an intentional part of a formal learning experience. However, my use of the metaphor includes Stone's extension of the image to reflect the fluidity of the process that builds a continually evolving mutual perspective on how to conceive the situation, and also includes Rogoff's image of mutuality where the learner takes more initiative and responsibility. As such, my interpretation of what might be considered scaffolding may be broader than the vision of some scholars.

While, from my perspective, this broader vision of scaffolding is in many ways the essence of the teaching/learning process, Bruner cautions that 'pedagogy is never innocent' (1996, p. 63)—that 'it is not just . . . that the medium is the message,' but that 'the message itself may create the reality that the message embodies and predispose those who hear it to think about it in a particular mode' (1986, pp. 121–122). Freire (2003) offers a similar perspective in his discussion of the nature of pedagogical actions as containing not only content, but also presentation (p. 117). For Allsup (2002), scaffolding is a form of intrusion; he suggests that education itself is a form of intrusion—and that Vygotsky's theories presume the existence of a power structure (pp. 125–126).

In the case of scaffolded songwriting, the teacher's musical participation is never innocent because of the holistic nature of the product and process. For example, if the teacher is providing harmonic support for the work in progress, every action or decision of the teacher determines, to some extent, the direction the work will take. Because the product moves through time, it is often necessary to make these decisions rather instantaneously without discussion. A teacher may be accompanying students as they sing a portion of a song that has already been agreed upon. This performance often continues into a new not-yet-composed section. A teacher scaffolding this process may inadvertently take the lead in establishing the harmonic colour of the new section because, as the composing/performing continues into the new section, he must make an immediate decision about what to play.

In some instances in these data, generally those reflecting the work of more experienced composers, when the teacher shifts the harmony, the students resist and sing what they originally had in mind, causing the teacher to follow a harmonic path that better fits what the students are singing (and thinking). But more often, particularly in cases involving novice composers, the students tend to move their voices to follow the teacher's harmonic choice, even if it means slightly altering what they had intended to sing. In this kind of collaborative process, this is often unavoidable. As a teacher, I have experimented with just dropping the accompaniment out at that point and encouraging the students to continue. Because of the abrupt change in momentum that this creates, inexperienced composers often just stop singing when the accompaniment stops, halting the process awkwardly. This is one reason I found the 'Animal Palace' composers to be so sophisticated in their approach, despite their young age and lack of experience in this particular process of composing together with a teacher. For whatever reason—probably because the first few suggestions were made unaccompanied—in each case, I was able to play the part they had already composed and drop out while someone suggested a new line *a cappella*. In this case, they seemed to fall into this pattern of process fortuitously. A more reticent, inexperienced group of student composers would generally have needed more teacher support in order to be successful.

Scaffolding creative music process

Analysis of data from the various learning communities that informed the discussions in this chapter yielded information about the nature of both the musical and social scaffolding that supported these students' collaborative composing efforts. The following vignette describes an incident that occurred in one of my own third-grade general music classes; I had taught most of these students for two or three years prior to this composing experience.

A third-grade class was in the midst of composing a song they had named 'Pizza' for which they had already created several stanzas of lyrics. One student suggested (through singing, gesturing, and explaining) that the piano should play an accompanying bassline (Fig. 5.11):

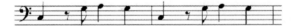

Fig. 5.11

As I played what he suggested, someone added that a cabasa should play the same rhythm doubling the bassline. Several students then asked to have the bassline and cabasa play continually while they figured out a melody that would fit with it. I made eye contact with the cabasa player and, with a nod, established the tempo, signalled the start, and began playing the bassline on piano, throwing in an occasional tonic chord in the right hand. I nodded to the class and the students joined in, all singing different melodies that fitted with the bass, and after a few repetitions it was agreed that the first two phrases should be (Fig. 5.12):

Fig. 5.12

To clarify for those who have never engaged in such a process with children, they all sing the lyrics simultaneously over the accompaniment, which of course means that multiple melodies are suggested simultaneously.[3] Not as many different melodies emerge as one might imagine because (a) from the children's perspectives, constructed through the music of their experience, there are only so many possibilities that stay within the predictable basic harmonic structure of the music they tend to know, and (b) leaders invariably emerge within the group and some students choose to follow their lead. In general, once a particular phrase is sung several times, students gravitate to a

---

[3] Goodman (1978) describes multiple perspectives as different 'versions' of the same world. When people make collaborative art in a situation mutually scaffolded by peers and teacher, many versions of the final product exist side by side. Within this context, the collaborative product is negotiated.

common idea—which they tend to identify as their own idea, even though it was likely the idea of only one or two children initially.[4]

The melodies produced through this kind of process tend to be predictable, often sequential. Innovation is almost always the idea of one individual who often sings out an idea unprompted, as in the 'Animal Palace' story. This might lead some to question the wisdom of engaging students in this process as a whole class. However, the point of the experience is that it promotes and empowers independent musical thinking in students who might never have dreamt they could engage successfully in this kind of work. The fact that initial attempts often result in predictable melodies often prompts second- and third-time songwriters to reject unimaginative, sequential repetitions and seek more interesting ideas, often suggested by individuals within the collaborative context. Ultimately, this teacher-scaffolded experience fosters their ability to write songs with small groups of peers or on their own, without (or with less) teacher support.

As the composers of 'Pizza' tackled the third line of text, they generated a sequence that implied a chord other than the tonic. Without discussion, I transposed the accompaniment pattern to support the sequence in a way that would 'sound good' or 'right' to them in the context of their musical experience. Eventually the song grew to (Fig. 5.13).

As the children worked to develop the melody, I did not realize immediately that they were conceiving the 2/4 measure as such. At first I continued to play that measure with the 4-beat accompaniment pattern. As the children continued to sing that portion of the melody as a 2-beat phrase, I adapted the accompaniment to support the sound they seemed to be seeking. Such musical decisions were made non-verbally, embedded in the flow of the musical process driven by the temporality of music. In this type of process, as ideas are suggested one after another, there is a sense that the momentum could be

---

[4] It should be noted that my purpose in engaging young or inexperienced composers in this type of process was to enable a successful songwriting experience (or series of experiences) that would provide students with sufficient understanding of the process and self-efficacy to enable them to work with peers to write their own songs in subsequent experiences. In those subsequent experiences, teacher scaffolding looks quite different for different groups and individuals. The weakest or least confident students may still require teacher support that is as influential as what was provided for the whole group. At the other end of the continuum, some small groups, pairs, or individuals may be able to work with complete independence and share only their final product with the teacher. And of course, there are many students whose needs lie between these poles. However, the nature of teacher scaffolding in a small group setting is not the purview of this chapter.

Fig. 5.13

destroyed if the mutual sense of flow through time were to be interrupted—which produces a quality of intensity in the process.

As is evident from this vignette and the 'Animal Palace' story, scaffolding the students' songwriting process involves both musical and social scaffolding. In the instances of whole-class song composing that were captured and analysed, musical scaffolding included:

- Helping students musically realize ideas they were able to conceive and communicate in some way, but not able to fully realize musically.

- Establishing a starting point from which they could travel (a suggested key or basic harmonic structure within which they could generate melodic ideas).

- Creating and playing a harmonic accompaniment that either fitted with what students' melodic ideas implied or served to lead the creation of new melodic material.

- Accompanying in a way that supported student singing of the sections that were already created, as a context for the development of new material.

- Sharing information about musical conventions to help them create a song that they would accept as musically valid (in terms of the music of their experience).

- Identifying interesting melodies as they were suggested within the group—sometimes softly and timidly from the rear of the room—coaxing them forward into the collaborative discussion.
- Supporting whole-group singing of the more complex ideas suggested by individuals to be sure they were accurately represented and appropriately valued in the product.

In the instances analysed, social scaffolding included:

- Providing time and space for students' musical thinking and process. Working in a way that supported and did not impede their flow of ideas.
- Establishing and maintaining an atmosphere in which all participants had an opportunity to think and to be heard.
- Recognizing, supporting, and validating ideas. Creating a positive, supportive atmosphere in which students could expect their ideas to be honoured and respected.
- Making space for students to take the lead wherever possible. Making it clear that the song was theirs—that the teacher was there to provide support, but not usurp or dominate.
- Stepping back to make space for and encourage peer interaction and scaffolding.
- Providing space and support for reflection and independent thinking throughout the process—in the context of the momentum necessary to support the flow and recall of musical ideas.

Through scaffolding, teachers enable learners to become increasingly knowledgeable participants in communities of practice (Lave & Wenger, 1991; Wenger, 1998), in this case, the practice of songwriting. With experience and over time, the nature of students' participation transforms in complexity and sophistication, enabling them to take on increasing personal responsibility for the work.

While students working in a formal learning setting may have need for and certainly have the right to teacher scaffolding, inevitable tensions may arise as teachers' efforts to scaffold may confront or inadvertently interfere with students' need for and right to learner agency. In reflecting further on the instances of classroom composing analysed for this chapter, I realized that the data actually included more recordings of the process in situations where the teacher had not worked long term with the students. In instances where the teacher had been a more integral, longstanding member of the community, these kinds of tensions came to the surface less frequently (see Wiggins, 1999b, 2005). It was not that the tensions did not exist in those settings, but that recognizing them, understanding them, and knowing how to negotiate them was an integral part of the ways of being of the students and teachers in those communities. When students are long-term members of a learning community in which their ideas and agency are valued, they tend to take the initiative when they are able and seek support when it is needed in ways that make the inherent tension between teacher support and student agency less of an issue. That said, we do need to consider such tensions, what they look like, how they emerge, and how they might be negotiated.

Negotiating tensions

Scholars who look at learning process through a cultural psychology lens have different ways of describing tensions that lie between teacher scaffolding and learner agency, but they share a common understanding that potential for negotiation and resolution of these tensions lies in the teacher's way of being (van Manen, 1991). In her exploration of emancipatory education, Lather (1991) articulates the issue as a question, 'How can we position ourselves as less masters of truth and justice and more as creators of space where those directly involved can act and speak on their own behalf?' (p. 137). Greene (1995) describes the teacher's process as provoking and releasing rather than imposing and controlling (p. 57). In setting forth a vision of schooling as a mutual community of learners, Bruner (1996) urges us to keep in mind that even in such a community, the teacher is still responsible for 'orchestrating the proceedings' (p. 21). In taking a more democratic approach, teachers do not abdicate the role of teacher, but add to their responsibilities by encouraging others to share authority in the community (pp. 21–22). For Freire (2003), the nature of pedagogical discourse is critical to the process; for it to be effective, the teacher must keep students' thinking at the core or risk becoming authoritarian and detrimental to student agency (pp. 116–117).

As part of his illuminating discussion of the nature of successful teachers' ways of being, van Manen (1991) cautions that we should not assume that teachers' efforts to influence learners are necessarily manipulative or reductive of the relationship to a situation in which one person is seeking to control the other. Rather, influence can connote 'the openness of a human being to the presence of another' (p. 16). As teachers, we need to become reflectively aware of our pedagogical influence, making sure that our orientation is always to what is good for the learner—that 'the intention is to strengthen the child's contingent possibility for 'being and becoming' (p. 17).

As teachers endeavour to walk the path between teacher scaffolding and learner agency, in the best of circumstances where teachers are actively reflecting on their process in the moment, these tensions often reside more in the mind of the teacher than in the atmosphere of the classroom. When tensions arise within the flow and momentum of the creative process, they must be sorted out and dealt with 'on the spot' to prevent them from becoming a source of interruption to the process. Examples from the data are discussed below.

Tensions in decisions about lyrics

Tensions can lie in discussions of, and decisions about, topics or lyrics for songs. Particularly with older students, this sometimes becomes a testing ground for just how far the teacher will allow the sharing of authority to go. There are examples in these data that are reminiscent of many experiences from my life in classrooms. In one case, a sixth-grade male student had composed a song at home that he brought to class to be performed by his peers as part of our annual songbook project,[5] which would be a highly public venue. The song, 'Man Put the Gun Down,' was extraordinarily well written and organized. He and his classmates had worked on it during the lunch hour that preceded music class, planning who would sing what and how it should be staged. The student was highly respected by his peers and had a history of perceiving himself to be 'way too cool' for music class. I had to make a decision about whether to honour this first positive effort on his part and respect the work he would share or to, in essence, censor what I felt might have been inappropriate material for schoolwork. My decision to welcome the work into our midst may not have sat particularly well with the building principal, but it went a long way in establishing the credibility of our work in music class as authentic and of the songbook as worthy and relevant from the students' perspective.

This particular incident and dozens like it in my experience are reflective of tensions between the students' experiences with the music of their lives outside of school and its relation to what comprises 'school music' (discussed by many, e.g. Green, 1988, 2002; Hargreaves, Marshall & North, 2003; Lamont, Hargreaves, Marshall & Tarrant, 2003; Ross, 1995) and of tensions that generally surround the worlds of children growing up in contemporary times

---

[5] For most of the years that I was an elementary music teacher, my students and I produced an annual songbook that consisted of notated and recorded versions of original songs created by all students in the school. Students in grades K-3 wrote whole-class songs, with one song representing each class in the songbook. Students in the upper elementary grades wrote songs in small groups, as pairs, or on their own. In some years, we produced 90–120 minutes of music that was duplicated and distributed to all classrooms in the school with copies also sold to families as a fundraiser. The project was always central in the children's school lives with some getting off the bus on the first day of school telling me they already knew what their songbook song was going to be.

(e.g. Elkind, 1981/2006; Postman, 1982/1994). The same kinds of tensions were mirrored in a study of choices made by students who were invited to produce their own videos (Grace & Tobin, 2002). The similarity of the children's judgements and decisions when engaged in these two real-life projects—composing a song and producing a video—is quite compelling. In both cases, the projects dealt with processes and media that are central to children's out-of-school lives. And, in both cases, their apprenticeship of experience[6] gives them a rich, authentic context from which to make decisions about how they should proceed with the work, and what work is valid and valuable. Grace & Tobin found that the children in their study were 'frequently fascinated with things that adults consider to be rude, uncouth, or gross,' noting that although this was not particularly surprising, it was unusual in this case, as behaviours that usually occurred outside the school agenda emerged within the authorized curriculum (p. 196). They suggest that:

> video production opens up a space where students can play with the boundaries of language and ideology and enjoy transgressive collective pleasures. This boundary-crossing and pleasure-getting by the children in the midst of the curriculum pushes teachers to think about their authority in new ways. (p. 196)

Further, they note that the children's work was 'greatly influenced by the media and popular culture,' but that the videos did far more than mimic popular culture. 'Rather than simply replicate remembered plots and themes, children play with aspects of the familiar and conjoin them in imaginative and pleasing ways. In the children's videos, the world of popular culture is interwoven with the world of school' (Grace & Tobin, 2002, p. 200).

This is also true of children's decisions during songwriting as a school project, and is exemplified by numerous instances from my own classroom. Instances of what could be considered inappropriate lyrics or topics arose more often during small group or independent work than in the whole-class context—because those more independent organizational contexts provided more opportunity for private, unsupervised conversation. There were the inevitable sexually explicit lyrics which, in my classroom, were always nixed as the creators fully expected they would be—but they had made their point nonetheless (that they knew how to write 'real' lyrics, comparable to those experienced through the media). There were songs about gang fights and other similar incidents that the students could not have experienced firsthand, but,

---

[6] Darling-Hammond (2001) talks about the 'apprenticeship of experience' of pre-service teachers, a concept that Lortie (1975/2002) developed years earlier as 'apprenticeship of observation'. I use Darling-Hammond's version here to describe the processes through which children learn the music of their lives.

again, reflected their knowledge of lyrics in the music of their experience; lyrics that they considered to be authentic (and would earn the respect of their peers). In other attempts at authenticity, some children tried to write love songs; too sweetly innocent to be truly successful. Decisions about how to scaffold such attempts without squelching the children's creative process and personal agency are always difficult. Each must be considered for its own merit in its own context. There is no simple formula.

Children use songwriting to share their views about what is important to them in life, from the joys of chocolate cake to the difficulties of wearing braces. I have seen students use songwriting as a vehicle for expressing what they perceive to be essential, important topics, like helping abused children ('Can You Help Me Please?'), ecological issues (which are often about their desire to have a say in their own fate), and a celebration of freedom in honour of the end of the Berlin Wall ('The Wall is Coming Down'). One fifth-grade girl whose father had been in prison for most of her life wrote an impassioned song about what a good father would be. The writer of 'It's Hard Being Small,' about the teasing she regularly endured, was quite surprised at the number of apologies she received once she decided to share her song publicly.

Sometimes what appears to be innocent is not, which can unknowingly put teachers into awkward positions—as when a commercial jingle for mouthwash was written as a statement about students' hopes that a particular teacher would use it more often, or when a song celebrating the joys of apple juice turned out to be a mockery of a cafeteria incident that was particularly embarrassing to one student in the class. These kinds of awkward moments seem to arise more frequently when the relationship between the teacher and students is relatively new or strained. On the other hand, experienced, comfortable songwriters tend to know and respect the process and choose paths that get them closer to their goals, rather than ones that waste their time. They also seem to be more focused on the musical aspects of the work than on the lyrics. Or perhaps I, as a more experienced teacher of songwriting, have learned better how to negotiate these tensions and turn them into more productive energy. Being so close to the process, it is hard to know.

Of importance, however, is the establishment of an environment in which students feel they have enough free choice for them to feel that the music is theirs. Within such an environment, difficult decisions arise that require the teacher to assert more authority than he or she seeks. The way these decisions are handled can positively or negatively impact students' feelings of ownership and agency. In these cases, talking *with* students instead of *at* them can create a situation in which students can be brought into the teacher's (more mature) understanding of the situation (Rogoff, 1990). Enabling students to make at least some choices in the situation can engender agency and enable them to 'buy in' and continue along a positive route to success.

Tensions in decisions about musical ideas

Once the lyrics are established, the process of turning them into a song may take a variety of paths. There are many possible points of entry into the process, including chanting the lyrics as a group and then singing them; chanting lyrics over a teacher-proposed accompaniment pattern; student-suggested ideas for the accompaniment (before the melody exists); student-suggested ideas about stylistic qualities, orchestration, or timbre (before the thematic material exists); and so forth. The process of collaborative songwriting requires a sensitivity and attentiveness, on the part of the teacher, to details that may emerge from individuals in any part of the room at any time. Capturing and embedding those ideas into the work in progress with everyone's approval require the teacher to be aware of, and highly in tune with, all that is happening in the room. Sometimes the process moves along smoothly; sometimes it feels more like a battle. Tensions can arise from within any aspect of the process.

The most central tensions lie in the process of interweaving the ideas of so many individuals while nurturing collaborative ownership of the product. Allsup (2002), who studied collaborative composing in settings where students worked independently from the teacher, found that 'ideas may be credited to individuals, but they eventually belong to the entire group' (p. 161). He describes the 'plural nature' of his students' compositional process. 'Every idea is negotiable, any member can make a request, judicial comments are rarely withheld, and decisions are finalized by consensus' (p. 177). The situation is similar for students engaged in composing under the guidance, and through the scaffolding, of a teacher. However, the added presence of the teacher as co-collaborator can potentially alter these feelings of collaborative ownership, depending on how assertive the teacher feels she needs to be at any particular time.

For one year, I taught in a private school in which students had never before composed original music as part of their music class experiences. It was nearing the end of the school year and my plan was for the sixth-grade students to work in small groups to write, orchestrate, learn, perform, and record original songs as a culminating project. As the first experience in this final unit, we would work together as a whole group to compose one song to provide a model for what the process might look like. Once the class song had been written, they would work in small groups, pairs, or as individuals to create their own songs. While we were composing the class song, I happened to be running a tape recorder and unknowingly captured a salient example of tensions created by the teacher's curricular goals coming into conflict with the students' vision of the product. (My pedagogical decisions in this instance were heavily influenced by my knowledge of the small number of contact times that remained in the school year and the amount and nature of the work I hoped the students would accomplish before time ran out.)

The class had chosen to compose an anti-war song that reflected their anger and fears about the Gulf War that was in progress at the time. As they thought about how to set their lyrics, strong sentiments were expressed about the song seeming to sit best as a rap—that it was fine the way it was, with lyrics alone and no melody. I tried to honour and respect their vision for the setting (which was certainly a musically valid one) while trying to negotiate the necessity (from my view) for the curricular experience—trying to be fair-minded, but asserting my position nonetheless. It was a role I was never comfortable with. My attempt at persuasion follows:

> We could. We could make it a rap . . . Would you mind if we try to write a tune and then, if you don't like it, we can throw it out? Because you need to learn how to take words and turn them into a song [thinking: so we will have enough time remaining for you to write your own songs]. That was the purpose of doing this [talking faster now, trying to be convincing] 'cause you're gonna do that by yourselves next week. And if we miss that step now, you might not know how to do it. I understand why you're saying that, because it sort of works, you know? But let's see if we can get a tune. [Then, moving forward despite their reticent looks] Do you think this would have a very melodic tune? You know, would it be pretty? It's going to be an angry kind of sound like we're saying anyway, so that's OK. It might work.

Without re-engaging them in conversation, I began to play the accompaniment pattern we had chosen before the conversation had turned to rap. They followed my lead (whether or not they agreed with my decision) and were soon deeply involved in creating what turned out to be a rather powerful and appropriately effective melodic setting. As they arranged, rehearsed, performed, and recorded the song, no one mentioned returning to the rap idea—and they seemed rightly proud of the product, eager to share it with their teacher and peers in other classes.

I remember thinking that if these students had responded by becoming more insistent about the rap setting of the text, I would have accepted their viewpoint and asked them to create a new set of lyrics through which we could learn songwriting process. As it happened in this case, they instead became swept up in the process of writing the melody, and in that process they seemed to forget about their initial ideas of setting the text as rap. In my experience with such circumstances, I have found that once the students are drawn into the compositional process, they rarely (if ever) opt to discard the melody they have created and return to their original idea of rap. In this case, fortunately, the situation remained positive and productive. It might not have, and then I would have needed to make a decision between plunging forward with my own curricular goals or accepting the preference of the students and modifying my plans. In formal school settings, teachers face such decisions constantly, and probably make some bad decisions along the way, in the name of 'progress'. However, we might also keep in mind that, as Wenger (1998) reminds us, 'the very presence of tension implies that there is an effort at maintaining some kind of coexistence' (p. 160).

Also relevant, in this instance, is the fact that this was our first collaborative songwriting effort. In my experience in longstanding learning communities, where time has enabled a more established curricular culture, the students would have had enough experience with their own original songs and those of their peers and predecessors to foster their understanding of, expectations for, and respect for the project. In such cases, had the situation described above occurred, peers would have explained to others why we had to at least make an effort to learn how to set the text. What remains most critical, though, is that honouring students' perspectives requires inviting them into an understanding of the situation and including them in the decision-making process.[7]

Engendering and honoring agency

Researchers who have studied children, adolescents, and young adults composing music in formal settings (e.g. Allsup, 2002; Barrett, 2003; Burnard, 1999; Espeland, 2006; Faulkner, 2001, 2003; Ruthmann, 2006; Savage, 2004) and informal settings (e.g. Campbell, 1995; Davis, 2005; Green, 2002) discuss the authorship, ownership, agency, power sharing, valuing, and positive

---

[7] While it might be important to interrogate the hegemonic implications inherent in such a pedagogical decision, this is part of a larger discussion that is, again, not the purview of this chapter. Such a discussion would consider how teachers go about creating environments and laying groundwork that enable and support students' own explorations of ideas. In this case, I knew that engaging these students in the final project of composing, arranging, performing, and recording their own original songs would provide them open-ended freedom to explore, create, and express their personal musical perspectives and ideas. I also knew from experience that, whereas some students are ready to jump right into such an open-ended project, others would require, prefer, and embrace a bit more structure and guidance at the start. In my experience, once students begin their more independent work, some students use composing processes that are remarkably different from the collaborative, scaffolded experience. However, there are also some who are clearly grateful to have a process in place that they know they will be able to use to be successful in what might otherwise be an intimidating, uncertain experience.

interdependence that the experiences seem to generate. The nature of creative music process itself can be empowering if the environment in which it occurs permits it to be.

For student composers to successfully generate original musical ideas, the culture of the classroom must allow time and space for students to think aloud musically. The musings that can be heard throughout a classroom, on such occasions, are audible musical thinking in action, not unlike the egotistical voice that Vygotsky (1978) describes in processes of internalization of verbal ideas, as discussed earlier. For this enactive musical thinking to occur, the teacher must be prepared to accept a certain level of sound in the classroom. The musical learning of young children is rarely silent, because they often need to think aloud musically to be able to invent, work with, evaluate, and formulate understanding of musical ideas.

The data from which the following vignettes were generated were collected during a study of learning and teaching in a general music class. (In this case, I was the researcher, but not the teacher.) Two key student informants carried small tape recorders and wore lapel microphones throughout the study. The data included their musical think-alouds during a teacher-scaffolded, whole-class song composition project.

Second-grade students were working with their teacher to develop a melody for the lyrics they had written for a song they called 'Aliens'. Their initial ideas for the melody were far too reminiscent of the theme from the film *Star Wars* to be considered original material. As many children sang the actual *Star Wars* theme to themselves, some sang permutations inspired by its rhythm, style, and mood. One student sang to herself (Fig. 5.14):

Nah   nah   nah   nah   nah   nah   nah   nah   Nah____

Fig. 5.14

Meanwhile, standing behind a keyboard, the teacher was encouraging the children to find a different melody. To 'plant a new seed' that might move their thinking away from the sound of *Star Wars*, she played and softly sang her own suggested idea for the first line (Fig. 5.15):

A - li - ens,   a - li - ens   are   ev   -   where.

Fig. 5.15

The room was abuzz with humming as the children privately and simultaneously invented and considered musical ideas, singing them softly under their breath, pondering whether the ideas were worthy of contributing to the group. From my perspective as observer, they had not seemed to attend to the theme the teacher had suggested, but the tape recorders in the pockets of the two key informants recorded both children humming and singing to themselves melodies that were clearly rooted in the teacher's subtle suggestion. One sang to himself a long, extended exploration of the suggested idea (Fig. 5.16):

Fig. 5.16

On the other side of the room, the second key informant sang to herself (Fig. 5.17):

Fig. 5.17

As the class continued, the first student contributed several ideas to the group's composing effort; the second continued to generate original ideas to herself, but never ventured to share them with the group. Through this project, however, both children had experiences that had potential to support their agency as independent composers. Both had engaged in setting text to music, even though only one had chosen to make his ideas public.

In addition to creating a classroom culture that allows for and enables musical thinking, teachers must also ensure that all students are given opportunities to develop a sense of agency—even children who, for whatever reason, may be less popular with their peers. As is evident in the vignette that follows, turning a potentially negative situation into a positive one can be transformative in the school life of a child who has had trouble relating to his peers. This incident took place in one of my own second-grade classes, when I was a general music teacher.

For the student who suggested the idea that became the basis for the opening melody for a class song called 'Freckles,' sharing this melodic idea produced the first moment of respect his classroom teacher or I could recall his earning from his peers in a classroom setting. As is quite common in young children, his idea was shared through singing combined with a physical representation—in this case, leaping to his feet and drawing an ascending zigzag in the air with his index finger, exuding an energy that seemed to emanate from his very toes: 'Wait! It has to go (singing on an ascending chromatic scale) neh, neh, neh, neh, neh, neh, neh.' As he finished his statement, much to his amazement and delight, I played the scale he had just sung. As his peers shouted, 'Yeah!' I sang and played (Fig. 5.18):

Fig. 5.18

Merging his idea with the lyrics on the board, scaffolding the realization of his idea in the context of the song in progress. The class enthusiastically embraced his suggestion as the basis for subsequent development of the entire melody of the chorus of their song. (The song also included a verse that had a contrasting melody. Only the chorus appears Fig. 5.19.)

Fig. 5.19

It is not uncommon for an idea suggested by an individual child to be adopted by the group in a way that gives rise to the general form, shape, and/or style of a song. In these instances, one can see the originator of the idea sitting a bit straighter, eyes gleaming a bit brighter, for the remainder of the experience.

Feelings of ownership and agency abound in the level of energy, enthusiasm, and intensity with which students finalize and then rehearse their songs again and again—carefully assessing the overall effect of their choices, making constant suggestions about the orchestration and organization of the performance, correcting peers who are performing something incorrectly, cheering when the group has achieved the desired effect. Sometimes the work persists as the class lines up to leave the room, and continues down the hallway. Sometimes it resumes unannounced when they pass the music teacher in the hallway midweek, or as they re-enter the classroom during the following class session. It sometimes seems as though they would happily work on their songs forever.

When the song belongs to the children, the process is self-motivational—exciting and rewarding for all involved. Scaffolding such a process in a way that enables and allows student ownership to flourish is an art born of sensitivity, respect, musicianship, and experience. Well-scaffolded collaborative composing allows students to create their own musical narratives, narratives that may become powerfully meaningful in their lives. When the process becomes a deeply embedded part of the culture of the classroom and school, children begin to see themselves as creators of music, and begin to see musical creative process as an integral part of their private lives. For some, it becomes one of their primary means of personal expression.

For Bruner (1986), 'conceiving of a possible world includes conceiving of procedures for operating upon it' (p. 106). Engaging music learners in creating original music provides opportunities for them to operate within and upon the structures of their musical world, and contributes to the development (construction) of their capacity for conceiving of, and operating within, this world and beyond. Creating original music is one means of enabling children to become architects of their own destiny, worldmakers (Goodman, 1978), stirred to imaginative action and consciousness of possibility (Greene, 1995), operating as valued interpreters and creators of the culture they (and we) share.

References

Allsup, R. E. (2002). Crossing over: mutual learning and democratic action in instrumental music education. Unpublished doctoral dissertation, Teachers College, Colombia University, New York.

Bakhtin, M. M. (1981). *The dialogic imagination* (M. Holquist, Ed.; C. Emerson & M. Holquist, Trans.). Austin, TX: University of Texas.

Barrett, M. S. (2003). Freedoms and constraints. In M. Hickey (Ed.), *Why and how to teach music composition* (pp. 3–27). Reston, VA: MENC.

Belenky, M. F., Clinchy, B. M., Goldberger, N. R., & Tarule, J. M. (1997). *Women's ways of knowing*. New York: Basic Books.

Bruner, J. (1966). *Toward a theory of instruction*. Cambridge, MA: Harvard University Press.

Bruner, J. (1986). *Actual minds, possible worlds*. Cambridge, MA: Harvard University Press.

Bruner, J. (1990). *Acts of meaning*. Cambridge, MA: Harvard University Press.

Bruner, J. S. (1996). *The culture of education*. Cambridge, MA: Harvard University Press.

Burnard, P. (1999). 'Into different worlds': children's experience of musical improvisation and composition. Unpublished doctoral dissertation, University of Reading, UK.

Campbell, P. S. (1995). Of garage bands and song-getting: the musical development of young rock musicians. *Research Studies in Music Education, 4*, 12–20.

Cole, M. (1996). *Cultural psychology*. Cambridge, MA: Belknap Press of Harvard University Press.

Darling-Hammond, L. (2001). Standard setting in teaching: changes in licensing, certification, and assessment. In V. Richardson (Ed.), *Handbook of research on teaching* (pp. 751–76). Washington, DC: American Educational Research Association.

Davis, S. G. (2005, December 8). 'That thing you do!' Compositional processes of a rock band. *International Journal of Education & the Arts, 6*(16). Retrieved 8 December 2005, from http://ijea.asu.edu/v6n16/

Elkind, D. (1981/2006). *The hurried child: growing up too fast too soon*. Cambridge MA: Da Capo Press.

Espeland, M. (2006). *Compositional process as discourse and interaction*. Unpublished doctoral dissertation, Danish University of Education, University of Aarhus.

Faulkner, R. (2001). *Socializing music education*. Unpublished doctoral dissertation, University of Sheffield, UK.

Faulkner, R. (2003). Group composing. *Music Education Research, 5*(2), 101–24.

Freire, P. (1970/2002). *Pedagogy of the oppressed*. New York: Continuum.

Freire, P. (2003). *Pedagogy of hope*. New York: Continuum.

Goodman, N. (1978). *Ways of worldmaking*. Indianapolis, IN: Hackett.

Grace, D. J., & Tobin, J. (2002). Pleasure, creativity, and the carnivalesque in children's video production. In L. Bresler & C. M. Thompson (Eds.), *The arts in children's lives* (pp. 195–214). Dordrecht: Kluwer.

Green, L. (1988). *Music on deaf ears: musical meaning, ideology, and education*. Manchester, UK: Manchester University Press.

Green, L. (2002). *How popular musicians learn*. Aldershot, UK: Ashgate.

Greene, M. (1995). *Releasing the imagination*. San Francisco: Jossey-Bass.

Greenfield, P. (1984). A theory of the teacher in the learning activities of everyday life. In B. Rogoff & J. Lave (Eds.), *Everyday cognition* (pp. 117–38). Cambridge, MA: Harvard University Press.

Hargreaves, D., Marshall, N. A., & North, A. C. (2003). Music education in the twenty-first century: a psychological perspective. *British Journal of Music Education, 20*(2), 147–63.

Huong, L. P. H. (2003). The mediational role of language teachers in sociocultural theory. *English Teaching Forum, 41*(3), 32–35.

Ladson-Billings, G. (1994). *The dreamkeepers*. San Francisco: Jossey-Bass.

Lamont, A., Hargreaves, D., Marshall, N. A., & Tarrant, M. (2003). Young people's music in and out of school. *British Journal of Music Education, 20*(3), 229–41.

Lather, P. (1991). *Getting smart: feminist research and pedagogy with/in the postmodern*. New York: Routledge.

Lave, J., & Wenger, E. (1991). *Situated learning: legitimate peripheral participation*. New York: Cambridge University Press.

Lortie, D. (1975/2002). *School teacher: a sociological study*. Chicago: University of Chicago.

Nealon, J. T. & Giroux, S. S. (2003). *The theory toolbox: Critical concepts for the new humanities*. Lanham, MD: Rowman & Littlefield.

Postman, N. (1994). *The disappearance of childhood* (2nd edn). New York: Vintage Books.

Rogoff, B. (1990). *Apprenticeship in thinking*. New York: Oxford University Press.

Rogoff, B. (2003). *The cultural nature of human development*. New York: Oxford University Press.

Rogoff, B., & Gardner, W. (1984). Adult guidance of cognitive development. In B. Rogoff & J. Lave (Eds.), *Everyday cognition* (pp. 95–116). Cambridge, MA: Harvard University Press.

Rogoff, B., & Lave, J. (Eds.) (1984). *Everyday cognition: its development in social context*. Cambridge, MA: Harvard University Press.

Ross, M. (1995). What's wrong with school music? *British Journal of Music Education, 12*(3), 185–201.

Ruthmann, S. A. (2006). Negotiating learning and teaching in a music technology lab. Unpublished doctoral dissertation, Oakland University, Rochester, MI.

Savage, J. (2004). Re-imagining music education for the 21st century. Unpublished doctoral dissertation, University of East Anglia, Norwich, UK.

Stone, C. A. (1993). What is missing in the metaphor of scaffolding? In E. A. Forman, N. Minick & C. A. Stone (Eds.), *Contexts of learning* (pp. 169–83). New York: Oxford University Press.

van Manen. M. (1991). *The tact of teaching: the meaning of pedagogical thoughtfulness*. New York: SUNY Press.

Vygotsky, L. S. (1978) *Mind in society*. In M. Cole, V. John-Steiner, S. Scribner & E. Souberman (Eds.). Cambridge: Harvard University Press.

Wenger, E. (1998). *Communities of practice: learning, meaning, and identity*. New York: Cambridge University Press.

Wertsch, J., Tulviste, P., & Hagstrom, F. (1993). A sociocultural approach to agency. In E. A. Forman, N. Minick & C. A. Stone (Eds.), *Contexts of learning* (pp. 336–56). New York: Oxford University Press.

Wiggins, J. (1992). *The nature of children's musical learning in the context of a music classroom*. Unpublished doctoral dissertation, University of Illinois.

Wiggins, J. (1994). Children's strategies for solving compositional problems with peers. *Journal of Research in Music Education, 42*(3), 232–52.

Wiggins, J. (1995). Building structural understanding: Sam's story. *Quarterly Journal of Music Teaching and Learning, 6*(3), 57–75.

Wiggins, J. (1999a). The nature of shared musical understanding and its role in empowering independent musical thinking. *Bulletin of the Center for Research in Music Education, 143*, 65–90.

Wiggins, J. (1999b). Teacher control and creativity. *Music Educators Journal, 85*(5), 30–35.

Wiggins, J. (2001). *Teaching for musical understanding*. New York: McGraw-Hill.

Wiggins, J. (2002). Creative process as meaningful musical thinking. In T. Sullivan & L. Willingham (Eds.), *Creativity and music education* (pp. 78–88). Toronto: Canadian Music Educators Association.

Wiggins, J. (2003). A frame for understanding children's compositional processes. In M. Hickey (Ed.), *How and why to teach music composition* (pp. 141–66). Reston, VA: MENC.

Wiggins, J. (2005). Fostering revision and extension in student composing. *Music Educators Journal, 91*(3), 35–42.

Wiggins, J. (2006). Compositional process in music. In L. Bresler (Ed.), *International handbook of research in arts education* (pp. 451–67). Amsterdam: Springer.

Wiggins, J. (2009). *Teaching for musical understanding* (2nd edn). Rochester, MI: Center for Applied Research in Musical Understanding.

Wood, D., Bruner, J., & Ross, G. (1976). The role of tutoring in problem solving. *Journal of Child Psychology and Psychiatry, 17*, 89–100.

Chapter 6

Making music or playing instruments: secondary students' use of cultural tools in aural- and notation-based instrumental learning and teaching

Cecilia Hultberg

Two vignettes of students' learning from teachers' perspectives

Helen, a piano teacher, comments on Nina's performance

'It is really stuck in her', Helen comments when she and I are looking at videos showing her lessons with Nina, a 16-year-old student, who is studying *Notturno* by E. Grieg (*Lyrical pieces*, No. 4, book 5, op. 54). Helen refers to her own comment to Nina concerning Nina's performance of two parallel passages, the notation of which she has misunderstood, despite Helen presenting model performances and instrumental solutions to her in a couple of lessons. Nina's misreading makes the melodic line 'stumble', and she performs without noticeable expression. 'I ought to be able to help her solve such problems better', Helen reflects.

Maria, a marimba teacher, comments on Eve and Doris' performance

'Look at that, they're playing straight', Maria exclaims. She and I are viewing videos that I have recorded from aural-based lessons with a group of her pupils aged 12–13 years. Maria pays special attention to Eve and Doris, who are standing beside each other at one of the alto marimbas, playing their repetitive part of a traditional Zimbabwean narrative song rather mechanically. Maria continues: 'I don't know how to make them *feel* the music. To them it's just a part. They should dance as well, but they don't want to. The older students do; it works much better then.'

These vignettes demonstrate the area which is the focus of this chapter: Eve and Doris use the marimba to play a correct series of tones rather than to express music, and Nina plays inaccurately from the printed score without musical expressivity; the three girls are playing instruments rather than making music. They do so in contexts of aural-based and notation-based tuition, contexts in which the cultural tools at their disposal in their learning processes differ.

Also exemplified in the vignettes are tensions that may occur in teaching and learning. Maria's disappointment at having failed to help her students feel the music and Helen's reflection on the challenge to support her student better, in order to solve problems that prevent musical development, raise questions about students' ways of using the tools for learning provided to them by their teachers. Hence, in this chapter, students' ways of using cultural tools in aural-based and notation-based instrumental music lessons will be discussed. This discussion will draw on the findings of exploratory case studies of Maria and Helen's teaching, and some of their students' learning.

Theoretical background

The cultural psychological perspective used in these studies implies a special interest in the relationship between individuals and traditions: in how people are influenced by participation in cultural activities, and how they use the tools provided by the culture (Säljö, 2000). In the study that has informed this chapter, students participate in music activities in pedagogical settings, interacting with their teachers who are established representatives of the culture in question. In this interaction, the teachers' ways of using cultural tools to 'distribute' knowledge to students is of particular importance to students' learning. This interactive social and cultural dimension of human learning is central to Vygotsky's (1934/1981) theory of cultural history, from which the cultural psychological perspective has been developed.

According to a cultural psychological perspective, cultural tools function as mediators of the real world, and, hence, strongly influence individuals' thoughts and actions (Bruner, 1996/2002; Vygotsky, 1934/1981) and contribute to their development. However, because of the close interrelation between different kinds of cultural tools and artefacts, Bruner proposes the idea of a box of tools as a complex entity rather than that of separate tools. He exemplifies this by referring to J. S. Bach, whom he suggests would not have been able to create his music if he had been living in a different cultural context (Bruner, 1996/2002, p. 136). Having access to knowledge developed by other composers, musicians and instrument builders, Bach became familiar with a tradition in which there were established ways of structuring and expressing music. Compositions, improvised music, instruments, performance practice and music notation provided a toolbox which he was able to use to assist him to develop his competence.

The complex impact of cultural tools in the studies presented in this chapter is evident. Instruments are both artefacts and tools, whereas works of music are artefacts, which may function as tools contributing to individuals' musical development. In instrumental tuition, works of music may, for instance, be represented in two ways: first, by teachers' or other musicians' performances to which students listen; second, by printed scores, from which they read and play. The printed score, which incorporates complex symbols representing sounded music, may be used in different ways as a tool for musical learning: reading and/or playing from it, individuals may develop their image and their understanding of the music (Hultberg, 2002). Music performances may also function as cultural tools. When listening repeatedly to a certain style of music, for example, individuals accumulate familiarity without necessarily paying special attention to what they hear (Davies, 1994). Listening attentively to their teachers' performances, students learn about representative practice to which they can relate when listening to their own playing. In parallel, teachers relate to their own ideas of representative practice in their model performances, and, listening to their students' playing, they may learn about the ideas and needs of individual students. Thus, conventionalized ways of structuring and express-ing music in a certain style (performance practice) are important musical gestures, tools, by means of which students and teachers may develop their images and understanding of music (Hultberg, 2006).

Generally, conventions represent collective knowledge and are related to cultural practices that individuals participating in a tradition follow, mostly without reflecting on them (Rolf, 1991). Thus, established cultural practices may function like rules of a game to which people adapt their actions; accord-ing to Gadamer (1997) they may even be so strongly influenced by the rules that they are played by these. He refers to Huizinga's (1939/2004) theory that conceptualization in original human cultures is connected to game-like rituals with clear rules, and states: 'The nature of the game consists of the rules and agreements telling how to fill the space of acting' (Gadamer 1997, p. 85, my translation). In instrumental tuition, such cultural influence concerns not only music traditions but teaching traditions. Some teachers might use established practices without reflecting on them or questioning them, whereas others may be more deliberate and reflective. Likewise, some students may take teachers' musical and pedagogical practices for granted and adapt to these without reflecting, using them repeatedly. However, students who misinterpret their teachers' intentions, like the girls in the introductory vignettes seem to do, may develop diverging practices to which they become accustomed. The effect that repeated experiences have on individuals' learning is described by Vygotsky (1934/1981) as traces in the mind, like folds in a piece of paper, which are difficult to replace once there. Consequently, students' comprehension of musical and pedagogical practices is an important factor in their further learning.

According to Bruner (1996/2002), established cultural representatives distribute cultural knowledge to other individuals who gain access to the tradition in question by internalizing and transforming their experiences of this knowledge in different ways. In this distribution, he emphasizes, *conventionalization* of practices is of great importance (p. 181), that is, when these are taken for granted without being questioned (as described above). By using cultural tools, and relating new experiences to earlier ones, learners create cultural 'works' (Bruner, 1996/2002), by which they present, that is, externalize, their ideas. In this chapter, music performances are 'works', created by students, by teachers, or by students and teachers working together. Being cultural representatives, the music teachers distribute knowledge to their students, whose learning may be further facilitated when they are making music together.

According to Vygotsky (1934/1981), the interaction between cultural participants who are working at different levels of skill and expertise activates learners' zones of proximal development (ZPD). When learners work with others more expert in their ZPD they tend to perform at higher levels than they would have managed on their own, facilitating their future independent learning in similar tasks. Vygotsky also underlines the mutuality of such learning contexts, maintaining that such mutuality supports individual development of both participants (1934/1981). Transferring this understanding to instrumental tuition means that both students and teachers learn by collaborating in music activities.

The idea that individuals develop new knowledge not merely by interacting with other individuals but by interacting and communicating with and through works of art, is one aspect of the cultural dimension in Vygotsky's theory of human learning. According to Wells (1999), the works of art themselves function as cultural representatives for the individuals who interact with them. This view is consistent with the notion that both a music performance and a printed score may function as a cultural tool and contribute to personal development. In instrumental tuition, students and teachers interact with each other, bringing into this interaction their individual experiences from communicating with works of music, as well as their experiences from and expectations of being a student or a teacher in this context. Consequently, two forms of traditions need to be taken into account: the music traditions in question and the pedagogical traditions on which the teachers draw.

Students, however, do not always experience their instrumental tuition as supportive. Musicians from different epochs and traditions, as well as researchers, give evidence that students' learning and musical development may be obstructed rather than supported by teaching. This may be the case when students experience an expectation that they will 'correctly' reproduce printed music or exactly follow teachers' instructions without being encouraged to develop their own musical judgement (Booth, 1999; Brändström & Wiklund, 1995; Folkestad, 1996; Green, 2001; Hultberg, 2000, 2002; Quantz, 1752/1974; Rostvall & West, 2001). These conditions may provide students with limited possibilities to use music notation, teachers' performances, and verbal instructions as tools for learning, as their own experiences and reflections on these are not taken into account. By contrast, the role of reflection is emphasized by representatives of aural as well as Western music traditions. For instance, Alagi Mbye, a *jali* (established cultural representative) of the oral West African Mandinka tradition, maintains: 'You have to be intellectual in music to satisfy the people' (as cited in Sæther, 2003, p. 110), while the pianist Alfred Brendel (1977/1982) advises musicians to reflect on implicit musical meaning in a composition rather than to slavishly follow everything as it is written.

According to Vygotsky (1934/1981), good conditions for fostering students' reflection, as described above, and to develop independent judgement, require a dialogic teaching approach in which both students and teachers are given opportunities to act and react. This implies demands on teachers, not only to collaborate with students to support them working in their zones of proximal development, but to take students' experiences into account and support them according to their individual needs. In this chapter, students' ways of using cultural tools in instrumental tuition are explored in contexts representing these conditions. The students participating in this project appreciate their lessons, and their teachers are concerned about their students' musical development. In the introductory vignettes, this is exemplified by Maria's and Helen's reflections on the need for developing strategies that facilitate students' implementation of knowledge about traditional musical expressivity that they, as teachers, have tried to communicate to them. It should be acknowledged that the vignettes merely allow small glimpses of the longitudinal processes of teaching and learning.

Method

This project, which explored strategies in instrumental teaching and learning, consisted of two parallel collaborative case studies in which the participating teachers acted as co-researchers: they planned their respective data collection and analysed their own data in collaboration with me. The aim of this approach was to account for the teachers' perspectives, to explore aspects of general/ particular relevance to practitioners and to contribute to the trustworthiness of the data and findings. To capture students' longitudinal learning the teachers and I agreed that I would follow some of their students during two time periods of three weeks each, with a break of about two months between these periods. Maria selected two groups on primary and secondary levels, and Helen two students who were having one-to-one tuition. The participating pupils, and their respective parents, accepted the conditions of participation. Together, the teachers and their students decided which span of lessons to select for the study, and invited me to attend their lessons, as an observer. Before beginning my observation of the first lesson, both teachers introduced me to their students. I videotaped the lessons with a camera placed close to a wall in order to create as little disturbance as possible, and, for the same reason, I remained sitting beside the camera during the entire observation. During my observations, students and teachers seemed to take little notice of me as soon as they turned their attention to each other and to their lessons.

After the second lesson of the first period, each teacher described her strategies, and these descriptions were videotaped. During the fieldwork I analysed the data continuously and, in addition, conducted further analysis and interpretation in collaboration with the respective teachers after each series of lessons. These collaborative analyses took place about a month after the final lesson of each series. This timing facilitated the participants' development of enough perspective to become their own observers. This was a decision based on findings from an earlier study of pianists' approaches to notation (Hultberg, 2000, 2002). This earlier study showed that some participants had difficulty maintaining distance from their actions when they commented on their own video-taped performances during the phase of stimulated recall which took place on the same day. For example, some participants' comments on and accounts of interpretation contradicted the musical actions recorded and presented to the participants. For instance, a piano teacher commented on a certain articulation that she actually did *not* play and explained *why* she had 'chosen' this articulation, thus taking up the attitude of an actor in an imagined and ongoing process of interpretation-finding, rather than that of being her own observer (Hultberg, 2000, 2002). Hence, in the present studies I met with each teacher for the collaborative analyses at a time when a similar influence could be avoided.

Both teachers were keen to watch their own lessons in detail, to comment on them and discuss them with me, especially after the first period of documentation. Thus, the first collaborative analytic sessions with each teacher lasted an entire working day. When we had revisited each lesson in detail, the teacher summarized her observations and I presented video excerpts that had informed my preliminary analysis. We then discussed our observations and reflections. After the second span of lessons, both teachers, independently of each other, asked me to present significant excerpts based on my preliminary analyses. In addition, Maria and Helen, again independently, complemented these by suggesting further excerpts showing incidents that had drawn their attention. Then we discussed the entire documentation based on an overview of extracts representing both series—selected by me.

During all analytic sessions I took notes of the teachers' comments and our discussions. Comments made during the video-documented lessons were transcribed verbatim, and the teachers' and my own observations were thoroughly described. The notes from the collaborative analyses and the transcripts of the videos were sent to the respective teacher together with copies of the videos. Both Helen and Maria approved of the text, and neither of them wished to add anything. Altogether, these data informed a re-analysis that I undertook. Finally, in three seminars at different universities, excerpts of crucial importance to the analysis were independently examined by groups of researchers. This chapter presents findings that have been confirmed in these seminars.

Two case studies in different contexts

For this chapter, I have selected the case studies of Maria and Helen's lessons in secondary level education in order to discuss students' ways of using cultural tools in contrasting contexts of music education. In the following two subsections, findings from the two case studies are presented and commented on separately. Descriptions that go beyond what has been documented on video are based either on teachers' statements during the collaborative analyses or on students' spontaneous comments to me, made in connection with their lessons.

Helen and Nina

Helen is a Swedish piano teacher teaching in the Western music tradition at a Swedish community music school. After her exam for teaching piano and ensemble, she studied Suzuki pedagogy in Sweden. Helen tries to maintain a friendly atmosphere in her teaching room; comfortable furniture complements the instruments and shelves. Each lesson begins with a short conversation about the students' preceding week, mainly musical, but Helen also takes her time to listen briefly to other events of importance to her students. She performs works that are new to them before they begin to study these, but otherwise—after the small talk—her students begin and end each lesson with as complete a performance as is possible of the music they are studying.

Describing her teaching strategies, Helen emphasises the four main points in Suzuki pedagogy: 'to work with hand and arm gestures, to breathe, that is, to *wait* before you begin to play a piece of music or a new section, to *listen* while playing, and to *take* the tone from the piano' (Helen's emphases).

Nina is 16 years old and has played the piano for several years; during her first years of tuition she was in one of Helen's Suzuki groups after which she shifted to having one-to-one lessons. She plays for her own pleasure and does not intend to study music professionally. Like the rest of Helen's students she plays repertoire partly selected by herself, partly by her teacher [Nina, interview following second documented lesson]. Now she is preparing for a public performance of music of her own choice—*Notturno* by E. Grieg, (*Lyrical pieces*, No. 4, book 5, op. 54)—planned to take place in a music café in two-and-a-half weeks. Before Nina begins to play, Helen reminds her to 'imagine the grandiose Norwegian landscape, and then, take a calm breath.' After the performance, Helen comments kindly that Nina is making progress and asks her to play from the beginning again. After a few phrases Helen interrupts Nina:

> *Helen*: Do you know that you have fallen back into your old mistake?
> *Nina*: Well . . .
> *Helen*: That is stuck in you somewhere. You see, the suspension should come before the downbeat. You performed that [points at the beginning] very well, but here . . . [plays the chord after the suspension in the first bar of the third staff in the score (see Fig. 6.1)], the suspension comes first and then the thumb [plays the entire bar with clear emphasis on the downbeat, repeats the bar with exaggerated finger gestures while explaining], the 'A' comes with the bass [turns smiling to Nina].
> *Nina*: Well, it's rather similar, isn't it?
> *Helen*: No, you played like this [plays as Nina did, the suspension emphasized on the downbeat and the 'A' afterwards, just before the D minor chord in the left hand on the second quaver].
> *Nina*: [reads the phrase in the score carefully while listening] Oh, yes, I see . . . [places her hands above the keyboard, preparing herself to play].
> *Helen*: But before that, it was very good.
> *Nina*: Yes, I think so, too.
> *Helen*: Fine. Could you, please, play from there?
> *Nina*: Yes. [She plays the two phrases from the last bar on the second staff, with the suspensions *before* the downbeats, as indicated in the score, leaving the suspensions without stress and emphasizing the following downbeats. She shapes both the melodic line and the harmonic progression more clearly than in her first performance, in which the musical flow 'stumbled' slightly when she played the suspensions on the downbeats and the A[1] the G[1] afterwards respectively, without clear emphases in the phrases.]
> *Helen*: Yes, that's it. Fine.

Before Nina begins to play, Helen uses the image of 'the grandiose Norwegian landscape' as a tool for communicating the general character of *Notturno*, and

Fig. 6.1 Excerpt from Nina's printed score of E. Grieg: Lyriska stycken (Lyrical pieces), No 4, book 5, op. 54; Ed. Peters 7637

Reprinted with friendly permission of C. F. Peters Musikverlag Frankfurt, Leipzig, London, New York.

refers to one of the Suzuki strategies that she finds especially important: to wait before playing. However, then she leaves her planned strategies aside to react to Nina's performance instead. Helen aptly describes the way in which Nina's experience of the suspensions is stuck in her, like a fold in a paper as described by Vygotsky (1934/1981). Although Helen has presented model performances of these phrases before, these have not been able to dislodge Nina's strongly memorized misinterpretation from practising at home on her own. On the contrary, she maintains that the performances sound rather similar; her memory prevents her from using her teacher's performance and the printed score as learning tools. Not until Helen has shown the correct phrasing, and explained in which way Nina's version is diverging from the notation and Helen's performed model, does Nina grasp the musical gestures of these phrases. From now on, Helen's performance functions as a tool by which Nina develops her understanding of the music. She does not even have to try out her new image of these phrases before implementing the change. The more elaborate expressivity in her subsequent performances indicates that Nina now also uses the printed score as a tool for developing her image of the music by reading while playing.

For her next lesson, one week later, Nina has prepared a performance of *Notturno* by heart. She puts the score aside, takes her seat at the piano and asks, 'Shall I begin?'

Helen: Do you remember what we talked about last time?

Nina: I should wait before I begin.

Helen: Exactly. And take a deep breath at these breaks, too, and while breathing you take the gesture with you [makes a soft gesture with her right arm] to begin the follow-ing section. What else did we talk about?

Nina: We talked about the breaks.

Helen: Yes, well, have you figured out something about them?

Nina: Well, that there should be stillness at the endings [of the sections].

Helen: Does that feel good, then?

Nina: Yes, I think so.

Helen: Well, let's try, then.

Nina: Should I hold the pedal down when I begin? I'm uncertain about that.

Helen: I don't know—have you tried out some alternatives?

Nina: Yes, I have [Nina shows different ways of performing the beginning, which Helen imitates].

Helen: I almost think you should take the tone first [points at the 'C' introducing the piece] and then capture it with the pedal.

Nina: Mm [puts her hand above the keyboard, concentrates, and then she performs the entire *Notturno*, seemingly with self-confidence].

Helen: [when Nina has ceased to play] Bravo, bravo, it is certainly becoming more and more like an entity!

Nina: Yes, it is.

Helen: The breaks were great, you know.

Nina: Yes [laughs a little].

Helen: You listened, and there was stillness in your hands, and then you took a breath, and it continued; very good!

Nina and Helen refer to strategies arising from the Suzuki pedagogical tradi-tion, strategies Helen has adopted and described as central to her teaching; to wait, to take a breath before a new section, and to listen. Nina's progress in performance indicates that Helen's advice during the previous lesson has helped Nina develop her image of the music further. For instance, while prac-tising on her own, Nina has maintained stillness at the section endings, a strat-egy praised by Helen.

Asking about how to perform the beginning (Fig. 6.1), Nina refers to a pedal marking in the score that has made her explore the music as far as the possi-bilities provided by the piano (the pedal) allow. However, while practising at home Nina has not incorporated her new knowledge into her interpretation; on the contrary, rather than making her own decision on how to use the pedal she turns to her teacher expecting an instruction. When Helen returns the question to her, Nina plays her alternate suggestions; excerpt performances

function as tools for Helen in developing her understanding of Nina's preferences, by listening and imitating. Referring to one of her main pedagogical
strategies—to take the tone—Helen shows a possible solution. Their collaborative exploration helps Nina perform according to her own preferences while
maintaining her self-esteem and convincing expression—on a higher level
than she would have mastered without Helen's support.

Later, during this lesson, Helen pays special attention to the passages leading
to the culmination of *Notturno* (Fig. 6.2). Nina plays the rising part in the left
hand unevenly, without noticeable expression, missing a couple of tones.
Helen leaves this without comment, but asks her to play the left hand part
carefully again, reminding her to 'maintain continuous arm gestures and to
take the tones.' When Nina has played the passage a couple of times, paying
attention to the position of her hand and her fingering, Helen says:

> Yes, that fingering. Well [puts the printed score on the piano, plays the D^{m7}-chord on
> which the bass part is based], let's proceed a little. The second time you have that
> [plays the chord again], that seventh chord, it requires even more sound, and then you
> still have two further tones left [makes a gesture as if she were holding something small
> and very precious between her left thumb and finger], which really emphasize the
> crescendo ['draws' a circle around these notes with her finger] to that culmination. So,
> your idea is fine. Imagine even more elasticity in your arm that you can feel [plays with
> exaggerated arm gestures].

Nina plays the passage, first with her left hand and then, a couple of times
with both hands, each time with more expressivity. The attention to fingering
facilitates Nina's playing of the correct keys. She has tried it out on her own as
Helen has emphasized that all pianists ought to figure out fingerings individually and adapt these to their own hands. However, directing her attention
towards her arm and hand gestures Nina develops mainly her *instrumental*
skill. Not until Helen shows and explains the harmonic fundamental and the
extraordinary character of the bass theme—stretching over more than two
octaves—does Nina grasp more of the *musical* ideas of the passage. Helen
refers implicitly to an established convention practised since the baroque era
(see, for example, Quantz, 1752/1974), to make unexpected events come clearly to the fore, a tool by which she, as a cultural representative familiar with the
convention, develops her understanding of the music. Helen's explanation,
her performance and completing gestures, function as tools for Nina, who
develops her idea of this passage further by reading the printed score and playing the left hand repeatedly. Afterwards, she presents her individually created
performance, her cultural work at this stage of performance preparation.

In her complete performance of *Notturno* which concludes this lesson,
Nina misses the tone she is heading for in a passage, which she now plays more

Fig. 6.2 Excerpt from Nina's printed score of E. Grieg: Lyriska stycken (Lyrical pieces), No 4, book 5, op. 54; Ed. Peters 7637

Reprinted with friendly permission of C. F. Peters Musikverlag Frankfurt, Leipzig, London, New York.

agitato than she has done before. Helen, who usually listens quietly to her student's complete performances while she reads the score, comments: 'Nice try!' When Nina has ceased to play, she praises:

> Helen: Bravo [applauds, silently clapping]; how do you feel about it?
> Nina: [takes her time before answering] It feels good [reflects silently]. The breaks were a little shaky, I think.
> Helen: Some of the breaks at the end were a little shaky but others were fine. Most of what we have been going through was fine.
> Nina: Was it, really?
> Helen: Yes, it *really* is. You maintain a flow that does not stop, all through. There [points at the passage leading to the culmination] it is just rolling on, until there [points at the falling motives rounding off the middle section after the culmination].

In her feedback, now 10 days before Nina's performance in the music café, Helen gives priority to aspects of special importance in public performance. She praises Nina's new interpretational idea instead of commenting on how to manage to hit the intended key, and follows up their work on the passage leading to the culmination of *Notturno* by relating it to the flow maintained by Nina 'all through' the entire piece of music. Helen uses Nina's performance as a tool for developing her understanding of how listeners may receive her interpretation.

Nina's last lesson before her public performance is a class lesson with two other students of her age who are also going to perform in public, although on different occasions. They comment mutually on each other's performances, after each of which Helen adds minor comments. They also comment on videos of their performances made during this lesson, which allows the students to take a listener's perspective of their own interpretations. Thus, they use their own complete performances as tools for learning about what may be further refined. Since all of them are playing by heart, the printed scores now mainly function as tools of reference in their discussions, rather than as tools for developing further ideas. Contrary to this, the instrument—the piano—and their performances remain important tools by means of which they continue to develop their interpretations in connection with the other listeners' (students' and Helen's) comments, which also function as tools for learning.

During the collaborative analysis of these lessons, Helen comments positively on Nina's development as an interpreter. She also assesses her own teaching according to the four points in Suzuki pedagogy, the only strategies that she has described as being important to her. For instance, watching the excerpt that shows the passage leading to the culmination, Helen states that she is quite satisfied with the response she has given to Nina in this respect, but she does not comment on her references to performance practice in relation to musical structure—in this case, the long thematic line of the bass and its harmonic ground. As I direct her attention towards this aspect, she reflects: 'I think I should do more of that in my lessons but explain it better. That's something I ought to develop.' When we summarize the lessons of this series, Helen reflects that she might have helped Nina to reveal the actual notation of the passages in Fig. 6.1 of the score by explaining the *harmonic* progress, dissonances that are resolved, in combination with her model performances. Rather, she merely emphasized the *order* of the tones in her right hand. Thus, Helen uses the video as a tool for evaluation and development of her own teaching in relation to her students' development.

Maria and her marimba students

Maria grew up in Zimbabwe but moved to Sweden with her husband, a music ethnologist. She has Swedish degrees for teaching music at primary and secondary school, and for teaching piano and ensemble in music schools. However, for the past two years she has only taught marimba groups, partly at a community music school, partly at her private studio, which she has decorated with wall carpets from Zimbabwe. She schedules beginners' lessons early in the afternoon, and, the more advanced the student groups are, the later they have their lessons. Like Helen, Maria lets her students begin and end by presenting a complete performance of a piece of music, on which she gives feedback. Unlike Helen, though, she varies the beginnings within this frame. Quite often she lets a couple of students stay longer to participate in the introductory performance of the following group. Thus, within a few weeks all students but the most advanced ones get the opportunity to perform with more experienced players.

Based on her husband's reconstruction of Zimbabwean marimbas, Maria has had sets of instruments built: sopranos, altos, tenors and basses. She teaches aurally, a repertoire mainly consisting of original marimba music that she has collected in Zimbabwe, but now and then she arranges popular songs suggested by her students. A short story and a specific character are connected to each Zimbabwean song, all of which have the same general structure: each part consists of one or a couple of phrases that are repeated and sometimes varied. Maria adapts them to the respective level of the groups to allow her students to experience the joy of making music together despite their beginner status. She also wants them to learn all parts to understand the relationships between: 'the pulse function of the bass, the counter function of the tenor [related to the melody], the accompanying motor function of the alto and the leading function of the soprano.'

Maria maintains that she prefers not to talk very much during her lessons but to support her students' learning by playing with them. Related to this is her strategy to let students 'find their way back into the ensemble when they lose the thread. They learn quickly to find the beginning of the next phrase.' Hence, complete performances are important to Maria who also wants her students to share the strong experience of the music with listeners.

The students in the group selected for study in this chapter, six girls and four boys, are about 12–13 years old and most of them have played together for two years. Unlike Nina, they play their instruments only during lessons, public performances and marimba camps organized by their teacher; practice and performance are overlapping rather than separate activities. All these students play for their pleasure; none of them intend to become musicians. At the beginning of the lesson, during which Maria observed Eve and Doris 'playing straight' (in the opening vignette), some of the students enter the marimba room while most of the pupils from the younger group, whose lesson just ended, are leaving. Maria goes with them to see them out. Meanwhile, the older students start playing around on the instruments, but soon a few of them take the lead suggesting they play a song they call 'Strawberry'. This nickname, created by Maria, refers to the rhythm of the alto part that consists of four parallel themes played by two players on each alto marimba: 'Strawberry, strawberry, strawberry, lingonberry' (Fig. 6.3). Being familiar with the form of this song, the students begin to play their respective parts: tenor, soprano, alto, and bass. Late-coming students go to an empty place, and await the beginning of the next phrase at which they join the ensemble.

Maria enters the room while they are still performing, listens for a while and shows some remaining pupils from the younger group where to play, beside more experienced players. Then she gives support where this is needed by joining to play different parts standing and facing the students on the opposite side of the marimba. In a loud voice she reminds them of the form they have agreed on for the middle section of the performance: 'Now without the sopranos, and then, the basses . . .' The parts stop two periods after each other until only the tenors are playing, after which a *tutti*, built up as at the beginning, leads to the end.

Maria: Bravo!
Karen: But Maria, it became slower and slower!
Maria: Yes—why?
John: Because we didn't listen.
Maria: [Turns to the girls playing the bass] Well, the basses are the ones who should keep up the tempo, and the rest of you should listen back to them. Play a 'C' on the bass [one of them plays; the C sounds jarring and somewhat dull]. Did you notice? It takes a *very* long time to hear this sound, so you must come a little before the other ones.

Peer teaching is central to Maria's practice, although she does not explicitly refer to this when describing her deliberate strategies. At the beginning of most lessons she lets her students conduct and assess their own ensemble performance. These complete performances initiated by the students are their cultural works, which also function as tools for them to reflect on how to go about learning the music. Hence, although Maria maintains that she prefers not to talk very much, spoken language—the students' as well as Maria's comments—is an important cultural tool by means of which the students develop musical understanding. Karen's and John's assessment initiates Maria's explanation of characteristics that they need to take into consideration. In learning about functions of the bass part and the sound characteristics of the bass marimba, they develop understanding of the music and how to perform it. While all of them are playing together, the performances of students who are already familiar with traditional ways of expressing the music function as tools of learning to other students in the group. The students from the younger group learn by playing beside more experienced peers and by participating in an ensemble working at a higher level than that of their own.

Maria continues: 'Please, once again! Let's take it a little faster.' During this performance she helps the students to maintain a stable tempo by marking the pulse playing maracas. Eve and Doris seem to be concentrating on their own playing but without following Maria's tempo. After the performance she comments:

Maria: Ok, it was fairly good. What happened this time?
Karen: We got faster.

> *Maria*: [turns to the sopranos and the altos] When you are playing 'Strawberry, strawberry, strawberry, lingonberry,' don't play 'lingonberry' [makes an exaggerated *accelerando* while speaking 'lingonberry'] as if you were a high speed train. Let's clap it together. [She begins to clap and speak, the students join her. When the tempo tends to accelerate Maria ceases to clap and marks the pulse on a djembe drum instead.] Good, excellent!

During the performance which follows, Maria plays the maracas while dancing between the instruments. She moves from one instrument to another, facing the students while saying: 'You know, you shouldn't be standing straight. Your bodies should *express* that you are dancing, so, dance before each other!' She continues to dance and play, and, in addition, she talks/sings emphasizing important rhythmical gestures of the part closest to her at the time. 'Yes, ok!' she shouts when the students follow her. Some of them manage to perform with a similar expression, while others, for example Eve and Doris, are still 'playing straight', now and then slightly out of tempo.

> *Maria*: [after this performance] Does it feel different now?
> *Betty*: It feels as if you are in it with all of you.
> *Maria*: Well, dance is very important; most of the songs you play are dances, you know.
> *Doris*: It is so difficult to concentrate on dancing when you are playing; it's really hard.
> *Maria*: Well, you don't have to, you know, but inside yourself you should *imagine* that you are dancing.

In practising the rhythm of the alto part, Maria first leaves all kinds of material artefacts aside; the rhythmical gesture, spoken and clapped, is the only cultural tool that she makes use of. Then she inserts the djembe drum as a supporting teaching tool. Her own performance of the pulse marking the main emphases of the phrases functions as a tool to the students. In the ensemble performance, her dance is another tool, supporting some students' learning, but restricting others'. Betty gets more into the music, while Doris finds it hard to coordinate dancing and playing. Like Eve, she continues to play her instrument rather than to make music.

The beginning of the subsequent lesson is similar to the previous one. When Maria enters the room after seeing the younger pupils off, the students of this group have already begun to play 'Strawberry'. Maria picks up a couple of sticks, goes to an empty place and performs with them for a while. Then she goes around supporting some of the students by playing their parts face-to-face or speaking the rhythm while pointing at the respective keys with her sticks. While Maria is directing her attention towards the sopranos, Betty and Cindy, who are playing the bass, lose the thread after having become slightly out of tempo. Sara, who is standing beside them, plays the tenor, the energetic counterpart of the melody. Quickly glancing and nodding at the bass players she shifts to their part on her own instrument and continues to play this until their performance is stable again. At the beginning of the next period, Sara shifts back to the tenor. Maria does not seem to notice this incident. After the complete ensemble performance she greets the students:

> *Maria:* Hello, everybody! How are you? Are you ok? [takes her time to listen to the students, answers kindly; then she faces the entire ensemble] It sounded fairly well. Do you know why it was not *very* good? There was too much pounding. You should take it easy. Even if African music can be fast it needs that underlying pulse that is very, very light. The listeners should get that impression but they should *not* get the impression of ten young people struggling hard to play the marimbas.
>
> *Albert:* [has played the soprano part which, contrary to the other parts, consists of several different phrases] What should I play after the first ones [phrases]?
>
> *Maria:* [plays the soprano in a lower tempo together with Albert, shifts the order of the phrases, adds small embellishments] You may choose for yourself and improvise, too, if you like [turns to the ensemble].
>
> Once again, don't stress! [Shortly after the students begin to play some of them develop slightly diverging tempi. Maria interrupts the performance and turns to Betty and Cindy, the bass players]. Do you remember what I said last time? If you make too big a gesture it takes too much time [makes exaggerated arm gestures followed by small ones]. Let's try again! The fantastic tenors begin, the sopranos follow, then the altos and finally the basses.

This time the performance of the entire ensemble is well coordinated. All students are maintaining a stable tempo and a swinging character similar to that of Maria's models.

As happened in the preceding week, Maria uses the students' performance as a tool for understanding what kind of support they need, and to provide that support for them while playing. Her own performance as a common ensemble member is a tool by which all students may develop their stylistic idea of the music, while her supporting performances facing some of them are tools by which the respective students may develop their ability to play the correct keys of their parts or refresh their memory of these.

Sara is one of the students who has developed a personal way of playing within the stylistic frame provided by Maria. She has never had other instrumental tuition and does not want to, either, but she enjoys playing in the marimba group [Maria, first collaborative analysis]. Although she is deeply engaged in playing her own part, she manages to support the bass players during the ongoing performance. Since she has not yet played the bass herself, this indicates that she keeps the music as an entity in her mind. Sara has used Maria's earlier performances of the different parts as tools by which she has developed her structural and stylistic image of them in relation to the entity. Now, this enables her to recognize mistakes in the bass, to jump into it, perform as long as is needed and then switch back to her own part.

To most other students, the mere image of a part, developed from listening to it, is not sufficient to perform it with traditional expression. In addition, many of them need a stable visual and motor memory of what and how to play; which keys in which order, with which hand or stick, which rhythm and emphases. On the one hand, the excerpt above illustrates that a partial lack of this aural–visual–motor memory may prevent students from taking into account exemplary models provided to them, and from using these as tools for further learning. Albert, for instance, seems not to pay attention to Maria's comments on the light character, because he is uncertain about the order of the phrases in the soprano part. Without knowing what is expected of him in this respect, he cannot concentrate on other aspects. On the other hand, a partial lack of this complex memory may prevent students from making use of stylistic familiarity they have already developed. Even though Betty and Cindy, both of whom have played other parts with stylistic expressivity, have been reminded about how to play the bass in 'Strawberry', they are only partly capable of imitating Sara; they still play with exaggerated gestures, with too much pounding. They do not manage to adapt their performance stylistically to the frame set by Maria until she repeats her advice concerning the need to achieve a light character through the use of smaller gestures.

The following week, John, one of the boys in this group, is late. When he arrives, the other students have already begun to perform a song about strength and power. John goes to an empty place at one of the alto marimbas, waits for the next period and begins to play. During the previous two lessons, he was able to play this part with bodily engagement, stylistic expression and good timing. However, now it seems as if he is playing without any deliberate expressivity, rather mechanically and with slightly accelerated tempo, standing on one foot with crossed legs in a relaxed manner. Sara, who plays the alto this lesson, too, is standing behind him playing with a driving character and physical engagement. All of a sudden, John gives a start and changes his position to standing on both feet, after which he adapts his performance to that of Sara, exhibiting engagement, drive and stylistically characteristic expression.

For his age, John has become quite a virtuoso on the marimba, and he likes to show his talent in his improvisations when playing the first soprano. In spite of his instrumental mastery, and although he has performed this part with stylistic expression earlier, he plays the marimba as a mechanical, rather than as a musical, instrument. For some reason, he does not pay attention to the music around him. He seems to play for himself, gaining pleasure from hitting the correct keys without any effort, faster and faster; being the master of his own game that goes on until his tempo is clearly diverging from that of the ensemble. As soon as he realizes this, he regulates his own tempo to match Sara's performance, a tool by which he enters the music as an ensemble player, from now on using the marimba as a musical instrument rather than merely a mechanical one.

During the collaborative analysis of her lessons, Maria comments on her students' actions and reflects on her teaching in relation to these, considering the ways in which she may need to develop her strategies to support students' learning better, as, for example, in the introductory vignette with Eve and Doris. Based on my preliminary analysis, I describe how these girls, one week after the lesson described in the vignette, adapt their performance to incorporate the conventions presented repeatedly by Maria in different ways. I also direct her attention towards the learning that takes place between the students during their performances. On the one hand, this makes her reconsider her critical self-assessment, and, on the other hand, it helps reveal the value of peer teaching and learning as practised by her and her students.

Discussion

The two contexts of music education, described previously, display very different conditions due to the respective music traditions, the complexity of the repertoire in these group or one-to-one lessons, and the aural or notation-based teaching and learning. In some respects, the teachers' and the students' intentions are also divergent within and between the contexts. Helen's teaching aim is to support her students to independently master a wide and complex repertoire in the Western music tradition. Maria, too, aims to foster her students to become independent amateur musicians, but their future marimba repertoire will be drawn from the same kind of music they are already playing. The challenges faced by Maria's students concern how they might vary the structure of performances, to add percussion and dance, and to develop the style of the ensemble. 'To practise at home' is one of the rules taken for granted by Helen's students, while Maria's students play solely in settings in which their teacher is present. These differences between the two contexts of music education provide an opportunity to discuss similarities in strategies and ways of using cultural tools. Beginning from these considerations, the strategies of the teachers and the students are discussed separately in the following two subsections. These lead on to concluding reflections on the implications of this study for music education.

Straw- ber - ry, straw- ber - ry, straw- ber - ry, lin-gon-ber-ry

Fig. 6.3 The alto rhythm with Maria's string.

Helen and Maria's strategies

A common denominator in the teaching approaches of Maria and Helen is the strong focus on the music itself, framed by the music tradition, and the students' learning related to this. The teachers' attitudes make evident that they are both convinced about the quality of the music they are teaching and the value of learning how to play it. Both teachers have arranged their teaching rooms in personal, welcoming ways in order to maintain a focus on music learning during their lessons; Maria has even given her studio the character of the Zimbabwean marimba music tradition. During greeting procedures at the beginning of the lessons, both teachers take their time to listen to the students, all of whom know that only a short time is to be spent on this interaction. As soon as they have completed these personal inquiries and interactions the teachers jump directly into the music, striving to meet their students at the stage of learning they have reached. Altogether, these underlying strategies are basic 'rules of the game,' once set up by Maria and Helen and now taken for granted by them; rules that direct their teaching and their students' learning (Gadamer, 1997; Huizinga, 1939/2004).

Both teachers let their students influence the selection of repertoire and leave space for them to present their cultural works, and complete performances of music, which they, as teachers, use as tools for developing their own understanding about what kind of advice would be suitable in the specific situation. They encourage their students to develop ideas on their own and challenge them to assess their own performances, thus putting them into the position of being their own listeners for whom the performances function as tools for reflection. This strategy supports the students' preparation of public performances, which are part of the teachers' goals. However, it needs to be emphasized that no degree or level assessment is connected to these performances.[1]

While helping students to be well prepared for their concerts, the teachers are both demanding and supportive. They expect their students to concentrate

---

[1] At the community music schools at which Helen and Maria are teaching, degree and level assessments do not exist, as is the case in many similar schools in Sweden.

on characteristics of the music tradition, to approach the music they are going to perform in respectful and responsible ways necessary for presenting its qualities to future listeners. To support the students in this, Maria and Helen pay attention to their students' actions and adapt their response to this, partly using established strategies, and partly developing new ones to support their learning. For instance, Maria develops new strategies in the exercise on maintaining tempo and developing a swinging character in the alto part of 'Strawberry': She models by speaking and clapping the rhythm in a stable tempo, repeats this with the students, shifts when needed to a djembe drum to maintain the tempo and adds traditionally established emphases, continues to mark the tempo during the following ensemble performance, and, in addition, dances and explains the character. Altogether she uses a complex mixture of tools belonging to the cultural toolboxes of the music tradition and her pedagogy. This example may be compared with Helen's support of Nina in the passage leading to the culmination of Grieg's *Notturno* (Fig. 6.2), in which tools from pedagogical and musical traditions are also intertwined. First Helen focuses on the points in Suzuki pedagogy that she refers to as important to her: to maintain a movement in the arm, for example. Then, pointing at the long rising bass line in the printed score, performing the D^{m7}-chord and explaining the harmonic structure, she combines notation, performance, and a general convention of expression to make unexpected events come to the fore to facilitate listeners' attention to these. To emphasize this she uses bodily gestures in a completely different way compared with Maria.

Although Helen uses a complex blend of cultural tools and approaches, she refers only to the four points in Suzuki pedagogy when describing her main teaching strategies: to work with hand and arm gestures, to wait before beginning to play, to listen carefully while playing, and to take the tone from the instrument. Maria describes her strategies more substantially, but leaves out one of her most central ones, peer teaching, which, incidentally, Helen also applies in her class lessons. One reason for not mentioning some strategies may be that these are included in the 'rules of the teaching game', which teachers and students, alike, take for granted. In Gadamer's terms (1997), they are played by the rules of the respective musical and pedagogical traditions when they follow conventions without reflecting upon them.

Students' strategies

Like their teachers, the students are 'played' by the rules (Gadamer, 1997). These rules are set up by their teachers, but this by no means implies that there is no space for students' to contribute their own initiatives. On the contrary, their teachers expect them to become independent and to take responsibility for their own performances. However, the students do not always make use of the space left for their own initiatives, but, instead, interpret the teachers' rules as more restrictive than these are intended to be. Albert, for instance, wants to know precisely in which order he is expected to play the phrases of the soprano part, and Nina expects Helen to tell her exactly how to use the pedal at the beginning of Grieg's *Notturno*, although she has already tried out different alternatives very carefully. Feeling uncertain about how to use the cultural tools available in their respective situations, the students turn to their teachers to learn more about conventions to structure (Albert) and to express (Nina) the music they are playing. In collaboration with their teachers, the students work within their zones of proximal development, and master challenges that they would not have mastered on their own. Once they have learned about the frames and space for individual freedom for acting they do not need any further support. They have reached a space in which they feel safe to use their instruments in combination with the conventions of musical structure and expression.

Like Albert and Nina in the examples above, many students prefer to ask their teachers, the experienced representatives of the music tradition, for advice in order to avoid taking risks when they are about to present new performances of their own. They want to be assured that they are learning how to use the respective cultural tools according to established rules. This approach may be considered a strategy for reproducing conventions rather than for learning how to cope with these in individual ways. However, even if this limits the students' learning at the moment it may be a successful strategy for them to adopt in order for them to be able to reach a space for further learning.

Knowing that they have solved their immediate problems in adequate ways, Nina and Albert, for instance, can concentrate on other aspects of their performance presentation. They also know about individual freedom in acting because their teachers have put the problems into the contexts of the music traditions, and have shown them that their individual decisions are required. For now, Nina relies on Helen's approval, knowing that this means that she uses the pedal as a tool in a relevant way, but she also knows that she has the freedom to revise this decision later on. Albert, too, can rely on his teacher's approval by imitating Maria's model performance of the alternate phrases of the soprano part. Feeling safe as a performer he may use the musical structure as a tool for adding his individual note to the ensemble performance, changing the order of, and improvising on, the themes when he wishes.

Now and then, some of the students prefer another limiting strategy; to use instruments as mechanical rather than as musical tools, despite their teachers' advice to relate their playing to performance practice. Playing only in a mechanical way may certainly result in strong memory traces persisting (Vygotsky, 1934/1981), but this does not necessarily imply that the traces based on motor memory prevent students from including stylistic musical expressivity, later on—especially when students use their instruments mechanically because they feel uncertain about their performance as an entity. As long as Nina does not grasp the musical gestures of the phrases with the suspensions (Fig. 6.1), her misunderstanding leaves a strong motor trace because she is uncertain about the musical intention. As far as these passages are concerned, she is unable to use the printed score as a tool for developing her understanding. On the contrary, she uses it in a restricting way; it makes her use the piano merely as a mechanical tool. However, as soon as Helen has helped her to grasp the *musical gestures* she develops her understanding of the music by using these as cultural tools in combination with the model performance and the printed score; she manages to perform according to the notation without first trying out the phrases on the piano. When Nina understands the motives as these are notated, it seems as if they reveal musical intention that makes the phrases become meaningful to her. Grieg's intended way of structuring the music, which is related to established conventions—cultural tools—helps her develop her idea of *Notturno*, and her performed interpretation of it, now using the piano as a musical tool.

Contrary to the example above, in which Nina revises her performance of the suspensions after merely listening, reading and imagining how to perform, many students need to practise on their instruments to establish a stable motor memory. For instance, some of Maria's students who sometimes use the marimbas as tools mainly for developing motor skills, playing mechanically or straight, may need to concentrate on learning *what* to play before they manage to take stylistic aspects into account. Even if it seems as if they do not use Maria's performances as cultural tools to develop their images of the music, they may do so as listeners, without yet being capable of taking this knowledge into account as performers. The ensemble performance, in which all students play with bodily engagement and a stylistic drive, as modelled by Maria, is an indication of this. All of a sudden, the students, who until then have lacked physical engagement and a swinging drive, are capable of incorporating this into their performance. At this time, Eve and Doris, who found it difficult to play and dance one week earlier, may have repeated their parts, playing the correct keys so many times that this has left mechanical memory traces that facilitate their concentration on further aspects, such as the stylistic expression of the ensemble. Betty and Cindy's pounding way of playing may be a deliberate or an intuitive strategy to establish a similar stable motor memory of the bass part of 'Strawberry'. Irrespective of whether their strategy is deliberate or intuitive, to them this stable memory seems to be a presumption for taking their familiarity with this music tradition into account while playing, and adapting to the expressive performance within this frame.

Since Maria's students are playing the marimbas only during their lessons, they are learning their parts predominantly while the other students in the group are playing. The music playing around them may cause some students to lose concentration on the music style when they feel uncertain about their part; the proximity of other players and the continuing musical experience may disrupt their capacity to imagine their part in their mind and remember which keys to use. Using the marimbas as mechanical tools for learning how to play the correct keys in a correct rhythm, these students may reach a space of know-how in which they can include other cultural tools at their disposal more easily, including: performances by Maria, by their peers, and by themselves, as well as conventions to structure and express the music. The inclusion of conventions of expression, specifically, allows them to use the marimba as a musical tool.

The close connection between familiarity with conventions to structure and express music, and instrumental mastery, is also exemplified by Nina's development of her interpretation of the long rising bass line leading to the culmination of *Notturno* by Grieg (Fig. 6.2). She plays without noticeable expressivity, before she has grasped the relation between musical structure and expression, but as soon as Helen has explained and shown this to her, Nina manages to use the piano as a tool for presenting a far more convincing performance.

Contrary to the situations described above, in which students use instruments as rather mechanical tools in order to achieve instrumental mastery as a platform for developing their ability to perform with stylistic expression, John's initial performance in the last lesson referred to above exemplifies the pure pleasure of instrumental mastery for its own sake. John plays mechanically, even though he is quite capable of playing with stylistic expressivity. Having had his pleasure for a while, he easily shifts his approach as soon as he pays attention to Sara's drive and the tempo of the ensemble. John uses Sara's performance specifically as a cultural tool to enter the performance as an ensemble musician, a point at which he begins to use the marimba as a cultural rather than as a mechanical tool.

Hence, even if students sometimes do not immediately make use of the space left to them by their teachers, they do so later, when they feel capable of mastering the challenges that have bothered them. They are aware of the permanent invitation to take responsibility for their own development, to assess their own performances and those of other students. Assessment of performances of their own, as well as of other students and the entire ensemble, is a strategy imposed on all students by both teachers. Following this invitation—a rule of the game—students contribute to their own learning, and most of them also support other students as peer teachers. Thus, they get used to coping with performances as crucial cultural tools. This applies to the marimba students as well as to Nina and her peers, who comment on each other's performances during the class lesson.

Implications for music education

The aim of the discussion should not be mistaken for a plea to limit learning strategies or teaching directed at playing mechanically. On the contrary, both case studies show that Maria's and Helen's underlying strategy, to maintain dialogic teaching focusing on traditional expression, supports rather than restricts the students' development, even while the students may follow instructions or play mechanically now and then. The fact that the students are the ones who initiate this is important; the teachers do *not* expect their students to reproduce the printed score 'correctly' or just follow instructions on performance without reflecting on these. Hence, on a general level, the outcome of these studies implies a need for teachers to be prepared to cope with students' preferences for such strategies, while still maintaining a frame of traditional expression to facilitate their adaptation to this when they are ready for it. Reflection on students' ways of using cultural tools may facilitate teachers in responding to students' needs; to guide them in problem-solving in the present as a platform for further development.

For instance, when students seek advice because they hesitate, uncertain of how to progress, as Albert and Nina do, they profit not only from their teachers' advice on how to act at present, but from the knowledge their teachers provide about framing traditional conventions and expectations on individual decisions. Even if Helen and Maria do not mention the concept 'cultural tool', they respond to their students in ways that support their students' use of musical structures, both in the present, and, in a longer perspective, to develop their individual competences as performers. During the collaborative analysis, Helen reflects that she ought to develop strategies for explaining the relationship between performance practice and musical structure; that is, she considers it supportive to direct students' attention towards combinations of cultural tools in the music tradition.

When students use instruments as mechanical tools it is important for teachers to understand why they do so. One reason may be that the printed score functions as a restricting tool, as is the case when Nina misreads the notation of the phrases with suspensions (Fig. 6.1). For a couple of weeks Nina neither managed to use the piano and the notation as tools for improving her performance, nor as a means to developing her idea of the music; the score even prevented her from taking Helen's advice and model performances into account as tools for learning. As referred to in the presentation of findings, Helen reflects during the collaborative analysis that an explanation of the harmonic progression in combination with model performances might have supported Nina's learning in a more efficient and effective way. In terms of cultural tools this might have drawn Nina's attention to four kinds of tools, all of which need to be combined in a performance of an interpretation with convincing expressivity: conventions of structuring music, conventions of expressing these, notation, and instrument.

Another reason for playing instruments mechanically is illustrated by the students who do not yet manage to master the technical requirements of their parts. Observing that some of her students are playing straight and rather mechanically, Maria blames herself for not having succeeded in making them feel the music in their bodies. In her critical assessment of her teaching, she does not take learning over a longer space of time into account; a couple of weeks later these students do perform with some stylistic drive. At first, when the students are playing mechanically, the instruments are preventing them from using conventions of expression as tools for learning because their entire concentration is needed to hit the right keys, preventing a musical use of the instruments. At the same time, however, or, little by little, they may very well pay attention to Maria's advice, even if this cannot be revealed in their playing. In each lesson Maria uses complex blends of tools to demonstrate stylistic musical expressivity to her students: model performances, supportive performances where needed during ensemble performances, rhythmic support, bodily gestures, dancing, verbal explanation—of the character of a song, musical structure, characteristics of instruments and parts—as well as specially designed exercises to solve specific problems. Maria's frequent emphasis on stylistic character in combination with other cultural tools may function as a box of interconnected tools, which the students use as soon as they are capable of mastering their parts technically.

Concluding remarks

The mutual responsibility taken by teachers and students in both teaching contexts is of general importance. Expecting students to act in responsible ways, the teachers have to do so, too: they have to try to find out what kind of problems the individual student may have and develop teaching strategies to help in solving these specific problems. Allowing students the time they need to grasp a part instrumentally is one kind of support, during which teachers may leave an underlying consideration of the music tradition aside, as exemplified by Maria and Helen. However, as soon as the students master the particular task instrumentally, both teachers expect them to act within a frame of the music style.

The strong emphasis on the music tradition, maintained by both Maria and Helen, is worthy of general consideration. Both teaching contexts are indeed contexts of *music* education in which instrumental tuition is a means for the students' musical development. Certainly, some students find a great pleasure in mastering their chosen instrument for its own sake but their teachers connect this firmly to the music tradition, supporting their students' development as musicians at the level of instrumental mastery they have achieved. Maria may be a marimba teacher and Helen a piano teacher, but primarily both of them are music teachers.

According to the saying, 'learn the conventions before you break them', students learn how to relate the cultural tools, that is, the instrument, performance and—as far as Helen's students are concerned—notation, to conventions of the music tradition. Having achieved a solid familiarity with the 'rules' of performance practice and musical structures, students generally become representatives of the tradition, capable of developing personal styles not only in performance of music created by others, but also in improvisation. This allows, for instance, Maria's students to develop individual expressivity and to improvise in the leading soprano part. Helen's students create their personal interpretations based on their familiarity with the respective styles in Western music tradition.

References

Booth, W. (1999). *For the love of it: amateuring and its rivals*. Chicago: University of Chicago Press.

Brändström, S., & Wiklund, C. (1995). *Två musikpedagogiska fält. En studie om kommunal musikskola och musiklärarutbildning* [Two music-pedagogy fields: A study of municipal music schools and teacher education]. Umeå, Sweden: Pedagogiska institutionen, Umeå universitet.

Brendel, A. (1977/1982). *Nachdenken über Musik*. München: R. Piper & Co. Verlag.

Bruner, J. (1996/2002). *Kulturens väv. Utbildning i kulturpsykologisk belysning* [The culture of education, 1996]. Göteborg: Bokförlaget Daidalos AB.

Davies, S. (1994). *Musical meaning and expression*. Ithaca, NY: Cornell University Press.

Folkestad, G. (1996). Computer based creative music making: young people's music in the digital age. Göteborg: Acta Universitatis Gothoburgensis.

Gadamer, H.-G. (1997). *Sanning och metod (i urval)*. [Truth and method (selected)]. (A. Mellberg, selection and translation.) Göteborg: Daidalos.

Green, L. (2001). *How popular musicians learn*. Aldershot, UK: Ashgate.

Huizinga, J. (1939/2004). *Den lekande människan*. (Original: Homo Ludens. Vom Ursprung der Kultur im Spiel.) [Homo Ludens. A study of the play-element in culture.] Stockholm: Natur och Kultur.

Hultberg, C. (2000). *The printed score as a mediator of musical meaning. Approaches to music in Western tonal tradition. Dissertation.* Studies in Music and Music Education, 2. Malmö, Sweden: Malmö Academy of Music, Lund University, Lund.

Hultberg, C. (2002). Approaches to music notation: the printed score as a mediator of musical meaning in Western tonal music. *Music Education Research, 4*(2), 185–97.

Hultberg, C. (2006). *Tolkning förpliktar—teori, metod och resultat* (Interpretation obliges—theory, method and results). Report on the project 'Musicians' processes of performance preparation' to The Swedish Research Council, Stockholm.

Quantz, J. J. (1752/1974). *Versuch einer Anweisung, die Flöte traversiere zu spielen . . .* (Original: Berlin: 1752. Reprint, fifth edition (1974) of the facsimile print of the third edition. H.-P. Schmitz, Ed., 1953/74) [On the flute . . .]. Kassel/Basel: Bärenreiter-Verlag.

Rostvall, A.-L., & West, T. (2001). *Interaktion och kunskapsbildning. En studie av frivillig musikundervisning* [Interaction and formation of knowledge. A study on voluntary music education]. Skrifter från Centrum för musikpedagogisk forskning. Dissertation. Kungliga Musikhögskolan i Stockholm. Stockholm: KMH-förlaget.

Rolf, B. (1991). *Profession, tradition och tyst kunskap: en studie i Michael Polanyis teori om den professionella kunskapens tysta dimension* [Profession, tradition and tacit knowledge: A study of Michael Polanyi's theory of the tacit dimension of professional knowledge]. Lund: Bokförlaget Nya Doxa AB.

Sæther, E. (2003). *The oral university. Attitudes to music teaching and learning in the Gambia.* Studies in Music and Music Education, No. 6. Malmö: Malmö Academy of Music, Lund University.

Säljö, R. (2000). *Lärande i praktiken. Ett sociokulturellt perspektiv* [Learning in practice: a socio-cultural perspective]. Stockholm: Bokförlaget Prisma.

Vygotsky, L. S. (1934/1981). *Thought and language.* Cambridge, MA: MIT Press.

Wells, G. (1999). *Dialogic inquiry: towards a sociocultural practice and theory of education.* New York: Cambridge University Press.

Chapter 7

A century of music listening in schools: toward practices resonating with cultural psychology?

Magne Espeland

Introduction

When Haldis, my 18-month-old granddaughter, comes to visit, it does not take long before she toddles over to me, stretches both hands upwards, points at the CD player and exclaims: 'Dansa! (dance!)'. I know very well what she wants, so I pick out the right CD, find the right track, lift her up and we start bouncing about as soon as the music starts. What she actually means is: 'Lift me up, put on the music I want and let us dance together.' I have noticed lately that she smiles and seems very happy when I try to transfer aspects of the music—the rhythm, the phrasing of melody and the dynamics—into my bouncing and movements. If I try to put on a different piece, she exclaims 'No, no' and wants to be put down. Sometimes she wants to get down anyhow, to dance herself, swaying and turning, eagerly inviting me and anyone else around to join in.

As I write this chapter, my happy moments with Haldis—because there is no doubt that we both enjoy our listening and dancing sessions—keep puzzling me. What is actually taking place here? Am I trying to add to her musical listening ability and skills by attempting to connect interpretations of musical phraseology and our movements? Am I initiating her into a particular style and musical work, and into appreciation of music I consider universally or culturally important? What are the connections here between the specific piece of music, the cultural and social situation where it takes place, and Haldis as a meaning-making individual? What is it that appeals to her in this special music, and what does she learn from listening to it? What goes on in her mind and body, and how can I find out? If she hears this music in ten years time will she remember it, and what will she remember?

It is not my intention in this chapter to try to answer any of the questions above. But, as a professional music educator, I realize that these are questions I might have asked myself—or rather, should have done—when practising as a listening pedagogue. Questions about the relationship between individual perception and those cultural objects called music, between what is situated and what is more or less universal, between bodies, cultural contexts and the individual mind, and between our actions and the formation of our mental capacity, are crucial questions for music educators.

Similar questions have, for the past hundred years or so, become increasingly important in the social and cultural sciences, including philosophy (e.g. Bowman, 2004; Bresler, 2004; Elliott, 1995; Langer, 1943/1960; Merleau-Ponty, 1962; Reimer, 2003), anthropology (e.g. Geertz, 1973), musicology (e.g. Cook & Everest, 1999), sociology (e.g. DeNora, 2000), and psychology (Bruner, 1966, 1990, 1996; Cole, 1996; Lave & Wenger, 1991; Vygotsky 1978; Wertsch, 1998). Answers to questions of this sort lie at the heart of different theories of music learning and pedagogy, and they illustrate the immense scope of practical decisions to be made—consciously or unconsciously—by a music teacher, or a grandfather, who embarks upon the important task of trying to impart, or perhaps rather to co-construct, knowledge in its widest sense about the sounding aspects of musical works, culture, genres, and styles to future generations.

In this chapter I shall examine, describe and discuss the practice most often called 'music listening' in Western school music education. The first part of the chapter focuses on early developments of music listening practices in modern schooling and serves as a historical backdrop for the last part of the chapter where I reflect on past and present practices of music listening in schools from the perspective of 'cultural psychology'. The field of cultural psychology is by no means clear-cut in terms of tenets, theories and connections to other fields of psychology. Jerome Bruner (1996), however, identifies nine different tenets—drawn from different theories—as a sort of common denominator guiding a psychocultural approach to education. In his 1996 book, *The culture of education*, he lists the following tenets: perspectival tenet (p. 13); constraints tenet (p. 15); constructivism tenet (pp. 19–20); interactional tenet (p. 20); externalization tenet (p. 22); instrumentalism tenet (p. 25); institutional tenet (p. 29); tenet for identity and self-esteem (p. 35); narrative tenet (p. 39). I will make use of a number of these as a basis for my reflection and discussion as the chapter unfolds.[1]

---

[1] See Bruner (1996, pp. 15–43), Cole (1996), and Chapter 1 of this book.

My starting point, however, is not psychological theory, but my 'pragmatist' knowledge about music listening as primary and secondary classroom practices and methodologies; that is, the everyday professional life worlds of many music teachers, rather than the immense amount of research devoted to music listening, or rather music-listening skills, in relevant academic sciences.[2] I am aware, of course, that classroom methodologies have been and are influenced by a number of scientific disciplines other than psychology, for example, musicology, philosophy, ethnomusicology, and sociology. As the chapter unfolds, the reader will find that I am paying short visits to some of these sciences in order to throw light on some of the characteristics of different traditions and practices of music listening.[3]

The evolving topology of music listening

The rationale for the very existence of a curriculum practice called music listening in school music seems obvious. Without the phenomenon of meaningful listening to music—and I guess this is a cross-cultural fact—there would probably be no music to listen to. Music listening is integral to all aspects of music education, be it performing or composing, singing or music-making in all styles and in all genres across the primary, secondary and tertiary levels. Music listening as a specific curriculum practice, however, constitutes an important part of music as a school subject at different levels in many countries, where it exists as a set-aside and specific subject component. The topology of this curriculum practice—understood as the way in which the

---

[2] The research on different aspects of music listening has, over the past 50 years, been dominated by psychological issues and research questions. However, there seems to have been a decreasing interest in this kind of research for the past fifteen years. The extensive review on music listening in the *Handbook on music teaching and learning* by Paul Haack (1992)—which defines music listening as the fundamental music skill—concludes that although 'research in teaching for the acquisition of music listening skills' seems less important in the 1980s than in the 1960s and 1970s, 'quality work continues to be done' (p. 461). In an overview of research in this field, Blair (2006) comments that *The new handbook* (Colwell, 2002) has only one chapter devoted to listening.

[3] However, I emphasize that I don't think there is a direct link between the shaping of the practicalities of the listening classroom and research in academic disciplines. It is my experience that classrooms, to some extent, are life worlds on their own where practices start, develop, continue, and end, sometimes because of research findings, but very often for a number of other reasons. In the case of music listening practices, I can think of a number of very different influences including politically motivated school reforms, innovations in technology, music polls, local community or national music events. These influences can be described as cultural rather than psychological influences, and although relevant in a cultural psychology perspective, they will not be dealt with here.

constituent parts are interrelated or arranged—is by no means clear-cut. Its closest roots as discipline concepts—even to the extent as to be directly overlapping—are music appreciation and ear training, which, still in many countries, are used as concepts to denote this part of the school subject.[4] Other 'listening' disciplines such as music history, music analysis, and music theory—especially in upper secondary and tertiary education—are also closely associated with the term 'music listening'. Despite these varied and overlapping uses, the focus of the present chapter is educational music listening defined as different ways of educating young people to recognize, understand, and appreciate central aspects of the sounding essences of particular pieces of music and their respective contexts. In music education, this normally takes place via different listening approaches, drawing on different kinds of theory, information and reflection connected to the selected music, and in most cases through different kinds of listening assignments linked to the pieces or aspects thereof.[5]

A number of issues in recent practices in music listening build on a long and gradually evolving music-listening history. Some of these issues—highly relevant in a discussion about music listening as a curriculum practice in schools and its relationship to cultural psychology—are connected to questions such as what music to listen to, what to listen for in the music, how to listen, when to listen in an educational process, and, lastly, how to allow—or rather encourage—students to express learning and understanding in the listening classroom. We shall look more directly into these questions in relation to recent practices later in the chapter. First, however, to provide an appropriate context for our discussion, it is necessary to take a closer look at some aspects of music listening as it evolved in the first decade of the twentieth century, here referred to as early listening practices.

Early listening practices: a historical backdrop

Music listening as a curriculum practice in education owes much to the appearance of the gramophone and the development of the wireless radio. These developments (in a number of countries and continents),[6] not only offered the

---

[4] I will return to the connections between music listening and music appreciation later in the chapter.

[5] Keith Swanwick denotes this discipline as audience-listening (Swanwick, 1994). I prefer the term music listening, as I do not consider pupils or students in any form of classroom to necessarily become an audience in the traditional sense of that concept. To me, 'audience' has connotations of passive reception rather than the active interaction often seen in recent music listening practices.

[6] By the late 1920s, the gramophone was widely used and national radio was established in many countries, most of them in America and Europe, but also in countries like Japan

opportunity of repeated listening at any time, but also of listening across vast distances. They revolutionized the potentials for music education in general, and music listening in particular, on a broad scale for young people as well as for adults. The early pioneers in the development of music listening at the beginning of the twentieth century in the UK and USA, often referred to as the Music Appreciation Movement (Scholes, 1935), and their educational practices were deeply affected by such revolutionary technical devices. The appearance of these devices generated a very lively debate, not only about the potential of the gramophone and the radio in education, but also about the formation and contents of music education in general, including the role of aural or ear training, the position of live music making in the classroom and the introduction of 'masterpieces' of music to young people.

To understand the essence of the debate on the use of the gramophone in music education, it is important to be aware that music appreciation as a curriculum practice was well-established before the gramophone made its appearance. Prior to this event, all music listening was listening to live music, and for music educators the piano was a natural vehicle to present students with composed music as well as ear-training exercises. In 1910, a music professor at the Royal Academy of Music in London, Stewart MacPherson, published a text entitled *Music and its appreciation, or the foundations of true listening*. This pioneering work established a new practice (Scholes, 1935, p. 22).[7] Professor MacPherson subsequently invited a former student, Ernest Read, to collaborate with him on a series of three books: *Aural culture based upon musical appreciation* (MacPherson & Read, Part I, 1912, Part II, 1915a, Part III, 1915b).[8] In the first book he also included an important appendix written by Miss Marie Salt entitled 'Music and the Young Child'. MacPherson wrote:

> Since the appearance in 1910 of *Music and its Appreciation* . . . I have been repeatedly asked to write something in the nature of a class-book, or teacher's guide, for those desirous of systematically training their pupils in the aural perception of music. Certain ideas had begun to shape themselves in my mind in this direction when I discovered with pleasure that my friend and former pupil, Mr. Ernest Read, A.R.A.M., was planning a series of lessons in which the basic facts of music, such as Pitch, Time,

and China. The BBC established music programmes for schools, as did its Australian counterpart (Gestalt Psychology, 2009).

[7] Percy A. Scholes describes Stewart MacPherson as being the person who 'is rightly looked upon as the Father of the Music Appreciation movement in Britain' (Scholes, 1935, p. 22).

[8] Stewart MacPherson authored a number of other books for music education, among them *Form in music* (1910), *Studies in phrasing and form* (1912), and *The musical education of the child* (1915).

Rhythm and Character, were revealed to the pupil *through the medium of definite musical compositions.* This design—so far as I know, original in its conception—seemed so eminently in consonance with the whole idea of Music Appreciation Study, that I at once proposed to Mr. Read that we should collaborate on the present work. ... Although actually independent of the scheme of work herein set forth by my colleague and myself, the interesting and attractive Free Rhythmic Movements for young children described by Miss Marie Salt in the Appendix entitled "Music and the Young Child," are, in my opinion—based upon close observation for some time past—of the utmost value in preparing the way for a more formulated musical training of ear and mind. (MacPherson, 1912, Editor's note)

MacPherson and his colleagues, then, seem to endorse a music-listening practice that not only included movement, but that also was based on a systematic integration between ear-training exercises and specific musical works *before* recorded music and the gramophone entered the educational scene.[9] Not unexpectedly, when the gramophone finally did find its way into music education, the introduction to society of a revolutionary technology of this kind challenged existing pedagogical as well as cultural practices.[10] In an article in the English journal/magazine *The Musical Times* in 1934, MacPherson, referring to an ongoing debate at the time regarding the position of the appreciation movement in music education, wrote:

Having spoken already of the advantage, and the disadvantages, of broadcast music to the young and immature mind, and of the need for some kind of guidance in the practise of listening, let us now turn to the uses of the wireless and the gramophone—particularly the latter—in the actual business of teaching. I have more than once been accused of belittling the importance of the gramophone in the Appreciation lesson, and of being unsympathetic towards those teachers (professional or lay) who may be full of enthusiasm for the art and musicianly in their outlook, but who have not the pianistic ability to play the works they wish to present to their classes. I should like to make my attitude in this respect perfectly clear. I do *not* underestimate the value of the gramophone in the very least—far from it; in the hands of a competent teacher it can be of the greatest possible help . . . But there are two points, which, I feel, need to be taken into consideration. First, the gramophone, however it is used, is necessarily an impersonal thing, and—as I know from experience—it is not, and never can be,

---

[9] In MacPherson's book from 1915, *The musical education of the child*, he refers to the use of 'players', probably meaning 'pianolas' that were being produced from the 1890s onwards (MacPherson, 1915, p. 36).

[10] In a letter to the Editor of *Musical times* in the December issue, 1919, a teacher, Mr J. Bernard McElligott, discusses 'the gramophone as an aid to music appreciation'. His main concern was the development of records lasting more than four minutes. However, he also discloses that 'many of your readers no doubt have discovered the value and importance of good gramophone records for educational purposes', and muses that 'it would be interesting to hear their experiences' (McElligott, 1919, p. 697).

> capable of bringing a class into that close and sympathetic relation to the music which is possible by means of the teacher's own playing. (MacPherson, 1934, p. 55)

MacPherson's article echoes in many ways the discussion in education today about the challenges connected to the introduction of digital technology into schools and classrooms.[11] The belief—and fear—that today's technology is emerging as one of the most powerful changing and shaping forces in relation to educational goals as well as practices, is mirrored in MacPherson's observation that even if the gramophone has solved some challenges for the goals of music listening, new ones seem to appear. In his case, it was the need to preserve the pianistic skills of the teacher, the quality of live musicianship as opposed to gramophone listening, and the position and quality of the Aural Training Class that were at stake.[12]

Revolutionary cultural events of this dimension are illustrative—to the point of being exemplary—of one of the major foci of cultural psychology, specifically, the processes:

> by which psyches and cultures construct each other, elucidating how cultures create and support psychological processes and how these psychological tendencies in turn support, reproduce and sometimes change the cultural systems. (Fiske, Kitayama, Markus & Nisbett, 1998, p. 916)

Along with the technical innovations entering the educational field in the first decades of the twentieth century, other cultural institutions such as the radio, the gramophone companies and the symphony orchestras contributed to the shape and contents of music listening in schools in major ways. The Lausanne Resolution encapsulates much of the discussion and debate that these institutions precipitated internationally.

The Lausanne Resolution

In MacPherson's article (1934), quoted above, he refers briefly to The Lausanne Resolution; a resolution put to the 1931 meeting of the members of the

---

[11] In his article MacPherson also refers to the discussion of music listening and 'work with young children' and comments on a number of methodological questions, such as the role of physical action in the listening process, unwise lessons, and 'stages in Appreciation work'. We shall return to some of these questions and MacPherson's viewpoints later in this chapter.

[12] Today, one of the common errors in much of the available research on technology in education seems to be to compare its contribution to that of more traditional instructional means, thus using as criteria for comparison the lowest common denominator (e.g. Cuban, 2001). The same line of discussion seemed to be the case with the introduction of the radio and the gramophone way back in the early 1930s.

Anglo-American Music Education Conference in Lausanne, Switzerland. In a letter to the Editor of *The Musical Times* the resolution is quoted in its entirety, and I have chosen to include it here because it illustrates some major discussion topics in early listening history as well as in more recent and contemporary music-listening practices. The Lausanne Resolution reads:

1. The aims of the study of music appreciation, as we understand it, are a) the development of a high degree of sensitiveness to the medium of the art, and b) an intensive and critical study of representative examples of admitted masterpieces.

2. This implies, first, the ability to hear music *in its own terms, and not in terms of association with other experiences*, and secondly, an insight into all those factors which constitute style.

3. In our opinion, the development of a high degree of sensitiveness to the medium of the art represents the scope of the Aural Training Class, and is primarily the work of the school. Let it be clearly understood, however, that at all points in aural training, actual examples of music most appropriate for the purpose must be presented to the class. In this way aural training and the study of the literature of music are at no time divorced from each other.

4. The *intensive* and *critical* study of musical masterpieces follows naturally from this foundational training, and it is obviously appropriate to more mature students, and entirely unsuitable as a subject in elementary education. (Forbes Milne, 1931, p. 829)

The Lausanne Resolution demonstrates clearly some familiar issues and—to some extent—debates within the music education community and in music listening specifically, some of which are still with us in different forms or practices. It also introduces us to three major issues in the development of the discipline of music listening: the parenthetical position in music listening; absolute or referential meaning-making; and, the role of masterpieces of music.

The parenthetical position in music listening

The first issue illustrated in the Lausanne Resolution confirms MacPherson's view that music listening should be a combination of aural culture—which for MacPherson meant ear training and music theory—and music appreciation, and that there should be a *parenthetical* relationship between these two components. According to the Lausanne Resolution, the mother discipline is still aural training, in the sense that it provides the foundational training necessary to study great masterpieces. This position seems to be slightly different from

MacPherson's views in his pioneering books on Aural Culture (1912, 1915a, 1915b) where the argument was that 'all ear training work must be based on Musical Appreciation' (MacPherson & Read, 1912, p. 2).

Looking more closely into MacPherson's methodology for music listening, however, it seems that his main emphasis—with regard to *what* to listen to—is on the analysis of formal aspects of music compositions, including rhythm, pitch, time, form and notation.[13] Even so, it is interesting to notice that MacPherson's parenthetical position also includes the discipline of composition. His fifth stage in his recommendation for each listening lesson reads:

> The home-preparation given to the pupil should aim at drawing out his power of doing things for himself. Most children are capable of a certain amount of original invention, and it will be found that many will, after a short time, be able to construct little tunes for themselves, embodying the main point of the preceding lesson . . . (1912, p. 5)

MacPherson comments extensively on the inclusion of composition, suggesting that the influence from recent developments in the school subject of drawing has convinced him of the wisdom in 'the application to music-study of the saner ideas now gaining ground with reference to the training of the pupil's powers of observation and imagination' (1912, p. 6). However, he is quick to maintain that 'the object, it need hardly be said, of such constructive work is not to endeavour to breed a race of *composers*' (p. 6).[14]

MacPherson's parenthetical position is even more clearly demonstrated in his advice on how to deal with what he calls subconscious listening. After having emphasized the importance of training the child to 'observe with his ears' he continues:

> On the other hand, it is of course true that the pupil may be brought into touch at an early age with a good deal of music to which—although he will not be able to grasp it consciously or fully—he will yet enjoy listening, in a general sort of way. This is a branch of musical education, which it is most important to carry on side by side with the more conscious assimilation of the *material* of the music, to which allusion has already been made. (1912, p. 3)

A common characteristic of the parenthetical position, as established by the 1930s, seems to be a clear focus on what MacPherson calls the 'materials' of music, such as form, pitch and scales, rhythm, pulse and time, and solmization,

---

[13] Scholes (1935) describes his educational position as a 'remarkable synthesis of Sight-Singing, Aural Training, and Appreciation' (p. 165).

[14] In 1912, MacPherson also referred to the influence of Emile Jacques Dalcroze and the Rhythm Gymnastics system. The influence of Dalcroze on MacPherson's work must have been substantial. In 1934, MacPherson was the chairman of the Dalcroze Society in England with Mrs Ernest Read as the Society Secretary.

although 'the technical side', as MacPherson calls these elements of music, 'must never be divorced from the aesthetic, and the whole aim of the study must be the fostering of real musical perception in the pupil' (1912, p. 2). Whilst MacPherson's position does not exclude what is referred to as 'aesthetic perception' and 'subconscious listening', it is apparent that educational items associated with music listening in modern practices, such as personal and creative response to music and issues concerning expression and individual interpretation, are only partly included.

Absolute or referential meaning-making

The second issue coming to the fore in the Lausanne Resolution—and this is the one that seemed to arouse the most heated debate—is the view that a masterpiece of music should be listened to '*in its own terms, and not in terms of association with other experiences.*'[15] This statement not only indicates *what* to listen to, but also *how* to listen. In an article about the child and aesthetic response, Margaret Barrett (2006), referring to Kant's theory of disinterestedness (1790), and later Hanslick's aesthetics of music (1854), ascribes this position to the view of the aesthetic that arose during the eighteenth and nineteenth centuries. This view, she writes, 'sought to identify engagement with the arts as rational, cognitive, and separate from the powerful and seductive effects of the emotions and the sensuous' (p. 174). The urge to identify universal and eternal qualities, she claims, necessitated the 'discarding of all reference to context or qualities external to the work itself: the arts work became 'autonomous', an object or event to be judged solely through an analysis of its 'internal' features, its form' (Barrett, 2006, p. 174).

The discussion outlined above—the conflict between referential and emotional interpretation and meaning-making on the one hand and absolute and formal interpretation and meaning-making on the other—was central in the formation of music listening as a curriculum practice throughout the greater part of the past century. As we can observe in the Lausanne Resolution, this grand debate also surfaced in music education in the 1930s.

With this background in mind, we might begin to understand—from what might be characterized as an elitist and academic point of view—what was at risk with the introduction of the gramophone and the radio in the music education community in the first decades of the past century. Not only did the new technology threaten to open up unprecedented access to musical masterpieces to everyone, everywhere, it also empowered teachers, lay as well as

---

[15] Italics as per original publication. It is also an important argument in MacPherson's 1934 *Musical Times* article quoted earlier in this chapter.

professionals, to teach music listening and thereby provide access to works of great art, even in the elementary school, and also without the necessary professional aural training. And—what seemed to be even more disturbing—music-listening teachers began to include irrelevant contextual and referential aspects of the music, which from an elitist and purist point of view was 'harm done', to quote MacPherson (1934, p. 56). In his article, under the subheading 'Unwise lessons', he wrote in *The Musical Times*:

> It may not be inappropriate to refer at this point to the harm that has been done to the Appreciation cause by some teachers through attempting to associate music, to an unwise extent, with ideas external to itself—stories or scenes, perhaps—which they think may make it more attractive and interesting to the class. And lurid pictures have been drawn by various critics of the absurdities to which such practise may lead. In regard to this let us on the one hand preserve a sense of proportion, while on the other hand we admit the excesses, which may have been committed. It should be clear that pictorial music, i.e. music with some definite poetic or literary connection, or inspired by some aspect of nature, has its distinct use in helping to gain an entrance to the young child's mind, and so to stimulate his imagination; its chief danger is that, if the teacher is not careful, it may eventually encourage his pupils in the fatal impression that all music 'means something'. (MacPherson, 1934, p. 56)

MacPherson, who in 1934 was in his late sixties, appears to have been aware of an ongoing conflict in the music education community regarding the use of ideas external to music in music listening. He tries to advocate a middle position to 'preserve a sense of proportion', suggesting that the practice of music listening has changed since he launched his pioneer books on music appreciation and aural culture. Even so, it is interesting to notice that the Appendix in *Aural culture based upon musical appreciation* (MacPherson & Read, 1912) on 'Music and the Young Child', written by Miss Marie Salt—and warmly recommended by MacPherson—contains a number of passages pointing forward to the issues in the 'ideas external' debate.

Miss Salt builds her methodology on two 'fundamental'—as she denotes them—principles of child development. The first states that 'mental assimilation is incomplete without expression' (Salt, 1912, Appendix, p. ii). 'Development', she wrote:

> takes place as a result of the interaction of the environment upon the individual, and of the individual upon the environment. This is to say, that there are two aspects in the process of learning—(a) Impression, and (b) Expression. (p. ii)

In her methodological recommendation for music listening for 7- and 8-year-olds, she relies heavily on the use of expressive movement, and with regard to 'ideas external' she wrote:

> They are encouraged to tell stories and make pictures suggested to them by the music; such pieces, for example, as the following, usually being effective in this connection:– Hall

of the Mountain King (Grieg), Knight Rupert (Schumann), Pastoral Dance (German). At other times the children's power to read meaning into music is increased by a background of environment and story supplied by the teacher. (Salt, 1912, Appendix, p. iii)

Salt goes on to refer to Coleridge Taylor's *Song of Hiawatha* and Mendelssohn's *Midsummer night's dream*, explaining that 'before this music was introduced, the children were well acquainted with the environment of the story' so that when the music was introduced 'to the children the music expressed the same ideas in a wilder and more wonderful way' (1912, p. xiii).

In her small, but important, Appendix to MacPherson's and Read's 1912 book, Marie Salt reveals to us a listening practice that to some extent is narrative and expressive—and even action-based—thus touching on the questions of how to listen and when to listen, as well as the question of expression of learning and meaning in the listening classroom. Thus, she is pioneering later and more recent practices.

The role of masterpieces of music

The third issue in the Lausanne Resolution is the insistence on the Western canon of classical masterworks as the only worthy object of art to be used, not as education for the masses and elementary education, but for the mature student who has been given foundational training through the '*intensive* and *critical*' process of the Aural Training Class (Forbes Milne, 1931, p. 829).

The insistence on the non-use of this kind of music for the elementary classes may be attributed to the widespread belief in phylogeny in the early twentieth century and the Darwinist recapitulation theory developed by the German philosopher and artist Ernst Haeckel.[16] In 1912, Marie Salt, in her appendix to *Aural culture*, states that the second of her two principles in theories 'of child development' is that 'child development is analogous to race development' (Salt, 1912, Appendix, p. ii). Salt maintains that because of this principle, music for young children is required to be 'primitive in character in the early stages' (p. iii). Her recommended selections of music for children aged 6 years and upwards, however, seem, as we have just seen, to include pieces by Grieg, Schumann, Dvorak, Tchaikovsky and Mendelssohn in addition to a mixture of folk tunes and other short classical works.

---

[16] Haeckel promoted Charles Darwin's work in Germany and developed the controversial 'recapitulation theory' claiming that an individual organism's biological development, or ontogeny, parallels and summarizes its species' entire evolutionary development, or phylogeny: 'ontogeny recapitulates phylogeny' (see *Encyclopædia Britannica*, 2007; see also Cole, 1996, p. 146).

The Lausanne Resolution illustrates a seemingly growing conflict in the music-listening community of the 1930s about what music to select for education, a conflict fuelled by the increasing access to recorded music and technology. The use of masterpieces of classical music in educational environments in schools (including elementary education) seemed to have established itself in England—in spite of the advice from the Lausanne Resolution—along with the development of the use of the gramophone for appreciation and listening classes. In a letter to the Editor of *The Musical Times* (1919) concerning the gramophone, the author, a school teacher, discloses that his school had:

> found it possible to obtain a large variety of records of the best music by composers such as Palestrina, Bach, Mozart, Beethoven, Schubert, Schumann, Wagner, Brahms, Tchaikovsky, Borodin, Rimsky-Korsakov, Glazunov, Dvorak, Debussy, Franck, Ravel, Elgar, Grainger, Vaughan Williams and Frank Bridge. (McElligott, 1919, p. 697)

What is surprising about this information is the degree to which this school had included contemporary art music in their gramophone resource bank, something that hardly is the case in schools in more recent times.

Summary of early educational listening history

From this scrutiny of some—and only some—of the writings on different aspects of music listening in the first three decades of the twentieth century, it seems reasonable to conclude that a number of issues, debates and practices characteristic of music listening, as conceived of in more recent times, were well established. The following points should be noted:

+ The topology of music listening as an evolving school music practice was characterized by efforts to link the separate components of ear training, music theory and music appreciation. Music listening was still in its infancy and characterized by a parenthetical relationship between aural training and music appreciation. As music listening evolved, there was a stronger emphasis on the connections between formal and material elements of music and interpretation of composed music.

+ The main component, aural training, seemed to be under pressure from music appreciation and an increasing access to musics of different genres, primarily classical masterpieces, due to new technology. Classical music masterpieces had an unrivalled dominant position in music appreciation and also in aural training.

+ The belief in phylogeny dominated views on child development, and, consequently, listening to 'primitive' music was recommended for young children. However, the musical pieces selected did not necessarily follow this advice.

- ◆ The advocated focus of music listening was by and large on the material or formal aspects of music. However, some practices approached music listening via stories and the narrative.

- ◆ Some early practices demonstrated music-listening approaches via movement, composition, expression and student agency.

It seems, then, that early practices and debates on music listening were quite complex and nuanced. The debate we have been examining points forward to issues that recur in contemporary practices in music listening in many ways, for example, the focus on stories versus a focus on formal qualities in the music, the balance between impression and expression in the listening situation, the issue of passive reception versus active mental listening, and the role of contemplation versus creative multimodal interactivity. Before turning our full attention to some of these issues and their relationship to a psychocultural approach to education, let us for a moment turn to connections between early music-listening practices and some contemporary theories in music psychology.

Early listening practices and psychologies of music

The different positions regarding music listening in the music education community discussed above seemed to mirror parallel debates in the development of contemporary music psychology. These positions included different viewpoints on the need to focus on the materials of music versus response and reaction to music, the importance and position of individual components of music versus holistic aspects, and viewpoints on the relationship between, on the one hand, auditory and rhythmic perception and, on the other hand, associations and emotion.

In the late 1930s, this debate surfaced nowhere more clearly than in the work of James Mursell and Carl E. Seashore. Their two books with the almost identical title of *(The) Psychology of music*, published in 1937 and 1938 respectively—and both building on 'Gestalt' psychology[17]—illustrate the essence of the debate. Whereas Mursell dedicates a whole chapter in his book to the psychology of musical listening, including sections on intrinsic and extrinsic factors in listening, Seashore gives preference to chapters on the relationship between perception, memory and intelligence and music materials such as pitch and timbre. Their different viewpoints are demonstrated in many ways, some of

---

[17] Charles Plummeridge points out that in essence Gestalt psychology was concerned with form. It 'laid stress on the power of the perceiver mentally to organize whatever objects or situations he encounters, and to do so in formal terms rather than terms of individual components and his previous experience of them' (2007, n.p.).

which refer directly to those assumptions underpinning different music-listening practices.

'There are four—and only four—fundamental things', wrote Seashore, 'to be learned in musical hearing: the hearing of pitch, intensity, time and timbre. Unless this is recognized', he continued, 'the task may seem, to both teacher and pupil, endless and unreasonable' (Seashore, 1938, p. 157). 'It is a basic error', wrote Mursell, 'to suppose that we ever have a response to all aspects of the music, or that it is always and for all persons substantially the same thing' (Mursell, 1937, p. 201).

Mursell's book was a major breakthrough for the belief in the importance of what he called 'extrinsic factors in listening', specifically: the general mood or affective set of the listener; the flow of association and the arousal of imagery; and visual experience of various kinds (Mursell, 1937, pp. 205–209). His 'listening chapter' challenged the dominant views in the music education community—as demonstrated in the Lausanne Resolution—and strengthened the more progressive practices already in operation. By identifying and describing extrinsic factors in music listening, Mursell legitimated existing progressive practices connected to response, expression, imagery and movement.

Seashore, with his emphasis on sensory capacities, formal aspects of the music and musical memory, seemed to be underpinning the prevailing music-listening practice, the parenthetical position, with its major emphasis on aural training. Even Seashore, however, warned against music listening becoming too intellectual. In his chapter on 'The musical mind', he warns that the great intellect in music 'may dwell so exclusively upon the musical forms and upon conceptions of new musical structures as to become calloused to the more spontaneous appreciation and expression of music' (Seashore, 1938, p. 8). Neither Mursell nor Seashore, however, questioned the selection of music for music listening and their prime foci were not on cultural, but on the universal and individual, aspects of person and mind.

The question of what music to select for listening

Today, with the massive change in music production and the introduction of a great variety of genres into academia and education, insisting on the exclusive use of classical masterpieces and 'primitive' music, as seemed to be the case in early listening history, would be regarded as an extreme elitist and romantic position. This position is very much in opposition to the tenets of cultural psychology with regard to the question of what music to select for music listening in schools. The critique of the elitist and purist position has been extensive, more or less along with the increasing acceptance of alternative artistic values in objects of arts in a variety of cultures, musical styles and genres, and the critique of regarding certain styles of music and the music of certain cultures as primitive in comparison with Western art music (e.g. Born & Hesmondhalgh, 2000; Small, 1998, Walker, 2001).

It is hardly surprising, therefore, that this 'purist' position is genuinely problematic with regard to values in our multicultural societies and at odds with what Bruner characterizes as the central thesis of cultural psychology. He writes: 'For its central thesis is that culture shapes mind, that it provides us with the toolkit by which we construct not only our worlds but our very conception of our selves and our powers' (Bruner, 1996, Preface, p. x). Surely, says Bruner, referring to what he calls 'the instrumentalist tenet' of cultural psychology, the school:

> can never be considered as culturally 'free standing'. *What* it teaches, what modes of thought and what 'speech registers' it actually activates in its pupils, cannot be isolated from how the school is situated in the lives and culture of its students. (p. 28)

This cultural awareness seems only gradually to have grown into music-listening practices despite early advocacy against the singular use of works from the Western musical canon. The MENC-supported Tanglewood Symposium[18] in the USA in 1967, for example, took a giant step away from the elitist position in music education when it was resolved that the first two paragraphs of the final Symposium Declaration should read:

- ◆ Music serves best when its integrity as an art is maintained.
- ◆ Music of all periods, styles, forms, and cultures belongs in the curriculum. The musical repertory should be expanded to involve music of our time in its rich variety, including currently popular teen-age music and avant-garde music, American folk music, and the music of other cultures. (Choate, 1967, pp. 38–40)

Even so, it is worth noting that the formulations of the Tanglewood Declaration underline the notion of music as art, and that the admittance of non-classical musical works is recommended as expansion, not replacement. It is indeed expansion rather than replacement that has taken place in Western music education—and in a number of nations modelling their music-listening practice on the traditions of the appreciation movement. A number of the classical 'masterpieces' from the Romantic period, for example, Beethoven's *Pastoral symphony*, Grieg's *Peer Gynt suite*, and others, continue to play a

---

[18] The Tanglewood Symposium in July–August, 1967 in Tanglewood, Massachusetts. Musicians, educators, and representatives of corporations, foundations, communications, as well as government, assembled at a ten-day symposium. The theme was 'Music in American Society' (Choate, 1967).

central role in music-listening curricula on many levels. The influence of early listening practices and the music appreciation movement has been strong; not only in terms of content but also in terms of the attendant pedagogical practices developed around the Western classical canon, practices which are often applied to musics that might require different pedagogical approaches.

The grand discussion about what music to select for listening programmes is connected to a number of other issues in music education, directly and indirectly. It is, for example, a crucial question in the discussion about viewing music education primarily as 'aesthetic education' or 'praxial music education'.[19]

Praxialism, as advocated by David Elliott (1995), illustrates that the parenthetical positions regarding music listening as a subject discipline in general, and the selection of music in particular, are still with us today; not primarily with regard to its relationship to ear training, but to performing and music making. Elliott's parenthetical view on this question might be looked at as an alternative and culture-oriented route into solving the challenges of what music to select for listening. Elliott writes:

> But achieving *an* experience of the special kind of event-performance we call a musical work requires an understanding of musical performing; it requires that students learn how to perform and improvise competently themselves, as well as to compose, arrange and conduct. (1995, p. 102)

The main criteria for the selection of music for listening in Elliott's view are thus linked to performing and composing, not to aural training as claimed by the authors of the Lausanne Resolution. Elliott gives little advice about what specific qualities and criteria listening curricula should adhere to, except being in direct relation to the musical practices students are being inducted into. In other words, the performance and composition practice adopted in different educational settings should directly influence the selection of music for listening. Elliott's position appears to be in keeping with the tenets of cultural psychology because it gives priority to the production of, as well as the listening to, tangible 'works' in relevant cultural and contextual settings. Bruner calls this 'the externalization tenet' of cultural psychology, and claims that:

> the main function of all collective cultural activity is to produce 'works'—oeuvres . . . The benefits of 'externalizing' such joint products into oeuvres have too long been

---

[19] The debate between Bennett Reimer and David Elliott following the publication of Elliott's *Music Matters* in 1995 was not only a North American debate. It affected—and still does— music education debates in a number of countries. For example, a comprehensive 423- page report on a 'Music Education National Debate for Ireland' contains a chapter with the following title: 'The American Philosophical View on Music Education. Towards a reconciliation of the Reimer/Elliott Counterpositions' (Henegan, 2001, pp. 373).

> overlooked . . . Works and works-in-progress create *shared* and *negotiable* ways of thinking in a group . . . Externalization produces a *record* of our mental efforts, one that is 'outside us' rather than vaguely 'in memory' . . . 'It' embodies our thoughts and intentions in a form more accessible to reflective efforts. (Bruner, 1996, pp. 22–23)

Elliott has modified his position somewhat in later writings, stating that he supports the use of recordings to enhance and extend students' listening beyond the works or styles they are working in as performers, improvisers, composers, and so forth. He maintains, however, that educational listening should have a direct relation to the musical practices into which students are being inducted (D. Elliott, personal communication).

Although Elliott's position is a valuable attempt to contextualize music listening in terms of what music to select, it does not—in my opinion—present a satisfactory solution to the challenges facing us today. In many ways, modern technology has created challenges to music education similar to those created by the gramophone and the radio in the first decades of the twentieth century. A global situation with unlimited access to music of all sorts cannot be solved by parenthetical solutions in music listening alone, especially not at a time when technology challenges the very necessity of performance as a basic and compulsory skill in music education (Savage, 2005, 2007).

It seems to me that the shift in emphasis and attention during the last 30 years or so, from a focus on music listening to performing and composing in many curricula around the world, has delayed the development of a comprehensive debate on the criteria for the selection of music for listening in music education.[20] A technology-based society has created a new situation for music education in general, and for music listening in particular. Future practices have to deal with this situation on the basis of priorities in cultural values as well as in theories of learning and an effective listening education for all.

Today, Western music still dominates music education. A report from the International Music Council's (IMC) action programme, 'Many Musics', concludes that from their research of the situation in 20 countries across continents, Western classical musics were most widespread in terms of the range of musics taught in schools and teacher training, as well as in the range of musics available as resources and for learning in communities. 'The education systems of the world', says the report, 'are in general doing little if anything to encourage musical diversity' (Drummond, 2003, p. 1).

---

[20] In his introduction to 'Symposium on Music Listening. Its Nature and Nurture', Bennett Reimer, writes that 'we have amassed an extensive body of research in arts education, but, so far little in the way of definite or reliable bases for our work, especially in regard to the teaching of aesthetic responsiveness' (Reimer, 2006, p. 3).

I suggest that the reasons for the continued practice of music listening, with an emphasis on Western music, are threefold. First, many of the musical works in this tradition have a rich potential for educational processes and motivation for listening, something that many teachers consider important. Second, teachers do not necessarily, in my experience, consider these pieces primarily as works within a Western classical canon, but as a canon of educational music listening. As a canon within a framework of music education, they have incorporated the educational processes connected with them, and appear—from a practising music-listening teacher's point of view—inseparable from these educational processes. Third, I believe that music education, just like other sectors of education, is shaped by what Bourdieu describes as 'doxa'—the fundamental beliefs, taken as self-evident universals, that shape actions in a particular field (Bourdieu, 1984). According to Bourdieu, doxa will shape a particular arrangement of a certain field, often enhancing the dominant and believing this to be self-evident and universally favourable.

This does not mean that the music education profession is not—or should not become—aware of cultural issues when selecting music for listening. In the big picture, cultural issues are not only a question about methodologies, educational processes and learning, but questions about equity and justice. 'Music educators in our times', writes Bennett Reimer:

> have the same obligation as all other citizens, and all other educators—to support and promote ideals of equity and justice in all we do. But we have the particular obligation to relate those ideals to the field—music—in which we are professionals. Attention to equity and justice need not and should not contradict our responsibility to musical learnings, the two seemingly different concerns being entirely compatible. (Reimer, 2007, p. 191)

It is only by looking more closely at music listening as *living learning processes* in classrooms, that we can approach a more nuanced, albeit tentative, answer to the question we set out to discuss in this chapter; namely, to what extent music listening as a school discipline is resonating with the tenets of psychocultural theory.

The learning processes of music listening

The concept of *process* is probably one of the most used educational concepts since Dewey's early writings on education (1897).[21] It has come to mean a

---

[21] The very opening sentences in Dewey's *My Pedagogic Creed* (1897) describe education as a process. He writes: 'I believe that all education *proceeds* [italics added] by the participation of the individual in the social consciousness of the race. This process begins unconsciously almost at birth, and is continually shaping the individual's powers, saturating

range of different things in different contexts and sometimes different things in the same context. The etymological meaning of the concept of process closest to my understanding and use of the term stems from Latin 'procedere', meaning 'go forward'. In this sense it means 'course or method of action' or a 'continuous series of actions meant to accomplish some result' (Harper, 2002,).

Music-listening activities in a classroom lend themselves easily to being viewed as different forms of learning processes. A common scenario is as follows. The teacher has a specific piece of music s/he wants to use or present to the class at some time during the lesson. The students will listen to the music at some time. Goals for the lessons can be of different kinds, but in any case the teacher wants the students to benefit or learn from their listening in some way or other. In order to make this happen, the teacher has to plan how to start, continue and end the lesson, and include some considerations about what kind of learning processes s/he wants to involve the students in. One of the many challenges of such a situation is to make sure that students listen to what the teacher intends should be listened to at certain times during the process. In a traditional class of thirty students, this often means trying to control thirty individuals and their attitudes, attention, mental foci, and responses—a formidable task for experienced as well as novice music teachers.

In my first year as a beginning music teacher, I was invited to a new music resource book demonstration lecture in a classroom with 10-year-olds. The topic of the lesson was listening to Edvard Grieg's work *Morning Mood* from Ibsen's *Peer Gynt*. I no longer remember the details of the lesson, but one particular part stands out. Somewhat into the process, the teacher asked the children to lean forward on their desks, heads and arms on top of the desk and with eyes closed, listen to the music and to raise their arms and heads gradually reaching the top after 53 seconds of music. I can still hear the teacher's 'Now!' ringing in my ears, and I remember how impressed I was seeing all those hands flying into the air illustrating the students ostensible 'learning' of the sunrise climax of this piece.

Liora Bresler presents a 'thick description' of another listening situation in an American school in the early 1990s in the following way:

> 11.45. The listening is done in preparation for tomorrow's concert. Copland's work, along with Sousa and the others, is featured in the program. Louise [the teacher] starts a tape. The sound flows, energetic, picturesque. A girl in the front row makes horse-riding movements. Most of the boys in class have a good time, laughing and talking

his consciousness, forming his habits, training his ideas, and arousing his feelings and emotions' (Dewey, 1897, p. 77).

with friends. Louise: 'Hear the horses? Now the shooting', and makes shooting gestures with her hands. Copland's picture, an added source of distraction, is still being passed around. A boy bumps his head against the picture. Another, in his turn, plays with it, turning it in all different directions. Jeremiah forgets himself in the noise, stands up and gets sent to the last row. Change of location makes little difference: he is active and restless still. Finally, the first section is over. Two girls clap their hands in applause. (Bresler, 1991, pp. 59–60)

In both of the situations depicted above, the teacher tries to control and direct the children's attention, for example, in terms of identifying a climax or a composer's use of musical references to American life, as well as *when* in the process learning should take place.

This approach to teaching and learning is hardly in keeping with cultural psychology's insistence on what Bruner refers to as 'the constructivism tenet' (Bruner, 1996, p. 19ff.). Citing Nelson Goodman (1978), Bruner underlines that in any meaning-making situation, 'reality is made, not found' (p. 19). In music listening, important goals from early listening history onwards have suggested that learning processes involve finding, categorizing and identifying *something already found* by the teacher, rather than students discovering and responding to something individually. Within this framework, an increased pressure from progressive Deweyan education—with its child-centred, problem-oriented and discovery approach—must be felt as a dilemma to listening pedagogues.

Music listening and progressive education

The influence of progressive education is, nevertheless, evident in many of the methodologies for music listening introduced during the past 50 years. In Radio Corporation of America's (RCA) famous *Adventures in Music* (1961) series—an immense source of inspiration for listening methodologies to follow—Gladys and Eleanor Tipton (1961) paid credit to early listening history with its emphasis on 'conscious recognition', as well as to the ideals of progressive education, when they wrote:

> For, at the moment when *conscious recognition* of a familiar piece, or interest in a unique feature of a new piece of music engages children's attention, then voluntary participation, in the form of *thoughtful listening*, is likely to result. The key to an enjoyable and stimulating adventure in listening to music consists of 'alerting' the children's musical ears so that, as they sample the vast literature of the ages, they make some of it their own. However, a passing acquaintance is not enough. In order to take music into their hearts, children must have ample opportunity to find out for themselves what the music has to *say* to them. For only through a process of gradual, interested 'discovery' of the music itself, on their own terms, will children really remember and treasure it. (Tipton & Tipton, 1961, p. 5)

The Tiptons' insistence on discovery on the children's own terms reflects the emphasis in progressive education on problem-solving and active doings in the learning process (e.g. Dewey, 1916). In *Adventures in music* the overall emphasis on formal elements in the music is still there. The relationship between ear training and composed pieces, however, is no longer a parenthetical one, but integrated into an educational process trying to balance information about highlights in the music and children's responses in a process of discovery.[22]

Active mental listening

Another memory from my freshman days back in the 1970s has to do with the educational buzzword at the time in music listening: active listening. Coloured by my sympathy for the educational tenets of progressive education, active listening was to me an attempt to introduce Deweyan activity pedagogy into the educational process of music listening. I was never convinced, however, that 'learning by doing' could be regarded as learning by *mental* doing. Active listening in music listening was strongly advocated already in early listening practices by Professor MacPherson. In the previously quoted article from *The Musical Times* (1934), he wrote:

> And we hear a good deal today in certain quarters of the 'uncreative attitude of mind' that is content with 'mere listening.' Now it is perfectly clear that there is a form of hearing (I will not call it listening) in which the hearer's intelligence can hardly be said to function at all. This is very common in connection with the use of the wireless; but it cannot be too strongly asserted that the true listening to music, far from being a passive indulgence in a merely sensuous gratification, *is an active mental process* [italics added]—an endeavour to re-create for ourselves what the composer has already created. (MacPherson, 1934, p. 57)

---

[22] In light of early music listening history, *Adventures in Music* is just that, an 'adventure'— considering time and educational frameworks available—in creative and multimodal approaches to music listening. Its importance as a renewer of Western music listening methodology first dawned on me in my first year as teacher educator in the mid-1970s, when I visited a remote school deep in one of the Norwegian fjords. In a cupboard at the very back of the only classroom of this school I found a complete collection of the American RCA music listening package (Tipton & Tipton, 1961), which consisted of nine long-playing records and accompanying and comprehensive teacher guidelines. I think it was then that I started to wonder about the great variety in approaches in everyday classroom work that already existed, the global aspects of music education, and the seemingly international consensus and canon-like character of the selection of musical pieces for music listening.

The view of music listening as a process of *rational* or mental recognition and discrimination of structural and formal aspects or constructs in the music was strengthened with the appearance of cognitive psychology.[23] Influential writers such as Leonard B. Meyer (1956) claimed that the central meaning of music was to be found in the structural interplay of its elements and form, rather than in associations to non-musical events (Aiello & Sloboda, 1994, p. 3). This view, naturally, influenced what should be considered as *learning* in music-listening classroom practices.

This *rationalification*, as I will call it, of the music-listening process can be viewed as an important trajectory in music listening as a discipline from early listening practices till today. Nicholas Cook (1994), in a chapter on perception with a perspective from music theory, argues that psychology in this respect has been influential because it seems to have been a psychology of ear training rather than a psychology of music. Claiming that psychological research has placed too much emphasis on the psycho-acoustical parameters of music and too little on meaning and cultural values, he writes:

> We have studies of how listeners distinguish the voices of polyphonic music, dis-criminate intervals, follow chord progressions, and judge key centres. Now people can do all these things, at least within certain constraints . . . Such training—called ear training, aural training or aural analysis—creates the interface between musical sound and the theoretical knowledge in terms of which musicians create, notate, and repro-duce music. So we have a lot of psychological studies of ear training. The trouble is they are not called studies of ear training. They are called studies of music listening. And as such they are thoroughly unsatisfactory, because they begin with the premise that people hear music in terms of music-theoretical categories. (Cook, 1994, p. 81)

Cook's suggestion that the use of cognitive psychology in music listening primarily seems to be a psychology of ear training, and 'thoroughly unsatisfac-tory' in terms of student learning about music, confirms my view that the trajectory of rationalification in music listening has severe shortcomings.

---

[23] The so-called 'cognitive revolution' is referred to by a great number of writers, in par-ticular Anglo-American theorists. In his retrospective article 'The Cognitive Revolution: A Historical Perspective', American George A. Miller, a pioneer in the development of cognitive science in the USA, describes how 'the cognitive revolution' in psychology orig-inated in the USA in the 1950s. He argues that it was a 'counter revolution' (Miller, 2003, p. 141). 'The first revolution', according to Miller, 'occurred much earlier when a group of experimental psychologists, influenced by Pavlov and other physiologists, proposed to redefine psychology as the science of behaviour. They argued that mental events are not publicly observable. If scientific psychology were to succeed, mentalist concepts would have to integrate and explain the behavioural data. We were still reluctant to use such terms as *mentalism* to describe what was needed, so we talked about cognition instead' (p. 142).

The combination of structural listening and the tradition in ear training for finding and controlling 'something already found' by the teacher is not—as already pointed out—in keeping with a constructivist view of learning. However, I am not sure that the blame should be placed entirely on cognitive psychology.

Musicological practices—such as mainstream music theory, musical analysis, and the emphasis on the understanding of the work of geniuses—played an important part in this development. Rose Subotnik, in her characterization of 'structural listening', leaves no doubt of its inappropriateness in dealing with aspects of culture and society. 'Of all methods,' she writes:

> structural listening, even in its 'replete' version, seems the least useful for entering the semiotic domain of sound and style. Carried to its logical conclusion, this method in all its versions, as an exclusive or even as the primary paradigm for listening, cannot define much of a positive role for society, style, or ultimately even sound in the reception of music. Discounting metaphorical and affective responses based on cultural association, personal experience, and imaginative play is at best secondary, not only in musical perception but also in the theoretical accounts we make of such perception, this method allows virtually no recognition of non-structural varieties of meaning or emotion in the act of listening. Since these are, of course, precisely the varieties favoured by the overwhelming majority of people, structural listening by itself turns out to be socially divisive, not only in what it demands but also in what it excludes or suppresses. (Subotnik, 1996, p. 170)

What remains to be asked about the relationship between the methods of structural listening, the psychology of music and music listening in schools with regard to learning about music, is the following. If the child is conceived of as an adult growing into adulthood and knowledge primarily through learning processes focusing on rational meetings with music, how does such a practice deal and resonate with interpretational, contextual, cultural, and situational aspects?

Jerome Bruner would probably answer that a rationalification-oriented learning process in music listening could be incompatible with two other tenets of cultural psychology, the 'perspectival' tenet and the 'constraint' tenet. The first tenet implies that the meaning of any fact, proposition, or encounter is 'relative to the perspective or frame of reference in terms of which it is construed. To understand well', Bruner (1996) continues:

> what something 'means' requires some awareness of the alternative meanings that can be attached to the matter under scrutiny, whether one agrees with them or not . . . In a word, the perspectival tenet highlights the interpretive, meaning-making side of human thought while, at the same time, recognizing the inherent risks of discord that may result from cultivating this deeply human side of mental life. (pp. 13–15)

The whole point, then, is not whether the focus in the listening process is on enhancing active mental processes in students. What is decisive in a psychocultural approach is *the different ways* in which constructs in the music, like themes, motives, form, harmonies, and the musical and cultural context can mean something, and *the ways* in which they are introduced by teachers and discovered by the learning student. David Best calls this 'interpretative reasoning' and argues that this form of reasoning is of central importance in the arts for 'giving understanding and evaluation' (Best, 1992, p. 2).

The constraints tenet in a psychocultural approach to education argues that the forms of meaning-making accessible to human beings 'in any culture are constrained in two crucial ways'. 'The first', writes Bruner:

> inheres in the nature of human mental functioning itself. Our evolution as a species has specialized us into certain characteristic ways of knowing, thinking, feeling, and perceiving . . . They can be considered as limits on human capacity for meaning making . . . The second comprises those constraints imposed by the symbolic systems accessible to human minds generally—limits imposed, say, by the very nature of language—but more particularly constraints imposed by the different languages and notational systems accessible to different cultures. (Bruner, 1996, pp. 15–18)

Any monophonic listening process, therefore, using only one—or rather, the one and only—channel in the enculturation of young people into musics and its secrets, risks, in my view, becoming subject to constraints in cultivation as well as in the reaping of benefits of the educational investments.

Music listening and narrative

In the rationale arguing for a psychocultural approach to education, Bruner (1996) also includes what he calls *the narrative tenet*. Narrative thinking, he says, can be considered as one of two broad ways in which human beings organize and manage their knowledge of the world. We have already discussed aspects of the first one, logical-scientific thinking, in relation to music-listening processes. 'No culture', writes Bruner:

> is without both of them, though different cultures privilege them differently . . . None of us know as much as we should about how to create narrative sensibility. Two commonplaces seem to have stood the test of time. The first is that a child should 'know', have a 'feel' for, the myths, histories, folk tales, conventional stories of his or her culture or cultures. They frame and nourish an identity. The second commonplace urges imagination through fiction. (Bruner, 1996, pp. 39–41)

Educational music listening, as experienced as a student in my Norwegian teacher education context in the late 1960s, was mostly a story about musical narratives in the form of programme music and classical works like *Moldau*,

Peer Gynt suite, Peter and the wolf, Carnival of the animals, Vivaldi's *The seasons,* and others. Our professor never appeared to question this selection, nor did he question the accompanying assignments and intended learning processes, their position in the listening repertoire and connected curriculum.

There is little doubt that narrative has played—and is playing—an important role in music-listening processes. We have touched on it in connection with Marie Salt's early listening practices (1912) and we have seen it as a hot discussion topic in the Lausanne Resolution (Forbes Milne, 1931). Programme music and music with titles or other narrative suggestions still constitute an important part of the music-listening repertoire for classrooms to the extent that it might be meaningful to identify a trajectory of *narratification* in addition to that of rationalification.

Different aspects of narratification and the use of programme music in education have been heavily criticized from the time of early listening practices and onwards. The philosopher Suzanne Langer compared narrative programmes in music with a crutch, characterizing their use in education as a disaster (Langer, 1942). Di Rocco, echoing the Lausanne Resolution debate, warned that the possibility for any aesthetic encounter with the music might be eliminated for the child by offering him/her a substitute—namely, story. 'Shouldn't music educators', she wrote:

> use the unique syntax of music to evoke a response of delight, and not usurp the role of literature? The child who has been presented primarily with music like 'Peter and the Wolf,' 'Pictures at an Exhibition,' 'The Sorcerer's Apprentice,' and 'Billy the Kid,' has this variety of program literature from which to choose when asked the meaning of some other musical composition. Every oboe is a duck, every timpani roll a storm, and every strike of the stick on the snare drum is a gunshot. (Di Rocco, 1969, p. 35)

Even if a psychocultural approach to listening processes might endorse the use of narrative in music-listening processes, existing traditions in the field, as seen in the example of identifying 'the horses' in Copland's music (Bresler, 1991, p. 59), do not easily lend themselves to music-listening practices based on cultural awareness. Challenges connected to narrative-oriented learning processes, however, *can* be met with increased emphasis on discovery and interaction, for example, as demonstrated in *Adventures in music.*[24]

The real challenge, however, for narrative as a method in music listening, as well as for any other approach, is to connect a balanced selection of music to

---

[24] For example, when the Tiptons (1961) introduced 'mood' and 'pictures in music' alongside structural and formal categories in their assignments, they avoided the traditional programme pieces and encouraged processes where the child would listen for clues in the music that might help them *discover* narrative or pictorial ideas that the composer had in mind.

culture-specific and culture-based learning items, and to use effective and interactive learning processes adapted to the music selected as well as to the educational context. In such learning processes, one needs to listen to what Marie Salt wrote as early as 1912. 'We are working against Nature', she wrote, 'when we stimulate thought, perception and feeling, and do not provide for adequate expression through action' (Salt, 1912, Appendix, p. ii). Her statement is mirrored in today's discussion and critique of cognitive psychology and Cartesian dualism, a critique where contemporary writers like James Wertsch (1998) and Wayne Bowman (2004) argue for an embodied account of cognition and knowing as inseparable from action. And what is closer to music educators as a vehicle for the expression of embodied knowing and meaning than artistic expression itself?

The 'artification' of music listening

I have borrowed the term *artification* from a chapter by Ellen Dissanayake (2007) in the *International handbook of research in arts education* (Bresler, 2007). Dissanayake uses this concept to explain how cultural ceremonies and rituals use 'artified' materials—spaces, bodies, sounds, words, movements and ideas—as expressions of meaning. She argues that artification is a basic and culturally and genetically developed aspect of human behaviour. 'It implies', she writes: 'basic performative operations including repetition, formalization, exaggeration, dynamic variation, and manipulation of expectation upon vocal, visual and kinesic modalities' (Dissanayake, 2007, p. 790). A little later in her chapter, she describes 'a behaviour of art, or artification' as 'making use of and responding emotionally to aesthetic operations' (p. 793).

When applying this concept to characterize aspects of music listening in schools, I refer to the use of the arts and the application of artistic expression in listening processes when responding to music. My investigation of early listening practices demonstrates that the use of arts as an expressive device for students has been a part of music-listening methodologies for a long time. We can see important elements of it in Marie Salt's Dalcroze-inspired practice and methodology (1912);[25] in the Tiptons' *Adventures in music* (1961) in their use of poetry, expressive movement and drama; and in a range of recent classroom literature in different countries.[26]

---

[25] In her early school practice she emphasized a balance between 'impression' (being exposed to music) and 'expression' in the form of meaningful expression through movement (Salt, 1912, Appendix p. ii).

[26] This is a major characteristic in my own listening methodology *Music in Use* [Musikk I bruk] (Espeland, 1987, 1991, 1992a, 2001, 2004). This research-based listening

The emphasis on artification and meaningful expression in relation to learning processes in music listening can also be identified in contemporary research on music listening in general (e.g. Dunn, 2006; Peterson, 2006; Zerull, 2006), as well as on particular aspects thereof, for example, in research on invented notation (e.g. Barrett, 2001, 2004; Upitis, 1992) and on creative student mapping (Blair, 2006).

In Debbie Blair's (2006) review of some of the research undertaken in natural classroom settings (e.g. Cohen, 1997; Dunn, 1997; Espeland, 1987; Kerchner, 1996, 2000), she points out six important threads that emerge from the activities used by these researchers, which have informed recent listening practices in schools: (a) the projects/problems were open-ended in nature; (b) the teacher used modelling to provide groundwork and scaffolding; (c) each activity involved solving a problem while listening—requiring the listener to 'do something' that reflected their thoughts about the music. These activities included movement, writing, drawing, manipulating or creating visual graphics, and discussions; (d) repeated listenings were an important aspect of the activities; (e) the activities included discussions that valued multiple perspectives; and (f) the results of each activity were varied and reflected both similarities and differences in the students' interpretations of the music (Blair, 2006, p. 42).

In her own research on student-created musical maps, Blair places herself in this tradition. Her concluding paragraph, however, is not about repeated listenings, scaffolding, or doings. It is about responses to music, and the value of understanding and of being understood (Wiggins, 2001): 'By noticing the various and similar ways that we each respond to music,' she writes:

> we notice that we, as people, have commonalities that we share, yet each with our own unique perspective. This is the valuing that students so desire—that others in their learning communities recognize in each one of them that they know something about this thing called music and that what they know is very special—they understand. It is in knowing this about each other that we come to be understood. (Blair, 2006, p. 241)

---

methodology focuses on responsive music listening in primary schools, basing the educational approach on the belief that response on the part of the listener is crucial in musical understanding and learning, and that children therefore need to be involved in a variety of activities which, while primarily related to the music itself, engage also with experiences in verbal, visual, musical and kinetic artistic expression (Espeland, 1987, pp. 283–297). Similar approaches can be found in a number of resources for schools and teachers over time, for example, *The Experience of Teaching General Music* (Atterbury & Richardson, 1995); *Musical Growth in the Elementary School* (Bergethon, Boardman, & Montgomery, 1997); *Music in the Primary School* (Mills, 1993); *Teaching for Musical Understanding* (Wiggins, 2001); *Upbeat* (Murphy & Espeland, 2007).

By focusing on the value of understanding as a common and mutual experience, Blair is very close to describing the essence of one of the most important tenets of a cultural–psychological approach to education as described by Bruner (1996), namely the interactional tenet:

> Consider the mutual community for a moment. Typically, it models ways of doing or knowing, provides opportunity for emulation, offers running commentary, provides 'scaffolding' for novices, and even provides a good context for teaching deliberately . . . . One of the most radical proposals to have emerged from the cultural–psychological approach to education is that the classroom be reconceived as just such a sub-community of mutual learners, with the teacher orchestrating the proceedings. Note that, contrary to traditional critics, such sub-communities do not reduce the teacher's role, nor his or her 'authority.' Rather the teacher takes on the additional role function of encouraging others to share it. (Bruner, 1996, p. 21)

To me it seems that artification needs to be an important characteristic of music listening in schools for a number of reasons. It has the potential of involving creativity in the learning process—invention, expression, manipulation of forms and structures and patterns in the music—leading to the sharing of 'something found' with a 'sub-community of mutual learners'. It may unify and integrate rationality with feeling into embodied knowledge about multiple interpretations. And it reflects a way of responding, expressing and communicating that is basically human and universal for all cultures. According to Dissanayake,

> Although we live today in societies very different from those in which human nature evolved, recognition of the aesthetic nature inherent in humans from infancy is a potent ally as we help children to satisfy their emotional needs for mutuality, belonging, meaning, competence, and artful participation along with the academic and social skills they need for a modern life. (Dissanayake, 2007, p. 794)

When, or rather, if, such 'artful participation' is open to situational, cultural and contextual adaptations with regard to the selection of music as well as to other aspects of music-listening processes in schools, we might be on our way to practices resonating with the basic tenets of a psychocultural approach to education.

Conclusions and future challenges

By characterizing music-listening classroom practices over time as a story of three different trajectories in music listening—rationalification, narratification and artification—I hope to have given some tentative answers, at least, to a discussion about the relationship between these three trajectories and a psychocultural approach to music listening as a music education discipline.

All of them are a necessary part of Western classroom traditions developed over the past hundred years or so. All of them have their historical roots in early educational listening practices as described by Professor MacPherson, Marie Salt, and their colleagues. All of them rely on the practices of engaged and dedicated music educators harbouring different positions in aesthetics, philosophy, music theory, educational theory and, of course, psychology. None of these practices, however, have, in my opinion, so far solved—in a satisfactory way—the immense challenge of developing a culture-based and sound rationale for a practice of music listening in schools in our global society.

Let there be no doubt that I think some of the recent practices in music listening are much closer to being in accordance with the tenets of cultural psychology than others.[27] I have argued that practices relying on students' responses, artistic expression, interpretive reasoning, discovery and problem solving—in short practices building on artification—are closer to such a claim than other practices. This approach is not the only recommendable one. To repeat: any monophonic listening process, using only one—or rather, the one and only—channel in the enculturation of young people into music and its secrets, risks becoming subject to constraints in cultivation as well as in the reaping of benefits of the educational investments.

However, there are some major challenges ahead. As we have seen, a psychocultural approach to music listening necessitates important changes in many existing practices in terms of what music to select for listening as well as in terms of what learning processes to include. In my view, however, those methodologies and practices that emulate the Brunerian tenets, as discussed in this chapter, are vulnerable in everyday educational settings in their implementation, which in turn requires teachers who combine artistic and educational competence, and the capacity to withstand the increasing accountability pressures of educational authorities and society (Murphy, 2007). Music teacher education is challenged to find better ways of developing students' music-listening competencies in the artistic field and the educational field, in similar ways to those we have seen in the areas of performing and composing.

---

[27] My use of Bruner's tenets for a psychocultural approach to education should not be considered as something fixed beyond discussion. Some of these tenets, for example, the constructivism tenet, are being challenged in important ways by writers building more on phenomenology than psychology, for example, Dreyfus (2004), Bowman (2004) and Nielsen (2004). Similar concerns can be expressed regarding Bruner's categorization of thinking into logic-scientific and narrative. Other important writers, for example, Kieran Egan (2005), have other categorizations appearing to be very relevant for music listening. Egan, focusing on the importance of imagination, identifies some of our primary cognitive tools as the use of story, metaphor, binary opposites, mental imagery, rhyme-rhythm and pattern, jokes and humour, gossip, play, and mystery.

A major and far-reaching challenge—not only in primary and secondary education—is to find ways to develop the inheritance from traditional musicology and 'early educational listening' towards newer approaches to music listening involving elements like intensity, dynamic form, layers and genre-specific approaches to music.[28] In this process we might need to rethink music, as well as our approaches to music listening in schools (Cook & Everest, 1999).

When moving from a western art music-based tradition and practice in music listening towards a more equitable, diverse, and culturally and context-situated music-listening practice in schools we might reach a state where 'we no longer know what we know' (Cook & Everest, 1999, preface). Nevertheless, a major challenge in this transformation will be to utilize what we think we know—as well as recognizing what we don't know—in a discussion about some basic criteria for the selection of music for educational listening.[29] In this discussion, we need to avoid destroying or belittling the lessons learnt from early listening approaches and the great genre of Western classical music, and look ahead in a true spirit of *transformation* rather than aiming for transplantations of contents, ideas and methods (Jorgensen, 2003, p. 118).

Coda

Music listening as a discipline in contemporary school music education is, as I see it, more important now than at any other time in modern history. The pioneers, as well as contemporary listening pedagogues, over the approximately 100-year-long existence of school music listening, have produced a number of ways of introducing and educating young people into appreciating and learning about composed music. We call these ways *methods*. When it

---

[28] The field of newer aural-based research in musicology and music analysis holds, in my view, many promises for such a renewal. The Norwegian composer Lasse Thoresen, for example, presents his theories within the framework of something he calls the Aural Sonology Project. Here he writes about music analysis in terms of concepts like time-fields (the temporal segmentation of the musical discourse), layers (the synchronous segmentation of the musical discourse), dynamic form (time directions and energetic shape), thematic form (recurrence, variation, and contrast) and formal transformations (looser and firmer Gestalts, transformations between them) (Thoresen, 2007).

[29] In all modesty; 15 years ago I gave a talk at the International Society for Music Education World Conference in Seoul, Korea with the title: 'What are they going to listen to? Problems and opportunities in the selection of music for educational music listening'. I ended up advocating the selection of music for listening to be based on three groups of criteria: (1) contextual criteria: duration, contrast and method; (2) musical criteria: structure, communication, and interpretation; and (3) cultural criteria: tradition, versatility and identity (Espeland, 1992b, p. 68).

comes to the challenge of what methods to develop further, I return to John Dewey and what he wrote in *My pedagogic creed* (1897) more than a hundred years ago: 'I believe', he wrote, 'that the question of method is ultimately reducible to the question of the order of development of the child's powers and interests. The law for presenting and treating material is the law implicit within the child's own nature' (Dewey, 1897, Article IV, introduction).

Dewey's belief in the importance of paying attention to 'the child's own nature'—whatever that is—brings me back to what I described in the beginning of this chapter, to my listening and dancing sessions with my little granddaughter, Haldis. Next time she comes around, I will be thinking about Dewey's first specification of his beliefs with regard to determining the spirit in which education should be carried on rather than reflecting on my own role as being a grandfather *or* a listening pedagogue—and act accordingly. 'I believe', wrote Dewey in 1897:

> that the active side precedes the passive in the development of the child's nature; that expression comes before conscious impression; that the muscular development precedes the sensory; that movements come before conscious sensations; I believe that consciousness is essentially motor or impulsive; that conscious states tend to project themselves in action. I believe that the neglect of this principle is the cause of a large part of the waste of time and strength in schoolwork. The child is thrown into a passive, receptive or absorbing attitude. The conditions are such that he is not permitted to follow the law of his nature; the result is friction and waste. (Article IV, p. 1)

There is not much to add—is there, Haldis?

References

Aiello, R., & Sloboda, J. (Eds.) (1994). *Musical perceptions*. New York: Oxford University Press.

Atterbury, B., & Richardson, C. (1995). *The experience of teaching general music*. New York: McGraw-Hill.

Barrett, M. S. (2001). Constructing a view of children's meaning-making as notators: a case-study of a five-year-old's descriptions and explanations of invented notations. *Research Studies in Music Education*, 16, 33–45.

Barrett, M. S. (2004). Thinking about the representation of music: a case study of invented notation. *Bulletin of the Council for Research in Music Education*, 161/162, 19–28.

Barrett, M. S. (2006). Aesthetic response. In G. E. McPherson (Ed.), *The child as musician: a handbook of musical development* (pp. 173–91). Oxford: Oxford University Press.

Bergethon, B., Boardman, E., & Montgomery, J. (1997). *Musical growth in the elementary school* (6th edn). Fort Worth, TX: Harcourt Brace.

Best, D. (1992). *The rationality of feeling*. London: Falmer Press.

Blair, D. V. (2006). Look at what I heard! Music listening and student-created musical maps. Unpublished doctoral dissertation, Rochester, MI: Department of Music, Oakland University.

Born, G., & Hesmondhalgh, D. (Eds.) (2000). *Western music and its others. Difference, representation, and appropriation in music.* Berkeley, LA: University of California Press.

Bourdieu, P. (1984). *Distinction: a social critique of the judgement of taste.* Cambridge, MA: Harvard University Press.

Bowman, W. (2004). Cognition and the body: perspectives from music education. In L. Bresler (Ed.), *Knowing bodies, moving minds: towards embodied teaching and learning* (pp. 29–50). Dordrecht: Kluwer.

Bresler, L. (1991). Washington and Prairie Schools, Danville, Illinois. In R. Stake, L. Bresler, & L. Mabry (Eds.), *Custom and cherishing: the arts in elementary schools* (pp. 55–94). Urbana, IL: University of Illinois at Urbana-Champaign.

Bresler, L. (2004). *Knowing bodies, moving minds: towards embodied teaching and learning,* Dordrecht: Kluwer.

Bresler, L. (Ed.) (2007). *International handbook for research in arts education.* Dordrecht: Springer.

Bruner, J. (1966). *Towards a theory of instruction.* Cambridge, MA: Harvard University Press.

Bruner, J. (1990). *Acts of meaning.* Cambridge, MA: Harvard University Press.

Bruner, J. (1996). *The culture of education.* Cambridge, MA: Harvard University Press.

Choate, R. A. (1967). Music in the American society: the MENC Tanglewood Symposium Project. *Music Educators Journal, 53*(7), 38–40.

Cohen, V. W. (1997). Explorations of kinaesthetic analogues for musical schemes. *Bulletin of the Council for Research in Music Education, 131,* 2–13.

Cole, M. (1996). *Cultural psychology: a once and future discipline.* New York: Harvard University Press.

Colwell, R. (Ed.) (2002). *The new handbook of research on music teaching and learning.* New York: Maxwell Macmillan.

Cook, N. (1994). Perception: a perspective from music theory. In R. Aiello & J. Sloboda (Eds.), *Musical perceptions* (pp. 64–95). New York: Oxford University Press.

Cook, N. & Everest, M. (Eds.) (1999). *Rethinking music.* New York: Oxford University Press.

Cuban, L. (2001). *Oversold and underused: computers in the classroom.* Cambridge, MA: Harvard University Press.

DeNora, T. (2000). *Music in everyday life.* New York: Cambridge University Press.

Dewey, J. (1897, January 16). My pedagogic creed (Article IV). *The School Journal, LIV*(3), 77–80.

Dewey, J. (1916). *Democracy and education: an introduction to the philosophy of education.* New York: Macmillan.

Di Rocco, S. T. (1969, April). The child and the aesthetics of music. *Music Educators Journal, 55*(8), 34–36, 105–108.

Dissanayake, E. (2007). In the beginning: Pleistocene and infant aesthetics and 21st-century education in the arts. In L. Bresler (Ed.), *International handbook of research in arts education* (Vol. II, pp. 783–97). Dordrecht, the Netherlands, Springer.

Dreyfus, H. (2004). *A phenomenology of skill acquisition as the basis for a Merleau-Pontian non-representationalist cognitive science.* Regents of the University of California. Retrieved May 10, 2007, from http://socrates.berkeley.edu/ hdreyfus/html/papers.html

Drummond, J. (2003). *Musical diversity in music education*. Paris: International Music Council.

Dunn, R. E. (1997). Creative thinking and music listening. *Research Studies in Music Education, 8*, 3–16.

Dunn, R. E. (2006). Teaching for lifelong, intuitive listening. *Arts Education Policy Review, 107*(3), 33–38.

Egan, K. (2005). *An imaginative approach to teaching*. San Francisco: Jossey-Bass.

Elliott, D. (1995). *Music matters: a new philosophy of music education*. New York: Oxford University Press.

Encyclopædia Britannica (2009). Gestalt psychology. *Encyclopædia Britannica Online*. Retrieved 4 February 2009 from http://search.eb.com/eb/article-9036624

Encyclopædia Britannica (2007). Phylogeny. *Encyclopædia Britannica Online*. Retrieved 29 September 2007 from http://search.eb.com/eb/article-9059861

Espeland, M. (1987). Music in use: responsive music listening in the primary school. *British Journal of Music Education, 4*(3), 283–97.

Espeland, M. (1991). *Music in use: selections of music for schools* (Volume 1). Stord: Stord lærarhøgskule (Stord University College).

Espeland, M. (1992a). *Musikk i bruk* [Music in use]. Stord: Stord lærarhøgskule (Stord University College).

Espeland, M. (1992b). What are they going to listen to? Problems and opportunities in the selection of music for educational music listening in schools. In H. Lees (Ed.), *Music education: sharing the musics of the world. Proceedings of the 20th world conference of ISME* (pp. 67–72). Christchurch: Christchurch University Press.

Espeland, M. (2001). *Lyttemetodikk. Studiebok* [Listening methodology. Study book]. Bergen: Fagbokforlaget.

Espeland, M. (2004). *Lyttemetodikk. Ressursbok* [Listening methodology. Resource book]. Bergen: Fagbokforlaget.

Fiske, A. P., Kitayama, S., Markus, H. & Nisbett, R. (1998). The cultural matrix of social psychology. In F. L. Gilbert (Ed.), *The handbook of social psychology* (pp. 915–68). New York: MacGraw-Hill.

Forbes Milne, A. (1931, September 1). Musical appreciation: a Lausanne Resolution (in Letters to the Editor). *The Musical Times, 72*(1063), 829.

Geertz, C. (1973). *The interpretation of cultures*. New York: Basic Books.

Haack, P. (1992). The acquisition of music listening skills. In R. Colwell (Ed.), *Handbook of research on music teaching and learning* (pp. 451–64). New York: Maxwell Macmillan.

Harper, D. (2002). *Process*. Online Etymology Dictionary. Retrieved 17 April 2002 from http://www.etymonline.com/index.php?search=process&searchmode=none

Henegan, F. (2001). Report: a review of music education in Ireland, incorporating the Final Report of the Music Education National Debate (MEND Phase III). Dublin: Dublin Institute of Technology.

Jorgensen, E. R. (2003). *Transforming music education*. Bloomington: Indiana University Press.

Kerchner, J. L. (1996). Perceptual and affective components of the music listening experience made manifest through children's verbal, visual, and kinesthetic responses. Unpublished doctoral dissertation, Northwestern University, Evanston, Illinois.

Kerchner, J. L. (2000). Children's verbal, visual, and kinesthetic responses: insight into their music listening experience. *Bulletin of the Council for Research in Music Education, 146*, 31–50.

Langer, S. (1942). *Philosophy in a new key: a study in the symbolism of reason, rite, and art.* Cambridge, MA: Harvard University Press.

Lave, J., & Wenger, E. (1991). *Situated learning: legitimate peripheral participation.* Cambridge, MA: Cambridge University Press.

MacPherson, S. (1910a). *Form in music.* London: Joseph Williams.

MacPherson, S. (1910b). *Music and its appreciation, or the foundations of true listening.* London: Joseph Williams.

MacPherson, S. (1912). *Studies in phrasing and form.* London: Joseph Williams.

MacPherson, S. (1915). *The musical education of the child.* London: Joseph Williams.

MacPherson, S. (1934). The present position of the appreciation movement in musical education. IV (Concluded). *The Musical Times, 75*(1091), 55–57.

MacPherson, S., & Read, E. (1912). *Aural culture based upon music appreciation* (Part I). London: Joseph Williams.

MacPherson, S., & Read, E. (1915a). *Aural culture based upon musical appreciation* (Part II). London: Joseph Williams.

MacPherson, S., & Read, E. (1915b). *Aural culture based upon musical appreciation* (Part III). London: Joseph Williams.

MacPherson, S. (1915c). *The musical education of the child.* London: Joseph Williams.

McElligott, J. B. (1919). The gramophone as an aid to musical appreciation. *The Musical Times, 60*, 696–97.

Merleau-Ponty, M. (1962). *Phenomenology of perception.* New York: Routledge.

Meyer, L. B. (1956). *Emotion and meaning in music.* Chicago: University of Chicago Press.

Miller, G. (2003). The cognitive revolution: a historical perspective. *Trends in Cognitive Sciences, 7*(3), 141–44.

Mills, J. (1993). *Music in the primary school.* Cambridge: Cambridge University Press.

Murphy, R. (2007). Harmonizing assessment and music in the classroom. In L. Bresler (Ed.), *International handbook of research in arts education* (Volume I, pp. 361–79). Dordrecht: Springer.

Murphy, R., & Espeland, M. (2007). *UPBEAT—Teacher's resource books (Infants through sixth class).* Dublin: Carroll Education.

Mursell, J. L. (1937/1971). *The psychology of music.* New York: Greenwood Press.

Nielsen, F. V. (2004). Music education and the question of musical meaning. A theory of music as a multispectral universe: basis for a philosophy of music education. RAIME Seventh International Symposium, Bath, England.

Peterson, E. M. (2006). Creativity in music listening. *Arts Education Policy Review, 107*(3), 15–21.

Plummeridge, C. (2007). Schools, §III: From the 19th century: the growth of music in schools. *Grove Music Online.* Retrieved 20 April 2007 from http://www. oxfordmusiconline.com/subscriber/article/grove/music/43103?q=Schools%2C+§III%3 A+From+the+19th+century%3A+The+growth+of+music+in+schools.+&search=quic k&source=omo_gmo&pos=14&_start=1S43103.3

Reimer, B. (2003). *A philosophy of music education.* New York: Prentice Hall.

Reimer, B. (2006). Introduction to symposium on music listening, its nature and nurture. *Arts Education Policy Review, 107*(3), 3–4.

Reimer, B. (2007). Roots of inequity and injustice: the challenges for music education. *Music Education Research, 9*(2), 191–204.

Salt, M. (1912). Music and the young child: the realization and expression of music through movement. In S. MacPherson & E. Read (Eds.), *Aural culture based upon musical appreciation* (pp. i–xv). London: Joseph Williams.

Savage, J. (2005). Information communication technologies as a tool for re-imagining music education in the 21st century. *International Journal of Education & the* Arts, *6*(2). Retrieved 10 January 2007 from http://www.ijea.org/v6n2/

Savage, J. (2007, November). Reconstructing music education through ICT. *Research in Education, 78*, 65–77.

Scholes, P. A. (1935). *Music appreciation: its history and technics.* New York: M. Witmark & Sons.

Seashore, C. E. (1938/1967). *Psychology of music.* New York: Dover Publications.

Small, C. (1998). *Musicing. The meanings of performing and listening.* Hanover: Wesleyan University Press.

Subotnik, R. R. (1996). *Deconstructive variations. Music and reason in western society.* Minneapolis: University of Minnesota Press.

Swanwick, K. (1994). *Musical knowledge: intuition, analysis and music education.* London: Routledge.

Thoresen, L. (2007). Form-building transformations: An approach to the aural analysis of emergent musical forms. *Journal of Music and Meaning.* Retrieved 12 December 2007 from http://www.musicandmeaning.net/issues/showArticle.php?artID=4.3

Tipton, G., & Tipton, E. (1961). Adventures in music, Grade 2. *Adventures in music.* New York: Radio Corporation of America.

Upitis, R. (1992). *Can I play you my song? The compositions and invented notations of children.* Portsmouth, NH: Heinemann Educational Books.

Vygotsky, L. S. (1978). *Mind in society: the development of higher psychological processes.* Cambridge, MA: Harvard University Press.

Walker, R. (2001). The rise and fall of philosophies of music education: looking backwards in order to see ahead. *Research Studies in Music Education, 17*, 3–19.

Wertsch, J. (1998). *Mind as action.* New York: Oxford University Press.

Wiggins, J. (2001). *Teaching for musical understanding.* Boston: McGraw-Hill.

Zerull, D. S. (2006). Developing music listening in performance ensemble class. *Arts Education Policy Review, 107*(3), 41–46.

Chapter 8

Learning in and through music performance: understanding cultural diversity via inquiry and dialogue

Susan O'Neill

Introduction

> Tolerance, inter-cultural dialogue and respect for diversity are more essential than ever in a world where peoples are becoming more and more closely interconnected. People of different religions and cultures live side by side in almost every part of the world, and most of us have overlapping identities which unite us with very different groups. We can love what we are, without hating what—and who—we are not. We can thrive in our own tradition, even as we learn from others, and come to respect their teachings. (Annan, 2004)

In this quotation, Kofi Annan, the former Secretary-General of the United Nations, reminds us of two concepts that are central to theory and research in cultural psychology—self and culture. He also articulates one of the central principles of cultural diversity in education—to foster 'tolerance, inter-cultural dialogue and respect for diversity'. At the same time, Annan highlights the inherent tensions that exist when educators try to fulfil two contradictory social agendas: acknowledging and mediating the unique identity of individuals or groups while at the same time occupying a shared space where all people, regardless of their cultural background, feel a sense of value and belonging. Although these social agendas are both rooted in notions of equality and respect; they often come into conflict in social and educational situations (Taylor, 1994). How do we learn to 'love what we are, without hating what—and who—we are not'? How do we 'thrive in our own traditions' while also learning about the cultural traditions of others in a way that will foster mutual respect? These are key questions facing today's music educators, who acknowledge the importance of cultural diversity in education and seek ways to foster it *in and through* their music performance practices.

Recent work in cultural psychology has begun to explore theoretical frameworks that involve the mutual inclusion of *self and culture in action* (Hermans, 2001; Sullivan, 2007; Sullivan & McCarthy, 2005). These frameworks draw on the concepts of *dialogue* and *experience-based inquiry* to illustrate the ways that learning in and through our experiences offers the potential and possibility for changing our perceptions of both self and other. This chapter discusses these ideas in relation to music performance and cultural diversity in education. But first, I describe some of the challenges that music performance educators face as they respond to the growing and problematic cultural–political agendas associated with *multiculturalism*.

Multiculturalism and challenges facing music performance educators

Music educators, like their counterparts in other disciplines, have responded to the growing public discourses on multiculturalism by developing curriculum initiatives aimed at promoting multicultural awareness. Expectations are high in terms of what music educators have to offer for increasing students' acceptance of, and respect towards, cultures that differ from their own (Boyce-Tillman, 2004; O'Neill, 2008, 2009). And yet, according to Gutmann (1995), the concept of multiculturalism in education is insufficiently debated and poorly understood. Rarely comprehensive or contextualized, many multicultural curriculum initiatives fail to take into account (among other things) the multiple perspectives of those who are involved. The outcome tends to produce 'watered down' classroom or school cultural events that have little impact on students' mutual respect for the artistic practices that take place in the world around them. Huddleston Edgerton (1996) provides a familiar anecdote that illustrates this approach:

> In one elementary school I visited, a Christmas program was produced in which the children sang a variety of songs. Out of ten songs (performance of which included costumes and some acting), eight were traditional Christian songs, one was "Hanukkah Is Here," and the other was "Calypso Noel." I suppose the intent was to foster multi-cultural awareness and tolerance. How even this modest and misguided ambition would be realized within the clear centrality of an Anglo-Christian holiday and ceremony is beyond me. It was clear whose religious tradition set the scene for any others. (p. 13)

Although the multicultural strategy described above may be supplemented by examining particular historical periods and regions of the world, this often amounts to no more than a superficial overview. Too often 'facts' are interpreted as 'truths' about particular people and events. At best, this approach merely adds a multicultural patina to standard curriculum structures or practices by incorporating a few token gestures that are often bounded, inauthentic, and stereotypical representations. What we learn by being involved *in music performance*, even when the performers and/or the choice of repertoire are culturally diverse, does not necessarily translate into increased mutual respect and intercultural dialogue. Instead, any culturally diverse variation in music performance is likely to be evaluated (albeit implicitly) in terms of the dominant cultural model and either accepted, assimilated, ignored, or rejected by students without any thoughtful discussion of their *lived experience*. According to McCarthy (1988), the strategies that educationalists use for adding multiculturalism to the school curriculum only serve to legitimatize the dominance of Western culture. Indeed, pedagogical approaches to 'multicultural' or 'world' music in the classroom typically involve strategies in which the dominant cultural norm forms the basis for interpreting all other musical practices. Such performance practices are more than likely to strengthen inherently privileged cultural traditions, making them the norm against which all other musical practices are considered different and therefore deviant (Huddleston Edgerton, 1996).

Many multicultural music performance practices emphasize the importance of bringing learners from different backgrounds together in ways that will help them 'find common ground'. However, finding common ground does not necessarily encourage students to respect each other's rights and differences (e.g. Shehan Campbell, Dunbar-Hall, Howard, Schippers & Wiggins, 2005; see also review by Russell, 2007). Working toward a consensus or sharing a common experience are frequent goals in music performance education that do not necessarily provide opportunities for mutually constructing understanding in a way that will foster growth, new insights and learning transformations. Although multicultural events provide minority students with a voice and visibility, they create a situation in some schools where students in the majority become mere spectators who can sit back and enjoy the music without having to think about the meaning of the songs and their importance to others. Further, Perry (2001) contends that in schools where white students represent the majority, these students may see themselves in a privileged position but they lack an understanding of how this situation arose.

When children enter school they are enculturated into what is often referred to as *school music*. Deeply rooted within the Western classical music tradition, school music in many countries consists of learning to perform in various music ensembles, such as the school band, orchestra or choir. Despite sharing many similar features or qualities, school musical performances are deemed 'different' from the dominant cultural model of music-making that learners experience in the world outside of school. This is not to say that school performance practices are not valued. Rather, their worth is judged through a different set of criteria and expectations that seem to coexist alongside those used to evaluate performance practices associated with the dominant cultural model. For most learners, the two coexist in a way that is potentially mutual and yet autonomous (i.e. school versus the 'real world' outside school). As such, learners develop a passive acceptance of what constitutes school versus non-school performance practices (O'Neill, 2002).

Once learners come to understand what constitutes a musical performance within a particular school or outside school context, their perceptions are often resistant to change and disconfirmation. Instead of accommodating or accepting new performance practices, there is a tendency for students to ignore or reject those practices that do not conform to their existing models (see for example, Harrison & O'Neill, 2000, 2002, 2003, and O'Neill, 1997, for related examples associated with gender stereotypes and musical instruments). This poses particular difficulties for educators who wish to develop multicultural or pluralistic musical understandings alongside the dominant and traditional school music curriculum.

In order to bring about change in our musical and cultural understandings, I believe it is necessary to move through and beyond utilitarian notions of music performance education. Although the performances that typically take place in concert halls, school auditoriums and outdoor playing fields serve as dominant cultural models of what constitutes legitimate musical practices, they become problematic in an educational setting if the learning outcomes that are explicitly valued and expected only concern the acquisition and display of music performance skills. This approach reinforces the idea that music teachers can neglect wider sociocultural and moral agendas provided that their students are producing legitimate forms of conventional music-making. By not providing an opportunity for students to *examine and question their involvement in music performance* beyond the skills needed to produce a particular performance, it is unrealistic to believe that music education will function in any meaningful way beyond one of training and indoctrination in 'classical conservatoire' or other such narrowly defined traditions. It is even less likely that students will be given the opportunity to consider the 'taken-for-grantedness' of their music performance practices in a way that avoids a mere rapprochement of existing perspectives.

There are various ways in which musical performances are experienced and negotiated as the process is complex and infused with multiple layers of meaning for teachers and students. As such, music performance provides an opportunity for learners to do more than demonstrate their knowledge and skills. It can also actively engage students in a learning process that will deepen their understanding and increase their sense of the different cultural lenses through which they come to see themselves and others (Skelton, 2004). What is needed is an approach that fosters cultural diversity in education by learning in and through music performance. This approach would need to encourage students to view music performance not only as a form of music-making, but also as a lens through which teachers and students, together, may awaken a part of themselves and those musical and cultural understandings that might otherwise remain dormant or frozen. For this to occur it is first necessary to create a momentary space for interaction that encourages the exploration of difference and hope; a space that facilitates the transformation of perspectives.

The recent and pervasive public discourses on cultural diversity have encouraged a new emphasis, across disciplines, on the social practices associated with the interdependence of people, cultures and language. As such, the notion of cultural diversity in education has moved beyond the 'inclusiveness' agenda of multiculturalism and evolved into a form of social action where meanings and symbols of cultures are actively produced through complex processes of translation, negotiation and dialogue. In order to address some of the problems music educators face in fulfilling the social responsibility agendas described above, I will outline some recent theorizing in cultural psychology that offers a useful framework for examining our existing practices and developing future research in this area.

Cultural diversity and cultural constructionist psychology

Since at least the early part of the twentieth century, with the so-called 'linguistic turn' theorists have been focusing on the performative role of language, and the interconnectedness of culture in actively producing forms of knowledge and meaning-making (Rorty, 1992). In cultural psychology, this movement gained considerable momentum with Jerome Bruner's assertion that psychological research must take into account the cultural context, thereby blurring the lines between psychology and anthropology (Bruner, 1990). Cultural anthropologists also began to argue that cognition 'cannot be extricated from the historically variable and culturally diverse intentional worlds in which it plays a coconstitutive part' (Shweder, 1990, p. 13).

One of the most influential conceptualizations in the field of cultural psychology draws heavily on the work of Lev Vygotsky and his view of human development as an emergent process from which higher mental functioning develops out of social interaction. Vygotsky (1978) described learning as embedded within social events and occurring as a learner interacts with people, objects, and events in the environment (Kublin, Wetherby, Crais & Prizant, 1989). His ideas form the basis of sociocultural theory (see further, Wertsch, 1991, 1998), which has had a substantial influence on contemporary educational theory and practice.

One of the most significant contributions to our understanding of how language and culture are interdependent is found in Kenneth Gergen's (1985, 1991, 1994) theoretical work on social constructionist psychology (see further, Burr, 1995). Central to the social constructionist approach is the idea that our understanding of the world is historically and culturally specific and that knowledge of the world is negotiated or constructed. Our negotiated understandings of the world take place primarily through language. Words gain meaning within communicative relationships from which new forms of social action can emerge. From within a framework of cultural constructionist psychology, Gergen and Gergen (1997) purport that:

> because meaning is a human construction, precariously situated within ongoing patterns of coordinated action, it is always open to transformation. Transformation may begin with play, poetry, experimentation, or any other form of action that falls outside the reiterative patterns of daily life. It may also begin with new arrangements of communication, new models of dialogue, which invite exploration of the forgotten, the suppressed, or the other. (p. 33)

Simply put, if we engage dialogically with others, particularly with those who are not like us, we have the potential to transform ourselves through the process.

Increasingly, cultural psychologists have been considering the significance of dialogue as a form of *self and culture in action* (Hermans, 2001; Sullivan, 2007; Sullivan & McCarthy, 2005). According to Hermans (2001), this conception of self and culture provides for 'a multiplicity of positions among which dialogical relationships can develop'. while at the same time avoiding 'the pitfalls of treating the self as individualized and self-contained, and culture as abstract and reified' (p. 243). Drawing on the work of the American psychologist William James and the Russian literary theorist Mikhail Bakhtin, Hermans proposes a model for understanding the dialogical self that incorporates both temporal and spatial characteristics. Temporal characteristics are a fundamental feature of stories or narratives and have also been central to the work of Bruner (1986), Gergen and Gergen (1997) and McAdams (1993). The spatial dimension of self is expressed through the notion of 'positioning', which is also found in the work on positioning theory proposed by Harré and Van Langenhove (1991). However, Hermans emphasizes Bakhtin's recognition of the spatial dimension of narrative as 'juxtaposition' in order to acknowledge that dialogical voices, such as those that take place between people from different cultures, are 'neither identical nor unified, but rather heterogeneous and even opposed' (2001, p. 249). These oppositional spaces provide what Hermans refers to as 'contact zones' that offer a meeting point between cultural groups where 'meanings and practices of the contacting partners change as a result of communication, understandings and misunderstandings' (p. 273). From this perspective, a focus on self and culture in action provides opportunities for music educators and researchers to explore questions such as: What happens to the beliefs and values of individuals, and their own musical practices, when they engage in extensive contact with another cultural form of music-making? How do learners respond to discrepancies between real and imagined experiences resulting from prolonged experiences in these 'contact zones'?

In building on and extending the work of Hermans (2001), and incorporating other key theorists such as McNamee and Shotter (2004), Sullivan and McCarthy (2005) explore the concepts of dialogue and experience-based inquiry. Sullivan (2007) provides an interesting example of how dialogue changes the way we look at situations beyond those we might have intentionally set out to change. When Sullivan was studying artists' experiences of making art, he hoped that by making art himself he might understand the artists he was studying better. Instead, he believed that by making art he changed 'to viewing his academic work as being much closer to the artists' experience than his nascent art experience. This opened up his view of the text as material for a more artistic, creative participation than he had previously felt' (Sullivan & McCarthy, 2005, p. 635). His work encourages a focus on dialogism in cultural psychology. According to Sullivan (2007):

> 'spirit' and 'soul', sense of action and action, are two dimensions of dialogue that potentially offer contemporary cultural psychology a significantly different view of the self–other boundary. The struggle for meaning, in particular, lies at its core as an ambiguous, creative and dilemmatic process. Taking account of this struggle may help us to understand the variety and complexity of social action and self-identity. (p. 125)

Although the above outline offers only a brief introduction to recent theorizing in cultural psychology, it illustrates how these approaches might begin to challenge existing cultural models, thereby opening up possibilities for meaning-making and developing students' understandings of cultural diversity in and through music performance. In the next section, I will outline the ways in which inquiry-based dialogical approaches have developed in educational theory and practice, and highlight some of the implications for music performance education.

An inquiry-based dialogical approach to music performance education

Historically, both philosophical and pedagogical approaches have emphasized the importance of inquiry and dialogue in the pursuit of knowledge and understanding. The fundamental position that dialogue has occupied in approaches to education dates back to the time of Socrates and Plato. More recently, the moral and political ramifications of inquiry and dialogue in the pursuit of egalitarianism and democratic education have been discussed by influential scholars such as Dewey (1916), Bruner (1966), Rogers (1969), and Freire (1994).

Inquiry refers to the process of using selected questions to guide our learning in a way that is exploratory and responsive, yet focused on something of importance to us. Inquiry is often triggered by experiences that challenge us. We might feel excited, curious, uncertain, confused, or frustrated by what is happening in a particular situation. The questions that come to mind at these times signal a learning opportunity. We can let the questions and uncertainties overwhelm us, or we can use them deliberately to focus attention on what we might learn from the situation. Inquiry in education is a student-centred approach that encourages students to ask questions which are meaningful to them, and which do not necessarily have easy answers (Awbrey & Awbrey, 1995; Hubbard & Power, 1993). Inquiry-based programmes encourage music performance educators to be reflective problem solvers and agents of change, critical consumers of published research, and generators of their own knowledge by examining their own understandings of music performance practices. The process of inquiry is defined as 'critical and transformative, a stance that is linked not only to high standards for the learning of all students but also to social change and social justice and to the individual and collective professional growth of teachers' (Cochran-Smith & Lytle, 1993, p. 38).

An inquiry-based approach asks learners to consider a driving question about the nature or function of music performance in school and outside school contexts. The question would emerge through a conversation with the student about his or her understanding of a particular performance, for example, such as its origins and history. Once a driving question has been identified, it is necessary for students to make active investigations that will dispel myths and allow space for new truths and understandings to emerge. Finally, an inquiry-based approach encourages collaboration among students, teachers, and others in the music community with the aim of sharing knowledge, music and stories so that a new understanding of cultural diversity is both fostered and established. Some key characteristics of inquiry include: (a) 'driving questions' that are anchored in a real-world problem; (b) opportunities for students to make active investigations that enable them to learn concepts, apply information, and represent their knowledge in a variety of ways; and (c) collaboration among students, teachers, and others in the music community so that knowledge can be shared.

At the heart of an inquiry-based approach is dialogue. Dialogical learning focuses on developing the skills and qualities necessary for students to become effective communicators and active citizens in today's fluid and multicultural society. It requires a learning environment that builds trust and facilitates the development of caring relationships and a learning community. Education dating back to the time of Plato is premised on the notion that to be educated in music and other disciplines depends on developing the specific knowledge, competence and character that will enable individuals to make reasoned judgements and become responsible and engaged members of their community (Nussbaum, 1997). Thinking about music performance as dialogue enables us to see more clearly what is distinctively valuable in education by pointing out the centrality of the moral and intellectual virtues in civilized life and educative teaching (T. Kazepides, unpublished manuscript; McNamee & Shotter, 2004).

Although inquiry and dialogue provide useful heuristics for thinking about music performance education, not all musical learning situations lend themselves to developing children's understandings of cultural diversity. However, by creating a musical environment that builds trust and facilitates the development of caring relationships and a 'community of knowers', it is more likely that students will unite in a shared experience of trying to make sense of the musical practices and lived experiences of themselves and others. In considering the role of dialogic inquiry in education, Wells (2000) draws on Vygotsky's concept of artefact-mediated joint activity, which involves change and transformation of participants and settings over time. From this concept follow a number of important implications for thinking about learning and teaching cultural diversity in education. These implications, which are also related to the previously discussed cultural psychology theoretical perspectives, provide a useful framework for music performance educators to consider the role of cultural diversity in education as an integral part of their music performance practices. I have therefore adapted them as a beginning set of overarching principles for music performance education, as follows:

1. *Music performance groups should be encouraged to view themselves as a collaborative community of learners.* According to Wells (2000), 'joint activity, by definition, requires us to think of the participants not simply as a collection of individuals but also as a community that works toward shared goals, the achievement of which depends on collaboration' (p. 60).

2. *Music performance activities should be purposeful and involve 'self and culture in action' by taking into account the lived experiences of the whole person.* 'Learning is not simply the acquisition of isolated skills or items of information, but involves the whole person and contributes to the formation of individual identity' (Wells, 2000, p. 60). As Gergen and Gergen (1997)

remind us, engaging dialogically with others, particularly with those who are not like us, offers the potential to transform ourselves through the process. Learning activities should be aimed at increasing learners' sense of the different cultural lenses through which they come to see themselves and others.

3. *Music performance activities are situated in place and time; each encounter offers unique 'contact zones' of interaction.* Hermans (2001) refers to these 'contact zones' as a meeting point between cultural groups where 'meanings and practices of the contacting partners change as a result of communication, understandings and misunderstandings' (p. 273). Stories are shared and meanings are negotiated among individuals 'all of which have their own histories, which, in turn, affect the way in which the activity is actually played out' (Wells, 2000, p. 61).

4. *Music performance activities are a means, not an end, to achieving cultural diversity in education.* Music performance should not be seen as part of a cultural 'tool kit' but as a means for carrying out activities that are of personal as well as cultural significance to all participants. Sullivan (2007) reminds us that it is in the struggle for meaning, as an ambiguous, creative and dilemmatic process, that we may begin to understand the variety and complexity of self and culture in action.

5. *Music performance outcomes are both aimed for and emergent.* According to Wells (2000), outcomes of activity cannot be completely known or prescribed in advance. 'Although there may be prior agreement about the goal to be aimed for, the route that is taken depends on emergent properties of the situation—the problems encountered and the human material resources available for the making of solutions' (p. 61).

6. *Music performance activities must allow for diversity and originality.* 'Development involves "rising above oneself," both for individuals and for communities. Solving new problems requires diversity and originality of possible solutions. Without novelty, there would be no development; both individuals and societies would be trapped in an endless recycling of current activities, with all their limitations' (Wells, 2000, p. 61).

To move beyond traditional, dominant and narrow conceptualizations of music performance education, teachers need to expand their focus beyond practical concerns, such as how to teach music performance skills effectively, how to increase students' motivation, and how to create a successful ensemble programme. Innovative approaches are needed that will encourage dialogue and forms of participation in music that lead to thoughtful and collaborative explorations of a wider range of voices and cultural practices. It is necessary for teachers to make a concerted commitment to fostering students' musical and cultural understandings through a vision of music performance as 'alive' and capable of generating meaning. This type of music performance education is saturated with a motivational force that is not found in homogenized musical activities. As Deleuze (1995) purports, 'we set against this fascism of power active, positive lines of flight, because these lines open up desire' (p. 19). Opening up positive lines of flight, enhancing desire, and generating motivation are worthy educational aims for music educators in and of themselves. In order to provide students with opportunities to experience a measure of excellence that is coupled with both an emotively charged experience and an enduring growth of character, we need to consider innovative approaches to music performance education that hold the possibility of being more than a way to teach people how to sing or play instruments.

Cultural diversity in education and learning transformations

Perspective transformations or transformative learning is about creating 'possibility and potential' as well as 'mutuality and interdependence' so that learners can be active co-constructors in the pursuit of understanding *self and culture in action*. Perspective transformations refer to the processes of becoming aware and critical of how and why our assumptions about the world act as barriers and constraints to our understandings and actions. According to Mezirow (1991), changing our meaning schemes (specific beliefs, attitudes, and emotional reactions) 'make(s) possible a more inclusive, discriminating, and integrating perspective' (p. 167). In other words, perspective transformations occur when individuals change their frames of reference by becoming aware of, and reflecting critically on, their assumptions and beliefs, and consciously making and implementing plans that bring about new ways of defining their cultural understanding (Goldblatt, 2006).

Mezirow's (1990) theory of transformative learning describes learning as an intricate process of integrating new information with the personal perspectives and values that have developed through life experience. According to Mezirow (1991), for learners to change their 'meaning schemes' (specific beliefs, attitudes, and emotional reactions such as those encountered during a musical performance), they (the learners) must engage in critical reflection on their experiences, which in turn leads to a transformation in their perspective.

> Perspective transformation is the process of becoming critically aware of how and why our assumptions have come to constrain the way we perceive, understand, and feel about our world; changing these structures of habitual expectation to make possible a

more inclusive, discriminating, and integrating perspective; and, finally, making choices or otherwise acting upon these new understandings. (Mezirow, 1991, p. 167)

In other words, transformative learning occurs when individuals change their frames of reference by reflecting critically on their assumptions and beliefs and consciously making and implementing plans that bring about new ways of defining their worlds (Mezirow, 1997). Dialogue-directed reflection is central to this process, encouraging listeners to test their own perspectives about unfamiliar personal paradigms that can accommodate different points of view (Mezirow, 1990).

In arts education, scholars argue that it is ethically and morally necessary to embrace cultural diversity as a vehicle for social action that can be used to inform, challenge, and broaden conceptualizations and representations of self and other (e.g. Kuster, 2006; Schensul, 1990). According to Balin (2006), arts education offers:

An articulated experience into the beliefs and practices of other cultures . . . It helps us to see our assumptions, to recognize the contingency of our beliefs and practices, to notice they are embedded in larger networks of beliefs and social arrangements, to see other possibilities. But there is still the need to evaluate, to see how and whether aspects of other beliefs and practices are relevant to ours, to see to what extent our views are mutually compatible or whether there may be more than one possibility, to compare them in accord with the standards of rational inquiry as well as with criteria related to our human goals and purposes, and with moral principles which we have good reason to believe are fundamental. And, in light of all this, there is still, ultimately the need to make judgments about what to accept, about whether to alter any of our beliefs and practices – or not. But whatever we end up deciding, we come to the evaluative enterprise with a fuller and more complex repertoire of resources. And we come from the enterprise with a richer, subtler and more nuanced understanding; and with better justified beliefs.

There is growing recognition among music educators that acquiring the knowledge and skills necessary to sing or play an instrument is not the same as being *educated in music* or an *educated musician*. To be educated in music, an individual must also develop his or her mind and character. At the very least, music education must reflect the cultural values of a given society. However, a musically educated person is more than just knowledgeable about music from his/her own and other cultures. According to T. Kazepides:

Well-educated people are able to pursue any subject in some depth describing phe-nomena with clarity and precision, explaining the reasons why certain things are the case, talking about works of art, music and literature in an informed way, evaluating arguments with appropriate criteria and knowledge, examining their and others' beliefs, assumptions, commitments and the like. They are not passive recipients of ideas; they are active and able to distinguish between those things that are required by reason and those that are allowed by reason; they can see what is literally true and what might be metaphorically appropriate or suitable in specific circumstances. "To be educated," said R. S. Peters very aptly, "is not to have arrived at a destination; it is to travel with a different view." ('Education as dialogue', unpublished manuscript, p. 43)

An inquiry-based dialogical approach to learning may help to increase our awareness of the momentary relational and dialogical spaces occurring in and through music performance education and provide opportunities to foster cultural diversity in education. However, there are few conceptual frameworks or research findings to help us further our understanding of these practices in music education. The problem with philosophical approaches is that they can be idealized and prescriptive; they tell us little about how students and teachers actually experience dialogue-based learning approaches in real educational settings. An important first step in developing the necessary conceptual frameworks is for researchers to examine existing practices to further our understanding of how students and teachers experience dialogue as both a learning process and as a pedagogical approach within the context of music performance education. To promote discussion and ideas that may inspire the development of research in this area, I will next explore the significance of inquiry-based dialogical approaches to cultural diversity in education through a story that serves as both a metaphor and an illustration of the types of musical and education encounters researchers might explore.

Dwelling in the margins of culture through dialogue and inquiry

The appropriation of the 'linguistic turn', the application of cultural constructionist psychology, and the advances in inquiry-based dialogical education have broadened and deepened our conceptualization of cultural diversity in education. The ways in which groups, individuals and ideas come to be marginalized in a given culture, society, and/or community have much to do with what is considered to be knowledge and whom is considered to possess it—whom is perceived as knower and whom/what is perceived as known (Isar, 2006). In many ways, the marginalized are in a position to know more about the group, community, culture, society or other forces that keep them from the centre than can members of that centre know about the margins (Freire, 1970). Also, those in the centre have marginal aspects of self through which they gain a broader or differentiated perspective or a distance from self from which to reflect. Yet, the margin and the centre cannot exist without each other—they are relational—they define and are defined by each other. Both are necessary, although the margin must gain knowledge of the centre to survive (however, the reverse is not necessarily true to the same extent). It is therefore a choice to dwell in the margins and gain multiple perspectives around self, other, and community.

According to Huddleston Edgerton (1996), stories that take place in the margins 'offer us alternative ways of constructing and performing meaning in our lives, which affect the ways we read texts and the world' (p. 39). A curriculum of marginality refers to this storytelling approach–one that focuses on autobiography and provides an opportunity for us to 'choose to dwell in the margins' (p. 39). For educators, creating a curriculum of marginality is also about excavating excluded stories, or telling stories with 'unique outcomes in the interest of constructing and performing alternative meanings and ways of being in the world' (p. 39). Egan (1992) tells us that 'stories are good for "educating us into the virtues" because the story not only conveys information and describes events and actions but because it also engages our emotions . . . The story, in short, is the ability to exchange experiences' (Benjamin, 1969, as cited in Egan, 1992, p. 55). This story-telling approach is also an inquiry-based dialogical approach that can help explore cultural diversity by encouraging divergent stories to come together and form ways of making new meanings possible by creating spaces where no one owns the truth and everyone has the right to be heard and understood.

In exploring these ideas further, I will draw on Toni Morrison's 1993 acceptance speech for the Nobel Prize in Literature. Morrison provides both an exemplar and a metaphor for the notion of inquiry and dialogue in music education. To illustrate her point (which I will later recreate as a metaphor for music performance education), Morrison tells a story of an old, wise Black woman who is blind but believed to have special powers to see and heal by people in her rural community. One day, the old woman is approached by some young people from the city. They want to expose her as the fool and fraud they believe her to be. Knowing the old woman is blind, they demand that she tell them whether the bird one of them is holding is alive or dead. The old woman's response is soft but stern: 'I don't know. I don't know whether the bird you are holding is dead or alive, but what I do know is that it is in your hands. It's in your hands.' (p. 11) The repetition is Morrison's and it is not repeated for emphasis. The shift in stress (apparent in the oral version but not in the published written text) from 'in your hands' to 'in your hands' signals the young people's responsibility for the bird—its life or death.

Morrison develops the old woman's reprimand into an extended metaphorical passage, treating the bird as language: either alive (generating meaning) or dead (destroying or denying meaning). Morrison says:

> If the bird in the hands of her visitors is dead, the custodians are responsible for the corpse. For [the old woman] a dead language is not only one no longer spoken or written, it is unyielding language content to admire its own paralysis . . . Ruthless in its

policing duties, it . . . actively thwarts the intellect, stalls conscience, suppresses human potential. Unreceptive to interrogation, it cannot form or tolerate new ideas, shape other thoughts, tell another story. (pp. 13–14)

Let us re-enact the story and make the old woman a music teacher who is well-respected in his or her school or community, but who is approached by a group of new students who want to know if the teacher believes the music they are playing is alive, exciting, and interesting, or dead, dull, and boring. Now the story would involve the music teacher telling the young people that the life or death of the music is in *their* hands—they have the power to make the music interesting and exciting or dull and boring. If, however, the students are content to play only music that they predetermine to be interesting and exciting, they are being 'ruthless in [their] policing duties' and '[suppressing their] potential'. Only by creating a space for all music to 'form . . . new ideas, shape other thoughts, tell another story'. can we truly begin to understand the transformative power of musical performance education—the performance of music that is deeply embedded in our cultural understanding and sense of who we are and who we could become.

The story could end there and the old woman's words—extended by Morrison's metaphorical treatment—could be taken as profoundly wise and generative. It seems a good example of the concept of generativity—a concept that can be traced back at least 2,500 years to Plato's notion of immortality and the externalization of the self. It is a concern for establishing and guiding the next generation. It is about caring for and educating young people by assuming the role of responsible adult—a parent, guardian, mentor, teacher. It is also about being a responsible citizen, a contributing member of a community, a leader, and an enabler (see further, O'Neill, 2006).

But Morrison's story does not end there. In Part Two, Morrison returns to the 'cruel and misguided youth' and shows them the inadequacies and limitations of the *old woman's words*—words that at first seemed full of potential for teaching and transforming. Instead, the words are shown to be a way of ignoring and closing down meaning, completely shutting the young people out. It turns out that the children had no bird in their hands, and, refusing to be silenced or put in their place by the old woman, they responded:

Your answer is artful, but its artfulness embarrasses us and ought to embarrass you. Your answer is indecent in its self-congratulation . . . Why didn't you reach out, touch us with your soft fingers, delay the sound bite, the lesson, until you knew who we were? . . . You trivialize us and trivialize the bird that is not in our hands (pp. 25-26)

The children speak back. They demand that the old woman gives them authentic language, the true and rich particularities of her own life stories, and in turn tell her a poignant story of their own, as an example of what they are looking for from her.

The old woman, once given access to *their* story, comes to know and trust them. The two parts of the story come together and intertwine. Everyone is changed in the process: the old woman and her young interlocutors (and, of course, the listeners to Morrison's speech). The old woman's parting words are, 'I trust you now. I trust you with the bird that is not in your hands because you have truly caught it. Look. How lovely it is, this thing we have done— together.' (p. 30)

Morrison's faith in stories and language as a route toward transformative learning inspires us to be willing and active co-constructors of connections between music, performance and learning. Among other things, Morrison provides us with an insight into how we might learn to 'love what we are, without hating what—and who—we are not' (Annan, 2004). She also offers us an insight into how we might 'thrive in our own traditions' while also learning about the cultural traditions of others in a way that will foster mutual respect (Annan, 2004). But first we need to embrace the value and importance of the two parts of the story. We might refer to Part One of the story as creating opportunities for 'possibility and potential' as students discover that the responsibility for their musical performance is 'in their hands'. The students are given the responsibility for keeping the music and the performance practice alive (generating meaning) or dead (destroying or denying meaning). However, it is not until Part Two that we encounter the necessary reciprocal relationships that are associated with 'mutuality and interdependence'. Morrison shows the limitation of one-sided monologues—of only telling one story or completely shutting the young people out of the story—as a way of ignoring or closing down meaning. Mutuality and interdependence provide an opportunity for worlds and stories to be made and re-made through contact with one another.

Revisioning opportunities and enabling cultural diversity in education

Morrison's notion of the transformative power of narrative offers a powerful metaphor for exploring the transformative power of music performance education within a cultural constructionist psychology framework that fosters cultural diversity in education. As Buber (1965) points out, dialogue is situated in the 'between-ness' of an interpersonal relationship rather than with one point of view or another. In other words, dialogue has a performative function as an effective means of ongoing communication that is based on notions of equality, openness and mutual respect. Initial research and practice in the use of inquiry-based dialogical education have revealed it to be a powerful approach to teaching and learning (Burbules, 1993; Schoem & Hurtado, 2001). Audiences and applications are varied but are united in approaching dialogue-based education as a meaning-making exercise that transcends the downloading of facts and information to become a form of pedagogy that emphasizes growth in students' understanding in a socially relevant and productive manner.

Dialogue establishes patterns of interaction and a framework for inquiry while encouraging students to remain open to new knowledge and insights into the diversity of musical cultures (Burbules, 1993). I recently attended a conference where a colleague told me about an innovative programme at her prestigious institution where children were composing their own opera that was later performed by a professional opera company. A teacher would work with the children in the music classroom to 'create' the opera through discussion of a storyline and improvisations by the children using electronic keyboards. The 'themes' produced by the children were recorded and later transcribed by the teacher using a synthesizer and arranged into an opera score. This 'opera composed by children' was then choreographed and staged by professionals. The children and their families were invited to attend the first performance of the opera where the children were celebrated as talented young composers.

To what extent might we consider this music curriculum initiative an illustration of an inquiry-based dialogical approach to understanding cultural diversity through musical performance? On the surface, we could offer a translation of this experience that would map onto Part One of Morrison's story in terms of 'possibility and potential' since the children initially discovered that the responsibility for the opera's creation was 'in their hands'. The students were given the opportunity to generate meaning through their musical improvisations. The conditions of an inquiry-based approach may well have been met in terms of allowing the children's ideas for the opera to emerge through discussions, having the children explore their own musical ideas for the opera, and then sharing the opera with a wider musical community beyond the school context. Seemingly, the teachers, parents and others involved in this initiative would be fulfilling the role of generative educators (cf. Postman & Weingartner, 1969).

It is not until we examine this curriculum initiative through Part Two of Morrison's story that shortcomings begin to appear. Despite the obvious limitations of sloganeering generated by this initiative (e.g. 'children compose opera'), Morrison's lens of 'mutuality and interdependence' reveals how the children are actually shut out of the musical performance, made to sit on the sidelines while the adults engage in the 'real' musical meaning-making and performance experience. Instead of fostering a developing sense of character and musical growth, and enabling an opportunity for the children's understandings of the cultural diversity of their opera to emerge through the actual performance, the children are pushed into the role of mere spectators. It is likely that the teachers have led themselves into believing that they have created an authentic educational experience for the children. Instead, the children appear to remain content to sit on the sidelines and wonder about the self-congratulatory righteousness and satisfaction that the adults appear to gain by giving them credit for a musical performance that the children themselves no longer recognize or understand. Unlike Morrison's story, the children in the opera story do not speak back. They do not know how to demand an authentic musical experience; one that would take them beyond simply meeting the opera performance criteria, and one that would enable them to move into soulful work that might awaken a part of themselves and their musical and cultural understanding.

Postmodernist and critical pedagogical approaches have tended to omit from their accounts the reflexive capacity of students and teachers (i.e. their ability to reflect inwardly about connections between the self and the social environment). As Deleuze (1995) suggests, there is a knowable domain of information about teaching that is situated 'in-between' at the border of two things that can reframe our thinking by reflecting on the beliefs, values, moral and political positionings and the particular ideologies or frames of reference used by those involved. An inquiry-based dialogical approach to music performance education provides students with a framework that encourages them to examine discursively their own perspectives about unfamiliar ideologies and conflicting values in a safe, supportive and musical environment that fosters deep reflections about music, as well as respect and intercultural dialogue, conducive to understanding cultural diversity via musical performance.

As with many innovative approaches to curriculum, inquiry-based dialogical learning draws on a number of pedagogical strategies that redefine the parameters of what constitutes the traditional form and content of what is taught (Giroux, 1994). For example, rather than view dialogue as a mere 'tool' for developing communication and problem-solving skills, it is viewed as a sociocultural process that is contextually determined, politically reactive, and inherently reflexive. It is situated within 'real-world' understandings that draw on experiential and participatory approaches to learning music in a non-judgemental and supportive environment, thereby stimulating opportunities for transformative learning and for developing a community of learning relationships. In this way, power and knowledge are united as students interact musically with the ways in which people talk about, or construct, the meaning of music performance in the world around them.

Final remarks

In response to the growing public discourses on multiculturalism, new curriculum initiatives have emerged with an epistemology that differs markedly from traditional notions of teaching and learning. Educators from across the disciplines have responded with innovative approaches such as collaborative inquiry, peer instruction, participatory learning, problem-based learning, reflective learning, service learning and others. Interestingly, each of these models uses the terminology, concepts and practice of inquiry and dialogue. Inquiry-based dialogical learning involves multiple aspects or layers of curriculum elements that address core themes in an interrelated, relational and critically reflective manner. This involves collaborative teaching and learning to discover meaning among diverse participants, and underscores a fundamental goal of the student experience: to enhance citizenship, inspire societal service, and promote mutual respect for cultural diversity.

Throughout this chapter, I have drawn on recent theorizing in cultural psychology and have incorporated frameworks that involve the mutual inclusion of 'self and culture in action' (e.g. Hermans, 2001; Sullivan, 2007; Sullivan & McCarthy, 2005). In exploring these frameworks and the concepts of 'dialogue' and 'experience-based inquiry', I have opened up the possibility for future dialogue that I hope researchers and educators will continue to join and develop. This way of learning in and through musical performance may help educators spark students' curiosity of the unknown, and guide students toward the values of a liberal education and what it means to be thoughtful citizens in a pluralistic society (O'Neill, 2002, 2005). There is a need for future work to explore the extent to which learning in and through our music performance experiences offers the potential and possibility for changing learners' perceptions of both self and other. Since cultural understanding is not a set of principles that can be acquired but rather an ideal that can be pursued, it is the pursuit of cultural understanding that needs to be the focus.

References

Annan, K. (2004, March 21). Speech by the Secretary-General of the United Nations for the International Day for the Elimination of Racial Discrimination. Retrieved 10 September 2008 from http://www.un.org/News/Press/docs/2004/sgsm9195.doc.htm

Awbrey, J., & Awbrey, S. (1995). Interpretation as action: the risk of inquiry. *Inquiry: Critical Thinking Across the Disciplines, 15*, 40–52.

Balin, S. (2006). *An inquiry into inquiry: (how) can we learn from other times and places?* Presidential address of the Philosophy of Education AGM, 62nd Annual Meeting, Puerto Vallarta, Mexico, April 21–24.

Boyce-Tillman, J. (2004). Towards an ecology of music education. *Philosophy of Music Education Review, 12*(2), 102–24.

Bruner, J. (1966). *Toward a theory of instruction*. Cambridge, MA: Harvard University Press.

Bruner, J. (1990). *Acts of meaning*. Cambridge, MA: Harvard University Press.

Buber, M. (1965). *Between man and man*. New York: Macmillan.

Burbules, N. C. (1993). *Dialogue in teaching: theory and practice*. New York: Teachers College Press.

Burr, V. (1995). *An introduction to social constructionism*. London: Routledge.

Cochran-Smith, M., & Lytle, S. L. (1993). *Inside outside: teacher research and knowledge*. New York, NY: Teachers College Press.

Deleuze, G. (1995). *Negotiations* (M. Joughin, Trans.). New York: Columbia University Press.

Dewey, J. (1916). *Democracy and education. An introduction to the philosophy of education* (1966 ed.). New York: Free Press.

Egan, K. (1992). *Imagination in teaching and learning: ages 8 to 15*. London: Routledge.

Freire, P. (1970). *Pedagogy of the oppressed*. New York: Herder & Herder.

Freire, P. (1994). *Pedagogy of hope: reliving pedagogy of the oppressed*. New York: Continuum.

Gergen, K. J. (1985). The social constructionist movement in modern psychology. *American Psychologist, 40,* 266–75.

Gergen, K. J. (1991). *The saturated self*. New York: Basic Books.

Gergen, K. J. (1994). *Realities and relationships*. Cambridge, MA: Harvard University Press.

Gergen, K. J., & Gergen, M. M. (1997). Toward a cultural constructionist psychology. *Theory and Psychology, 7,* 31–36.

Giroux, H. A. (1994). *Disturbing pleasures: learning popular culture*. New York: Routledge.

Goldblatt, P. F. (2006). How John Dewey's theories underpin art and art education. *Education and Culture, 22*(1), 17–34.

Gutmann, A. (1995). Challenges of multiculturalism in democratic education. *Philosophy of Education*. Retrieved September 5, 2007 from http://www.ed.uiuc.edu/eps/ PESYearbook/95_docs/gutmann.html

Harré, R., & Van Langenhove, L. (1991). Varieties of positioning. *Journal for the Theory of Social Behaviour, 21,* 393–407.

Harrison, A. C., & O'Neill, S. A. (2000). Children's gender-typed preferences for musical instruments: an intervention study. *Psychology of Music, 28*(1), 81–97.

Harrison, A. C., & O'Neill, S. A. (2002). The development of children's gendered knowledge and preferences in music. *Feminism and Psychology, 12*(2), 148–53.

Harrison, A. C., & O'Neill, S. A. (2003). Preferences and children's use of gender-stereotyped knowledge about musical instruments: making judgments about other children's preferences. *Sex Roles, 49,* 389–400.

Hermans, H. J. M. (2001). The dialogical self: toward a theory of personal and cultural positioning. *Culture & Psychology, 7*(3), 243–81.

Hubbard, R. S., & Power, B. M. (1993). *The art of classroom inquiry: a handbook for teacher-researchers*. Portsmouth, NH: Heinemann.

Huddleston Edgerton, S. (1996). *Translating the curriculum: multiculturalism into cultural studies*. New York: Routledge.

Isar, Y. R. (2006). Cultural diversity. *Theory, Culture & Society, 23*, 372–75.

Kublin, K. S., Wetherby, A. M., Crais, E. R., & Prizant, B. M. (1989). Prelinguistic dynamic assessment: a transactional perspective. In A. M. Wetherby, S. F. Warren & J. Reichle (Eds.), *Transitions in prelinguistic communication* (pp. 285–312). Baltimore, MD: Paul H. Brookes.

Kuster, D. (2006). Back to the basics: multicultural theories revisited and put into practice. *Art Education, 59*(5), 33–39.

McAdams, D. P. (1993). *The stories we live by: personal myths and the making of the self*. New York: William Morrow.

McCarthy, C. (1988). Rethinking liberal and radical perspectives on racial inequality in schooling: making the case for nonsynchrony. *Harvard Educational Review, 58*, 265–79.

McNamee, S., & Shotter, J. (2004). Dialogue, creativity, and change. In R. Anderson, L. A. Baxter, & K. J. Cissna (Eds.), *Dialogue: theorizing difference in communication studies* (pp. 91–104). Thousand Oaks, CA: Sage.

Mezirow, J. (1990). *Fostering critical reflection in adulthood*. San Francisco: Jossey-Bass.

Mezirow, J. (1991). *Transformative dimensions of adult learning*. San Francisco: Jossey-Bass.

Mezirow, J. (1997). Transformative learning: theory to practice. In P. Cranton (Ed.), *New directions for adult and continuing education: No. 74. Transformative learning in action: Insights from practice* (pp. 5–12). San Francisco: Jossey-Bass.

Morrison, T. (1993, December 7). Nobel Lecture: Nobel Prize in Literature. Swedish Academy. Retrieved 1 January 2000 from http://nobelprize.org/nobel_prizes/literature/laureates/1993/morrison-lecture.html

Nussbaum, M. C. (1997). *Cultivating humanity: a classical defense of reform in liberal education*. Cambridge, MA: Harvard University Press.

O'Neill, S. A. (1997). Gender and music. In D. J. Hargreaves, & A. C. North (Eds.), *The social psychology of music* (pp. 46–63). Oxford: Oxford University Press.

O'Neill, S. A. (2002). The self-identity of young musicians. In R. A. R. MacDonald, D. J. Hargreaves & D. Miell (Eds.), *Musical identities* (pp. 79–96). Oxford: Oxford University Press.

O'Neill, S. A. (2005). Youth music engagement in diverse contexts. In J. L. Mahoney, R. Larson, & J. S. Eccles (Eds.), *Organized activities as contexts of development: extracurricular activities, after school and community programs* (pp. 255–73). Mahwah, NY: Lawrence Erlbaum.

O'Neill, S. A. (2006). Positive youth musical engagement. In G. McPherson (Ed.), *The child as musician: a handbook of musical development* (pp. 461–74). Oxford: Oxford University Press.

O'Neill, S. A. (2008). *What is cultural diversity and how is it a paradox for music educators?* Paper presented at the 28th International Society for Music Education World Conference, Bologna, Italy, July.

O'Neill, S. A. (2009). Revisioning musical understandings through a cultural diversity theory of difference. In L. Bartel (Series Ed.), E. Gould (Vol. Ed.), J. Countryman, C. Morton, & L. Stewart Rose (Eds.), *Exploring social justice: How music education might matter* (Vol. 4). CMEA Biennial Series: Research to Practice (pp. 70–89). Toronto: Canadian Music Educators Association.

Perry, P. (2001). White means never having to say you're ethnic. White youth and the construction of 'cultureless' identities. *Journal of Contemporary Ethnography, 30*, 56–91.

Postman, N., & Weingartner, C. (1969). *Teaching as a subversive activity.* New York: Dell.

Rogers, C. (1969). *Freedom to learn: a view of what education might become.* Columbus, OH: Merrill.

Rorty, R. M. (Ed.) (1992). The linguistic turn: essays in philosophical method. Chicago: University of Chicago Press.

Russell, J. (2007). [Review of the book *Cultural diversity in music education: directions and challenges for the 21st century*]. *British Journal of Music Education, 24*(1), 128–30.

Schensul, J. (1990). Organizing cultural diversity through the arts. *Education and Urban Society, 22*(4), 377–92.

Schoem, D., & Hurtado, S. (Eds.) (2001). *Intergroup dialogue: deliberative democracy in school, college, community, and workplace.* Ann Arbor: University of Michigan Press.

Shehan Campbell, P., Dunbar-Hall, Howard, K., Schippers, J., & Wiggins, R. (Eds.) (2005). *Cultural diversity in music education: directions and challenges for the 21st century.* Brisbane: Australian Academic Press.

Shweder, R. A. (1990). Cultural psychology: what is it? In J. E. Stigler, R. A. Shweder, & G. Herdt (Eds.), *Cultural psychology: essays on comparative human development* (pp. 1–43). New York: Cambridge University Press.

Skelton, K. D. (2004). Should we study music and/or as culture? *Music Education Research, 6*(2), 169–77.

Sullivan, P. (2007). Examining the self-other dialogue through 'spirit' and 'soul'. *Culture & Psychology, 13*(1), 105–28.

Sullivan, P., & McCarthy, J. (2005). A dialogical approach to experience-based inquiry. *Theory & Psychology, 15*(5), 621–38.

Taylor, C. (1994). The politics of recognition. In A. Gutmann (Ed.), *Multiculturalism* (pp. 25–74). Princeton: Princeton University Press.

Vygotsky, L. (1978). *Mind in society.* Cambridge, MA: Harvard University Press.

Wells, G. (2000). Dialogic inquiry in education: Building on the legacy of Vygotsky. In C. D. Lee, & P. Smagorinsky (Eds.), *Vygotskian perspectives on literacy research: constructing meaning through collaborative inquiry* (pp. 51–85). New York: Cambridge University Press.

Wertsch, J. V. (1991). *Voices of the mind: a sociocultural approach to mediated action.* Cambridge, MA: Harvard University Press.

Wertsch, J. V. (1998). *Mind as action.* New York: Oxford University Press.

Chapter 9

Culture, musicality, and musical expertise

Susan Hallam

Introduction

Psychological research focusing on the role of different cultures in development explores the reciprocal relationship between person and culture which leads to both the modification and creation of new cultural forms, and individual change, as a result of acculturation (Kagntcibasi, 2006). Early conceptions of culture viewed it as a given; a shared way of life of a group of socially interacting people transmitted from generation to generation through the processes of enculturation and socialization (Munroe & Munroe, 1997). More recent social constructive perspectives see culture as being interpreted and created daily through interactions between individuals and their social surroundings (Gergen & Gergen, 2000). This approach has led to a focus on the role of culture in development (e.g. Cole, 1996; Rogoff, 2003; Wertsch, 1988) with less emphasis on the biological underpinnings of human behaviour, despite the fact that cross-cultural similarities have been identified which are difficult to explain without consideration of species-specific potentials. Examples of this are the use of 'motherese', the tendency of adults in all cultures studied to date to talk to babies in a higher tone of voice and with more variations in tone (e.g. Fernald, 1992), and what has become known as 'infant-directed' singing which has particular characteristics relating to timing, phrasing and dynamic not in evidence when singing to adults (Trehub, 2003).

There are three broad theoretical approaches to understanding behaviour–culture interactions: absolutism, relativism, and universalism (Berry & Poortinga, 2006). The absolutist position assumes that human behaviour is qualitatively the same in all cultures with culture playing a very limited role. The relativist approach assumes that human behaviour is culturally defined, explaining human diversity in terms of the cultural context in which people have developed. Universalism assumes that basic human characteristics are common to all members of the species and that culture influences the development and display of them. An extension of this, the ecocultural approach, attempts to understand similarities and differences in cognition and social behaviour assuming that all human societies exhibit commonalities (cultural universals) and that basic psychological processes are shared (Berry, Poortinga, Segall & Dasen, 2002). From this perspective, cultural differences are explained in terms of ontogenetic development that differs systematically because different cultures facilitate particular routes through biologically given trajectories along which each child potentially can develop (Keller, 2002).

This chapter focuses on the processes concerned with learning and the development of musical expertise which are common to all human beings but which develop differentially depending on the environment (cultural and ecological) within which individuals are located. It considers what we know about human learning, the way that the brain develops in response to the particular musical environments to which the individual is exposed, and how these changes are expressed as musical expertise develops. The evidence regarding the importance of long-term engagement with music for expertise to develop is considered and how beliefs about personal efficacy can influence commitment to active music-making. The chapter concludes with a consideration of the different cultural perceptions of 'musicality' and changing perceptions of it in Western culture.

The universality of music

Music is universal and found in all cultures. Along with language, it distinguishes us from other species. It is at the very essence of our humanity. While the sounds that contribute towards making music exist as objective reality, for those sounds to be defined as music requires human beings to acknowledge them as such. What is acknowledged as 'music' varies between cultures, groups and individuals. In some cultures, there is no separate word for music. For instance, the Igbo of Nigeria use the term *nkwa* to denote 'singing, playing instruments and dancing' (Gourlay, 1984). The Kpelle people of Liberia describe a beautifully performed song, drum pattern or dance with the same term 'sang' which reflects the blending of the arts into one entity (Stone, 2004). Similarly, traditional Japanese music is closely connected with drama, dance and songs, the term 'geino' referring to all categories of 'humanly organized sound and movement' (see Kikkawa, 1959, p. 28). In Western culture, music is conceptualized as a separate entity. The *Oxford English Dictionary* definition describes music as 'the art of combining sounds of voice(s) or instrument(s) to achieve beauty of form and expression of emotion'—a definition which relies on subjective judgements which may vary from individual to individual.

Despite the variability in what constitutes 'music', there is general agreement that music is a universal trait of humankind (Blacking, 1995) which may have evolutionary significance. This is supported by the discovery of musical instruments from a range of early cultures (see Carterette & Kendall, 1999). Music exemplifies many of the classic criteria for a complex human evolutionary adaptation (Miller, 2000) and a range of evolutionary purposes has been suggested (Huron, 2003), although some have argued that music, along with the other arts, has no evolutionary significance or practical function. Pinker (1997), for example, suggests that music exists simply because of the pleasure that it affords, and its basis is purely hedonic.

Underlying these debates is the assumption that *Homo sapiens* as a species has the propensity for musical development and that musicality is as universal as linguistic ability (Blacking, 1971; Wallin, Merker & Brown, 2000). Recent neurological research supports this view, suggesting that there are two key elements to musical processing, one concerned with the encoding of pitch, and one ascribing regular beat to incoming events. Musical structures in the brain to support such processing are present and functional early in human development (Peretz, 2003).

Human learning

Learning is a natural process for human beings. We are preprogrammed to learn. In our everyday lives, during our interactions with others and with the environment, we are constantly engaged in learning. This may be deliberate and intentional or incidental and without conscious awareness. Whether what we have learned is retained in the long term depends on the extent of our ongoing engagement with it and how important it is to us. Indeed, whether we attend to particular stimuli in the environment at all depends on the brain's assessment of the extent to which these stimuli may be important to us. We begin to develop musical representations from the first moment that we are exposed to the music within our culture. As we shall see later in the chapter, this can occur before we are born.

In the same way that they can be bilingual, individuals can be bimusical (Hood, 1960), having an understanding of and being proficient in the technical requirements and stylistic nuances of two distinct musical systems either between or within cultures (O'Flynn, 2005). Cultures may be multimusical (Nettl, 1983), and are becoming increasingly so with recent technological developments and globalization which have made music from all cultures available worldwide. The underlying neural mechanisms which enable us to perceive, understand, and perform music in our own culture are capable of facilitating understanding of the music of any culture if we spend sufficient time engaging with it. This has long been illustrated in 'intermusicality', a process where musicians import specific practices and nuances from one style or performance context to others (Monson, 1996).

What can studies of the brain tell us about learning in music?

Human beings have not changed biologically or genetically over the past 7,000 years, although the environment is constantly changing. Our physiology provides us with the basis for learning, but what we learn is determined by our environment, both within the family and the wider groups within society with which we engage (Kim, Yang & Hwang, 2006). The culture to which we are exposed therefore shapes the musical structures which we develop, and the way that we enact these in our lives.

Although our knowledge of the way the brain works is in its infancy, some of the fundamental processes involved in learning have been established. The human brain contains approximately 100 billion neurons, each of which has considerable processing capacity (some estimates suggest that each is the equivalent of a modest-sized computer). A considerable proportion of the 100 billion neurons are active simultaneously and information-processing is undertaken largely through interactions between them, each having approximately a thousand connections with other neurons. During the learning process there are changes in the growth of axons and dendrites and the number of synapses connecting neurons, a process known as synaptogenesis. When an event is important enough or is repeated sufficiently often, synapses and neurons fire repeatedly indicating that this event is worth remembering (Fields, 2005). In this way changes in the efficacy of existing connections are made. Over time, as learning continues and particular activities are engaged with, myelinisation takes place. This involves an increase in the coating of the axon of each neuron which improves insulation and makes the established connections more efficient. Pruning also occurs, a process which reduces the number of synaptic connections, enabling fine-tuning of functioning. Through combinations of these processes, which occur over different timescales, the cerebral cortex self-organizes in response to external stimuli and our learning activities (Pantev, Engelien, Candia & Elbert, 2003). These are determined by the culture in which the individual is located.

Much learning occurs without our conscious awareness (Blakemore & Frith, 2000). For instance, when we listen to music or speech we process an enormous amount of information rapidly. The ease with which we do this depends on our prior musical and linguistic experiences and the culturally determined tonal scheme or language to which we have become accustomed (Dowling, 1993). This knowledge is implicit, learned through exposure to particular environments, and is applied automatically whenever we listen to music or speech. Permanent and substantial reorganization of brain-functioning takes considerable time. Research on Western classical musicians has shown that long years of active engagement with particular musical activities are associated with an increase in neuronal representation specific to the processing of the tones of the musical scale, with the largest cortical representations found in musicians playing instruments for the longest periods of time (Pantev et al., 2003). Changes are also specific to the particular musical learning undertaken (Munte, Nager, Beiss, Schroeder & Erne, 2003). Processing of pitch in string players, for example, is characterized by longer surveillance and more frontally distributed event-related brain potentials attention. Drummers generate more complex memory traces of the temporal organization of musical sequences, and conductors demonstrate greater surveillance of auditory space (Munte et al., 2003). Compared with non-musicians, string players have greater somatosensory representations of finger activity, the amount of increase depending on the age of starting to play (Pantev et al., 2003). Clearly, the brain develops in very specific ways in response to particular learning activities, and the extent of change depends on the length of time engaged with learning. Although the research to date has been undertaken with Western classical musicians, the assumption is that the underlying neurological processes are the same for groups of musicians in other cultures.

The ways in which we learn are also reflected in specific brain activity. When students (aged 13–15) were taught to judge symmetrically structured musical phrases as balanced or unbalanced using traditional instructions about the differences (including verbal explanations, visual aids, notation, verbal rules, playing of musical examples), or participating in musical experiences (singing, playing, improvising or performing examples from the musical literature), activity in different brain areas was observed (Altenmuller, Gruhn, Parlitz, & Kahrs, 1997). This suggests that the tools and practices used to support the development of particular musical skills in any culture will have a direct influence on brain development and, subsequently, on preferred approaches to undertaking musical tasks.

Taken together, the evidence suggests that the brain substrates of processing reflect the 'learning biography', of each individual (Altenmuller, 2003, p. 349). Individual learning biographies in turn reflect the available opportunities and influences within the prevailing culture. As we engage with different musical activities over long periods of time, permanent changes occur in the brain.

These changes reflect not only what we have learned but also how we have learned. These processes underpin cultural variation in musical processing. What neuropsychological research cannot tell us is how these long-term changes in the brain affect information-processing, learning, problem-solving, and undertaking creative activities. We must turn to the literature on the development of expertise to explore these issues.

Learning as the development of expertise

Research on the development of expertise is characterized by exploration of the ways in which individuals acquire specific skills and knowledge in a domain, and how thinking and learning processes change as expertise develops, reflecting the changes in the brain described above. Across a range of domains, a number of common characteristics of expert performance have been identified (Chi, 2006; Glaser & Chi, 1988). While much research has focused on expert performance in Western cultures, the overarching features have been explored across sufficient domains for us to have reasonable confidence that the broad principles will transfer to expert performance across different musical cultures.

Experts perceive large meaningful patterns in their domain

In music, for example, when reading notation, skilled readers do not fixate on each note, their fixations are directed across line and phrase boundaries, scanning ahead and returning to the current point of performance (Goolsby, 1994). They scan the page more efficiently and require shorter and fewer fixations to compare or encode material for execution than novices because they are able to grasp more information in one fixation (Waters, Underwood & Findlay, 1997). They can continue to read/recall about six or seven notes after removal of the printed page, whereas poor readers only manage about three or four (Goolsby, 1994). Similarly, professional composers take a more holistic view of compositions on which they are working, and maintain this global conceptual understanding while working on locally arising problems. Novices consider only local features or isolated individual sounds, whereas those working at a higher level adopt a Gestalt-like approach, demonstrating the ability to consider the detail of the task within the structured whole (Younker & Smith, 1996).

Experts are fast

Experts work faster than novices. Hours of engagement with relevant activities ensure that skills are automated to high levels, thus freeing up memory capacity for processing other aspects of the task. This has been demonstrated across a wide range of domains, including chess, music, typing, physics, and route planning (see Chi, Glasser & Farr, 1988).

Experts have superior short-term and long-term memory

Experts do not have a greater capacity in their short-term memory than novices, but the automaticity that they develop in relation to many of their skills frees up working memory for other tasks. Kauffman and Carlsen (1989) showed that musicians recalled musical material better than non-musicians especially when the material was structured to rules of tonality. Their superiority decreased when tonality rules were violated or when random note sequences had to be recalled. We would expect a similar phenomenon if musicians were asked to memorise sequences from a different cultural tonality.

Experts see and represent a problem in their domain at a deeper level than novices and spend a great deal of time analysing a problem qualitatively before attempting a solution

The conceptual categories which experts adopt in problem-solving are semantically and principle-based, whereas those of novices are syntactically or surface-feature-oriented. Experts spend time trying to understand the problem that they are trying to resolve, building a mental representation from which they can infer relations, define the situation, and add constraints to the problem. This can be seen most clearly when problems are ill-defined, for example in creative processes. Collins (2005), for instance, studying a single composer, demonstrated strategies operating at micro and macro levels. At the outset, a clear mental picture of the composition was in place, which acted as a loose framework throughout the process. Problem proliferation and successive solution implementation occurred not only in a linear manner, but also recursively. Moments of Gestalt creative insight were observed, which related to problem restructuring. Some insights were seen to overlap in real time, others indicated an element of parallelism in thinking. There were no clear boundaries between the various stages. For each problem arising, solutions themselves were conjectured, implemented, or deferred.

Experts have strong self-monitoring skills

Experts have well-developed metacognitive and self-monitoring skills. They know why they make errors, why they fail to comprehend, when they need to check their solutions, and what they need to do next. They are better than novices in judging the difficulty of a problem, and in selecting appropriate strategies to solve problems (Hallam, 1995, 2001a).

The way that expert skills are developed limits their transferability and can lead to rigidity (Chi, 2006). High levels of expertise in listening to and understanding music within a particular cultural tonality and idiom do not transfer to similar understanding in relation to music from other cultures. Even within the same musical tonality, transfer to a different genre can be problematic. For instance, Sudnow (1978), a highly skilled, adult, professional, classical musician, documented how tedious, effortful, frustrating and time-consuming was the experience of acquiring expertise in jazz improvisation, while some classically trained musicians experience difficulties in performing atonal or rhythmically complex music which does not conform to Western classical norms (Hallam, 1995). Similarly, Russell (2002), in a study of traditional cross-generational communal singing practices in the Fiji Islands, where children participate in a musical practice which is encountered in church, school, family and peer groups, found that replication of traditional practices limited innovation and constrained children's capacities to improvise.

Stages in the acquisition of expertise

Although much expertise in music-listening develops without our conscious awareness as a result of enculturation, three main stages have been identified in the acquisition of expert levels of musical performance (Fitts & Posner, 1967). There is initially a cognitive–verbal–motor stage at which learning is consciously controlled; the learner understands what is required and carries it out while consciously providing self-instruction. Learning is supported when the learner has a clear mental representation of both the process and the goal of learning, and when feedback is available, either directly from the environment or from observers. In the associative stage, the learner begins to put together a sequence of responses which become more fluent over time. Errors are detected and eliminated, and feedback from others or self-monitoring continues to be important. In the final autonomous stage, the skill becomes automated, is carried out without conscious effort, and continues to develop each time it is used, becoming quicker and more fluent. As automaticity develops, the component processes become unavailable to conscious inspection and learners have difficulty in explaining their actions to others (Fitts & Posner, 1967). Acquiring procedural skills and knowledge in a domain are inextricably intertwined. Knowledge-based mental representations of appropriate musical outcomes are required to check for errors, to select possible strategies, and to monitor progress (Hallam, 1995, 2001a, 2001b). These representations are acquired through enculturation, and differ depending on the culture within which the individual is raised.

The beginnings of the development of expertise

Musical expertise is acquired in relation to particular communities of practice which may operate at a number of different levels. Specific tonal and rhythmic structures, for example, can provide an overarching framework for a range of musical genres, which may then develop distinctive learning and performance contexts and related communities of practice. While all of these can evolve over time, tonal structures within cultures seem to be particularly resistant to change, perhaps because they are learned and automated early, alongside spoken language.

The incidental learning of musical structures which are predominant in any single culture begins before birth, the human auditory system being functional five to six months following conception. After 28 to 30 weeks of gestation, fetuses react to external sounds, their heart rates varying as a result of exposure to music (Woodward, 1992). The process of musical enculturation begins from that point. Infants show recognition responses to music that they have heard in the womb both before and immediately after birth (Hykin et al., 1999) and are significantly more soothed and attentive to music that their mothers have listened to daily during the last three months of pregnancy (Hepper, 1988). Lullabies to which infants have been repeatedly exposed in the latter part of their development are also preferred over unfamiliar melodies (Panneton, 1985). Trevarthen (1999) has argued that hearing external sounds and the rhythm of the mother's body provide the fetus with early musical experiences which impact on the structures and functions of the auditory system nervous pathways. Familiarization with specific sounds contributes to sensitivity to them and to subsequent infant preferences for given voices (particularly that of the mother), the maternal language, music sung by the mother, or particular musical sequences (Lecanuet, 1996).

From birth, the infant has well-developed systems for processing music. Infants are predisposed to attend to melodic contour, rhythmic patterning and consonant sounds, and are similar to adults in their sensitivity to the pitch and rhythmic grouping of sounds. However, the complex skills required for understanding and analysing music within any particular culture take time to develop, and depend on the type and extent of exposure to music. In early infancy, parents and the family play a crucial role in musical enculturation. There are long-established traditions of musical parenting, including singing, rhyming and moving infants rhythmically, and these occur across cultures (Gottlieb, 2004; Trehub & Trainor, 1998; Trehub, Unyk & Trainor, 1993). These processes, known as communicative musicality (Trevarthen & Malloch, 2002), share common characteristics (Trehub, 2003). When singing to infants, adults tend to sing at a higher pitch and slower tempo than normal, and exaggerate the emotional aspects of the song (Papousek, 1996). While there appear to be cultural variations in these interactions, with subtle differences in tempo, dynamic intensity, and rhythm, the basic structure within which they occur is similar for all, and facilitates the enculturation of the child into the particular musical tonality of his or her culture.

Although research on the development of musical skills has largely been undertaken within Western cultures, it is likely that there is commonality across cultures related to the time taken for appropriate musical representations to develop in the brain. In Western cultures, infants tend to begin to make spontaneous babbling or singing sounds, distinguishable from speech in terms of patterns of pitch and rhythm, which ultimately lead to spontaneous singing. Later, infants begin to spontaneously generate music which has systematic form, uses discrete pitch levels, repetition of rhythmic and melodic contours, and is recognizable as song (Ostwald, 1973). However, infants lack a stable pitch framework, and in any single song a very limited set of phrase contours is used (Dowling, 1984). It is not until about the age of five years that individual contours and intervals are produced accurately, and children can produce recognizable songs with stable tonality.

In Western cultures, there are wide individual differences in the extent to which pre-school children engage in singing; for some it is a part of almost all activity, whereas others only sing occasionally (Sundin, 1997). Home background plays a crucial role. Young, Street, & Davies (2007), in a study in England, found that babies and very young children experienced a wide variety of music at home from many sources, including toys, television, music-playing equipment and live music. Live singing of children's songs seems to be only one element of a wider range of musical stimuli to which children in modern Western societies are exposed (Street, Young, Tafuri & Ilari, 2003; Young & Gillen, 2006; Young et al., 2007). New technologies have vastly changed the musical environment, and as children play they are able to select from the wide array of cultural tools which are available to them. Children are not passive recipients of the musical culture within which they are located. They appropriate and adapt components of adult music-making and the popular media in their invented songs (Barrett, 2000, 2003), becoming 'meme engineers' engaged in the production and communication of musical culture.

Acquiring high levels of musical expertise

The Western classical tradition is one example of a community of practice, which, over the years, has spawned activity in a range of expert roles, including performance, composition, improvisation, evaluation, and analysis. Any or all of these may contribute to undertaking paid employment as a performer, composer, educator, therapist, critic, or more recently as a member of the music industries involved in the recording, production and promotion of music. The nature of what is now acknowledged to be expert musical skill in modern developed societies is much broader than was previously the case. Despite this, most research has focused on the nature of the acquisition of high-level performance skills. Undertaken within the expertise paradigm, findings have supported the importance of time engaged with individual musical practice as the key determinant of the level of expertise attained, as opposed to inherited ability. For instance, it has been established that classical Western musicians need to have accrued up to 16 years of individual practice to achieve levels which will lead to international standing in playing an instrument, the individual usually beginning to play at a very early age with increasing amounts of practice being undertaken, up to as much as 50 hours a week by adolescence (Sosniak, 1985).

While there are ongoing debates relating to the actual time required to be spent in individual 'deliberate practice' in order to attain high levels of expertise (Ericsson, Krampe & Tesch-Romer, 1993) as opposed to other musical activities—for instance, playing in a range of musical groups, playing more than one instrument, composing, or listening—there is powerful evidence that a considerable time investment in active engagement in music making is necessary. The specific amount of time is influenced by the demands of particular genres and instruments, for instance, jazz guitarists (Gruber, Degner, & Lehmann, 2004) and singers tend to begin formal training later than many classical instrumentalists (Kopiez, 1998), whereas different instrumental groups of conservatoire students practise for different amounts of time (Jorgensen, 2002). There is also evidence that cumulative practice does not predict the quality of performance at any particular point in time (Hallam, 1998a, 2004; Williamon & Valentine, 2000). Teachers' ratings of musical ability, self-esteem and involvement in extracurricular music activities are better predictors of examination marks than time spent practising (Hallam, 2004).

Studies of those dropping out of formal music tuition support the contention that time spent engaged with music may not be the only predictor of high levels of attainment. They show that complex relationships between prior knowledge, motivation, effort and perceived efficacy influence decisions to continue or discontinue learning (Hallam, 1998a, 2004; Sloboda, Davidson, Howe & Moore, 1996). When a child begins to learn an instrument, prior musical knowledge affects ease of learning and the time needed to achieve mastery of a task. Although undertaking additional practice may compensate for lack of prior knowledge, this has a time cost and requires perseverance.

If a task proves challenging, the effort required to complete it may be perceived as too great, and the individual may give up learning (Hurley, 1995). Difficulties may be attributed to a lack of musical ability, leading to a loss of self-esteem, loss of motivation, less practice, and a downward spiral, eventually leading to the termination of lessons (Asmus, 1994; Chandler, Chiarella, & Auria, 1987). Beliefs about musical ability can have a major impact on motivation and willingness to continue engagement with music. Cross-cultural differences in such beliefs may therefore impact on commitment to engage with music.

The focus on individual practice in much of this research has led to a relative neglect of the importance of engaging in a variety of group or other musical activities, including listening and analysis. Communal learning is very effective. Higher education music students in England reported benefits to their musical, technical, personal, and social skills, through learning in groups (Kokotsaki & Hallam, 2007), while Green (2001) showed that popular musicians acquired most of their skills through informal learning. Individuals learn from each other through processes of demonstration, discussion, and the actual practice of making music. These skills seem to develop early, with even quite young children being able to act as teachers. Studies of children's development of singing games in the school playground have shown that they adapt components of familiar games and songs using a variety of techniques, including reorganization of formulae, elaboration through addition of new material or expansion of known material, condensation through omission or contraction of formulae, and recasting of material (Marsh, 1995). Change is achieved through group processes of collaborative interaction that rely on close observation, kinaesthetic modelling, the shadowing of musical sound and action, and repetition of new games (Marsh, 1999). Similarly, Barrett and Gromko (2002), in a study of the learning and performance of three new works composed for a specific community project, found that participating children aged 9–12 years drew on the expertise of others, their previous experiences, and their observations of the learning experiences of their peers, and brokered their learning in adopting and adapting practices from other learning contexts such as private music lessons.

Explaining early attainment of high levels of expertise

Despite the growing neurophysiological evidence indicating the universality of the predisposition to learn music, and the growing consensus that the development of musical skills depends on committed and long-term active engagement with music, there continues to be an ongoing debate relating to the extent to which the propensity to develop musical skill is genetically determined at the individual level. Currently available research methodologies are unable to provide conclusive answers to this question. The evidence from

studies of identical and fraternal twins, and other family members, on meas-
ured musical intelligence is mixed (Gardner, 1999; Hodges, 1996; Shuter-
Dyson, 1999), and advances in research on genetics, to date, have been unable
to provide conclusive answers. Few human behaviours or traits have been
traced to specific gene pairs, and it is likely that those individuals who exhibit
high-level musical skills are drawing on a range of different gene combinations—which exert an influence on physical—in addition to cognitive and
emotional—development. The increasing recognition that there are complex
interactions between the environment and genetic inheritance make it unlikely
that there will be any simple answers (Ceci, 1990). This is particularly the case
as the acquisition of knowledge, in itself, affects the efficiency and effectiveness
of the processes by which more knowledge is acquired, alongside the ability of
the cerebral cortex to self-organize in response to external stimuli, including
music (Rauschecker, 2003).

Studies of savants and child prodigies, who attain high levels of expertise
early, stress the importance of the environment in the development of their
skills (Sloboda, Hermelin & O'Connor, 1985; Young & Nettlelbeck, 1995).
Many savants have language disorders and limited sight, perhaps increasing
development of auditory processing skills and the use of music as a means of
communication. Savants spend a great deal of time practising their skills, in
part because they receive considerable positive reinforcement for doing so
(Miller, 1989). Many of the musical characteristics of savants and child prodigies, and the supportive nature of their family environments, are similar,
despite the marked differences in relation to general intellectual functioning
(Ruthsatz & Detterman, 2003). Recent theorizing from neuroconstructivism
suggests that such marked developmental differences may be best conceived as
the outcome of atypical constraints operating on the normal developmental
process. An atypically developing trajectory affects the interactions of others
with the child, and the kind of experiences that the child seeks out, which further impacts on the trajectory (Mareschal, Johnson, Sirois, Spratling, Thomas
& Westerman, 2007). In instances in which parents designate their child as
having musical ability, they may provide musical resources and reward musical activity, leading the child to further engagement with music, supporting
increasing levels of expertise, and the development of particular neural structures, which makes future musical learning easier. Such familial responses may
occur in relation to savants and prodigies.

Musicality

There are no agreed definitions of the terms musicality, musical ability,
aptitude, talent, and potential, and they are often used interchangeably. The

meanings are constructed by each author who adopts them, and reflect the cultural, political, economic, and social factors pertaining in that place, at that time (Blacking, 1971). However, there has been a tendency for the term 'musicality' to be adopted when referring to the species-specific characteristics of human beings, the other terms being used to refer to individual differences. Music ability, often, although not exclusively, is used to refer to the current level of musical skills that an individual exhibits, whether acquired through genetic inheritance or learning, whereas aptitude, talent and potential tend to refer to musical skills perceived to be based on inherited factors. The use of such terms has reflected the needs of societies to differentiate between individuals on the basis of musical skills, for the purposes of selection to nurture what is perceived as developing talent.

In some parts of the developing world such selection is unnecessary, as the functions of music relate to cultural rituals which are shared by all. For instance, Blacking (1973) explored the nature of musicality in the Venda of the northern Transvaal in South Africa where everyone was regarded as capable of making music and no-one was excluded from participating in musical performance (Blacking, 1967). Goodale (1995), studying the Kaulong, an agrarian culture in Papua New Guinea, in which singing and dancing were an integral part of everyday life, also found that the children learned to sing, dance, hunt and make magic spells through observation and participation rather than systematic instruction. Singing was considered equal to speaking, with children learning to sing at the same time or prior to learning language. Despite this, 'some children were seen to be exceptional at a very early age' (Goodale, 1995, pp. 120) and were singled out for special treatment, with high standards expected of them. Similarly, if the Wolof Griots of Senegal identified a child as particularly talented, he was taken under the wing of a male relative and trained until he was sufficiently skilled to take a minor part in a public festival (Campbell, 2006). In some areas of Western Africa, there are secret societies in which older children are expected to leave their homes to live for a time in enclosures in the forest, Poro for males and Sande for females. There they receive instruction in the traditions and values of their culture, with music and dance featuring strongly. Once again there is specialized training for those perceived as talented to become solo singers, instrumentalists or dancers (Stone, 2004). It seems that the identification of those perceived as capable of high levels of musical achievement is not exclusive to developed societies, although it is particularly acute in those societies that wish their art to be of the highest quality, in order to reflect the wealth, power, and superiority of that society, or where there is a desire to control the arts. For instance, in China in the 1980s, the role of the musician was determined by the state and training was only available for a limited number of professional musicians who were assigned to fill existing places as players or teachers. These places were highly sought after. The family was crucial in identifying talent and ensuring that it was nurtured. Children started to play early, with the family instigating lessons and monitoring a strict regime of practice to ensure success (Lowry & Wolf, 1988).

A stark example of the way that musical ability is socially constructed comes from Japan where, in general, in common with other Eastern cultures, children's attainment is seen to depend on effort rather than innate ability (Stevenson & Lee, 1990). Western music was introduced into schools in Japan some 120 years ago. Prior to this there were no terms for music or musical ability. A clear link came to be established between 'ongaku-sei' (musicality) and the ability to perform Western music (Fujita, 2005), which did not apply to engagement with and learning in Japanese folk ensembles outside school. The introduction of Western culture brought with it Western beliefs about ability, but only in relation to Western music.

In the late nineteenth century, in the UK and the USA, the need to allocate limited resources to those perceived as most likely to benefit led to the development of the testing of 'musical ability', which paralleled the development of the testing of intelligence, sharing the same assumptions; that ability was genetically based, relatively immutable, and unchanging. The tests, and the way that the measures were interpreted, were based on their developers' beliefs about the nature of musical ability. For instance, Seashore et al. (1960) believed that musical ability was a set of loosely related basic sensory discrimination skills, which had a genetic basis, and would not change over time, except for variation due to lapses of concentration. They believed that a musical profile should be obtained which could be divided into pitch, loudness, rhythm, time, timbre, and tonal memory. In contrast, Wing (1981) believed in a general ability to perceive and appreciate music, rather than a profile. More recent developments have acknowledged that any measure of musicality can only be considered within prevailing musical cultural norms. For instance, Karma (1985) suggests that sense of tonality, rhythm and harmony are all culturally specific and that musical aptitude is the general ability to make sense of these various elements from whatever culture they derive. The most recent developments in musical ability testing reflect the technological advances of the latter half of the twentieth century. Individualized computer-based systems can now assess the recognition of change in synthesizer-produced melodies (Vispoel, 1993). These changes reflect the way in which assessment processes over time respond to developments in cultural tools.

Greater access to music in the modern world, through the media and increased educational opportunities, has led to a change in conceptions of musical ability, in that other factors—apart from aural perception—are now perceived to be key defining elements. A wide range of skills is now acknowledged to contribute to musical attainment, including motor skills (Gilbert, 1981); creativity (Vaughan, 1977; Webster, 1988); sight-reading; performing rehearsed music; playing from memory; playing by ear, and improvising (McPherson, 1995/6); and aural, cognitive, technical, musicianship, performance and learning skills (Hallam, 1998b). Few of these skills can be tested prior to the child actively engaging with music. In a study of perceptions of those engaged in identifying gifted musicians, Haroutounian (2000) found that general behaviours of 'sustained interest' and 'self-discipline' were considered more important in identifying potentially gifted children than music-specific characteristics indicative of music aptitude among educators. In another study, Hallam and Prince (2003) found that 71% of respondents defined musical ability as the ability to play a musical instrument or to sing. These responses reflect the process of identification of musical ability which seems to prevail in the cultures described earlier, in which ability is identified on the basis of developing practical skills. Overall, only 28% of the sample mentioned aural skills as indicative of musical ability. Personal qualities including motivation, personal expression, immersion in music, total commitment, and metacognition (being able to learn to learn), were cited most by musicians. A follow-up quantitative study (Hallam & Shaw, 2003) established that musical ability was most strongly conceptualized in relation to rhythmic ability, organization of sound, communication, motivation, personal characteristics, integration of a range of complex skills, and performing in a group. Having a musical ear came lower in the list than might have been expected, given its prominent position with regard to musical ability historically (Fig. 9.1). The conception of rhythm as being most important may reflect its central role in much Western popular culture. The high ratings given to motivation and personal commitment acknowledge the time needed to develop high-level skills. Overall, the conceptions of musical ability generated by the research were complex and multifaceted and reflected the wide range of expert end-states that occur in the music professions of the developed world.

Conclusion

There is now general acknowledgement that human beings as a species are preprogrammed to acquire a wide range of musical skills. The particular skills that are developed depend on the culture and environment within which the individual is located. These determine the type of music to which the individual is exposed and the opportunities that are available to them. Different musical cultures and traditions determine the way that music is learned and how

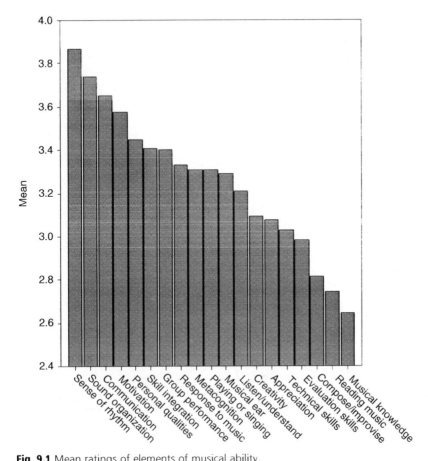

Fig. 9.1 Mean ratings of elements of musical ability.

the knowledge and skills relating to it are transferred from one generation to the next. Some traditions are inclusive, with everyone participating, whereas others require that some individuals develop high levels of expertise in performance. Where this is the case, it is important for society to identify those who, with appropriate training, will succeed in attaining the high levels of expertise required. In most cultures, this is undertaken through observing children engaged in music and differentiating on the basis of the speed of learning, and the quality of the learning outcomes. In developed countries, tests of musical ability have been devised to facilitate the identification of so-called 'musical children'. However, there is an increasing recognition that there is no measurement system which can assess 'innate' capacity, and that aural tests do not take account of the child's motivation to engage with music. They can only assess the level of musical expertise already acquired, which depends on prior experiences with music. Future research might usefully try to work in an interdisciplinary fashion, across the various research paradigms which contribute to our understanding of the development of musical skills, to provide further insights into the role of early experiences in different musical cultures, and how this contributes to the later development of expert specialist musical skills in those, or indeed other, cultures.

References

Altenmuller, E. O. (2003). How many music centres are in the brain? In I. Peretz & R. Zatorre (Eds.), *The cognitive neuroscience of music* (pp. 346–56). Oxford: Oxford University Press.

Altenmuller, E. O., Gruhn, W., Parlitz, D., & Kahrs, J. (1997). Music learning produces changes in brain activation patterns: a longitudinal DC-EEG-study. *International Journal of Arts Medicine, 5*, 2–34.

Asmus, E. P. (1994). Motivation in music teaching and learning. *Quarterly Journal of Music Teaching and Learning, 5*(4), 5–32.

Barrett, M. S. (2000). Windows, mirrors and reflections: a case study of adult constructions of children's musical thinking. *Bulletin of the Council for Research in Music Education, 145*, 43–61.

Barrett, M. S. (2003). Meme engineers: children as producers of musical culture. *International Journal of Early Years Education, 11*(3), 195–212.

Barrett, M. S., & Gromko, J. E. (2002). Working together in 'communities of practice': a case study of the learning processes of children engaged in a performance ensemble. Paper presented at the ISME 2002 conference Bergen, Norway (CD-Rom).

Berry, J. W., & Poortinga, Y. H. (2006). Cross cultural theory and methodology. In J. Georgas, J. W. Berry, F. J. R. van de Vijver, C. Kagitcibasi & Y. H. Poortinga (Eds.), *Families across cultures: a 30 nation psychological study* (pp. 51–71). New York: Cambridge University Press.

Berry, J. W., Poortinga, Y. H., Segall, M. H., & Dasen, P. R. (2002). *Cross-cultural psychology: research and applications* (2nd edn). New York: Cambridge University Press.

Blacking, J. A. R. (1967). *Venda children's songs: a study in ethnomusicological analysis.* Johannesburg: Witwatersrand University Press.

Blacking, J. A. R. (1971). Towards a theory of musical competence. In E. DeJager (Ed.), *Man: anthropological essays in honour of O. F. Raum.* Cape Town: Struik.

Blacking, J. (1973) *How musical is man?* Seattle: University of Washington Press.

Blacking, J. (1995) *Music, culture, and experience.* Chicago: University of Chicago Press.

Blakemore, S. J., & Frith, U. (2000). *The implications of recent developments in neuroscience for research on teaching and learning.* London: Institute of Cognitive Neuroscience.

Campbell, P. S. (2006). Global practices. In G. McPherson (Ed.), *The child as musician: a handbook of musical development* (pp. 415–38). Oxford: Oxford University Press.

Carterette, E. C., & Kendall, R. (1999). Comparative music perception and cognition. In D. Deustch (Ed.), *The psychology of music* (2nd edn, pp. 725–82). London: Academic Press.

Ceci, S. J. (1990). *On intelligence—more or less: a bioecological treatise on intellectual development.* Englewood Cliffs: Prentice Hall.

Chandler, T. A., Chiarella, D., & Auria, C. (1987). Performance expectancy, success, satisfaction and attributions as variables in band challenges. *Journal of Research in Music Education*, *35*(4), 249–58.

Chi, M. T. H. (2006). Two approaches to the study of experts' characteristics. In K. A. Anders, N. Charness, P. J. Feltovich, & R. R. Hoffman (Eds.), *The Cambridge handbook of expertise and expert performance* (pp. 21–30). Cambridge, UK: Cambridge University Press.

Chi, M. T. H., Glaser, R., & Farr, M. J. (1988). *The nature of expertise*. Hillsdale: Lawrence Erlbaum.

Cole, M. (1996). *Cultural psychology: a once and future discipline*. Cambridge, MA: Harvard University Press.

Collins, D. (2005) A synthesis process model of creative thinking in composition. *Psychology of Music*, *33*(2), 193–216.

Dowling, W. J. (1984). Development of musical schemata in children's spontaneous singing. In W. R. Crozier, & A. J. Chapman (Eds.), *Cognitive processes in the perception of art* (pp. 145–63). Amsterdam: North-Holland.

Dowling, W. J. (1993). Procedural and declarative knowledge in music cognition and education. In T. J. Tighe & W. J. Wilding (Eds.), *Psychology and music: the understanding of melody and rhythm* (pp. 5–18). Hillsdale: Lawrence Erlbaum.

Ericsson, K. A., Krampe, R. T., & Tesch-Romer, C. (1993). The role of deliberate practice in the acquisition of expert performance. *Psychological Review*, *100*(3), 363–406.

Fernald, A. (1992). Human maternal vocalizations to infants as biologically relevant signals: an evolutionary perspective. In J.H. Barkow, L. Cosmides, J. Tooby, (Eds.), *The adapted mind: evolutionary psychology and the generation of culture* (pp. 391–428). New York: Oxford University Press.

Fields, R. D. (2005). Making memories stick. *Scientific American*, *292*(2), 75–81.

Fitts, P. M., & Posner, M. I. (1967). *Human performance*. Belmont: Brooks Cole.

Fujita, F. (2005). Musicality in early childhood: A case from Japan. In S. A. Reily (Ed.), *The musical human: rethinking John Blacking's ethnomusicology in the twenty first century* (pp. 87–107). Aldershot: Ashgate.

Gardner, H. (1999). *Intelligence reframed: multiple intelligences for the 21st century*. New York: Basic Books.

Gergen, M. M., & Gergen, K. J. (2000). Qualitative enquiry: tensions and transformations. In N. K. Denzin & Y. Lincoln (Eds.), *Handbook of qualitative research* (2nd edn, pp. 1025–46). Thousand Oaks: Sage.

Gilbert, J. P. (1981). Motoric music skill development in young children: a longitudinal investigation. *Psychology of Music*, *9*(1), 21–25.

Glaser, R., & Chi, M. T. H. (1988). Overview. In M. T. H. Chi, R. Glaser & M. J. Farr (Eds.), *The nature of expertise* (pp. xv–xxviii). Hillsdale: Lawrence Erlbaum.

Goodale, J. C. (1995). *To sing with pigs is human: the concept of person in Papua New Guinea*. Seattle: University of Washington Press.

Goolsby, T. W. (1994). Profiles of processing: eye movements during sightreading. *Music Perception*, *12*, 97–123.

Gottleib, A. (2004). *The afterlife is where we come from: the culture of infancy in West Africa*. Chicago: University of Chicago Press.

Gourlay, K. A. (1984). The non-universality of music and the universality of non-music. *World Music, 26,* 25–36.

Green, L. (2001). *How popular musicians learn: a way ahead for music education.* London: Ashgate.

Gruber, H., Degner, S., & Lehmann, A. C. (2004). Why do some commit themselves in deliberate practice for many years–and so many do not? Understanding the development of professionalism in music. In M. Radovan & N. Dordevic (Eds.), *Current issues in adult learning and motivation* (pp. 222–35). Ljubljana: Slovenian Institute for Adult Education.

Hallam, S. (1995) Professional musicians' orientations to practice: implications for teaching. *British Journal of Music Education, 12*(1), 3–19.

Hallam, S. (1998a). The predictors of achievement and drop out in instrumental music tuition. *Psychology of Music, 26*(2), 116–32.

Hallam, S. (1998b). *Instrumental teaching: a practical guide to better teaching and learning.* Oxford: Heinemann.

Hallam, S. (2001a). The development of metacognition in musicians: implications for education. *British Journal of Music Education, 18*(1), 27–39.

Hallam, S. (2001b). The development of expertise in young musicians: strategy use, knowledge acquisition and individual diversity. *Music Education Research, 3*(1), 7–23.

Hallam, S. (2004). How important is practising as a predictor of learning outcomes in instrumental music? In S. D. Lipscomb, R. Ashley, R. O. Gjerdingen & P. Webster (Eds.), *Proceedings of the 8th International Conference on Music Perception and Cognition.* Evanston, IL: Cambridge University Press.

Hallam, S., & Prince, V. (2003). Conceptions of musical ability. *Research Studies in Music Education, 20,* 2–22.

Hallam, S., & Shaw, J. (2003). Constructions of musical ability. *Bulletin of the Council for Research in Music Education, 153/4,* 102–107. Special Issue, 19th International Society for Music Education Research Seminar, Gothenburg, Sweden, School of Music, University of Gothenberg, 3–9 August, 2002.

Haroutounian, J. (2000). Perspectives of musical talent: a study of identification criteria and procedures. *High Ability Studies, 11*(2), 137–60.

Hepper, P. G. (1988). Fetal 'soap' addiction. *Lancet, 1,* 1147–48.

Hodges, D. A. (1996). Human musicality. In D. A. Hodges (Ed.), *Handbook of music psychology* (pp. 29–68). San Antonio, TX: IMR Press.

Hood, M. (1960). The challenge of bi-musicality. *Ethnomusicology, 4*(2), 55–59.

Hurley, C. G. (1995). Student motivations for beginning and continuing/discontinuing string music tuition. *Quarterly Journal of Music Teaching and Learning, 6*(1), 44–55.

Huron, D. (2003). Is music an evolutionary adaptation? In I. Peretz & R. Zatorre (Eds.), *The cognitive neuroscience of music* (pp. 57–77). Oxford: Oxford University Press.

Hykin, J., Moore, R., Duncan, K., Clare, S., Baker, P., Johnson, I., et al. (1999). Fetal brain activity demonstrated by functional magnetic resonance imaging. *Lancet, 354,* 645–46.

Jorgensen, H. (2002). Instrumental performance expertise and amount of practice among instrumental students in a conservatoire. *Music Education Research, 4,* 105–119.

Kagntcibasi, C. (2006). Theoretical perspectives on family change. In J. Georgas, J. W. Berry, F. J. R. van de Vijver, C. Kagitcibasi & Y. H. Poortinga (Eds.), *Families across cultures: a 30 nation psychological study* (pp. 72–89). New York: Cambridge University Press.

Karma, K. (1985). Components of auditive structuring: towards a theory of musical aptitude. *Bulletin of the Council for Research in Music Education, 82*, 18–31.

Kauffman, W. H., & Carlsen, J. C. (1989). Memory for intact music works: the importance for musical expertise and retention interval. *Psychomusicology, 8*, 3–19.

Keller, H. (2002). Development as the interface between biology and culture: a conceptualisation of early ontogenetic experiences. In H. Keller, Y. H. Poortinga & A. Schoelmerich (Eds.), *Biology, culture and development: integrating diverse perspectives* (pp. 215–40). Cambridge, UK: Cambridge University Press.

Kikkawa, E. (1959). *Hogaku kansho nyumon* [Introduction to the appreciation of traditional Japanese music]. Osaka: Sogen sha.

Kim, U., Yang, K.-S., & Hwang, K.-K. (2006). *Indigenous and cultural psychology: Understanding people in context*. New York: Springer.

Kokotsaki, D., & Hallam, S. (2007). Higher education music students' perceptions of the benefits of participative music making. *Music Education Research, 9*(1), 93–109.

Kopiez, R. (1998). Singers are late beginners. Sangerbiographien aus Sicht der Expertiseforschung. Ein Schwachstellenanalyse [Singers' biographies from the perspective of research on expertise. An analysis of weaknesses]. In H. Gembris, R. Kraemer & G. Maas (Eds.), *Singen als Gegenstand der Grundlagenforschung* (pp. 37–56). Augsberg: Wissner.

Lecanuet, J. P. (1996). Prenatal auditory experience. In I. Deliege & J. A. Sloboda (Eds.), *Musical beginnings: origins and development of musical competence* (pp. 3–25). Oxford: Oxford University Press.

Lowry, K., & Wolf, C. (1988). Arts education in the People's Republic of China: results of interviews with Chinese musicians and visual artists. *Journal of Aesthetics Education, 22*(1), 89–98.

Mareschal, D., Johnson, M. H., Sirois, S., Spratling, M. W., Thomas, M. S. C., & Westerman, G. (2007). *Neuroconstructivism: how the brain constructs cognition* (Vol. 1). Oxford: Oxford University Press.

Marsh, K. (1995). Children's singing games: composition in the playground? *Research Studies in Music Education, 4*, 2–11.

Marsh, K. (1999). Mediated orality: the role of popular music in the changing tradition of children's musical play. *Research Studies in Music Education, 13*, 2–12.

McPherson, G. E. (1995/6). Five aspects of musical performance and their correlates. *Bulletin of the Council for Research in Music Education, Special Issue, the 15th International Society for Music Education*, University of Miami, Florida, 9–15 July 1994.

Miller, L. K. (1989). *Musical savants: exceptional skill in the mentally retarded*. Hillsdale, NJ: Erlbaum.

Miller, G. (2000). Evolution of human music through sexual selection. In N. L. Wallin, B. Merker & S. Brown (Eds.), *The origins of music* (pp. 329–60). Cambridge, MA: MIT Press.

Monson, I. (1996). *Saying something: jazz improvisation and interaction*. Chicago: Chicago University Press.

Munroe, R. L., & Munroe, R. H. (1997). A comparative anthropological perspective. In J. Berry, Y. H. Poortinga & J. Pandey (Eds.), *Handbook of cross cultural psychology, Vol 1: Theory and method* (2nd edn, pp. 171–213). Boston: Allyn & Bacon.

Munte, T. F., Nager, W., Beiss, T. Schroeder, C., & Erne, S. N. (2003). Specialization of the specialised electrophysiological investigations in professional musicians. In G. Avanzini,

C. Faienza, D. Minciacchi, L. Lopez & M. Majno (Eds.), *The neurosciences and music* (pp. 112–117). New York: New York Academy of Sciences.

Nettl, B. (1983). *The study of ethnomusicology: twenty nine issues and concepts.* Urbana: University of Illinois Press.

O'Flynn, J. (2005). Re-appraising ideas of musicality in intercultural contexts of music education. *International Journal of Music Education, 23*(3), 191–203.

Ostwald, P. F. (1973). Musical behaviour in early childhood. *Developmental Medicine & Child Neurology, 15,* 367–75.

Panneton, R. K. (1985). *Prenatal auditory experience with melodies: effects on postnatal auditory preferences in human newborns.* Unpublished doctoral thesis, University of North Carolina at Greensboro.

Pantev, C., Engelien, A., Candia, V., & Elbert, T. (2003). Representational cortex in musicians. In I. Peretz & R. Zatorre (Eds.), *The cognitive neuroscience of music* (pp. 382–95). Oxford: Oxford University Press.

Papousek, M. (1996). Intuitive parenting: a hidden source of musical stimulation in infancy. In I. Deliege & J. A. Sloboda (Eds.), *Musical beginnings: origins and development of musical competence* (pp. 88–112). Oxford: Oxford University Press.

Peretz, I. (2003). Brain specialization for music: new evidence from congenital amusia. In I. Peretz & R. Zatorre (Eds.), *The cognitive neuroscience of music* (pp. 192–203). Oxford: Oxford University Press.

Pinker, S. (1997). *How the mind works.* New York: W. W. Norton.

Rauschecker, J. P. (2003). Functional organization and plasticity of auditory cortex. In I. Peretz & R. Zatorre (Eds.), *The cognitive neuroscience of music* (pp. 357–65). Oxford: Oxford University Press.

Rogoff, B. (2003). *The cultural nature of human development.* New York: Oxford University Press.

Russell, J. (2002). Sites of learning: communities of musical practice in the Fiji Islands. In M. Espeland (Ed.), *Sampsel—together for our musical future! Focus area report* (pp. 31–39). Stord: International Society for Music Education.

Ruthsatz, J., & Detterman, D. K. (2003). An extraordinary memory: the case of a musical prodigy. *Intelligence, 31,* 509–518.

Seashore, C. E., Lewis, L., & Saetveit, J.G. (1960). *Seashore measures of musical talents.* New York: The Psychological Corporation.

Shuter-Dyson, R. (1999). Musical ability. In D. Deutsch (Ed.), *The psychology of music* (pp. 627–51). New York: Harcourt Brace.

Sloboda, J. A., Davidson, J. W., Howe, M. J. A., & Moore, D. G. (1996). The role of practice in the development of performing musicians. *British Journal of Psychology, 87,* 287–309.

Sloboda, J., Hermelin, B., & O'Connor, N. (1985). An exceptional musical memory. *Musical Perception, 3,* 155–70.

Sosniak, L. A. (1985). Learning to be a concert pianist. Developing talent in young people. In B. S. Bloom (Ed.), *Developing talent in young people* (pp. 19–67). New York: Ballantine.

Stevenson, H., & Lee, S.-Y. (1990). Contexts of achievement: a study of American, Chinese, and Japanese children. *Monographs of the Society for Research in Child Development, 55*(1/2). Chicago: University of Chicago.

Stone, R. (2004). *Music in West Africa*. New York: Oxford University Press.

Street, R., Young, S., Tafuri, J., & Ilari, B. (2003). *Mothers' attitudes to singing to their infants*. Proceedings of the 5th ESCOM conference, Hanover University of Music and Drama, Germany.

Sudnow, D. (1978). *Ways of the hand: the organisation of improvised conduct*. London: Routledge & Kegan Paul.

Sundin, B. (1997). Musical creativity in childhood—a research project in retrospect. *Research Studies in Music Education*, *9*, 48–57.

Trehub, S. E., (2003). Musical predispositions in infancy: an update. In I. Peretz & R. Zatorre (Eds.), *The cognitive neuroscience of music* (pp. 3–20). Oxford: Oxford University Press.

Trehub, S. E., & Trainor, L. J. (1998) Singing to infants: lullabies and play songs. *Advances in Infancy Research*, *12*, 43–77.

Trehub, S. E., Unyk, A. M., & Trainor, L. J. (1993). Maternal singing in cross-cultural perspective. *Infant Behaviour and Development*, *16*, 285–95.

Trevarthen, C. (1999). Musicality and the intrinsic motive pulse: Evidence from human psychobiology and infant communication. *Musicae Scientiae*, Special Issue, 155–215.

Trevarthen, C., & Malloch, S. (2002). Musicality and music before three: human vitality and invention shared with pride. *Zero to Three*, *23*(1), 41–46.

Vaughan, M. M. (1977). Measuring creativity: its cultivation and measurement. *Bulletin of the Council for Research in Music Education*, *50*, 72–77.

Vispoel, W. P. (1993). The development and evaluation of a computerized adaptive test of tonal memory. *Journal of Research in Music Education*, *41*, 111–36.

Wallin, N., Merker, B., & Brown, S. (2000). *The origins of music*. Cambridge, MA: MIT Press.

Waters, A. J., Underwood, G., & Findlay, J. M. (1997). Studying expertise in music reading: use of a pattern-matching paradigm. *Perception and Psychophysics*, *59*, 477–88.

Webster, P. R. (1988). New perspectives on music aptitude and achievement. *Psychomusicology*, *7*(2), 177–94.

Wertsch, J. V. (1988). *Vygotsky and the social formation of mind*. Cambridge, MA: Harvard University Press.

Williamon, A., & Valentine, E. (2000). Quantity and quality of musical practice as predictors of performance quality. *British Journal of Psychology*, *91*(3), 353–76.

Wing, H. D. (1981). *Standardised tests of musical intelligence*. Windsor, UK: National Foundation for Educational Research.

Woodward, S. C. (1992). *The transmission of music into the human uterus and the response of music of the human fetus and neonate*. Unpublished doctoral thesis, University of Cape Town, South Africa.

Young, L., & Nettelbeck, T. (1995). The abilities of a musical savant and his family. *Journal of Autism and Developmental Disorders*, *25*(3), 231–47.

Young, S., & Gillen, J. (2006). Technology assisted musical experiences in the everyday life of young children. *Proceedings of the ISME Early Childhood Music Education Commission Seminar, Touched by Musical Discovery: Disciplinary and Cultural Perspectives*, Chinese Cultural University Taipei, Taiwan, 9–14 July, pp. 71–77.

Young, S., Street, A., & Davies, E. (2007). The music one-to-one project: developing approaches to music with parents and under two-year-olds. *European Early Childhood Education Research Journal, 15*(2), 253–67.

Younker, B. A., & Smith, W. H. (1996). Comparing and modelling musical thought processes of expert and novice composers. *Bulletin of the Council for Research in Music Education, 128*, 25–35.

Chapter 10

Culture and gender in a cathedral music context: an activity theory exploration

Graham F. Welch

Introduction

> As soon as they have read the psalter attentively, small boys are able to understand the meaning of all books.
>
> (Guido d'Arrezo, 1025, as cited in Mould, 2007, p. 6)

The intention of this chapter is to use cultural–historical activity theory as a lens to explore the antecedents to the successful introduction of female choristers into English cathedrals in the late 20th century in musical, developmental, and sociocultural terms. In addition, activity theory is used to assess the contemporary impact of this major innovation and to offer an insight into how the established musical culture of the cathedrals shapes, promotes, and constrains the range of possible musical behaviours by the individual female choristers, but is also itself expanded.

Mapping the cultural–historical context

Choral activity has been part of the daily ritual in cathedrals, minsters,[1] and major chapels[2] across the UK since the foundation of the first Benedictine abbey by St Augustine at Canterbury in 597AD. This choral practice is believed

---

[1] Minsters are large and important churches that have the status of cathedrals and that were customarily part of a monastery.

[2] Depending on their original foundation status, there are three major categories of religious institution in the UK that have choristers. The vast majority are cathedrals, with a very small number of abbeys or minsters and a few so-called 'major chapels' (such as at Kings College, Cambridge). Throughout this chapter, the term 'cathedrals' is used as a collective term to signify this overall set of broadly similar settings for the performance of religious choral music.

to have its origins in the musical traditions of the song school of the Jewish Temple from the first century BC (Smith & Young, 2009). Subsequently, the Canterbury model of religious foundation was repeated at Rochester (604), London (St Paul's) (604) and York (627).

In Canterbury, young male novices were inducted from the age of 7 years to ensure a supply of new clergy and monks as part of Augustine's mission to bring Christianity from mainland Europe. Five years after the original foundation, a monastery was built at King Ethelbert's command alongside Augustine's church as part of the extension of the religious activity to other parts of the region. On entry to a religious foundation as a novitiate, an individual's new identity would be marked by a change in appearance (such as through special clothing—the 'habit'—and tonsured hair styling for boys, or perhaps the wearing of a ring to demonstrate betrothal to Christ for a nun[3]). In the relatively closed environment of the monasteries (compared to the more secularly organized cathedrals[4]), children would have had little subsequent contact with their family (Mould, 2007). The religious community was expected to provide the children with sustenance, both physical and spiritual, in order to ensure the continuation of the mission of the particular religious order. A central part of the children's education and induction into religious life would have included the singing of the daily liturgy (e.g. mass, lauds, vespers, psalms) by the quire (Mould, 2007). Some monastic buildings had an adjacent cathedral (the seat of the Bishop—such as at Canterbury) and all would have had their own quire.

Religious practices, including music, were often subject to severe disruption in many parts of the country during the Anglo-Saxon period. This was the result of attacks from Viking invaders from the latter part of the eighth century through to the eleventh century. Following the Norman invasion in 1066, there was a period of relative calm in which musical practices flourished with a large expansion in the numbers of churches and chapels (Mould, 2007). Nationally, by the time of the plague associated with the Black Death (1348–49), it is estimated that there were more than 1,000 monasteries and nunneries across Britain, embracing 14,000 monks and 3,000 nuns (Sackett & Skinner, 2006). Customarily, these religious foundations would have had boys (in the

---

[3] When taking their religious vows, young women wore white, as in a marriage ceremony, and had a ring placed in their finger (Laven, 2002, p. 23).

[4] By the twelfth century, 9 of England's 17 cathedrals were secular with boy choristers (Mould, 2007, p. 23). Each cathedral was (and is) managed by its own staffing 'foundation', headed by a 'dean' with support from a small number of appointed 'canons'. Religious activity is managed on a regional basis across the country, with each region being headed by a bishop whose 'throne' ('cathedra' (Latin): chair, one of the symbols of office) is located within a cathedral.

monasteries and a few nunneries) and girls (in the nunneries) involved in the musical life and daily worship. In contrast, music in the cathedrals would have continued to be all male.

The expansion was also characterized by the emergence of more diverse forms of musical polyphony, rather than plainchant, a change that required the singers to be highly expert musicians and vocal performers. At Canterbury, it was not until 1438 that a small group of eight almonry boys were identified separately in the abbey records as having been selected to sing in the Lady Chapel (Page, 2008). This number of male choristers appears to have been relatively commonplace at that time in choirs (which also included adult men), with the exception of the chapels at Winchester, New College (Oxford), Eton, King's College (Cambridge), and Magdalen College (Oxford). Between them, these five foundations 'employed . . . eighty singing boys, almost matching the ninety-seven required by the whole body of English secular cathedrals at their height' (Mould, 2007, p. 46). The 16 boys specified for New College (1379) and then Winchester College (1382) subsequently became a model for the numbers of choristers in major choral foundations that persist to the present day.

The split with the Church of Rome by King Henry VIII in 1534 led to the two Acts of Dissolution in 1536 and 1539 and resulted in the closure of many religious communities. Consequently, all the children who sang in monasteries and nunneries (the latter often responsible for the education of young boys as well as girls) lost their opportunities to perform the daily liturgy. Although there were continuing opportunities for boys to sing in cathedrals and chapels across the successive centuries (apart from the political hiatus of the Commonwealth in the seventeenth century when such musical practices generally ceased), no equivalent opportunity was to become available again for girls for more than 400 years.

The introduction of female choristers into English cathedrals in the late twentieth century, therefore, must be seen as a relatively unique historical event. Cathedral music has been all male in performance since its inception in Canterbury. Although Bradford (established as a cathedral in 1919 from an older parish church), Bury St Edmonds, and Leicester (established similarly in 1914 and 1927 respectively) had female choristers at various points during the 20th century (see 'Impetus for change' below), it was only in 1991 that Salisbury (established 1258) became the first old cathedral foundation in England to admit girl choristers.

Notwithstanding the controversy that surrounded this initiative, its powerful political impact has been reflected in a rapid increase in the establishment of choirs for female choristers in other cathedrals across England. As can be seen from Fig. 10.1, in the year before Salisbury's action (1990), 94% ($n = 45$ out of 48)

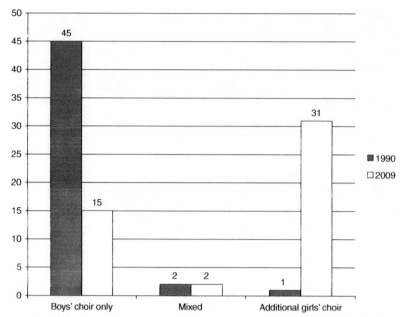

Fig. 10.1 Changes in the make-up of cathedral choirs in England by sex from 1990 to 2009.

of cathedrals, minsters and major chapels in England had boys-only choirs (Leicester being the exception at that time, with Bradford and Manchester being mixed), but by 2009 boys-only choirs were in the minority (31%, $n = 15$). Nearly two-thirds of English cathedrals (65%, $n = 31$) now employ both boys' and girls' choristers of the same age group, albeit usually singing the daily services separately and only occasionally performing together for particular major festivals or concerts.

Furthermore, Salisbury's initiative appears to have had a relatively rapid impact on other English cathedrals, with 17 new girls' choirs being created in the following six years (see Fig. 10.2), followed by a steady stream of others to the present day.[5]

Some cathedrals, such as Portsmouth and Salisbury, have created additional, more community-focused, choirs that bring together both sexes to sing on a regular basis. At Portsmouth, there is a new mixed choir called 'Cantate' for 12–18-year-olds that began in November 2006 and which sings Evensong each Thursday. Salisbury began a 'Junior Choir' of 70 members of both sexes aged 8–14 years in

---

[5] Original data provided by Claire Stewart (personal communication, August, 2009) and from additional correspondence with individual directors of music.

Fig. 10.2 Names and numbers (*n* = 31 to 2009) of English cathedrals by year of their introduction of female choristers in addition to their established boys' choirs to sing the daily services.

2007 that rehearses each Saturday morning, with performance opportunities within the cathedral services, as well as concerts. These are two examples of outreach activities by cathedral choirs into their local communities. The Choir Schools Association (CSA) report that the first such activity was in Truro, Cornwall at the turn of the millennium, followed by 21 similar programmes launched up to and including 2007. Most recently, cathedrals have been encouraged in their outreach development by an additional £1 million per year under the UK Government's National Singing Programme 'Sing Up' (2007–2011). This programme is focused on ensuring a high-quality singing experience for all primary school children (ages 5–11 years), with the cathedrals using their considerable expertise and experience in children's singing development by taking choristers into schools, promoting joint concerts for 'junior choirs' and encouraging wider music-making and sung performance within the cathedral itself.[6]

Each addition to an established cathedral foundation has necessitated the generation of new funding. Salisbury, for example, reported that £0.5 million was needed to endow sixteen scholarships and Wells Cathedral established a 'Girl Chorister Trust' to secure a permanent endowment fund to provide the 18 female choristers with the same ongoing opportunities (including choral scholarships) as their boys.

The impetus for change

The impetus for change in the first three cathedrals to admit female choristers (Bradford, Leicester, and Salisbury) embraced similarities and differences.

Prior to becoming a cathedral in 1920, Bradford had been a large parish church, in common with several other cathedrals of late nineteenth and early twentieth century foundation. By the early 1980s, Bradford had two large choirs of boys and men. However, a reported 'falling out' between the choir director and the cathedral authorities led to the former resigning his post and to many of the boy choristers leaving. As its musical traditions were relatively recent compared to those within the oldest English cathedrals,[7] there were no longstanding, substantial funds available with which to support the strong recruitment of boys at a time of unexpected shortage. By 1986, there had been a further change of musical director and it was around this time that girls were

---

[6] See http://www.choirschools.org.uk/2csahtml/outreach.htm. The CSA reports that 'more than 1,200 of the 21,500 boys and girls in choir schools are choristers' (Choir Schools Association, n.d.).

[7] Eighteen English cathedrals were founded between 597 (Canterbury) and 1133 (Carlisle), a further five were created in 1542, with the remainder dating from 1836.

recruited, probably to boost the number of choristers and perhaps also to improve the overall musical quality (C. Stewart, personal communication, February, 2008). A large influx of young female singers allowed the cathedral to create two mixed choirs, one to sing the morning services and one for the evenings. Since that time, Bradford has continued to have a mixed choir, not-withstanding recent discussions to create separate, single sex choirs (C. Stewart, personal communication, February, 2008).

Leicester Cathedral's female chorister initiative arose from a similar, related need.[8] It was customary for the cathedral to have two evening services on a Sunday. The first was held at 4:00 p.m. as a full choral evensong sung by the choir, with settings of the Responses, Magnificat, and Nunc Dimittis, followed by an anthem, but no sermon. At 6:30 p.m., there was another evensong that included a short psalm, the Canticles sung to Anglican chant, ferial responses, a short anthem, and sermon. Unlike the earlier service, the music of the second evensong was sung by eight boys, four of whom were probationers and the other four on a rota system from the main choir, supported by a small number of men (but not members of the main cathedral choir). As the musical quality was not reported to be particularly satisfactory, auditions were held in 1974 and a choir of 16 girls was formed from 1975, all aged between 12 and 14 years. Despite the choristers' success and competence, by 1984 the congregation for this 6:30 p.m. service had declined to such an extent that it was decided that a choir was not needed. The girls were offered the opportunity to transfer their singing to the Saturday evensong to replace the male-only choir (boys and men). However, the girls were reported as being reluctant to do this and so the choir was disbanded. A new female chorister choir was formed just for Saturday evenings and this continues to the present day.

Whereas the impetus for change at Salisbury has echoes of that in Bradford and Leicester, there were several other factors involved. Salisbury Cathedral was founded in 1075 and had existed for more than 900 years without the need for any innovation in the sex of its choir membership. Nevertheless, like many cathedrals, the regular and sustained recruitment of boy choristers was an ongoing challenge and the innovatory changes at Bradford and Leicester are likely to have prompted several discussions among cathedral authorities over whether or not this was an appropriate form of action to increase the pool of available choristers. There was also widespread interest at the time in the action of St Mary's Cathedral in Edinburgh where the first female chorister had been

---

[8] Detail provided by Geoffrey Carter, ex-Assistant Organist at Leicester Cathedral from 1973 to 1994, in correspondence with Claire Stewart.

admitted into the cathedral choir in 1978.[9] The organist, Dennis Townhill, had agreed to a suggestion six years previously by the headteacher of the cathedral's Music School that girls with a particular interest and ability in music should be accepted into the school (but not cathedral choir). Townhill gave a talk to the Cathedral Organists' Association (COA) in 1987 at their conference in Coventry, with the vote of thanks being provided by Richard Seal from Salisbury. Subsequently, the COA had a two-day meeting in Edinburgh in 1990 and its members attended daily services at St Mary's and also observed a choir practice with the boys and girls being rehearsed together.

Then a meeting took place in London at Church House, Westminster on Tuesday October 10, 1989 which included discussion of chorister recruitment.[10] The occasion was a joint meeting of representatives of two major cathedral groupings, namely senior clerics (the Deans and Provosts) and organists (Seal, 1991). Agenda item 7 focused on 'Cathedral Choir School and Chorister recruitment'. The official minutes record the following:

> There was a wide-ranging discussion of the desirability of training girls to sing in Cathedrals, perhaps in separate choirs. There was an agreement that the subject must be aired thoroughly . . . It was clear from the views expressed that this is an immense and complicated subject which cannot be tackled quickly. All agreed it is vital to maintain the excellent tradition of boys' choirs in the Cathedrals. (Seal, 1991, p. 2)

According to Richard Seal, who attended the meeting as Director of Music at Salisbury Cathedral at that time, this discussion provoked much thought and self-reflection about implications and possibilities. He recalled:

> To this discussion I contributed nothing of note, other than to take on board what had been said. When I boarded the train at Waterloo, however, for some reason best known to my maker, I began to address the problem of how on earth girls could be incorporated into this great tradition . . . By the time I reached Salisbury an hour and a half later, I had formulated a plan. (Seal, 1991, p. 2)

Reflecting on the customary weekly pattern of services for Salisbury's boy choristers, Seal recognized that the introduction of new, female choristers could be accommodated on the two evenings each week (Mondays and

---

9 Although Scotland has had a mixed sex cathedral choir at St Mary's Edinburgh since 1978 and is claimed to be 'the first British cathedral to establish a treble line of boys and girls of the same age' (Townhill, 2000, p. 121), there are reports that St David's cathedral in Wales had a mixed sex treble part from the early 1970s, initially because girls were drafted in at the last moment to cover for the boys who fell ill just prior to a radio broadcast. The girls were so successful that they remained until 1991 when they were separated into two single sex choirs, but with girls singing most of the services (Stevens, 1999, p. 12).

10 As recalled by Richard Seal in his notes for a speech given to the Precentor's Conference at Durham, 18 September 1991.

Wednesdays) when the boys were not required to sing. There was also an opportunity to reduce the boys' busy weekend workload from four services to three. Girls would, therefore, be able to sing three services each week, while the boys would continue to sing six, rather than seven services. An added bonus would be that the boys would have the same amount of rehearsal time, but for slightly fewer musical items each week.

The discussions on the possible introduction of female choristers into the all-male Anglican choral tradition in the late 1980s can also been seen within a wider political debate related to equal opportunities in society. The political landscape in England at that time included a significant concern on matters related to social justice. This was exemplified by the work of the Equal Opportunities Commission (established 1975) and included investigation of the ongoing impact of recent legislation concerning moves towards equal pay and the reduction of sex discrimination (HMSO, 1975), as well as legislation on race relations (HMSO, 1976) and disability provision, the latter specifically focused on special educational needs (Department of Education and Science, 1981; Warnock Committee, 1978).

Musicians and clergy in the cathedral were unlikely to have been immune to these public discussions and new legal imperatives.[11] In the case of Salisbury, this was exampled by the sister of a Salisbury boy chorister who sent in a request to a highly popular weekend BBC TV programme.

> I realise that I can never sing in a Cathedral choir like my brother, but please can you fix it for me to sing with them just once? (Seal, 1991, p. 4)

Her wish was granted on December 20, 1989 when the Cathedral choir travelled to London to sing with her on television. Just under 2 years later, Salisbury's 18 female choristers, including the TV performer, assembled on September 9, 1991 for their first rehearsal ('a truly historic moment'—Seal, 1991, p. 5) and one month later sang their first cathedral Evensong on October 7. Richard Seal subsequently recalled the television request as one of the key events at that time that confirmed his wish to implement change:

> What has really motivated me to go ahead with this project [the creation of a girls' choir] has been an overwhelming desire to see a cathedral church opening its choir stalls to both boys and girls, so that girls too can benefit from the unique education afforded at an English Choir School. (Seal, 1991, p. 6)

---

[11] In a small-scale survey of why cathedrals had introduced female choristers (Stewart, 2006), half (49%) of respondents reported on the importance of providing an equal opportunity for girls.

Seal was not alone in his push for change. He reports that he received much support from colleagues, including Richard Shephard from York Minster School (although it was another six years before York had its own female chorister choir) and the Director, as well as the ex-Director, of the Royal School of Church Music.

An underlying moral imperative for change was also emphasized by the Very Reverend Hugh Dickenson, Dean of Salisbury Cathedral, in his sermon on the occasion of the tenth anniversary of the founding of Salisbury's girls' choir on 15 July 2001 (Dickenson, 2001).

> Since the beginning of recorded history, patriarchal societies have systematically, institutionally, and personally conspired to oppress women and to deny them the freedoms which are their God-given rights . . . It is less than a hundred years since women were given the vote or allowed to sit for degrees and less than two hundred since married women were allowed to own property. Discrimination and male chauvinism still poison many of the transactions of our public life, in politics, business, the civil service—and the Churches. (p. 2)

In July 2001, Salisbury hosted a 'celebration weekend' to mark the first decade of the girls' choir. The weekend included a Gala Concert with the international soprano Emma Kirkby and more than 300 girl choristers from nineteen different cathedrals. An accompanying pamphlet contained interviews with ex-choristers who were part of the original female intake. They spoke of their sense of 'family' and of the longlasting 'friendships' that developed among choristers who were living a close life together, as well as of the advanced musical skills that they acquired and how these had been an asset in their subsequent engagement with music, whether as professional musicians or as relatively skilled musicians within the amateur community.

As demonstrated in Figs 10.1 and 10.2, throughout the 1990s and subsequently there has been a continuing shift towards the introduction of female choristers in English cathedrals. By 2006, the ground-breaking initiative at Salisbury, foreshadowed at Bradford and Leicester, had been copied by the majority of the English cathedrals. The two sets of choristers often come together for special musical events, such as radio and television broadcasts, concerts or major festivals. Nevertheless, with the exceptions of the mixed choirs at Bradford and Manchester (since 1992)—Bury St Edmonds was initially boys, then mixed from 1959 to 1984, then became boys-only again—they tend not to sing the daily services together. Instead, they alternate, usually with the boy choristers continuing to perform the majority of sung services each week.[12]

---

[12] For example, a small-scale survey for the COA (Stewart, 2006) revealed (a) that the ratio of boys to girls in the regular performance of the liturgy in cathedral services was 2:1 and

Reactions to change

These innovations in the composition of the traditionally all-male cathedral choir were not without controversy. The Dean of Salisbury Cathedral reported in his tenth anniversary sermon (mentioned above) that 'we knew that there would be screams of shock horror in some places' and 'we encountered stiff, sometimes almost venomous opposition' (p. 1). The professional music journals, such as *Cathedral Music, Church Music Quarterly, Classical Music,* and *BBC Music Magazine,* as well as other news media including *Le Monde* and *TIME* magazine have often carried articles expressing arguments for and against the innovation of girl choristers in the cathedrals.

One particular collective of concerned people created the Campaign for the Traditional Cathedral Choir (CTCC, formerly labelled the Campaign for the Defence of the Traditional Cathedral Choir) with the object 'To champion the ancient tradition of the all-male choir in Cathedrals, Chapels Royal, Collegiate Churches, University Chapels and similar ecclesiastical choral foundations'.[13] The CTCC website offers a 'guide in pictures to the demise of the all-male choral tradition'. They suggest that the introduction of female choristers will lead to fewer opportunities for boys and subsequent problems in the recruitment of adult male singers (male altos, tenors, basses) because they report that many of the men in cathedral choirs are ex-choristers.

The CTCC also expresses concern that the 'uniqueness' of the boy chorister voice will be lost, along with its centuries-old performance tradition. Several empirical studies have explored the extent to which the sound of trained boy choristers is 'unique' compared to that of girls, whether acoustically, perceptually or both. Certainly, there are acoustic and perceptual differences in the singing of untrained children's voices. A study of the singing of 320 (untrained) children aged 4–11 years found evidence that listeners were able to identify correctly the sex of the singer in more than 70% of cases, with older children more accurately identified than younger (Sergeant, Sjölander & Welch, 2005). Subsequently, the relatively consistent age and gender cues in untrained children's singing were examined acoustically though analyses of their 'long-term-average Spectra' (Sergeant & Welch, 2008, 2009). These revealed that there were no significant acoustic differences between the sexes for the youngest age group (4–5 years), but that the older two age groups (6–8 and 9–11 years)

(b) that boys tended to sing most of their services with the men as a full, four-part choir and fewer services on their own, whereas girls had fewer services to sing overall and these were approximately equally split between singing along or with the men.

[13] Retrieved 10 March 2008, from http://www.ctcc.org.uk/objects.htm

had demonstrable and statistically significant sex differences in their sung spectra. Shifts of spectral energy from higher frequency regions to lower frequency regions were found to be present in data for both sexes as they got older, and the fulcrum for these changes in spectral tilt was approximately 5.75 kHz, that is the energies at frequencies above 5.75 kHz decreased with increasing age, and energies below 5.75 kHz increased correspondingly. However, the shifts were not uniform between sexes, beginning earlier for girls than for boys.

By comparison, perceptual and acoustic studies of trained chorister voices, in choirs and singly, indicate that listeners' perceptual accuracy of singer gender varies according to the nature of the musical example (Howard, Barlow, Szymanski & Welch, 2001; Howard, Szymanski & Welch, 2002; Howard & Welch, 2002; Moore & Killian, 2000–2001; Sergeant & Welch, 1997). There is evidence of particular individual girl and boy soloists, as well as girls' and boys' choirs, being consistently identified or misidentified in relation to particular items of musical repertoire. It would seem that not all boys' cathedral choirs exhibit a 'unique' and archetypal male vocal timbre that is sustained over time; the experimental data reveal that some boys' choirs can be mistaken as female in their composition. Conversely, it is clear that some girl choristers, both singly and collectively, are able to produce vocal timbres that are perceived to be within a 'boy/masculine' category.

> With regard to perceived singer gender, a summary of recent research data indicates that, whilst it is possible for an untrained solo singer's sex to be identified relatively accurately from around the age of eight onwards, it is also equally possible for trained female choristers from the age of eight to be systematically mistaken as male, depending on the particular piece of music being performed. However, once the female chorister moves into her mid-teens, the voice quality becomes more characteristically identifiable as 'female' ('womanly').[14] (Welch, 2006, p. 321)

Furthermore, the concept of an 'appropriate' vocal timbre for all boy choristers in performance also appears to be socially located. For example, when appointed as organist of Westminster Cathedral in 1947, George Malcolm said that he disliked the 'artificial and unnatural sound' produced by English choirboys (Day, 2000, p. 131). He set out to produce a sound that was different and more 'natural'. The outcome was subsequently termed 'continental' by contemporaries, being perceived as not stereotypically 'English' because of a greater emphasis on vocal 'colour' and 'strength' (p. 131).

---

[14] For a detailed review of the literature on gender and chorister voice, including similarities and differences in the underlying anatomy and physiology for singing, see Welch and Howard (2002). For data on the perceived gender of untrained children's voices, see Sergeant et al. (2005).

Despite the durability of the male chorister tradition, one of the paradoxes of the research data on child and adolescent singing development is that girls tend to be reported as more competent singers in each age group and usually report that they enjoy singing more. Recent and ongoing research, under the auspices of the UK Government's National Singing Programme, into the singing development of 3,500 children between the ages of 7 and 11 years has found that, as they age, boys characteristically often dislike singing in school and in public contexts (Welch et al., 2008). Yet the cathedral choral tradition has been based around the singing skills of boys for more than a thousand years.

It remains to be seen whether the creation of girls' choirs alongside those for boys has any particular impact on traditional chorister recruitment. The *Liverpool Echo* (Riley, 2006) reported a Liverpool Cathedral administrator as saying, 'Only one boy chorister passed auditions in June, but we were overrun with girls'. The paper speculates that it may be the heavy schedule for boy choristers—Monday, Tuesday and Friday evenings, as well as half-day Saturday and all day Sunday—that was acting as a disincentive. Other press reports suggest that any difficulties with (male) recruitment are likely to be related to competition from other opportunities for play, recreation and exploration within contemporary childhood, such as offered by a wide range of technologically based media. It may also be that the recruitment of girls has a negative effect on the formerly exclusive status and identity of male choristers, not least because the females may be slightly older, more mature and able to remain in the choir for longer because of the relatively minimal impact of their adolescent voice change on singing performance compared to that of boys.

Although there were (and are) concerns that the innovation of girl choristers would weaken or even destroy the 'all-male' musical tradition, the evidence (such as in Fig. 10.2) suggests that this has not happened so far. Any particular challenges in boy chorister recruitment appear to be longstanding (at least as evidenced by the minutes of the meeting in Church House of 1989 cited earlier). Across the cathedral sector, there has been no change in the number of boys' choirs since the relative innovation at Salisbury. With the exception of the two cathedrals in England with mixed choirs (Bradford and Manchester), all the others continue to have choral activities in which boys sing on their own or with men. It may be that the introduction of female choristers has led to slightly fewer services for the boys to sing each week, but this reduction is likely to be a small proportion of their total workload; in general, boys continue to sing a greater number of services than their female peers. Furthermore, where girls' choirs have been introduced, the number of rehearsals for the boys is often the same as they experienced previously and so the level of their singing skill should be at least sustained, if not improved, under the new dispensation—a suggestion supported by the available data in survey responses from Directors of Music (Stewart, 2006).

Chorister tradition and innovation: an activity theory perspective

It is evident from the above cultural and historical narrative that the past two decades have been marked by a major cultural shift in cathedral music in England. From a social psychology perspective, one possible explanation is available through the lens of what has been termed as cultural–historical activity theory (e.g. Bedny, Seglin & Meister, 2000).[15] This theory (also known as 'activity theory') is concerned—*inter alia*—with how the structure of an organization generates messages and possibilities for its participants as to what is appropriate action (Daniels, 2004). The theory also takes the perspective that individual learning is mediated by action that is related to cultural artefacts and membership of groups within a wider community.

The grounding to the theory has been traced back to the work of Luria, Vygotsky, and Leont'ev in the early decades of the twentieth century (see Bannon, 2008; Cole, 1999). These Russian psychologists explored how learning and development were the product of inter- and intrapersonal behaviours that were shaped by cultural artefacts[16] (e.g. literature), alongside tools (including psychological tools, such as language and other symbol systems), expectations, 'rules'/conventions, and norms. The internalization of artefacts was also seen to facilitate the agency of the individual, such that the artefacts themselves became modified through personal use, enabling the possibility of consequent change within the culture.

A key concept is 'activity' which is defined as 'the engagement of a subject toward a certain goal or objective' (Ryder, 2008). One widely cited model of an activity system is that provided by Engeström in his discussion of the evolution of the theory (Engeström, 2001a, see Fig. 10.3; Engeström & Miettinen, 1999).

---

[15] An initial exemplification of how activity theory might be applied in music education, with examples from the introduction of the female chorister into cathedral choirs may be found in Welch (2007).

[16] According to Cole (1999, p. 90), an artefact is 'a material object that has been modified by human beings as a means of regulating their interactions with the world and each other. Artefacts carry within them successful adaptations of an earlier time (in the life of the individual who made them or in earlier generations) and, in this sense, combine the ideal and the material, such that in coming to adopt the artefacts provided by their culture, human beings simultaneously adopt the symbolic resources they embody.'

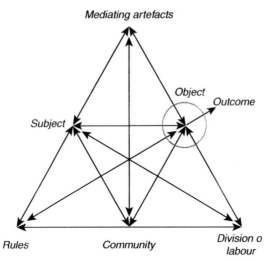

Fig. 10.3 The structure of a human activity system (redrawn with permission from Engeström, 2001b, p. 136). The circle indicates that 'object-oriented actions are always, explicitly or implicitly, characterised by ambiguity, surprise, interpretation, sense making and potential for change' (Engeström, 2001b, p. 134). Expansive Learning at Work: toward an activity theoretical reconceptualization, Engeström, Journal of Education and Work, 2001, Taylor and Francis, (Taylor & Francis Group, http://www.informaworld.com).

In the upper triangle in the figure, Engeström draws on a Vygotskian conception that the 'object' of an action by (or on) a 'subject' is culturally 'mediated' by some form of 'artefact'. This relates to Vygotsky's notion of the 'zone of proximal development' (Vygotsky, 1978), being the realisation of potential development under the guidance of an expert or more capable peers. The upper part of the figure is extended in the lower part to encompass Leont'ev's perspective of individual and group actions being embedded in a collective, interactive activity system (Leont'ev, 1978) in which 'rules', a sense of 'community', and 'division of labour' (division of effort) are also evidenced. In the overall model, the 'object' of the activity is perceived as a cultural entity (Engeström, 2001a) and the 'outcome' may or may not be the same as the intended 'object'.

Engeström also posits that several activity systems can coexist and interact, such that the 'object' is jointly shared or constructed, or is seen as an opportunity for 'expansive learning' (Engeström, 2001b, p. 137) where culturally new patterns of activity emerge[17] (see below).

---

[17] Engeström (2001b, pp. 140, 145) provides an example of how organizational tensions in children's health care in Helsinki were made explicit through an analysis of (minimally) three interconnected activity systems, representing the local children's hospital, the

Engeström (2001a, 2001b, 2005) articulates five basic principles for activity theory as follows:

The prime unit of analysis is 'a collective, artifact-mediated and object-oriented activity system, seen in its network relations to other activity systems' (2001a, p. 6). The activity system is the set of relationships between elements (see Fig. 10.3, Engeström, 2001b). 'Goal directed individual and group actions . . . are relatively independent but subordinate units of analysis, eventually understandable only when interpreted against the background of entire activity systems' (2001a, p. 6).

Activity systems are 'multi-voiced' (2001a, p. 7), embracing multiple viewpoints, traditions and interests: 'participants carry their own diverse histories and the activity system itself carries multiple layers and strands of history engraved in its artifacts, rules and conventions' (2001b, p. 136).

Activity systems 'take shape and get transformed over lengthy periods of time', suggesting a concept of 'historicity' (2001b, p. 136). History embraces both 'the local history of the [particular] activity and its objects', (p. 136) as well as the wider 'history of the theoretical ideas and tools that shape the activity' (p. 136).

Change and development arise from 'contradictions' that are 'historically accumulating structural tensions within and between activity systems' (2001b, p. 137).

Activity systems are subject to the possibility of 'expansive transformations' (2001b, p. 137). These are the product of the 'aggravation' of contradictions, such as when individuals 'question and deviate from established norms' which 'escalates into collaborative envisioning' towards an alternative collective viewpoint (p. 137).

Although it is possible to conceive of answers to such questions in any particular educational context without drawing on activity theory per se, Engeström (and others) believes that the theory provides a framework by which a more holistic and environmentally sensitive conceptualization of behaviour is possible.[18] Support for such an approach may be found in other

---

primary care health centre and the activity system of the child patient's family. The eventual outcome was a new, negotiated care agreement model for the improvement of healthcare for children.

[18] Activity theory has been applied to a wide range of studies into 'cultural practices and practice-bound cognition' (Engeström & Miettinen, 1999, p. 8), such as human–computer interaction (HCI) (e.g. understanding web-based activity, the process of software design), workplace learning, markets, healthcare, childhood play and certain categories of education. The theory's application in the field of music education and music psychology appears to be relatively recent (e.g. Barrett, 2005; Johansson, 2008; Smith & Walker, 2002; Walker & Smith, 2001; Welch, 2007).

relatively recent, educationally sensitive conceptualizations, such as 'situated learning' (Lave & Wenger, 1991) and 'communities of practice' (Wenger, 1998) in which the social location of individual action and understanding is central. Taken together, these perspectives suggest that individual and collective behaviour are grounded in situated practices (Johansson, 2008).

Activity theory and the introduction of female choristers into English cathedrals: a case study

One use of activity system theory is that it allows the investigator to combine both macro- and micro-perspectives.

> The analyst constructs the activity system as if looking at it from above. At the same time, the analyst must select a member (or better yet, multiple different members) of the local activity, through whose eyes and interpretations the activity is constructed. This dialectic between the systemic and subjective-partisan views brings the researcher into a dialogical relationship with the local activity under investigation. (Engeström & Miettinen, 1999, p. 10)

The underlying principles that inform Engeström's model of activity theory can be used to explore the recent introduction of female choristers into English cathedrals. For example, Wells Cathedral in the West of England introduced girl choristers in 1993, two years after the Salisbury innovation and in a context where male choristers have sung in the choir since 1354. In 1999, I began a longitudinal series of (ongoing) research visits to investigate the nature and development of the female chorister voice and the impact of the introduction of female choristers on the previously all-male cathedral culture. The multi-method, case-study approach embraced observations, semistructured interviews, analyses of printed materials (such as music and service schedules), field notes, and acoustic recordings of individual and collective singing behaviours in the different settings (including a vacant practice room in Wells Cathedral School, rehearsal spaces—the cathedral undercroft, cloister, new choir centre, and nave—and (with permission) choral performance at Evensong).[19] Opportunities have been taken during each visit to speak to individuals and small groups of female choristers, as well as to significant adults, such as the

---

[19] To date (October 2009), there have been 20 site visits, 357 recordings of 68 individual choristers (some recorded regularly over a period of up to six years), observations at 18 rehearsals and an equivalent number of evening sung services, as well as over 25 hours of semi-structured interviews. Two colleagues (Professor David Howard, University of York and, more recently, Dr Evangelos Himonides, Institute of Education) have been closely involved with the voice recordings and with the (ongoing) acoustic analyses. Part of the research was funded by the Arts and Humanities Research Board under grant B/SG/AN8886/APN14717 (2002–2003).

cathedral's organist and master of the choristers (with a change of post holder in 2004) and adult male singers from the choir (the 'vicars choral'), plus others with special responsibility for the general welfare of the choristers, including the head and deputy of the Wells Cathedral Music School where the choristers receive their specialist education. The prime focus for the interviews has been to explore the experience of becoming and being a female chorister and to contextualize these with views from adults who are closely involved in their support and development.

The semistructured interview data and observational field notes were transcribed into Microsoft Word and analysed using ATLAS.ti 5.0.[20] The analyses generated thirty-nine different elements that were identified as having a reported impact on chorister development. These clustered under four main umbrella categories and subcategories, with examples as follows.

Personal/individual identity

Under this heading, responses demonstrated the singers' sense of their emergent self and its development. Choristers commented on:

(a) improvements in their vocal technique: 'My voice is getting stronger. I am more able to do long phrases and sight read and all that'; 'I just use my diaphragm more'; 'I've got a lot stronger and I feel more confident with like intervals and stuff like that [as a probationer]';

(b) changes in the vocal quality, which can be positive: 'a clear sound'; 'a laser beam from your forehead'; 'Well, I listen to the older girls in the choir and they probably have the voice that you want to get . . .'; and sometimes negative: such as being frightened by the emergence of 'vibrato' [at 15 years old];

(c) a growing awareness of gender differences: 'Young boys' voices are 'pure', girls are 'more breathy', boys are sometimes 'annoying' and 'show off', as well as 'embarrassed to do certain things [singing in front of girls]';

(d) singing being an emotional experience: 'I loved it . . . I really enjoyed it' (ex-chorister); 'I would be lost without it'. They also commented on personal strategies for learning: 'I can't sight read, but I listen instead. If I can sing really quietly the first time, the next time it's all there.'

---

[20] This is a specialist qualitative analysis tool produced by ATLAS.ti Scientific Software Development GmbH.

Group identity

Comments revealed a sense of collectivity in their music-making and of belonging to the choir: 'I prefer singing with the girls' [rather than singing together with the boys]; 'We've got a bit more tone' [than the boys]; 'There was about a hundred of us' in the combined concert at Salisbury to celebrate their tenth anniversary which was 'great'; 'We get on really well, we like bond . . . That's part of being in a choir, bonding with people'; 'It's just fun . . . it's like really sociable'; and talking about the men in the choir: 'Well, I never used to like know them before we went on tour. But when we went on tour, I got to know them really well and it was good'. They also commented on the influence of others and of experiencing singing differences in shaping their musical identity: 'Mr A says "get a ping girls"'; 'It doesn't take that long' [to become part of the choral sound as a novice]; 'Sometimes I still get lost in some of the bits where it all gets loud'; 'She's louder than me. *And* I'm a year older than her'. 'On Saturday we did a concert in Bristol Cathedral. We each got a chance to sing a piece on our own, each choir. There was Exeter, Salisbury, Bristol . . . I think Wells is different in that it doesn't sound so girly'; Although comments from non-chorister peers may not always be positive, particularly as the girls grow older, these can also contribute to the sense of chorister identity: 'Gosh, you sing in the choir, why on earth do you do that?'; 'They sort of always assume that you're singing really strange stuff like operas, like totally sacred and everything, but that's not all, you know, we sing other stuff as well . . .'

Environment

The vocal sounds are shaped by the expectations of the religious rituals and buildings, as well as from within the musical culture: 'On Saturday we had a concert for the tenth anniversary of the girls' choir . . . and people in the audience were making comments that how on earth did we sound like boys so much'; 'My voice changed a lot [while I was in the choir] because mainly of the people around me'; 'The most important thing is vocal [music] first, then the words'; 'One girl left because her voice just broke, it just got too kind of rich. Too rich for the choir. She just didn't blend at all with the rest of the choir'; 'Mr A strongly advises that everyone plays the piano here [to improve their general musicianship skills]'; 'You have to put your hand up [when you make a mistake]'.

Relationships

This enfolds the sense of being part of a community of practice in which the senior choristers, for example, have a key role: 'Most of the seniors have very good voices'; 'It helps to listen to all the people around you'; 'When I was nervous, they were always telling me I'd be fine and everything'; '. . . they are supportive'; 'We went on tour last Easter to France, Belgium and Holland and we basically kicked ass 'cause we just sang everything and we sang really beautiful pieces. We did such a range of things that we really proved that we could do anything if we really wanted to'.

Although the data analyses are ongoing, a picture is beginning to emerge in which the female choristers may be seen both as part of an established tradition, but also as having a 'transformational' impact on it. The customary tripartite relationship in music (Small, 1999) between the physical setting, people (performers and listeners) and musical soundscape constrains the variety of possible musical outcomes, but this relationship has also been modified through the innovation of choristers who are female.

The introduction of female choristers has been in the context of a primarily all-male musical culture, with its established rituals, processes (including teaching and learning), rules, expectations, and communal perspectives. Although the prime purposes of those proposing the innovation embraced a moral imperative, they believed also (on the basis of experience elsewhere within the cathedral music community) that it was possible to introduce female choristers without risk to the musical quality or repertoire expected within the sung religious services. That this should be accomplished successfully, for example, as evidenced in the empirical perceptual data on the acoustic similarities of trained male and female voices (see Welch & Howard, 2002) and in the growth in the numbers of female choristers nationally, is testimony to the strength of the established musical culture. The lens of activity theory suggests that there is a dialectic development in which the novice cathedral chorister is nurtured and supported to become an accomplished performer. Yet, at the same time, there is evidence of cultural transformation as the dominant all-male culture adapts to unforeseen pressures from the creation of girls' choirs, such as exampled by the recent development of cathedral outreach activities that seek to address the moral imperative by bringing younger and older singers of both sexes together from outside the cathedral to perform with the more expert choristers.

At Wells, the data suggest that chorister development is nurtured, shaped, and constrained by systemized cultural practices (see Fig. 10.4, Welch, 2007). The novice female cathedral chorister is inducted into the musical culture by regular attendance at rehearsals (most days at least once, sometimes twice), as well as singing in religious services on selected weekday evenings and on a Sunday. A typical morning rehearsal of fifty minutes begins just before 8:00 a.m. with the twenty choristers (including 'probationers') processing from the School in pairs, led by the head chorister and with the senior

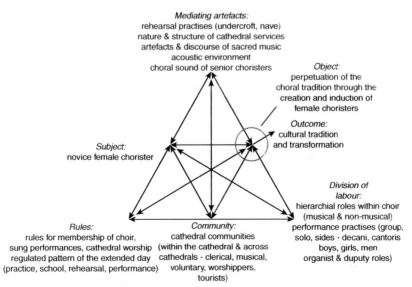

Fig. 10.4 An example of the activity system that frames the development of the novice (female) cathedral chorister (redrawn with permission from Welch, 2007). Welch, Research Studies in Music Education, 28(1), copyright © 2007 by Sage. Reprinted by permission of SAGE.

choristers keeping a close eye on the younger members, followed by the organ-ist and master of the choristers. They enter the rehearsal room (formerly the undercroft next to the chancel, now the new choir room complex) where they hang their cloaks and divide into two groups ('sides'—cantoris and decani) standing behind rehearsal pews (very similar to those in the Cathedral where they perform) either side of the grand piano, with some of the shortest and youngest members requiring small boxes to stand on so that they can see and be seen. The less experienced singers are placed between the senior choristers who provide support and guidance and who also act as vocal role models. Normally, two choristers give out the music to be rehearsed at each session. Choristers are expected to have pencils to annotate their copies of the music as necessary (such as to indicate particular elements of phrasing, or for the avoid-ance of errors in performance).

The rehearsal begins customarily with five minutes of vocalizes to 'warm up' the voices. These typically include such musical activities as nasalized hum-ming, ascending and descending on patterns across the first five pitches of the scale, with starting pitches transposed up by step and then down; then arpeg-gios up a ninth and back; then vocal glides on different vowels. On the morn-ing of 12 November 2007, for example, the warm-up session was followed by choristers singing through the Schütz 'Magnificat' in German for Evensong that day. Then they rehearsed Bach's motet setting of 'Lobert den Herrn' (Psalm 117). The vocal pitch range embraced an octave and a sixth from c4 (middle C) to a5 (top A) and much of the part writing is designed to be performed allegro. First the choristers sang through the piece without stopping, accompanied by piano. This was followed by the rehearsal of smaller sections that focused on aspects of pronunciation and phrasing, with and without accompaniment, including the final 'Alleluja' where the emphasis was on word stresses and with much evidence of pencils being used. There were also questions from the Master to be answered on aspects of the score. No errors in performance went unremarked and all prompted further rehearsal of that element until it was correct. Particular rhythmic phrases were modelled on the piano and sung by the Master. The singing was impressive, performed accurately at speed, in German. There was evidence of significant cognitive loading (see Owens & Sweller, 2008) during the rehearsal, as the choristers were required to process the auditory experience of the music, its notation, the text in a foreign language, as well as specific features required in performance by the Master. After 38 minutes, the focus shifted back to the Schütz with its double choir and two soprano lines. Particular foci were word rhythms that crossed bar-lines, pronunciation, entries, phrasing. The rehearsal ended just before 9:00 a.m. in time for the choristers to begin morning school. Throughout, the emphasis was on sustained sung performance, with little evidence of choristers being 'off task' and the behaviour being shaped (as in Fig. 10.4) by the ways that the 'tools' (musical and linguistic, over time) were used and shaped by the 'rules' (expectations and roles) for the rehearsal within the 'division of labour' (roles) as required by the choral community context.

This pattern of focused activity in which time is carefully managed is also characteristic of the school day as a whole. When asked to describe a typical day, a chorister reported a 14-hour series of activities, often from 6:30 a.m. to 8:30 p.m. The after-school period is particularly structured around music and community. At Wells, for example:

> On Choir day, I'll do like I do it today—you go to, at four o'clock you go to Cedars, have like a cake and a drink, then you line up in ranks at five past four and then at ten past four you set off down to the Cathedral. You have Evensong. You have a rehearsal from twenty past [four] till five o'clock. Quarter past five you get, um, to go into the service. Six o'clock it's, um, the service ends. You go back out and then at quarter past, it's tea and then after tea you go to Bat House, have salad, do your prep at seven. At half seven you come back from prep, have your tuck; quarter to eight upstairs, teeth and pyjamas, um, and a quiet read from quarter to eight till half eight and lights out half eight.

Similarly, at Canterbury, the modern boy choristers have an equally circum-scribed day:

> Here is a typical chorister's working day: 7:05 a.m.—rising bell at Choir House; 7:10 a.m.—first breakfast bell when half of the boys have breakfast while the other half have instrumental practice; 7:30 a.m.—the two halves swap. Followed by teeth clean-ing and changing from slippers to outdoor shoes; 8:00 a.m.—bell to line up for prac-tice. In crocodile (and silence). They file across to the song school for one hour's practice of scales and arpeggios and music for Evensong; 9:00 a.m.—all pack into the minibus and travel to St Edmund's and a normal school day follows; 4:00 p.m.—they have a drink and a slice of cake after which the minibus returns them to Choir House. Here they have shoe cleaning and hand washing supervised by a monitor; 5:00 p.m.—the boys are back in the cathedral where cassocks are put on and they practise for half an hour; 6:00 p.m.—fully robed and with surplices they process in. After Evensong they return to Choir House for supper.[21]

Another way in which the culture sustains itself is in the pattern of different ages within the choir. The female choristers represent overlapping annual populations because there is always some change of chorister personnel at the end of each summer term. When the female chorister choir was initially created at Wells in 1993, the senior female choristers were required to 'retire' from the choir at age 14 years, the same age as their male counterparts. Customarily, new, younger female singers, usually aged between 8 and 10 years, replace those who leave. However, a temporary shortfall in female chor-ister recruitment one year led to a membership rule change by which female choristers could opt to stay on to the age of 16 years, but without holding 'office' in the choir (such as head chorister). This, in turn, had the effect of changing the overall range of female vocal timbres available and allowed the (then) master of choristers to choose (and compose) new repertoire that exploited the opportunities afforded by this 'changed colour palette' (his words). A further outcome was that the more junior members of the choir had highly experienced, mature-voiced, senior colleagues whom they 'idolized' as powerful performers and role models; as a result, however, some also felt that their own individual contributions were overpowered.

One 'outcome' of the dominant culture is the way that it 'shapes' the indi-vidual chorister's singing towards an accepted acoustic product. Nevertheless, this singing style is only one of several that the choristers can employ. For example, as part of the research process, individual choristers have been recorded singing examples of the different vocal genres that are part of their daily lives, some public, some private, both within and without the cathedral

---

[21] Retrieved 4 January 2008 from http://www.ofchoristers.net/Chapters/Canterbury.htm

and school settings. These examples range from the sacred music of the cathedral, to individual pieces being studied in school (usually classical, but also some from popular music theatre), and to their 'own' music that they listen to at home or when relaxing with their peers. Each musical style has its own performance 'rules', established cultural 'artefacts', and implied musical identity.

Consequently, the success of the culture in creating accomplished young female singers who are capable of sustaining and enriching the existing musical programme with its characteristic vocal timbre may also contain 'contradictions' at a personal level. As these adolescent girls get older, their voices take on the acoustic characteristics of a young woman, both in speech and in singing, often with the latter embracing increased pitch and dynamic ranges and 'new' vocal colours, such as vibrato (see Gackle, 2000).

For some successful individual 14-year-old female choristers, the vocal mastery gained through choir membership, allied to a powerful emotional engagement with their own, non-sacred (popular) vocal music, has been sufficient for them to leave the choir to pursue their own musical interests, such as forming a rock group, learning music theatre repertoire, or 'just starting a new phase in my life'. Drawing on the proposition by Engeström (2001b, p. 137) that several activity systems can coexist and interact, it is possible to see how the collective 'object' within the choral tradition—to produce new, expert choristers—may, for some, become mismatched with their developing individual identity, both as an expert solo singer and as a performer drawn to other musical genres that are perceived to be more closely related to their peer identity (see Fig. 10.5). Object and outcomes can then become dissimilar. The vocal stylistics that characterize jazz or music theatre are not the same as required in classical music performance and the reference group for such genre-sensitive vocal behaviours—their communal membership—is less the cathedral and more the listening preferences and popular performers that are enjoyed by the peer group. The 'outcome' is an expert young female singer whose maturing vocal identity moves away from the 'object' expected in the collective performance of choral repertoire as this becomes less satisfying and aligned musically at a personal level. An ex-chorister, for example, reports on the benefits to her voice since leaving the choir:

> In the choir you sing every day. You sing how they want you to sing. You sing. I mean, really it doesn't give you much chance to be free, have your own really full voice. I mean, not having so many choir lessons has really helped not having so much pressure on my voice . . . it's fuller, less pure, um it's supported in a completely different way. To be free, you can't hold onto a pitch, but to get in tune, you have to get in tune some other way.

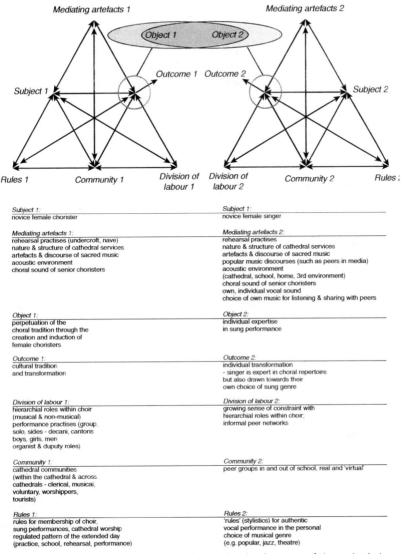

Fig. 10.5 Two activity systems: one that fosters the development of the cathedral chorister; the other that frames the development of the individual singer's identity, within and without sacred choral music.

Several choristers recognized that the possibility of individual singing lessons in the school from the age of 14 years could present challenges to their singing identities: 'If we all have separate singing lessons and our voices develop um . . . they won't blend 'cos we'll all have to develop our own techniques and stuff.' When asked about the future, one senior chorister said that she would like to transfer to a school that specializes in popular music: 'I went to look around there and it was just really friendly and you do all styles of music, 'cos I've only really been in a choir. I've only really done church music and stuff and so I want to do some different styles of music . . .'

Activity theory and the introduction of female choristers into English cathedrals: some general findings

The five summative principles that characterize Engeström's model of activity theory (2001a; 2005—see above) can be interpreted in relation to the historical–cultural introduction of female choristers across the cathedral music sector. This particular framing of activity theory provides explanations both for the maintenance of the choral tradition, as well as its relative transformation (termed by Engeström as 'expansion').

> Principle 1: '. . . a collective, artifact-mediated and object-oriented activity system, seen in its network relations to other activity systems . . .' (Engeström, 2001b, p. 136)

The musical culture and choral tradition are subject to ongoing sustenance each day through the combination of elements embraced by the theorized activity system (Fig. 10.4). Nevertheless, at the level of the group and individual, as well as the wider choral tradition, change is evident because there are social, cultural and musical processes embedded in the daily ritual. These processes generate opportunities for diversity and transformation—such as in musical repertoire, choral behaviour, individual voice development, role-play, leadership, apprenticeship, and in what counts as 'ideal' in sacred choral performance. Although the overarching 'object' may be the same across the cathedral music sector in terms of producing expert choristers (irrespective of sex) that are capable of performing the musical repertoire, there is variation within the sector in the organization of the choral activity at a local level.

Within each cathedral context, the local culture is characterized by various linked object-oriented activity systems. An individual student is likely to be subject to several of these, such as pupil, musician, or chorister—each with related, but different, educational 'objects'. For example, the female choristers of Wells Cathedral (with a few exceptions), normally attend the Specialist Music School at Wells—one of five within England—that is located within a co-educational independent (fee-paying, non-state-aided) school for pupils aged 4–18 years.

Physically, the three components (independent school, music school and cathedral) are in one complex that nestles around the original medieval buildings. The closeness and similarities of the geographical spaces are integral to the dominant musical identities and the way that these are shaped. These encompass the choristers' identities in music—as musicians, instrumentalists, singers, performers, as well as the way that music becomes interwoven with their personal identity, as young people, female, educated at Wells (see Hargreaves, Miell, & MacDonald, 2002 for a discussion on 'identity in music' and 'music in identity').

Principle 2: Activity systems are 'multi-voiced', embracing multiple viewpoints, traditions and interests

Members of the cathedral staffing—the clergy, administrators, voluntary helpers, musicians, caterers—each bring their own perspective, collective and individual, as to their purpose within the collective identity. The regular members of the cathedral congregation and the many thousands of visitors from the UK and overseas also bring different expectations to bear on the activity and how this is perceived. Although the music is a key component of cathedral life, its centrality will vary, depending on whether the perspective is from one of the professional musicians, including the choristers (and their parents), or consumers of, and audiences for, the music (whether official cathedral employees or others).

'Multi-voicedness' is evident in the multiple viewpoints that are made manifest, both between different cathedral choirs, as well as within the choral community, for example, with Wells girls often reporting that they see themselves as 'different' from the boys, in behaviour, maturity, and—sometimes—vocal sounds. A recent survey (cited earlier), for example, of why certain cathedrals had introduced female choristers reported diverse explanations at the local level (Stewart, 2006). Some Directors of Music suggested that it was a result of difficulties in male chorister recruitment; others said that female recruitment provided an opportunity to reduce the pressure on their boys, while many felt that they needed to address issues of equal opportunity.

Principle 3: Activity systems 'take shape and are transformed over lengthy periods of time' (Engeström, 2001b, p. 136)

The all-male cathedral choir in England has a 1,400 year history. This powerful tradition has managed to survive across the centuries despite major political and physical upsets in the country at large. Yet, even within this tradition there has been change, such as in the increased numbers of male choristers in the choir, the constant additions to the musical repertoire, including the design of the layout of the psalter (changed in the mid-eighteenth century to include 'pointing' to indicate changes in the chant in relation to the text—Mould, 2007) and the inclusion of hymns, as well as variations in the number of sung services across the week. Similarly, the introduction of female choristers at Salisbury in 1991 had several precedents earlier in the twentieth century, most notably in key cathedrals in Wales and Scotland and, for equally pragmatic and professional reasons, in the English cathedrals in Bradford, Bury St Edmonds, and Leicester. These examples would have been well known within the professional community of people with the responsibility for directing the cathedral choirs. This is a relatively small community—the Choir Schools Association, for example, has 44 members—with its own informal and formal professional networks, including the Cathedral Organists' Association. Members meet regularly, share experiences and are aware of what is happening locally, regionally, and nationally within the cathedral music community. The musical employment itself embraces an apprenticeship system where an Organ Scholar in one location might become an Assistant Organist somewhere else and then Organist and Master of the Choristers in a third location.

At Wells, there is evidence of 'historicity' in that the introduction of female choristers in 1993 after a period of more than 600 years of a male-only tradition had a profound effect on the local community, being strongly welcomed by all the parents of girls in the choir (past and present) and school, promoted as a sign of being 'in tune' with society's equal opportunities policy, and generating a formalized review of what features of the existing chorister tradition needed to be incorporated to ensure that the expected musical culture continued. When interviewed in 1999, having just finished their choir membership, the first female choristers to be appointed at Wells reported that they had a sense of being pioneers, not least because they all joined as a group, whereas the current senior choristers had entered an established choir a few at a time, with senior role models available to ease their induction into the choral tradition.

> Principle 4: Change and development arise from 'contradictions' that are 'historically accumulating structural tensions within and between activity systems' (Engeström, 2001b p. 137)

It is possible to recognize the importance of 'dialogicality' (the formation of ideas through dialogue), 'multi-voicedness' (a recognition that actions and ideas are informed by many voices—Daniels, 2004), and 'contradictions' in the ways that different organizations and groups responded to the innovation at Salisbury. The data suggest, for example, that the 'activity' of the all-male choral tradition needed to adapt to explicit sociopolitical expectations concerning the provision of equal opportunities in wider society. Individual members of the public and the cathedral music community challenged the basis for the all-male hegemony and the ongoing exclusion of females. Yet, the dominant patriarchal perspectives that supported traditional chorister membership had both physical and sociopsychological foundations. The perceived bias in the type of sound produced traditionally by boy choristers drew on the structure and function of the young male voice within liturgical and musical contexts. Because this sound was fostered by existing musical practices, as well as by expectations within the cathedral community, a gendered assumption was made that this type of vocal output was 'unique' to the young male voice and unavailable to the young female. Examples of gendered practice are evident elsewhere, such as in parental behaviour, mass media images, choices of children's toys and musical instruments. Not surprisingly, by the ages of 6 and 7 years, 'most children achieve gender constancy—a mature understanding that gender is stable and not influenced by superficial changes in body appearance or dress' (Lippa, 2002, p. 161).

However, notwithstanding the gendered discourse (see Mills, 2003), evidence began to accumulate from a small number of cathedrals in various parts of the UK to suggest that girls could sing as well as boys if they had the opportunity. Furthermore, the argument about the 'uniqueness' of the all-male sound was weakened subsequently by various empirical studies of gender attribution to chorister vocal products. These demonstrated that differences in physical sex need not equate to perceived differences in vocal output and also challenged the cultural stereotype of the chorister voice as 'male'.

In the case of Wells, change and development are evidenced in how the cathedral and school authorities and choir members have needed to address certain emergent 'contradictions' since 1993, such as in seeking additional female chorister recruitment from another local school; changing the ceiling of the female choir leaving age from 14 to 16 years at a time of low recruitment, which itself then offered new possibilities in the vocal timbre available for performance from the oldest choristers; adapting to changes in senior personnel, such as the appointment of a new Master in 2004—with concurrent subtle changes in rehearsal and performance expectations and practices; establishing appropriate financial support for female choristers; and in ensuring that the school and cathedral organization systems interrelate effectively.

Other 'contradictions' that have emerged from the introduction of choristers across the cathedral sector include dealing with the effects of boys singing less regularly. Although this could be a benefit if the rehearsal time remained constant, some directors of music have voiced concerns that the introduction of girls may mean insufficient practice of actual sung performance. Others suggested that the boys may be slower in learning new repertoire and have less opportunity to be expert in the complete Psalm repertoire if they do not sing all the services, as well as being less prepared to take part in radio broadcasts and recordings (Stewart, 2006).

> Principle 5: Activity systems are subject to the possibility of 'expansive transformations' (Engeström, 2001b, p. 137)

The few (rare) examples of successful female chorister introduction in a small number of cathedrals in England, Wales, and Scotland earlier in the twentieth century appeared to have had little impact on the all-male hegemony. But Salisbury's innovation—as the first old cathedral to embrace female choristers—was the catalyst for a major transformation (as portrayed in Figs 10.1 and 10.2). The contradictions that were evident across the sector (see Principle 4 above) produced seeds for change, yet within a way that has ensured the overall survival of the choral tradition.

The commonality of the liturgy provides a framework in which certain elements are known and recurrent, such as the customary organization of sung elements within Choral Evensong (Psalms, Canticles, Responses, and Anthem). But there is also variety across the sector in the choice of music, in the allocation of roles and responsibilities within the choir and in which elements of the personnel sing which services during the week. This inherent diversity provided a framework for expansive transformation. At Salisbury in 1991, the females began to share the services with the males by singing Evensong on Mondays and Wednesdays. At Portsmouth in 2006 the male chorister routine meant that they were not required to sing on Thursdays. This provided the opportunity for a new female and male (including ex-chorister) adolescent choir to sing Evensong without requiring any reduction in the weekly workload for the boys. The innovation of female choristers has been an 'expansive transformation' in the established chorister culture across the sector (with individual variability), as well as within the organization of a local cathedral activity system. For Engeström (2005, p. 321), an expansive transformation occurs when individuals question accepted practice 'and it gradually expands into a collective movement or institution'. That so many young females are now able to participate in cathedral music is testimony to the effects of questioning the all-male tradition, particularly at Salisbury.

Conclusion

'Once in place, gender stereotypes influence people's behaviour in many ways' (Lippa, 2002, p. 161). In terms of the appropriate sex for a cathedral chorister, there is a 1,400 year tradition to suggest that choristers stereotypically should be male. Nevertheless, the historical–cultural system that maintained this notion has been subject to various challenges since its English inception in

Canterbury in 597, some recent, others being much older. Until the sixteenth century, related religious foundations—nunneries—had both male and female intakes and their daily liturgy would have been celebrated around similar music being performed by young female voices. Then, for about 400 years, an all-male hegemony existed until, for various pragmatic reasons, individual cathedrals in different parts of the UK introduced females to sing daily services during the latter part of the twentieth century. However, the innovation at Salisbury was the 'tipping point' (see Gladwell, 2000) that encouraged the cathedral music community as a collective to engage formally with the possibility of including young female singers as choristers. Much has changed, yet the choral tradition—in terms of the musical repertoire and the characteristic vocal tone—persists. Boys continue to sing, either alongside girls (in two English cathedrals), or alternating with girls (now in the majority of cathedrals). The musical culture has adapted and, in doing so, has expanded (literally, in terms of the numbers of choristers across the country, as well as theoretically in relation to the activity theory notion of expansion as change). Some commentators have expressed concerns that the changes have created a persistent 'threat' to the continuing existence of the all-male choir. In contrast, supporters of female choristers note that there is not yet full equality across the sector, either in the numbers of services being sung, or in the funding available to support them. Overall, this range of perspectives is another example of the 'multi-voicedness' within the system (see Engeström, 2001a) and evidence of the possibility of further change in the future.

The application of activity theory (see Engeström, 2005) has been useful in suggesting that the dynamics of this tradition are identifiable and powerful, yet flexible. The theory has also been useful in illuminating how the development of an individual chorister's musical identity is shaped towards the dominant cultural model, yet, at the same time, is not immune to wider sociomusical forces within the dominant musical landscape outside the cathedral. Tradition and transformation coexist at different levels and are exampled in the individual pathways that young singers follow as they move from childhood into adolescence. Whatever the future brings, we should celebrate the cultural shift that has brought a widening of contemporary access to a unique choral tradition and the increased numbers of young people who are becoming expert in its sung performance.

Acknowledgements

The research that informs this article was supported in part by the UK Arts and Humanities Research Board under grant B/SG/AN8886/APN14717. I am also grateful to: Claire E. Stewart for her research into the details of Anglican choral foundations in UK cathedrals, including information on the background to the innovations in Bradford and Salisbury; Professor David Howard, University of York, for our ongoing collaborative work gathering acoustic data on female chorister singing; and Dr Evangelos Himonides for his specialist technical support and knowledge in our recording of individual choristers.

References

Bannon, L. (2008). *What is activity theory?* Retrieved 16 March 2008 from http://carbon. cudenver.edu/~mryder/itc_data/act_dff.html

Barrett, M. S. (2005). Musical communication and children's communities of musical practice. In D. Miell, R. MacDonald, & D.J. Hargeaves (Eds.), *Musical communication* (pp. 261–80). New York: Oxford University Press.

Bedny, G. Z., Seglin, M. H., & Meister, D. (2000). Activity theory: history, research and application. *Theoretical Issues in Ergonomics Science, 1*(2), 168–206.

Campaign for the Traditional Cathedral Choir (undated). Available from http://www.ctcc. org.uk/index.htm

Choir Schools Association (undated). *About the Choir Schools' Association.* Retrieved 16 March 2008 from http://www.choirschools.org.uk/2csahtml/aboutcsa.htm

Cole. M. (1999). Cultural psychology: some general principles and a concrete example. In Y. Engeström, R. Miettinen, & R-L. Punamäki (Eds.), *Perspectives on activity theory* (pp. 87–106). Cambridge: Cambridge University Press.

Daniels, H. (2004). Cultural historical activity theory and professional learning. *International Journal of Disability, Development and Education, 51*(2), 185–200.

Day, T. (2000). English cathedral choirs in the twentieth century. In J. Potter (Ed.), *The Cambridge companion to singing* (pp. 123–32). Cambridge: Cambridge University Press.

Department of Education and Science (1981). *Education Act 1981.* London: HMSO.

Dickenson, H. (2001). Salisbury Cathedral celebrations of the foundation of the girls' choir. Unpublished manuscript of the sermon preached 15 July 2001.

Engeström, Y. (2001a). *Expansive learning at work: toward an activity–theoretical reconceptualisation. With a commentary by Michael Young.* Learning Group, Occasional Paper No. 1. London: Institute of Education.

Engeström, Y. (2001b). Expansive learning at work: toward an activity theoretical reconceptualization. *Journal of Education and Work, 14*(1), 133–56.

Engeström, Y. (2005). *Developmental work research: expanding activity theory in practice.* Berlin: Lehmanns Media.

Engeström Y., & Miettinen, R. (1999). Introduction. In Y. Engeström, R. Miettinen, & R.-L. Punamäki (Eds.), *Perspectives on activity theory* (pp. 1–16). Cambridge: Cambridge University Press.

Gackle, L. (2000). Understanding voice transformation in female adolescents. In L. Thurman & G. Welch (Eds.), *Bodymind and voice: foundations of voice education* (rev. edn, pp. 739–44). Denver, CO: National Center for Voice and Speech, The VoiceCare Network, Fairview Voice Center.

Gladwell, M. (2000). *The tipping point: how little things can make a big difference*. London: Little, Brown & Co.

Hargreaves, D. J., Miell, D., & MacDonald, R. (2002). What are musical identities, and why are they important? In R. MacDonald, D. J. Hargreaves & D. Miell (Eds.), *Musical identities* (pp. 1–20). New York: Oxford University Press.

Howard, D. M., Barlow, C., Szymanski, J., & Welch, G. F. (2001). Vocal production and listener perception of trained English cathedral girl and boy choristers. *Bulletin of the Council for Research in Music Education, 147*, 81–86.

Howard, D. M., Szymanski, J. & Welch, G. F. (2002). Listener's perception of English cathedral girl and boy choristers. *Music Perception, 20*(1), 35–49.

Howard, D. M., & Welch, G. F. (2002). Female chorister development: a longitudinal study at Wells, UK. *Bulletin of the Council for Research in Music Education, 153/4*, 63–70.

Johansson, K. (2008). *Organ improvisation—activity, action and rhetorical practice*. Studies in Music and Music Education, No. 11. Malmö, Sweden: Malmö Academy of Music.

Lave, J., & Wenger, E. (1991). *Situated learning: legitimate peripheral participation*. Cambridge: Cambridge University Press.

Laven, M. (2002). *Virgins of Venice*. London: Viking/Penguin.

Leont'ev, A. N. (1978). *Activity, consciousness and personality*. Englewood Cliffs: Prentice-Hall.

Lippa, R. A. (2002). *Gender, nature and nurture*. Mahwah: Erlbaum.

Mills, S. (2003). Language. In M. Eagleton (Ed.), *A concise companion to feminist theory* (pp. 133–52). Oxford: Blackwell.

Moore, R., & Killian, J. (2000–2001). Perceived gender differences and preferences of solo and group treble singers by American and English children and adults. *Bulletin of the Council for Research in Music Education, 147*, 138–44.

Mould, A. (2007). *The English chorister: a history*. London: Hambledon Continuum.

Owens, P., & Sweller, J. (2008). Cognitive load theory and music instruction. *Educational Psychology, 28*(1), 29–45.

Page, A. (2008). *Of choristers—ancient and modern*. Retrieved 16 March 2008 from http://www.ofchoristers.net/index.htm

Riley, J. (2006, 20 January). Girls are taking over from the boys in choir. *Liverpool Echo*, p. 1.

Ryder, M. (2008). *What is activity theory?* Retrieved 16 March 2008, from http://carbon.cudenver.edu/~mryder/itc_data/act_dff.html

Sackett, E., & Skinner, J. (2006). *Abbeys, priories and cathedrals*. Salisbury, UK: Francis Frith Collection.

Seal, R. (1991). Notes for precentor's conference, Durham September 18, 1991. Unpublished manuscript.

Sergeant, D. C., Sjölander, P. J., & Welch, G. F. (2005). Listeners' identification of gender differences in children's singing. *Research Studies in Music Education, 24*, 28–39.

Sergeant, D. C., & Welch, G. F. (1997). Perceived similarities and differences in the singing of trained children's choirs. *Choir Schools Today, 11*, 9–10.

Sergeant, D. C., & Welch, G. F. (2008). Age-related changes in long-term average spectra of children's voices. *Journal of Voice, 22*(6), 658–70.

Sergeant, D. C., & Welch, G. F. (2009). Gender differences in long-term average spectra of children's singing voices. *Journal of Voice, 23*(3), 319–36.

Small, C. (1999). Musicking—the meanings of performing and listening. A lecture. *Music Education Research, 1*(1), 9–21.

Smith, J., & Young, P. (2009) Chorus (i). *Grove Music Online.* Oxford: Oxford University Press. Retrieved 5 October 2009, from http://www.oxfordmusiconline.com/subscriber/article/grove/music/05684?q=song+school+of+the+Jewish+Temple&search=quick&pos=5&_start=1#firsthit

Smith, R., & Walker, I. (2002). 'Oh no! Where's my recorder?': using activity theory to understand a primary music program. In R. Smith & J. Southcott (Eds.), *A community of researchers. Proceedings of the XXII annual conference of the Australian Association for Research in Music Education* (pp. 158–63). Melbourne: AARME.

Stevens, C. (1999, 12 December). Jobs for the girls. *Classical Music,* p. 12.

Stewart, C. (2006, 8 November). *Investigating female cathedral choristers.* Presentation to the Cathedral Organists Association, St Paul's Cathedral, London.

Townhill, D. (2000). *The imp and the thistle: the story of a life of music making.* York: G.H. Smith & Sons.

UK Government (1975). *Sex Discrimination Act 1975.* London: Stationery Office.

UK Government (1976). *Race Relations Act 1976.* London: Stationery Office.

Vygotsky, L. (1978). *Mind in society* (M. Cole, Trans.). Cambridge, MA: Harvard University Press.

Walker, I., & Smith, R. (2001, August 23–26). An activity theory perspective on a primary music program. In Y. Minami & M. Shinzanoh (Eds.), *Proceedings of the 3rd Asia–Pacific Symposium on Music Education Research and International Symposium on 'Uragoe' and Gender: Vol. 1.* (pp. 123–28). Nagoya: Aichi University of Education.

Warnock Committee. (1978). *Special educational needs: the Warnock report.* London: Department of Education and Science.

Wenger, E. (1998). *Communities of practice: learning, meaning, and identity.* Cambridge: Cambridge University Press.

Welch, G. F. (2006). Singing and vocal development. In G. McPherson (Ed.), *The child as musician: a handbook of musical development* (pp. 311–29). New York: Oxford University Press.

Welch, G. F. (2007). Addressing the multifaceted nature of music education: An activity theory research perspective. *Research Studies in Music Education, 28,* 23–38.

Welch, G. F., Himonides, E., Saunders, J., Papageorgi, I., Rinta, T., Stewart, C., et al. (2008). *The national singing programme for primary schools in England: an initial baseline study overview, February 2008.* London: Institute of Education.

Welch, G. F., & Howard, D. (2002). Gendered voice in the cathedral choir. *Psychology of Music, 30*(1), 102–20.

Chapter 11

On being and becoming a cathedral chorister: a cultural psychology account of the acquisition of early musical expertise

Margaret S. Barrett

Introduction

The life and learning experience of a cathedral chorister is a unique one. The domain of musical practice in which the cathedral chorister participates has been shaped around the sound of the boys' voice prior to adolescence and the attendant physiological changes that occur at that time. Unlike other musical practices in which young people participate, the performance peak for a chorister occurs around the ages of 12 or 13 years. Once the processes of voice change commence, the unique sound qualities of the cathedral chorister can be overlaid by the unpredictable 'cracks' and 'swoops' of the developing male voice. For some, the voice that emerges at the end of this process carries them on into further musical engagement as a singer. For others, continued musical engagement as a performer rests in the individual's capacity to play another instrument. Nevertheless, in a relatively short period of time—about five years—many cathedral choristers develop musical expertise and perform at the highest levels. How does this occur? What individual, social, and/or cultural conditions support the development of this early expert performance? What might we learn about the acquisition of expertise through the study of this practice? In this chapter, I explore these questions through an account of a longitudinal narrative case-study investigation of life and learning in an English cathedral choir.[1]

---

[1] An earlier version of this chapter was presented as the Jacinth Oliver Address to the XVIIth Conference of the Australian Society, for Music Education, Launceston, Tasmania, 10–14 July 2009.

Cultural psychology and music learning

Jerome Bruner reminds us that 'education is a major embodiment of a culture's way of life, not just a preparation for it' (Bruner, 1996, p. 13). This observation is peculiarly apt when considering the education of a cathedral chorister. Whereas the educational practice of the cathedral chorister might be seen as an intensive preparation for later learning and life in music, the day-to-day educational experience of a cathedral chorister embodies a particular culture's 'way of life', supporting and enabling the continuing spiritual practice of the Anglican Church, and contributing to the promulgation of sacred choral music as a Western musical practice. Through this process, not only are cathedral choristers part of a continuing educational tradition, but they also ensure that major cultural and spiritual traditions are maintained and developed through their efforts.

In writing of a cultural psychology approach to education, Bruner (1996) suggests that:

> Culturalism's task is a double one. On the 'macro' side, it looks at the culture as a system of values, thoughts, exchanges, obligations, opportunities, power. On the 'micro' side, it examines how the demands of a cultural system affect those who must operate within it. In that latter spirit, it concentrates on how individual human beings construct 'realities' and meanings that adapt them to the system, at what personal cost, and with what expected outcomes. (pp. 11–12)

As Bruner acknowledges, whereas humans create and construct cultural systems, these cultural systems, in turn, shape human engagement and interaction in and through culture, over time, at individual and collective levels. The macro system of the English cathedral choir embodies a particular history and system of values, thoughts, exchanges, obligations, opportunities, and power.[2] Although sometimes considered a unique English tradition, there are earlier and historically concurrent traditions that have 'employed' children in the service of religious and cultural practice, including those of the Abbey of Cluny (Boynton & Cochelin, 2006), and early-modern Seville (Borgerding, 2006). What is perhaps a distinguishing feature of the English cathedral choir tradition is the dedicated educational system embodied in the cathedral choir schools, the longevity of this system, and this cultural system's continuing efforts to respond to changes in the larger society of which it is a part, in order to maintain and sustain its existence. These efforts have included an emphasis on ensuring that the education provided in these schools is a 'first-class

---

[2] See Mould, 2007, for a history and account of the English cathedral choral tradition; also see Chapter 10 of this volume.

education' (Mould, 2007, p. 246), and increasing commercialization of many of the choir's activities, including demanding schedules of performance beyond those undertaken in service to the cathedral, touring, and recording. Writing in 2007, Mould asserts:

> Today, the picture of an association of fine schools, educating some 25,000 pupils and over a thousand choristers and probationers is little less than thrilling. Read the academic results table of the country's secondary schools published annually and there at or close to the top of their respective lists stand the secondary choir schools, whether independent and selective or Voluntary Aided and comprehensive. Go to the internet and read the latest inspection report of any choir school and one can find a picture of enlightened schooling and attentive pastoral care, the best reports outstandingly, even movingly, good. (p. 246)

Excellence and achievement, both academic and musical, are indicated as markers of the English cathedral choir tradition. Indeed, in terms of musical achievement, choristers experience and participate in music-making at an expert level. How is that expertise acquired? And what are the environmental conditions that support this early acquisition of expertise?

Describing expertise

Ericsson suggests that:

> Expertise . . . refers to the characteristics, skills, and knowledge that distinguish experts from novices and less experienced people. In some domains there are objective criteria for finding experts, who are consistently able to exhibit superior performance for representative tasks in a domain. For example . . . professional musicians can perform pieces of music in a manner that is unattainable for less skilled musicians. (2006, p. 3)

Chi (2006) identifies seven ways in which experts excel, including: generating the best solution to a problem or task; detecting and recognizing features that elude novices; qualitatively analysing problems and tasks over time; self-monitoring thought and action; identifying and selecting appropriate strategies; exhibiting greater opportunism in solving problems and undertaking tasks; and retrieving relevant domain knowledge and skills. As a counterpoint, Chi also identifies seven ways in which experts fall short, suggesting that they may be domain-limited, overly confident, context-dependent within a domain, inflexible, inaccurate in their prediction, judgment and advice, tend to gloss over the problem/task, and exhibit bias and functional fixedness (Chi, 2006, pp. 24–27).

The development of expertise

Expertise in a domain of practice has often been attributed to the possession of unique talents or skills, and viewed as the manifestation of 'innate gifts' in that domain, and/or genius. Such a view might be particularly tempting when considering instances of early expertise as evidenced in the musical practice of cathedral choristers. Recent research has begun to trouble the view that 'talent' or 'innate giftedness' is a necessary precursor to the development of expert performance (Ericsson, Nandagopal, & Roring, 2005; Howe, 1990, 1999; Howe, Davidson, & Sloboda, 1998).

Howe challenges the 'talent account' of high attainment (Howe, 1990, 1999; Howe, Davidson, & Sloboda, 1998), suggesting that variations in experience such as the quality and time spent practising, quality and length of education, and, individual motivation and commitment, provide alternative accounts (Howe, 1999, p. 195). He points to the potential dangers of an adherence to the 'talent account', commenting:

> Does it greatly matter whether the talent account is true or false? It matters immensely . . . The fact that the talent account is widely believed in has consequences that affect the lives of numerous young people. Within certain fields of expertise, such as music, unquestioning acceptance of the talent account is almost invariably accompanied by the belief that excellence is only attainable by those children who are innately talented. A frequent result of teachers and other influential adults having this combination of beliefs is that when scarce educational resources or opportunities are being allocated they are likely to be directed exclusively toward those young people who are thought to possess a special talent. Young children who are believed to lack innate talents are denied resources that are vital in order to gain any chance of succeeding. (Howe, 1999, p. 191)

Howe's concern at the potential deleterious effects of talent accounts, and the ways in which the label of 'giftedness' might lead to the withdrawal of educational resources and 'superior training resources' from some, is evident in the work of other researchers.

In disputing the 'innate giftedness' account of expertise, Ericsson et al. argue that the two necessary factors that support the development of expert performance are 'environmental conditions' and 'appropriate training (deliberate practice)', rather than 'the fixed constraints of a person's basic capacities' (2005, p. 291). Drawing on Simon and Chase's (1973) 10-year rule, these authors point to the incremental nature of the development of expert performance as a key indicator that expertise is not individually and uniquely 'gifted'; rather, they argue that 'expert performance results from acquired cognitive and physiological adaptations due to extended deliberate practice' (2005, p. 287). Importantly, they assert that the perception of giftedness in children 'gives children access to superior training resources, resulting in developmental advantages' (2005, p. 287).

Bloom's (1985) early interview study of internationally recognized performers in the domains of swimming and tennis, sculpting and piano performance, and mathematics and molecular biology, identified the two elements of early exposure and instruction, and strong family support, as key elements in the development of expertise. Early exposure and instruction and strong family support may be classified as 'environmental conditions.' These conditions have also been identified in Howe's (1999) study of 'genius' and, more recently, may be traced in Peter Doherty's (2005) autobiography, *The beginner's guide to winning the Nobel Prize.* Howe suggests that exceptional talents as exhibited by those distinguished as 'genius' arise from a combination of early life circumstances and opportunities, combined with individual drive, determination, and focus. In other studies of individuals who demonstrate high abilities (Csikszentmihalyi & Csikszentmihalyi, 1993; Csikszentmihalyi, Rathunde, & Whalen, 1993; Manturzewska, 1990), the nature and circumstances of individuals' early life are identified as significant features. In these studies the family's role is crucial in providing physical, emotional, and social support, through:

1. facilitating access to the best teachers, education opportunities, equipment and materials;

2. demonstrating positive values for the activity and the child's efforts in the domain; and

3. ensuring that the social structure of the family accommodates and supports a practice and performance regime.

For Ericsson (1996), expertise is acquired over four distinct phases of development, those of: playful interaction with the domain of practice; structured lessons and monitored practice; commitment to attaining excellence in the domain of practice and commencement of 'professional training'; and an original contribution to the domain. Through these phases the role of the parent is crucial in:

1. introducing the child to the domain;

2. monitoring practice and assisting the child to acquire the practice habits necessary for skills development;

3. seeking out the best teachers in the domain of practice and facilitating the child's access to opportunities (for example, residential camps, competitions, master classes, and other intensive education opportunities); and

4. demonstrating value for the activity and the domain of practice.

The role of 'practice'

What is consistent in all accounts of expertise is the role of 'practice.' Lehmann & Gruber suggest that 'we do not know whether practice is a *sufficient* condition for high achievement, but it is certainly a *necessary* one for invoking the cognitive, physiological, and psycho-motor adaptations observed in experts' (2006, p. 458). Various studies have identified 'deliberate practice' (Ericsson, Krampe, & Tesch-Römer, 1993) and the hours spent in that activity (Ericsson et al., 1993; Sloboda, Davidson, Howe, & Moore, 1996) as key to the attainment of high achievement in musical performance. The 'gold standard' of 10,000 hours of practice or the 10-year rule (Ericsson & Crutcher, 1990) to attain competence has been subject to some dispute. In the domain of music, for example, research suggests that the numbers of hours required for advanced performance varies from instrument to instrument (Jørgensen, 1997, 2008), with singers identified as the group that starts latest and practices least (Kopiez, 1998). The conditions of practice also vary from genre to genre with classical musicians tending to spend many hours in solitary practice whereas non-classical musicians including popular, jazz, and Scottish traditional musicians tend to spend the bulk of practice time working with others, and/or playing along to recordings individually and collectively, as a means to acquiring particular performers' characteristic licks and phrases (Gruber, Degner, & Lehmann, 2004; Papageorgi et al., 2010). Beyond these distinctions between instrument and genre, the most telling component of practice is that is it mindful practice, rather than mere repetition—in short that it is 'deliberate.' Deliberate practice focuses on two aspects of learning:

1. improving those skills you have; and

2. 'extending the reach and range of your skills' (Ericsson, Prietula, & Cokely, 2007, p. 119).

Ericsson et al. also emphasize the need for practice to be critiqued and monitored by a coach or mentor (2007, p. 120) as a key strategy in developing expertise. In relation to the important role of feedback in and through the practice process these authors note that 'a century of laboratory research has revealed that learning is most effective when it includes focused goals, such as improving a specific aspect of performance, feedback that compares the actual to the desired performance, and opportunities for repetition to achieve the desired level of proficiency' (Ericsson et al., 2005, p. 294).

The importance of adult monitoring (including providing feedback) and engagement in children's early practice has been demonstrated in a number of studies (Davidson, Howe, Moore, & Sloboda, 1996; McPherson & Davidson, 2002, 2006) and is seen as an important precursor to the self-regulation of practice (McPherson & Zimmerman, 2002). In recent research, McPherson (2009) has focused on the parental role in children's musical development, proposing that the development of musical performance hinges on the interaction between the goals and aspirations parents hold for their child, the parenting style of the family, and the parenting practices that are enacted. Children's competence and motivation to succeed are intrinsically linked to the sociocultural environment of the family, as well as that of the school and/or the music learning experience. Where children feel competent, autonomous, connected to family, and view the activities they engage in as purposeful (McPherson, 2009), their approach to these activities will be more positive. McPherson suggests that parenting practices are shaped by children's achievements in an interactive dialogue that continuously shapes and re-shapes the goals and aspirations parents hold for individual children, and consequently the communication of these to their child in both overt and covert ways. Importantly, an *authoritative* parenting style, characterized by 'high involvement in the child's learning, high structuring of the environment in which the learning takes place and high autonomy-support' (2009, p. 98) is the ideal.

It should be noted that the bulk of the music studies referenced above have focused on learning in Western classical music genres. Those studies that have expanded the investigative lens to include other musical genres suggest that family environment and parenting practices may have less impact on music learning and engagement. In a study investigating tertiary students' perceptions of musical performance education and the acquisition of musical expertise that included classical, popular, jazz and Scottish traditional musicians, age of initial engagement with music and family involvement in music engagement and learning were ranked as less relevant by non-classical musicians (Creech et al., 2008). Analysis of survey responses of 244 musicians across these genres indicated that non-classical musicians tended to commence their music education later than classical musicians and rated well-known performers and significant musical events as more important influences in their musical development than parents and/or teachers. Although these findings might suggest that genre specific differences exist in the environmental conditions that support the acquisition of expertise in music, the bulk of the research literature generated in domains as diverse as music, sport, mathematics, and chess suggests that there are some common factors in the development of expertise.

The research literature suggests that the twin factors of environmental conditions (including positive and supportive family values and structures, and early and continuous access to resources and education) and appropriate education (including deliberate practice that is goal-focused, and critiqued and monitored by an expert other) are key to the development of expertise. When these factors are considered in relation to the experience of the cathedral chorister an apparent paradox emerges. Many cathedral choristers leave their family at the age of 6 or 7 years to become boarders in cathedral schools, an experience that might be viewed as deleterious in some accounts of the development of expertise. This chapter explores the environmental conditions and education of cathedral choristers in an Oxbridge cathedral choir school in order to understand the acquisition of expertise in this setting.

Methodology

The research project on which this chapter draws aimed to investigate the meaning and function of music in the lives of cathedral choristers engaged in a highly demanding environment of musical practice, and to identify the music teaching and learning practices employed in this setting. The methodological approach was longitudinal narrative case study conducted over a two-year period (2005–2006). The case, an 'Oxbridge' cathedral choir school, provided the context for the investigation of the phenomena of musical meaning and function in the choristers' lives, and teaching and learning practices. This chapter focuses on the acquisition of musical expertise in this environment, specifically, teaching and learning practices that support the acquisition of expertise, including environmental and cultural factors (Bruner's 'values, thoughts, exchanges, obligations, opportunities, power'; 1996, p. 13). Although the case might be considered 'unique' and therefore intrinsic in nature, there are sufficient parallels between this case and others reported in the literature[3] to suggest that the case might also function instrumentally (Stake, 1995, 2000), that is, as a means to making 'petit generalizations' (Stake, 1995, 2000). The use of a narrative approach to the reporting of the case study is intended to provide readers with a rich account of the phenomenon in order to increase the possibilities of transfer to other settings and contexts.

The 'community of musical practice' (Barrett, 2005a, 2005b) at the centre of the case inducts boys (only) into the centuries-old tradition of choral practice. About four boys are admitted annually to the choir as probationers (aged 7 years), maintaining the choir numbers at 20 boys. Formal entry to the choir from probationary status generally occurs during year 4 of schooling (aged 8–9 years), with boys remaining in the choir until graduation from the school at the end of year 8 (aged about 13 years).

The project drew on rich and diverse data generation methods including: individual and dual observation (Barrett & Mills, 2009), small group and individual interviews with key participants in the community of musical practice, artefact analysis including cathedral service schedules, school publicity and

---

[3] See Chapter 10 of this volume, for example.

promotion material, curriculum documents, and repertoire. Project participants included the cathedral choristers (20 boys aged 8–13 years); other pupils
in the school (10 boys aged 8–13 years); school teachers including the school
music teacher, the boarding house matron, the headmaster; cathedral music
staff including the organist, the deputy organist, and two organ scholars; chorister parents (five mothers, three fathers); and several 'old boys' attending a
reunion of former choristers spanning the period 1936–1996. Small group
interviews were conducted with choristers and other pupils. Individual interviews were conducted with choristers across the year groups of the choir, and
all adults. Observations included dual and individual observation of rehearsals, secular and sacred performances including services (e.g. Easter Sunday,
Holy Eucharist, Christmas carol service), music lessons and other lessons over
a one-year period (June, 2005–June, 2006). These observations were 'natural-
istic' and recorded via field-note.

Interview, observation, and artefact data were analysed in order to identify
emergent themes that enlarged upon the phenomena of interest, the meaning
and function of music, and the teaching and learning practices evident in this
setting. In bringing a culturalist lens to this data, the analysis sought also to
identify those underlying values and cultural supports that enabled teaching
and learning, and, for the purposes of this chapter, the acquisition of musical
expertise to occur. The data were subsequently re-storied to provide a rich narrative account (Barone, 2001; Clandinin, 2006; Clandinin & Connelly, 2000)
of the acquisition of musical expertise in this setting.

The choir story

My first encounter with the choir took place one blustery Sunday in April
when I joined my colleague Janet Mills[4] at Sunday Eucharist at her 'local'
church. We were seated in a pew barely a metre from the choir stalls, a position
that afforded me an extraordinarily close view of the choir and director in
action. I recall my fascination as I watched the group of boys and men, ages
ranging from 8 years through to 20, 30, and beyond, working together to produce a sound glorious and mysterious in equal parts. My attention was drawn
to a young boy in the front row of the choir stalls; he was perhaps 8 years of age
and stood close by an older boy, eyes barely level with the music from which
both were reading. At times, the older boy would point to the page, or run his
finger under a line as he sang, glancing side-ways to check that the younger boy

---

[4] This chapter is dedicated to the memory of my co-researcher Dr Janet Mills.

was following the music. I noted that the younger boy did not always sing, his gaze alternating between the director, the score, the boy he stood next to, and those opposite. There were also times when, with his head lowered, he seemed more engaged with shuffling the kneeler cushion at his foot than with the musical activity that surrounded him. As the service continued through its various phases of contemplation and activity, I began to wonder how learning occurred in this environment; how young boys such as the lad who had caught my attention acquired the skills and expertise to sing enormously challenging choral music at a level to which many an adult choir could only aspire.

That curiosity led to long discussions between Janet and myself about the nature of learning and teaching in settings such as the cathedral choir to which these boys belonged, the environmental features that supported that learning and teaching, and how expertise in this musical practice developed. We were fortunate to be funded to undertake a research project to investigate these curiosities and so unfolded a relationship of some two years' duration with the choir.[5]

Gaining entry to the choir: selection

Selection into many cathedral choirs is via a comprehensive audition process that encompasses musical, academic, and social dimensions. The website for the King's School, Gloucester, for example, provides a detailed description of the dimensions of the music component of the voice trial process and the focus of selection:

> No special coaching or voice training is required or expected of those who attend a Voice Trial. The Cathedral Director of Music looks for boys who have an interest and ability in singing and a confident approach to challenges. A prospective chorister is asked to bring along one song that he enjoys singing: this can be a hymn, a carol, or even a nursery rhyme. Tests will also include those designed to measure the quality of the voice, the accuracy of the ear, the ability to pitch a note and the candidate's sense of rhythm. Reading aloud is also part of the test as a chorister has to be able to read old and contemporary English with reasonable confidence. (King's School Gloucester, 2009a)

The website of the cathedral choir at the centre of this project simply states that selection is via voice trial, academic test and interview.[6] Probing beyond the public description of the selection process with the choir director,

---

5 This project was funded by the British Academy Small Grants Scheme, 2004–2005, Mills, J. & Barrett, M. S. *Music as everyday life: a case study of learning and life in an English cathedral school.*

6 Information from the school website was retrieved on 5 July 2009. The url is not given due to de-identification of the school for the purpose of publication.

it emerges that for him two key qualities are necessary in a prospective chorister: musical potential and intellectual capacity.

> Well obviously potential. I think somehow one tries to make a decision about the musical ear, the quality of the ear—which is a bit hit and miss at that age, when they are 7 or 8. And the other is, how bright they are—intellectually how bright they are because, I think, for really good choirs . . . that if they are academically bright then they are able to understand some of the deeper concepts you might be trying to get across to them. So I find that the older ones . . . with those top two year groups, one can talk to them pretty much on the same level as you can to the adult members of the choir and they can understand more sophisticated concepts about musical issues, phrasing and structure and all those sorts of things . . . I suppose also, the other thing is that they get an understanding of what style means so if you are doing music by Vittoria, let's say, you don't have to say that you need them to do crescendo there—they just get used to the stylistic practice, their performance practice—in a way that those who have musical ears, lovely voices but they are not so bright—can't. And they have to be drilled more. (Choir director, interview 1)

Musical potential defined as the 'quality of the ear' and vocal range is assessed through 'very old-fashioned tests' according to the choir director.

> The most telling thing I do is where I get them to repeat a note that I have played on the piano and I tell them I am going to play a game and I generally go higher and higher and higher and, of course, many of them haven't realized that they can sing that high so they think that is quite funny. We are giggling away and suddenly I play a low note and I think those with the better ears get straight on to the low note. Those who have got less of an ear do a slide because they are expecting it to be up there because I have trapped them really. In a way that is almost the most telling thing that I do because picking the middle note out of three is something that you can learn to do really and some of them have been trained up to it. (Choir director, interview 1)

The school's music teacher elaborates on the musical component of the audition process identifying vocal range, pitch, rhythm, and general musicianship (in potential) as key considerations:

> We work on a number of things. The first thing is obviously voice range. If they have got no head voice access, I am always a bit cautious because it depends on how old they are . . . So that is one thing—range. Ear tests obviously—aural tests and they have to be able to pitch notes randomly—all over the keyboard—obviously within their range. Sing the lower note of two notes—the middle note of three and obviously that gets harder. The choir director has to play clusters and discordant stuff. Sing scales just to see if they can actually connect their voices from bottom to top. Playing their instruments if they offer an instrument but that isn't that important if they are young. We don't discriminate against them if they don't play an instrument but it is useful obviously as they would have made some sort of a start and we know what we are doing. Rhythm and rhythm tests. They clap back rhythms and various things that . . . get more complicated as we go along and they obviously sing a song that they have brought with them. That usually happens fairly early; and they do something familiar.

> They usually bring a hymn or something and the choir director tends to transpose up into different keys to see how they get on or he might start putting descant to put them off—the usual sort of stuff. And see if they can actually pitch for themselves or whether they have just relied on the piano. So it is pitch and rhythm and general musicianship is what we are testing. (Music teacher, interview 2)

When being judged in relation to intellectual capacity, prospective choristers undertake a series of reasoning tests. However, given reported increasing difficulties in recruiting, it emerges that the emphasis in this choir setting on intellectual ability might be outweighed by considerations of musical potential. As the music teacher remarked:

> In times when choristership was perhaps more attractive to parents, we had a lot more applicants and there used to be a benchmark that if the child had an IQ less than 125 he wasn't allowed to be a chorister. That is not something that we can afford to put into place now. (Music teacher, interview 2)

The audition process also considers a prospective chorister's social skills, and capacity for 'self-sufficiency'. In relation to this aspect of the selection process the music teacher remarked:

> As part of the audition process boys stay overnight in order to see how they cope with actually looking after themselves, to some extent. There is a matron there but obviously they need to be able to look out for themselves; brush their teeth and do whatever; get changed; put their washing in the bin. All these things . . . Self sufficiency. And perhaps seeing how they relate to other children in the classroom over a period of time. It is a difficult one—that, I think. We do have some quite unusual children auditioning, I would say . . . and we have to obviously think about how they are going to integrate with the other personalities that are already in their peer group or perhaps are going to be around in the dormitory or whatever because it is a very close environment up there and they need to be able to get on with children and to understand each other and have some sympathy or empathy with the other children. Just generally how they react to other children. (Music teacher, interview 2)

Given this range of tests and experiences the audition process in this choir school covers a two-day period and provides the prospective chorister with a 'taster' of the chorister life. In summarizing the qualities required of a chorister, one of the cathedral organ scholars suggested that choristers need:

> a mixture of intelligence, natural musicality, enthusiasm, dedication, team player . . . it doesn't matter whether they have had any musical experience before they arrive . . . If they have got the ear though, they will pick it up very quickly . . . and within a year or so, you can't tell which ones had done music before they arrived. (Organ scholar interview, visit 1)

Entering the choir

The commitment for the chorister family is a significant one and binds the chorister, and his family, to a major social contract with the school, the cathedral, the diocese, and the broader community. In one cathedral school, this commitment is made explicit very early in the process through placement of the following notice concerning chorister duties and cathedral expectations on the chorister recruitment website:

> Chorister's duties take priority over other school and social activities. As such there is a commitment required from both the Chorister and his family. Family holidays may only be taken during choir holidays. Parents have to be prepared to see that their son is brought to the Cathedral to meet all their commitments during term time, Holy Week, Easter, on the days between the end of Michaelmas up to and including Christmas Day.
>
> Choristers also take part in the Famous Three Choirs Festival held annually in August when the location rotates between Gloucester, Hereford, and Worcester. In addition special Diocesan and Civic services, radio and television performances, weddings and funerals involve the Choristers from time to time.
>
> Every effort is made to ensure that school lessons are missed on only a few occasions, equally the Choristers are encouraged to take as full a part as possible in school activities including drama and sport. The close liaison between the School and the Cathedral is complex and is managed by the chorister Tutor who has a role in both the King's School and the Cathedral. (King's School, 2009b)

Given the major disruption to 'ordinary' family life, the indication of substantial time commitments, and the potential interference with school and schooling outlined in the notice above, I am led to wonder 'Why do children and their families choose to take on the life of the chorister?' Several reasons emerged from interviews with parents, the boys, school staff—including the headmaster, teachers, the boarding housemaster and matron—and cathedral staff, including the choir director, the organist, and organ scholars. These ranged from an initiative of the prospective chorister himself, recognition of potential by others (generally a music teacher), the continuance of a family tradition, and/or the promise of a subsidized preparatory[7] school education (60% of full boarding fees) in a school of recognized quality, and the future prospect of attaining a music award to some of England's major public schools including Eton, Rugby, Shrewsbury, Wellington, Winchester.[8] Regardless of which of the above was foregrounded as the key component in the boys' entry into the choir, common features of every account were the boys' love of, or passion for, music, the evident valuing of music in the family environment, and active engagement in music-making of at least one of the parents and/or other family members.

---

[7] Preparatory school generally includes the schooling years of prep to grade 8.

[8] Information retrieved 5 July 2009, from the case study school's website. For the purposes of this study the school has been de-identified.

An initiative of the boy

Koji's[9] mother attributes her son's enrolment in the cathedral choir to three factors: his love of singing, his (initial) interest in being a boarder, and her encouragement of his piano playing. Her account of her son's ongoing involvement with the choir is tinged with reservation, however, as she acknowledges the difficulties of boarding, and the commitment to the cathedral through which the boys are given an early introduction to the obligations of service:

> My son, he loves singing. When he had a concert at his last school he made everyone laugh because he seemed so desperate to sing. So he sang a lot himself in the singing and everybody laughed because he was so happy . . . Koji insisted that he had a Voice Trial [and] said, 'I want to be a boarder, not a chorister but a boarder.' With children his soul, his soul does not belong to parents, it belongs to him so I can't stop him. After he was offered a place he decided to change his mind a bit but I said 'no' . . . I don't know if he likes boarding so much . . . They are talented but they also sacrifice some things. It seems they are desperate to sing. They are already making a contribution to society. They give service. They probably don't know this but they are giving service. Maybe service is not bad. It is a great discipline . . . it is like meditation where they have to sit down . . . it's [the choir] not a sort of showing off. (Mother interview, visit 2)

Philip's mother, a music teacher (as are the mothers of two of the other twenty boy choristers), also commented on her son's love of singing, describing her son as 'passionate about singing since before he could talk'. She characterizes her son as a 'live-wire', one for whom she 'thought the chorister life would keep him busy'. Philip started at the cathedral school in year 3 as there was no music at all in his previous primary school, and was quickly identified as a candidate for a voice trial by the music teacher at the cathedral school. Philip's mother describes music as:

> his passion. He has a CD of the choir in the car and he sings *all* the way home after 4 hours of singing on Sunday morning. From the back seat of the car he will cry 'Rewind it Mummy, I'm learning this one. Rewind it.' (Mother interview, visit 2)

Although she recognizes her son's passion for music and commitment to the choir, Philip's mother also remarks on the 'bitter-sweet aspect of the year', his first as a full chorister (aged 9 years). She continues:

> after a year it becomes apparent that not only is it as a chorister but also a music scholar—he just does what he really came here for—the singing. Last Sunday after service he said to me 'That piece of music was so beautiful, it made me tremble—I was so worried in case I got it wrong.'
> The choir is everything: you make sacrifices to do it. We had an aural tape on the way back in the car and I thought—can't you just relax? I feel torn between demands of the

---

[9] Pseudonyms are used throughout.

workload and pressure in terms of academic work, music scholar work, and choir work. And frustrated because he can't do more sport . . . But I have to recognize that he loves the standard of the music and singing with the men; he knows them all and they are his friends and he says, 'Would you be proud of me were I to come back as one of the men?' (Mother interview, visit 2)

An evident 'passion' for singing emerged also in Sam's mother's account of her son's early engagement with music. 'He could sing before he could talk', she began:

and at 1 year old—he would hear Beethoven, Mozart and sing back. He was bullied at his first school for singing. He used to sing when he's under pressure. The music teacher suggested a Voice Trial at 6 [years of age]. So we put him in [the cathedral school] in year 3—paid for that. That first year [in the cathedral school] nearly killed us [financially]. He started as probationer in year 4 when he was 8 [years old]. He liked being a probationer—although it was hard work in that first year to get his academic work up. (Mother interview, visit 2)

Sam's mother also spoke of the emotional strain of participation in the choir, commenting 'I don't come to many Evensongs because he can't handle it— him leaving' [for the boarding house]. Yet according to Sam's mother, that strain is tempered by other gains and her son's evident passion for and commitment to the choir.

He's gained in confidence, gained in knowledge and insight. It's making him more independent; he was having problems with other choristers and he's tackling these now in a more mature way. When I think of him with those children at his old school, he almost talks like an adult. He discusses what he has done during the week and the music and he'll sing the cadence of a melody that really thrills us. He loves it even more. When he's sick he'll say 'I'm letting the choir down.' He doesn't think of himself, he thinks of himself as part of an entity. He talks about the feeling he gets when he sings—he says 'you get this lump in your stomach and it rises into the chest and the hairs on the back of your neck stand up.' He loves Saturday school—even the theory, and he plays with the orchestra. He puts on tapes of *Songs of praise* in the car and sings all the way home. I still can't believe he's here. He fits in. He's like the other people. It's not an odd thing to love music or to sing. (Mother interview, visit 2)

For Sam and Philip in particular, belonging to the community of musical practice that is the choir, becoming 'part of an entity', plays a significant role in their participation and commitment to the choir.

Singing potential recognized by others

In many instances, parents, teachers, friends and/or family members noted a child's propensity to sing and evident enjoyment of music, and suggested that the boy attend a voice trial (as evidenced in Sam's case). Edward had attended the cathedral school since entering nursery school at 3½ years of age.

As his father describes it, a comment on a school report from the music teacher at the school precipitated the voice trial and subsequent offer of a place in the choir at the age of 7½ years. Given the family's valuing of music, with both parents involved in choirs and amateur music-making, the step to the choir seemed 'natural', although as Edward's father commented: the 'fees are a factor, the scholarship is a factor'. For Edward, his father suggests that 'generally he likes it, being boarders and being a little club together. As an only child he has twenty big brothers in the choir' (Father interview, visit 2).

Jonathon's story is similar to that of Edward's as he also comes from a family that values and practices music-making, with the initial suggestion to attend a voice trial again being made by the music teacher at the cathedral school where he attended first as a day boy (Mother interview, visit 2).

Tom's father's account of his son's entry into the choir indicates some of the extramusical reasons that might attract a child to become a chorister, and highlights the changes that have occurred early on in his son's experience of becoming and being a chorister:

> He started school in the state system and joined a local choir at age 5 for a brief period. He could always sing and my wife is very musical, and my brother took up music as a career. Tom learnt piano for 18 months or so and then joined as a chorister in September, 2005—aged 9. He loves it. He's the youngest and the smallest in the choir. He seems to enjoy the structure of the singing, the regimental life. He couldn't wait to be there as a full chorister. It was a bit of a Harry Potter effect going off to boarding school. His piano and cello are coming on in leaps and bounds. Our only complaint is having to leave home at the weekend. He's become so mature so quickly he's not the same little chap who came here two months ago.

At this point in the interview Tom's father fought back tears before continuing:

> He's streets ahead of his contemporaries that he left behind at the old school. We have a second child coming here. I don't know what we'll do with an empty house during the week. (Father interview, visit 2)

Continuing a family tradition

As a centuries-old tradition, it is not surprising that many young boys embarking on the life of a chorister are continuing a family tradition of some standing. Robert, a year 8 chorister, reflected on whose decision it was for him to audition for the choir, commenting:

> The whole family—literally the whole family did. My uncles were choristers, my Dad was a chorister at Durham Cathedral, and their Dad was a chorister . . . And so it was 'Wouldn't it be nice if Rob was a chorister?' (Robert interview, visit 2)

Continuing the family tradition was also evident in William's account:

> My Dad was a chorister at Litchfield and he wanted me to be in a choir and I went for this thing where you could be a chorister for a day at Salisbury. I tried for Salisbury but couldn't get in and I tried out Litchfield and [the case study] Cathedral School. I got in both and I decided to come here because it would be much closer to home. (William, boys' group interview, visit 1)

For some, the search for a chorister place was identified as a family 'quest', with one year 8 boy describing his Mum's search for a chorister place:

> I had already tried at Westminster but wasn't successful and I was going to go to Ely the next day but they gave me this place here. I had strong views about it and I talked to my Mum again [to take this place].

Securing a current and potential educational advantage

In considering what precipitated the decision to attend a voice trial and a family's subsequent commitment to the life of a chorister, the choir director initially remarked on the recognition of early 'potential' by a music teacher, or vicar or choirmaster, and suggestion by these individuals that the boy attend a choir school. He continued by outlining the dilemmas and opportunities that arise in such situations:

> There have been the cases where Johnny has been having piano lessons or something and the music teacher has said, 'Do you realize that he is really talented musically?', and perhaps they don't have—their child has been to the local primary school and they have never thought about spending any money on going to a private school. It is just not an issue so then the family gets thrown into turmoil because they think, 'How can we nurture this talent? Either we stick with going to the local school and we look at Saturday morning schools in the county . . .', or, 'Do we look at trying to plug him into what amounts to a sort of specialist musical education or something?' So they investigate and discover that they get 60% off the fees so it is a way into private education that they couldn't have otherwise considered. So that is one way it happens.
> Another way it happens is that a church-going family and the little boy has been with the parish church choir and either the vicar or the choirmaster has said that 'he is very, very good—have you thought about a choir school?' So there is that . . . The other issue for all of these people is that when they, particularly those who have always thought about private education for their child, [are at] the next stage, the subsidy is even more valuable because all the boys and even those who I was telling you about—those in the top end of our choir, they have all got top music scholarships to the sort of schools that they want to go to next and it is obviously worked out very closely between the headmaster and the parents, what is a suitable school to go to. But these scholarships are worth 50% of the fees and in some cases, I have got ex-choristers who have been to very expensive schools with fantastic music departments—private schools—where they have paid—picked up more or less the whole tab. Now when you have got fees at a senior private school that are about twenty thousand pounds a year,

that school has made a commitment for five years—that is 100k. That opens up opportunities for families who wouldn't have had that particular kind of opportunity. Whatever one may think about it, that is an opportunity for them. (Choir director, interview 2, visit 2)

This latter is not lost on the boys, who all sit for scholarship exams in year 8. In conversation with an exiting group of year 8 boys, the following exchange illustrates this issue:

Margaret: OK, what has it meant to you, Alistair, being here?
Alistair: It has meant a quite good education and a big step in musicality and I like making new friends and talking to them.
Davey: It has helped us get music scholarships.

For some younger boys, the scholarship support and the honorarium paid to the choristers were attractions, as evidenced by one year 7 student: 'First I didn't want to be in the choir and then my Mum told me about the money so I wanted to be here then and she got me an interview and basically I got it' (Group interview, visit 1).

Although the notion of participation in the cathedral choir as a means to achieve other life goals such as future placements at prestigious schools was not a dominant theme in the parents' or the boys' accounts of their entry to the choir, the record of cathedral chorister graduates who attain scholarships and bursaries to leading schools is considered of sufficient importance for this to feature in the school's marketing materials, and that of other cathedral schools. Financial considerations may not be a primary motivator for embarking on the life of being and becoming a chorister, but it has to be acknowledged that these are a factor, as outlined by the school headmaster:

I think they [parents] are often ambitious for their sons and they see the cathedral choir as the best . . . and therefore they want their sons to be in the best. But also it seems clear to me that our parents are probably not as wealthy as the typical [named public school] parent. Many of them are making considerable sacrifices to put their children through independent education. In that respect, a choristership is very helpful because although boarding fees are more than day fees, the college subsidizes every chorister to a considerable extent. (Headmaster interview, visit 1)

Regardless of the impetus for the prospective chorister's entry to the choir—boy's initiative, recognition of potential by others, the continuance of a family tradition, and/or the promise of a current and potential educational advantage—the boys participating in this practice have been provided with access to 'superior training resources' (Ericsson et al., 2005, p. 287), and a 'developmental advantage'. Few of the accounts of the boys' entry to the choir noted special 'gifts' or talents, beyond the enjoyment of music, and the capacity to 'hear', and to engage intellectually with the activity and the environment.

The service commitment

Embarking on the life of a cathedral chorister involves a commitment to a life in service to the cathedral, and, in this instance, a public concert schedule that takes the choristers on tour nationally and internationally during the annual holiday period. During the school year, beyond the expected absences from home of a boarder, Monday to Friday, choristers are also absent from home those weekends in which Saturday morning music school is held (about three in four weekends), and throughout the events of the Christian calendar such as Easter and Christmas. On those weekends where an *exeat* occurs from Friday evening, the choristers are expected back in the school by 4:30 p.m. Saturday afternoon to prepare for Evensong at 6:00 p.m., and the Sunday cycle of Matins, Eucharist, and Evensong. For those boys whose families live at some distance from the School, the short period of family life offered by an *exeat* is not possible. Chorister families become practised in constructing an alternative calendar of family rituals and celebrations. An 'old boy' whose two children, a boy and a girl, had taken up choristerships in separate cathedral schools described to me the family's Christmas ritual. Each year, he and his wife alternate between daughter and son, between cathedral schools, each driving a considerable distance across the country to spend Christmas eve alone in a bed & breakfast, and Christmas day in and around the cathedral in which their child is singing. This family's celebrations begin on Christmas night as each parent collects the respective child from the boarding house to drive back across the country to the family home.

The daily routine

Monday to Friday, the daily life of a chorister commences at 6:45 a.m. in the boarding house when the boys are woken by alarm in order to shower, dress, and present themselves at breakfast at 7:00 a.m. They have 15 minutes for breakfast, 5 minutes to clean teeth, and the first of two instrumental practice sessions commences at 7:20 a.m. Each boy learns two instruments; the piano and one other instrument. The decision concerning which instrument is to be practised at which time is made at term commencement to ensure access to the school pianos for every boy. At 7:50 a.m., instruments are packed away, and the boys collect themselves and their belongings for the 8 minute walk to the rehearsal room in the cathedral, and the first of two daily choir practices.

The morning practice: learning and teaching strategies

The hour-long practice with the choir director commences with a short vocal warm-up before launching into the repertoire. The choir is renowned for its

performance of early choral music—no 'Victorian war-horses in this environment' (headmaster interview, visit 1)—and the rehearsals move quickly
through repertoire that is either programmed into the cathedral services or to
be presented in concert, on tours, and recorded as part of the choir's performance profile. In one 55-minute rehearsal the choir moves through 12 separate
pieces of repertoire, ranging from Tallis and Tomkins, to Schubert, to Britten,
to Maxwell Davis, and emerging twenty-first century composers. None of
these works is sung in full as the choir director moves the boys through key
points of the work. He explains his strategy in part as one in which 'I have
just done a couple of pages a day because they half remember that (from last
year) . . . I reminded them of it.' Throughout the rehearsal boys 'own' errors
through the raising of a hand, a traditional chorister practice, and the choir
director makes good use of particular children to model the performance of
difficult sections and to provide opportunity for boys to self-correct:

> Obviously one is reliant, a lot of the time, on boys like Jonathon, who is extremely
> musical when he is concentrating, which he is most of the time. He can sing pretty well
> everything right the first time. Clearly there are quite a few of them there who are not
> like that and you will have noticed that—it is not premeditated from the beginning of
> the rehearsal but it is premeditated in the sense that I know that I am going to do it at
> some point in the rehearsal. I will pick on some of those children, who I know—they
> may have sung a few wrong intervals in the last 5 minutes or something but generally
> I know that they are not as quick and I do that stuff where I get one of the boys, who
> I know is going to get it right and they like doing that, of course, because they know
> that I am relying on them to set the example. Then I will get the younger child to do it
> and, of course, the others are listening in and learning whilst that is going on. So you
> can bet your life that everyone will get it right when they have heard little Harry do it
> three times or Tom. (Choir director interview, visit 3)

Sections of new works are sung as 'vocalise', the choir director commenting
to the boys: 'I quite like the tune actually and the harmony. It is quite fun so
I won't bother with the words with that—just yet.' He asks questions of the
boys about cadence points, the ways in which the cantoris will pick their starting note from the previous section, and their views on where and why a particular passage is not coming together. The choir founders at bar 37 of a Kyrie
and the choir director comments: 'That's interesting. The mistake was,
Christian, on your side, what was it?' 'It was the dotted note, Sir' Christian
responds. 'That's right, let's go . . .' And the choir recommences the section.
Less than a minute is spent on singing the section before another work is introduced: 'Let's do "When David heard." Tomkins isn't it? Let's read it. Can't
remember if we did it last year', the choir director comments. 'Which bright
boy wants to sing me a C? We start on a G. Come on, let's cut out the grade 7s'
he jests as hands go up, 'I mean a younger bright boy. Oh, come on Harry.

Let's try.' As Harry attempts to pitch the note the choir director listens intently and encourages him to 'try again. Good boy—it's a 4th', he confirms as the correct pitch is sung.

His manner is gentle, humorous. All is accompanied by a commentary that reinforces the meaning and use of musical terminology, provides contextual detail concerning specific works or musical practices, and focuses the boys' attention to issues of sound and voice production. The hour passes quickly and it seems only minutes before the boys are collecting their cloaks from the numbered pegs along the back wall of the rehearsal room and preparing to walk back to commence the school day at 9:00 a.m.

In this rehearsal, the elements of deliberate practice are evident, with the choir director focused on improving those skills the boys possess while extending the range of those skills. The rehearsal has clear goals related to immanent, tangible performance responsibilities. Constant feedback is provided to the boys both verbally and through musical modelling, and opportunities for repetition are provided until the boys are proficient (Ericsson et al., 2005, 2007).

The school day

The school day is long and busy, with the choristers moving in and out of classes to attend their weekly lesson on piano and other instrument, before finishing after their second instrumental practice session at 4:30 p.m. After a short break for 'a drink and a sandwich or biscuits or cake' (matron interview, visit 2), the choristers walk back to the cathedral at 4:45 p.m. to prepare for the day's service to the cathedral. The choristers are joined by the cathedral's lay clerks for a combined rehearsal from 5:00–5:45 p.m. In these rehearsals the choir director focuses on achieving a balance between the men's and boys' voices within the cathedral acoustic, and tightening phrase beginnings and endings. After a brief break for a drink, the choristers don surplices in readiness for Evensong or Eucharist (Thursday evening) at 6:00 p.m. At the end of the service, around 7:00 p.m., the boys return to the boarding house for dinner (7:10 p.m.) and an hour of prep commencing at 7:30 p.m. Lights out begins at 8:30 p.m. for the younger boys, with the older boys being able to watch television or play games through to 9:00 p.m. approximately. Although there might be some 'lee-way in the latter part of the day' (as described by the boarding house master), given the demands of the schedule and the boys' inevitable tiredness, most adhere to the schedule as set. The only variation to the above schedule occurs on Monday and Friday when the boys do not sing Evensong or attend afternoon rehearsal. On Sundays, the major day of service, the boys have a lie-in until 8:00 a.m. (matron interview, visit 2), to ensure that they are rested and prepared for the services. As noted by the music teacher: 'These children are working very long hours. I think it is 52 hours a week.' This is not lost on the choristers themselves. As one year 8 chorister comments:

> the thing that people don't realize is that they are not just little angels. They are hard-worked boys who get in bad moods and just like any other kid they act like normal. They are just exactly the same but just worked harder. (Chorister interview, visit 3)

The role of this routine is remarked upon by the headmaster who comments:

> I wouldn't underestimate the significance for boys of routine and ritual, which I see in some ways [as] two sides of the same coin. Children of all sorts find routine immense-ly reassuring and it is only a short step from that, I think, to ritual, the purpose of which I take to be the losing of yourself in a particular sort of routine. And I would expect these choristers, perhaps to be again gaining an appreciation of that, that might not come to other boys in the same way and certainly at the same age. (Headmaster interview, visit 1)

For the headmaster, it is this routine and highly structured timetable that provides the means by which the choir distinguishes itself as 'excellent':

> I think the way that he [the choir director] achieves those standards is because they are boarders; because they are here; they are very strongly committed to the cathedral and its pretty demanding regime of services and that business of living together, playing together, singing together—day by day for extended periods of time in the year—I think is what enables him to take the thing out of the merely 'very good' into the 'excellent'. (Headmaster interview, visit 1)

Dimensions of practice

Volume of practice

The literature suggests that 10 years or 10,000 hours of deliberate, thoughtful practice is required to develop expertise in a domain of practice (Ericsson & Crutcher, 1990), although it has been acknowledged that the time required differs between genre and instrument. Each week during term time, the chor-isters participate in about 11 hours of choir practice, 3 hours of piano practice, 3 hours of other instrumental practice, and sing Evensong four times, Eucharist twice, and Matins once (about 3 hours of performed music). Beyond this engagement, the choristers also participate in additional practice when rehears-ing for tours and concerts in non-term periods. Conservatively, by the time a boy has sung 14 hours per week, 35 weeks of the school year, from year 4 to year 8, he has participated in more than 2,450 hours of choral practice. In addi-tion, each boy participates in instrumental practice of about 6 hours per week across perhaps 40 weeks of the year, given some practice during holiday peri-ods, from years 4 to 8; a further 1,200 hours of practice. In summary, by the age of 13 years, these boys have accrued more than a third of the reported hours of practice on the journey to expertise.

Deliberate practice

Beyond the sheer volume of practice in which these boys participate, it is evident that in this environment the practice is deliberate, highly structured and monitored. The choir director's structuring of morning rehearsals attends to those aspects of the music and its performance that require thoughtful attention. In this setting, rarely does practice involve singing a work from bar one to the end. This approach to practice is perhaps a characteristic feature of the school as evidenced in the sports teacher's account of his approach to coaching:

> I suppose one of the problems is that it is the usual thing of pressure of time. So you have got 20 minutes or half an hour or whatever and you have got to really make that valuable time. It is a bit like in what I do with something that is say like training for a sport. The theory used to be that you would do 3-hour coaching sessions. Well I never believed it and most people don't believe it now. We tend to halve the time and make it absolutely intense for that time—it is concentrated, high quality rather than having a lot of time. There is no point standing around not doing very much. (Teacher interview, visit 1)

Deliberate and strategic practice is also modelled to the choristers by important figures including the cathedral organist—whom they hear practising as they attend the cathedral—and the headmaster. The latter, a former chorister and organist, describes his modelling of deliberate practice as intentional, commenting:

> By sheer chance—my practice organ happens to be here in school because it won't go into the house and it is in the entrance hall . . . I don't think it does any harm for boys to be passing and re-passing at the end of the school day and to see me practising—to see that I can't instantly sit down and play the piece; to see that, like them, I have to take the difficult bits apart and put them back together. (Headmaster interview, visit 1)

Further models of practice are provided to the boys each day through their participation in choir rehearsals, both in the rehearsal room and the cathedral. In the former setting, the physical structure of the choir places less experienced singers next to more experienced peers; in the latter setting, the participation of the cathedral lay clerks adds another model of practice to the boys' learning. Importantly, while it is evident that choral practice is closely monitored in the rehearsal setting, the boys' individual instrumental practice is monitored also, in overt and covert ways, by the school staff including the music teacher, the headmaster, the matron, and the boarding house master. With the exception of matron, all of these individuals have strong musical experience and the feedback that is given to boys is musically informed, focused, and encouraging. These boys develop the habits and strategies of deliberate and strategic practice early on.

Performance practice

In this environment, the choristers have an early introduction to the experience of performance. What is, perhaps, unique in this experience is that from an early age, and before a particular level of competence has been reached, the boys are placed in a performance setting in which they begin to participate in a performance practice that is exemplary, and operating well above the individual's current level of expertise. The choir director identifies year 6 as the 'pivotal year', commenting that:

> Year 6 . . . is when they start the year struggling a bit. There are three boys in that year . . . that year group is always a real struggle at the start of the year because they move from being—not exactly a baby but from being people that you expect to be tagging along a bit and learning by osmosis to people who make a difference. (Choir director interview, visit 2)

Although younger, less experienced boys might struggle in aspects of the performance practice, as I observed in my first encounter with the choir, they are valued as 'legitimate peripheral participants' (Lave & Wenger, 2002) in the practice and performance, attending and participating in services within the body of the choir, guided by the older boys, and encouraged by the choir director, to take up the practice of the community.

Environmental supports

Modelling and peer mentoring

Modelling and peer mentoring are key features of the choristers' teaching and learning experience. Every day, the choristers are exposed to a range of models of musical practice. Probationers and younger choristers are exposed to the practice of older and more experienced choristers who demonstrate the routines of the choir in practice and service, and provide overt models of vocal production, music reading and interpretation, and performance practice. As one organ scholar observed, 'the younger choristers do always learn from the older ones—that is the way it works in that team set-up, so the older ones setting a good example is really important' (organ scholar interview, visit 1). Peer mentoring is also identified as a learning strategy by the cathedral organist who comments 'I think it is brilliant if the older ones help the younger ones and there is a whole family atmosphere to it' (cathedral organist interview, visit 2). In an endeavour to structure peer mentoring into the choir, older choristers are matched with a younger chorister and are expected to assist 'in small ways, such as finding the right page for him and helping him find his place in the music' (chorister interview, visit 3). Such responsibilities are taken very seriously as outlined by Rob, a year 8 chorister: 'I think if you want to be a chorister, you don't have to be just good at singing; you have to be good at looking after and being responsible and acting on behalf of the whole choir instead of your own gain' (chorister individual interview, visit 3).

All choristers work 5 days a week with experienced male singers employed as lay clerks in the cathedral choir. Additionally, other models of musical practice are provided to the boys through their experiences of performing with orchestral musicians in concert, working with the music teacher in the school, their lessons with their instrumental teachers, and the example presented by the headmaster. Not only does the headmaster model practising techniques for the choristers through daily organ practice, he also sings on occasion in the choir, an experience he describes as 'a wonderful lesson for them, that I have to watch and listen and obey the conductor in the same way that they do' (headmaster interview, visit 2).

Independence and autonomy

The structure of the chorister's day and week contributes to the children's acquisition of time-management, self-regulation, and autonomy. In discussing the ways in which choristers learn to self-regulate their learning and manage their time, a teacher in the school comments:

> They are on a pretty tight schedule—a sort of regime. Therefore you have to say that when they—if they get a short amount of time, they usually like to use it as valuably as possible . . . Like, for example, in prep they'll say 'I have finished.' 'Right, you sit there and read for 20 minutes' I'll say, and they'll say back 'Right, in the last 10 minutes can I go to the IT room?' or 'Can I get ready to go and watch *The Simpsons*?' It doesn't matter what it is. It might be making a model upstairs—something like that. (Teacher interview, visit 1)

The older choristers comment on their perceptions of the shift in teaching style exhibited by the choir director over the course of their engagement with the choir. Rob, a year 8 chorister, describes this shift as follows:

> In your first year, he is a teacher. In your next years, he is not a teacher . . . he makes you become more independent. He doesn't teach you. He expects you, from what you have learned over the years, to apply that knowledge and become yourself and from your own musical knowledge to work out what you are going to do and what you are meant to do. When you get to year 8, he becomes more of an advisor than a teacher. (Chorister interview visit 3)

The younger boys describe the experience of the rehearsal somewhat differently; one boy describes the process as one in which:

> He tells us when we are going a bit slowly and he is really nice because he is a perfectionist at everything so . . . if we make a tiny mistake, he gets it perfect—not just good, but perfect. I think it [the approach] is good. (Chorister interview, year 4, visit 3)

Another year 4 chorister highlights the distinction between mere repetition and deliberate practice as experienced in the choir: 'if you are singing through it and singing through it, you are not really learning anything. Whereas if they are focusing and telling us about the sharp notes and how to improve that . . . then we are' (chorister interview, year 4, visit 3). The chorister routine is one that structures life yet promotes independence and autonomy.

Dimensions of family

For the choristers, the choir, the cathedral, school, and boarding house staff take on the role of an alternative family, and in that role exercise values, parenting styles and practices that support and value continued participation in and commitment to the choir. In an environment such as a cathedral choir school, the high values for music participation are self-evident, reinforcing those that prompted many of the parents to place their child in this environment. The chorister's highly structured schedule is illustrative of an 'authoritative' style (McPherson, 2009) of *parentis in locus*, that is, a style highly involved in the choristers' learning, ensuring that the environment is highly structured, yet allowing high autonomy and support in that environment. The boys' musical practice, whether as singers in the choir, or as instrumentalists in the school and boarding house, is strictly time-tabled, structured, and monitored by feedback from a range of 'family' individuals able to provide informed critical comment, including fellow choristers, boarding house, cathedral, and school staff.

Concluding comments

Reflecting on how expertise is developed in this setting, those key elements identified in the literature are borne out: early exposure to focused, goal-directed education, in an environment that provides constant and expert coaching and feedback; frequent and deliberate supervised practice; opportunity to observe initially, and, within a relatively short period of time, perform in an environment in which there is frequent exposure to multiple and varied models of expert performance; a structured and supportive family environment (albeit not the nuclear family that is the usual experience for children in many Western countries) that values and promotes the practice to be learned. Central to the development of expertise in this setting is the presence of an array of positive environmental supports (modelling and peer support, the promotion of independence and autonomy, dimensions of family), and appropriate education (frequent and deliberate practice, performance practice). Importantly, the choristers participate in a musical collective, a community of musical practice, in which individual musical goals and ambitions are negotiated in order to ensure continuing participation in the community (the service commitment), and adherence to the rules and structures (the daily routine) of that community.

Although the musical practice of the chorister is relatively short-lived (usually ending at the time of adolescent voice change, typically around the age of 13–14 years for males), it could be speculated that the values and habits of thought and practice that are developed in this environment may carry over into later learning and life experience. Ericsson and colleagues remind us that:

> The journey to truly superior performance is neither for the faint of heart nor for the impatient. The development of genuine expertise requires struggle, sacrifice, and honest, often painful self-assessment. There are no shortcuts. It will take you at least a decade to achieve expertise, and you will need to invest that time wisely, by engaging in 'deliberate' practice—practice that focuses on tasks beyond your current level of competence and comfort. You will need a well-informed coach not only to guide you through deliberate practice but also to help you learn how to coach yourself. Above all, if you want to achieve top performance . . . you've got to forget the folklore about genius that makes many people think that they cannot take a scientific approach to developing expertise. (Ericsson et al., 2007, p. 116)

What is retained from the experience of the choir? The boys, in their exit interviews over the years in which we worked with the choir, commented on their experience of working as a team, growing self-esteem and confidence, developing communication skills, responsibility, commitment, determination, discipline, organization, and independence. Their experience of the choir was at times bitter-sweet, echoing that of several parents. Through all of this, for most boys the commitment to the choir and to music remained paramount. As one year 8 chorister put it on his last day in the school:

> I would have to say, even though there were quite a few bad things about choir and how it affects my social life, I won't remember them. I will just remember the good things about it because they [the bad things] are not very important. The good things, I think, far outweigh it. There have been a few bad downsides but I wouldn't stop it for the world . . . in the five years which I have done most of my growing up and finding out who I am as a person in this school, music has become part of me . . . what I have been doing for the last three years has left an imprint on me. Music means to me everything at the minute. That is why it has been really difficult leaving choir because it has meant so much to me. (Chorister interview, visit 1)

Bruner (1996) reminds us that participation in a cultural system involves both 'macro' and 'micro' dimensions; that is, consideration of the 'system of values, thoughts, exchanges, obligations, opportunities, power' (p. 11), and the ways in which individuals adapt to this system, the 'costs' of their participation in the system, and the expected outcomes. The cathedral choir, as a cultural system, offers one pathway to the acquisition of early musical expertise. As is evident from this chorister's exit interview, to embark on that pathway requires the individual to work with the values and structures of the system, and weigh the personal costs against the outcomes. From a culturalist perspective, these processes may be viewed as mutually constitutive, as the individual chorister is shaped by participation in this environment, and in turn contributes to the shaping and continuation of the cultural system that is the choir.

References

Barone, T. (2001). *Touching eternity: the enduring outcomes of teaching*. New York: Peter Lang.

Barrett, M. S. (2005a). Musical communication and children's communities of musical practice. In D. Miell, R. MacDonald & D. Hargreaves (Eds.), *Musical communication* (pp. 261–80). Oxford: Oxford University Press.

Barrett, M. S. (2005b). Children's communities of musical practice: some socio-cultural implications of a systems view of creativity in music education. In D. J. Elliott (Ed.), *Praxial music education: reflections and dialogues* (pp. 177–95). New York: Oxford University Press.

Barrett, M. S., & Mills, J. (2009). The inter-reflexive possibilities of dual observations: an account from and through experience. *International Journal of Qualitative Studies in Education*, 22(4), 417–30.

Bloom, B. S. (1985). Generalizations about talent development. In B. S. Bloom (Ed.), *Developing talent in young people* (pp. 507–49). New York: Ballentine.

Borgerding, T. M. (2006). Imagining the sacred body: choirboys, their voices, and Corpus Christi in Early modern Seville. In S. Boynton & R.-M. Kok (Eds.), *Musical childhoods and the cultures of youth* (pp. 25–48). Middletown: Wesleyan University Press.

Boynton, S., & Cochelin, I. (2006). The sociomusical role of child oblates at the Abbey of Cluny in the eleventh century. In S. Boynton & R.-M. Kok (Eds.), *Musical childhoods and the cultures of youth* (pp. 3–24). Middletown: Wesleyan University Press.

Bruner, J. (1996). *The culture of education*. Cambridge, MA: Harvard University Press.

Chi, M. T. H. (2006). Two approaches to the study of experts' characteristics. In K. A. Ericsson, N. Charness, P. J. Feltovich & R. R. Hoffman (Eds.), *Cambridge handbook of expertise and expert performance* (pp. 21–30). New York: Cambridge University Press.

Clandinin, D. J. (2006). Narrative inquiry: a methodology for studying lived experience. *Research Studies in Music Education*, 27, 44–54.

Clandinin, D. J., & Connelly, F. M. (2000). *Narrative inquiry: experience and story in qualitative research*. San Francisco: Jossey-Bass.

Creech, A., Papageorgi, I., Duffy, C. Morton, F., Hadden, E., Potter, J., et al. (2008). Investigating musical performance: commonality and diversity among classical and non-classical musicians. *Music Education Research*, 10(2), 215–34.

Csikszentmihalyi, M., & Csikszentmihalyi, I. (1993). Family influences on the development of giftedness. In G. R. Bock & K. Ackril (Eds.), *Ciba Foundation Symposium 178: the origins and development of high ability* (pp. 187–286). Chichester: Wiley.

Csikszentmihalyi, M., Rathunde, K., & Whalen, S. (1993). *Talented teenagers: the roots of success or failure.* Cambridge, UK: Cambridge University Press.

Davidson, J. W., Howe, M. J. A., Moore, D. G., & Sloboda, J. A. (1996). The role of parental influences in the development of musical ability. *British Journal of Developmental Psychology,* 14, 399–412.

Doherty, P. (2005). *The beginner's guide to winning the Nobel Prize.* Victoria: Miegunyah Press (MUP).

Ericsson, K. A. (1996). *The road to excellence: the acquisition of expert performance in the arts and sciences, sports and games.* Hillsdale: Erlbaum.

Ericsson, K. A. (2006). An introduction to *Cambridge handbook of expertise and expert performance*: its development, organization, and content. In K. A. Ericsson, N. Charness, P. J. Feltovich & R. R. Hoffman (Eds.), *Cambridge handbook of expertise and expert performance* (pp. 3–19). New York: Cambridge University Press.

Ericsson, K. A., & Crutcher, R. J. (1990). The nature of exceptional performance. In P. B. Baltes, D. L. Featherman & R. M. Lerner (Eds.), *Life-span development and behavior* (Vol. 10, pp. 187–217). Hillsdale: Erlbaum.

Ericsson, K. A., Krampe, R. T., & Tesch-Römer, C. (1993). The role of deliberate practice in the acquisition of expert performance. *Psychological Review,* 100, 363–406.

Ericsson, K. A., Nandagopal, K., & Roring, R. W. (2005). Giftedness viewed from the expert-performance perspective. *Journal for the Education of the Gifted, 28*(3/4), 287–391.

Ericsson, K. A., Prietula, M. J., & Cokely, E. T. (2007). The making of an expert. *Harvard Business Review, 85*(7/8), 115–21.

Gruber, H., Degner, S., & Lehmann, A. C. (2004). Why do some commit themselves in deliberate practice for many years—and so many do not? Understanding the development of professionalism in music. In M. Radovan & N. Dordevic (Eds.), *Current issues in adult learning and motivation* (pp. 222–35). Ljubljana: Slovenian Institute for Adult Education.

Howe, M. J. A. (1990). *The origins of exceptional abilities.* Oxford: Blackwell.

Howe, M. J. A. (1999). *Genius explained.* Cambridge, UK: Cambridge University Press.

Howe, M. J. A., Davidson, J. W., & Sloboda, J. A. (1998). Innate talents: reality or myth? *Behavioural and Brain Sciences,* 21, 399–442.

Jørgensen, H. (1997). Time for practising? Higher level music students' use of time for instrumental practising. In H. Jørgensen & A. C. Lehmann (Eds.), *Does practice make perfect? Current theory and research on instrumental music practice* (pp. 123–39). NHM-publikasjoner 1997:1. Oslo: Norges musikkhøgskole.

Jorgensen, H. (2008). Instrumental practice: quality and quantity. *Finnish Journal of Music Education, 11*(1–2), 8–18.

King's School, Gloucester (2009a). Becoming a chorister. Retrieved 5 July 2009 from www.thekingsschool.co.uk/Choristers/Becoming-a-Chorister/

King's School, Gloucester (2009b). Chorister duties. Retrieved 5 July 2009 from www.thekingsschool.co.uk/Senior/Choristers/Chorister-Duties/

Kopiez, R. (1998). Singers are late beginners. Sängerbiographien aus Sicht der Expertiseforschung. Eine Schwachstellenanalyse sängerischer Ausbildungsverläufe.

In H. Gembris, R.-D. Kramer & G. Maas (Eds.), *Musikpädagogische Forschungsberichte* (pp. 37–56). Augsburg: Wissner Verlag.

Lave, J., & Wenger, E. (2002). Legitimate peripheral participation in communities of practice. In R. Harrison, F. Reeve, A. Hanson & J. Clarke (Eds.), *Supporting lifelong learning*, Vol. 1: *Perspectives on learning* (pp. 111–26). London: Routledge Falmer.

Lehmann, A. C., & Gruber, H. (2006). Music. In K. A. Ericsson, N. Charness, P. J. Feltovich & R. R. Hoffman (Eds.), *Cambridge handbook of expertise and expert performance* (pp. 457–70). New York: Cambridge University Press.

Manturzewska, M. (1990). A biographical study of the life-span development of professional musicians. *Psychology of Music*, *18*(2), 112–39.

McPherson, G. E. (2009). The role of parents in children's musical development. *Psychology of Music*, *37*(1), 91–110.

McPherson, G. E., & Davidson, J. W. (2002). Musical practice: mother and child interactions during the first year of learning an instrument. *Music Education Research*, *4*, 141–56.

McPherson, G. E., & Davidson, J. W. (2006). Playing an instrument. In G. E. McPherson (Ed.), *The child as musician: a handbook of musical development* (pp. 331–52). Oxford: Oxford University Press.

McPherson, G. E., & Zimmerman, B. J. (2002). Self-regulation of musical learning: a social cognitive perspective. In R. Colwell & C. Richardson (Eds.), *The new handbook of research on music teaching and learning* (pp. 327–47). New York: Oxford University Press.

Mould, A. (2007). *The English chorister: a history*. London: Hambledon Continuum.

Papageorgi, I., Creech, A., Haddon, E., Mortin, F., de Bezenac, C., Himonides, E., et al. (2010). Perception and predictions of expertise in advanced musical learners. *Psychology of Music*, *38*(1), 31–66.

Sloboda, J. A., Davidson, J. W., Howe, M. J. A., & Moore, D. G. (1996). The role of practice in the development of performing musicians. *British Journal of Psychology*, 87, 287–309.

Stake, R. (1995). *The art of case-study research*. Newbury: Sage.

Stake, R. (2000). Case studies. In N. K. Denzin & Y. S. Lincoln (Eds.), *Handbook of qualitative research* (2nd edn, pp. 435–54). Thousand Oaks: Sage.

Index

Note: 'n.' after a page reference indicates the number of a note on that page.